THE
ECONOMICS
OF STATE
AND LOCAL
GOVERNMENT

ECONOMICS HANDBOOK SERIES
Seymour E. Harris, Editor

THE BOARD OF ADVISORS

JOHN M. CULBERTSON
University of Wisconsin—Monetary Theory

SEYMOUR E. HARRIS
University of California, La Jolla—International Economics, Social Security; all other areas

FRANCO MODIGLIANI
Massachusetts Institute of Technology—Economic Theory

RICHARD A. MUSGRAVE
Harvard University—Public Policy

MARC NERLOVE
University of Chicago—Econometrics and Mathematical Economics

THE ECONOMICS OF STATE AND LOCAL GOVERNMENT

WERNER Z. HIRSCH

Professor of Economics
University of California, Los Angeles

McGRAW-HILL BOOK COMPANY

New York	Mexico
St. Louis	Panama
San Francisco	Sydney
Düsseldorf	Toronto
London	

THE
ECONOMICS
OF STATE
AND LOCAL
GOVERNMENT

Library of Congress Catalog Card Number 77–119821

29042

1 2 3 4 5 6 7 8 9 0   MAMM   7 9 8 7 6 5 4 3 2 1 0

This book was set in Bodoni Book by Monotype Composition
Company, Inc., and printed on permanent paper and bound
by The Maple Press Company. The designer was Marsha
Cohen; the drawings were done by John Cordes, J. & R.
Technical Services, Inc. The editor was Joseph F. Murphy.
Matt Martino supervised the production.

TO:
ESTHER
DAN
JOEL
AND LANI

PREFACE

Particularly in the United States, subnational governments play vital roles in people's lives; however, it is far easier to muse about our state, city, county, and special district governments than to understand their roles and devise economic doctrines to explain and guide their activities. These governments differ so widely —in size, character, leadership, administrative capacity, and circumstances—that generalizations are not easily made.

Rapid urbanization is making heavy demands on our city governments and school districts, so that in recent years they have found it increasingly difficult to cope with the demands of their constituents. These same constituents, however, are often reluctant to provide the financial means for providing the services they demand.

Many of our cities have been torn asunder by civil disorders, which have given impetus to economic as well as social change. However, governmental change is difficult to bring about because of numerous deeply entrenched interests, scarcity of resources, and inadequate rewards for tackling difficult jobs. Under such circumstances officials must orchestrate this diffuse and complicated system by establishing long-term strategies and by mobilizing all possible resources of expertise, ingenuity, leadership, and scientific inquiry. While a similar situation exists in many other countries, solutions to the particularly pressing social and racial issues in America, unprecedently affluent as she is, place especially heavy emphasis on the delivery of services by local governments.

States are significant factors in American life more because of the law and the logic of their position than because of their effectiveness. The Constitution has awarded them certain fundamental powers, including the chartering of cities. States appear to have survived but not necessarily prospered in this middle ground between Federal and local governments, most likely in the main because of their reluctance to become important in twentieth-century America. *Baker v. Carr* brought an end to the domination of state capitals by rural legislators. The shift from a rural to an urban America and the belated urbanization of state legislatures are only slowly making their effect felt on state governments as suppliers of services and as funders of local governments. Henceforth, states are likely to struggle toward greater relevance and a far greater piece of the action.

Working toward the solution of America's most urgent domestic problems in the seventies—in education, housing, health services, quality of the environment, and law and justice—will place heavy demands on the creativity and foresightedness of our state and local governments. These governments will be called upon not only to provide better services, but to distribute them in a more equitable and more efficient manner. Since services provided by subnational governments already represent a large percentage of gross national product—a proportion that is likely to increase in years to come—efficient performance will gain in importance. To stimulate efficiency, new incentive systems will have to be invented and instituted. At the same time, it appears that the process of intergovernmental bargaining will be sharpened and intensified.

There is a need to provide better ways of looking at the workings of the state and local government sector—an economic framework, tools of analysis, and techniques for operational decision making. Yet, until recently economists have shown only limited interest in this sector, even though it accounted in the late sixties for about 12 percent of gross national product and is a major employer. The economics of state and local government is a legitimate and promising field of inquiry for economists. Specifically, it appears attractive and rewarding to build inquiries into the economics of state and local governments on the base of available microeconomic theory, and particularly on modern public goods theory and welfare economics. With the aid of such tools, economists can make contributions to many decisions facing the officials of subnational governments. Such decisions cover a wide spectrum. State and local governments are key factors in establishing a favorable environment for the efficient operation of the private sector, in providing for a generally desirable distribution of government services and tax burdens, and in efficiently producing those goods and services in whose production they have a comparative advantage. Local governments must also be agents of social change and respond to observed needs, even though they may seek the necessary funds from other sources. In an affluent America they are expected to improve the quality of life by providing great diversity and variety of services.

Local governments, and to a lesser extent state governments, operate in an open economy. Because of numerous state and local jurisdictions and the great mobility of people and goods, costs and benefits spill across jurisdictional boundaries in a complex pattern. This phenomenon is unique to the economics of state and local government and distinguishes it from the economics of national government. This spatial spillover aspect of local and state governments must be kept in mind as we examine their planning and operations, develop analytic methods, and seek to improve the quality and results of their decision process.

My task of writing this volume would have been impossible without thoughtful stimulation and substantive help and collaboration from a large number of colleagues and students; this is especially true because the literature dealing with the economics of state and local government until recently has been quite limited. I have greatly benefited from discussing various ideas with my colleagues—Harvey S. Perloff, Sidney Sonenblum, Donald C. Shoup, James Buchanan, and Phillip E. Vincent. Richard A. Musgrave, Seymour E. Harris, Julius Margolis, Lyle Fitch, George F. Break, Carl C. Shoup, Michael Intriligator, and Harvey Brazer also offered helpful advice. But I owe no less appreciation to some of my students, most of whom served as research assistants at one time or another. Being able to explore ideas and concepts with them, both in and out of class, greatly broadened the scope of this volume and, no doubt, improved it. Foremost, I owe an expression of gratitude to Ronald Teeples, whose work and assistance on the subjects of user charges, taxation, and intergovernmental fiscal relations has been of great value. In many respects, treatment of these subjects represents collaborative efforts between Ronald Teeples and the author. Morton J. Marcus provided valuable substantive help in examining spillovers in general, and spillovers of intergovernmental fiscal relations in particular, as well as regulation of the transportation-communications network and fiscal outlook analysis; he greatly influenced the development of these subjects. Eugene J. Devine shared in the development of certain ideas relevant to the nature of public service supply functions. Sam Kline contributed to the section on analysis of land use regulation. Lawrence Revzan and Samuel Hale helped me think through certain aspects of government service demand. My thanks also go to Steven Mehay and Burck Burright, who participated in some of the discussions.

Special thanks are due Carl C. Shoup and Roland N. McKean for reading and criticizing Chapters 1 to 3; George F. Break for Chapters 4 to 6; and Seymour E. Harris and Julius Margolis for the entire manuscript.

Important editorial, typing, and secretarial help were provided by Thomas B. Moule, Lyda Boyer, Marilyn Schroeter, and Winifred Murck, to whom my sincere gratitude is expressed.

I also thank the *Review of Economics and Statistics* for permission to use portions of my articles "Expenditure Implications of Metropolitan Growth and Consolidation" (August, 1959), "Local Impact of Industrialization on Local Schools" (May, 1964), and "Cost Functions of an Urban Government Service: Refuse Collection" (February, 1965); the Regional Science Association for permission to use major portions of my article "State and Local Government Program Budgeting" in the *Vienna Congress Papers of the Regional Science Association,* 1966; The Johns Hopkins Press for permission to use major portions of my article "The Supply of Urban Public Services" in *Issues in Urban Economics,* edited by Harvey S. Perloff and Lowdon Wingo, Jr., copyright 1968; the Institute of Government and Public Affairs of the University of California at Los Angeles for permission to use major portions of *Spillover of Public Education Costs and Benefits* by myself, Elbert Segelhorst, and Morton J. Marcus; and the International Journal of Socio-Economic Planning Sciences for permission to use major portions of my article "Demand for Education, and Its Estimation" in *Proceedings of the Symposium on Operations Analysis of Education,* April, 1969.

Werner Z. Hirsch

CONTENTS

LIST OF
TABLES

LIST OF
FIGURES

CHAPTER 1
INTRODUCTION

THE MAGNITUDE OF THE STATE AND LOCAL GOVERNMENT SECTOR

Any doubts that state and local governments are major factors in the American economy can be readily dispelled. In the late 1960s about 9 million people worked for 80,000 state and local government units. Local governments, i.e., municipalities, counties, and special district governments, accounted for about three-fourths of this employment. State and local governments in the late 1960s incurred general expenditures of about $100 billion, or about $500 per person. State and local government general expenditures amounted to about 12 percent of gross national product, a steady increase from 5 percent in 1946. They were spent mainly on education, highways, public welfare, health and hospitals, and police and fire protection. One service, education, alone accounted for about one-half of state and local government employment.[1] Whereas at the end of World War II annual state tax receipts were $3.9 billion and those of local governments were $4.6 billion, twenty-five years later the amounts collected by each were about $30 billion. In constant (1957–1959) dollars, per capita total general revenues of state and local governments increased from $143 in 1942 to $436 in 1967.

WHY GOVERNMENTS PRODUCE GOODS AND SERVICES

Goods and services are provided by governments for a variety of reasons; the single most important economic consideration is their public good characteristic.[2] A public good in its "pure" form is a good which, if it is available to anyone, is equally available to all others because of two properties:

Joint consumption of public goods is possible, so that consumption by any one consumer in no way diminishes the amount of public goods that can be consumed by other individuals

The costs of excluding any one individual from enjoying a pure public good, without excluding all other individuals, are infinite.

State and local governments produce no public goods in their pure form and very few outputs of public goods have properties that closely approximate the two properties listed above. Outputs of public goods that are most nearly pure public goods are such services as mosquito abatement, air and water depollution, water fluoridation, and various acts that preserve for each individual recourse from injustices.

The second reason for goods and services being provided by governments is distributional. Some goods are considered merit goods and therefore are provided by governments and priced to change the allocation from that which would result from the workings of the market mechanism. Merit goods involve interdependencies in utility functions such that citizens receive pleasure or other benefits from knowing that some of their fellows are able to consume more of certain services than they would be able to consume if the market-place alone determined distribution.

The properties of joint consumption and interdependencies of utility are, of course, present in many of the goods we commonly associate with private market production. In later chapters we will consider government policy with regard to private production of goods having these properties, as well as the specific policy of government production and tax finance. In one chapter, government regulation of transportation-communications networks is discussed.

In addition to the properties of joint consumption and interdependencies of utility there are important circumstances of market supply that have led governments to intervene. A government may assume the major responsibility either for monopolizing or for regulating production when it expects significantly large economies of scale in the production of a good or service. In the presence of economies of scale, the number of active producers tends to be reduced; the industry tends to become concentrated.

A government may also furnish or regulate production of a good or service that requires a highly scarce and singly owned resource for which there are few close substitutes. It is believed that in such a case competition is unworkable and a natural monopoly will inevitably arise. This result is quite similar to the results in the presence of scale economies, mentioned above. Water supply and transportation systems as well as airport and seaport facilities are often viewed as being in this category.

Also, governments tend to become regulators if great uncertainties faced by private suppliers lead to private behavior that is socially costly but not necessarily socially beneficial. Government planning boards, regulatory agencies, zoning departments, inspection departments, and auditing agencies, for example, may be created to meet such a condition.

POLITICAL AND FISCAL FEDERALISM AND THE DISTRIBUTION OF POWER AND RESPONSIBILITY

We can look upon the seminal debate between the supporters of Alexander Hamilton and those of Thomas Jefferson as an argument about authority and responsibility under federalism. Hamilton called for centralization of power in the interests of efficiency and order; Jefferson demanded diffusion of power and the right of the citizen to be close to government and to participate in decisions, even at the price of efficiency. Philosophically Jefferson warned,

"When all government . . . shall be drawn to Washington as the center of all power, it . . . will become as venal and oppressive as the government from which we separated."[3] Materialistically, he contended, "Were we directed from Washington when to sow, and when to reap, we should soon want bread,"[4] and "If ever this vast country is brought under a single government, it will be one of the most extensive corruption, indifferent and incapable of a wholesome care."[5]

Thus the argument is that up to a point dispersion of power and responsibility to subsidiary governments produces more gains than losses to society. In recent years much centralization has taken place, perhaps to a point where the gains from decentralization may be on the increase. Modern technology has stripped us of the protections provided by distance and time, which once mitigated the effects of the actions of others, and has made us more vulnerable to imposed external costs. These interactions have been responded to in most cases by further centralization and national coordination. Thus, centralized and distant political decisions increasingly bear on our economic, social, and personal lives. A widespread feeling of powerlessness is produced by the sheer size, complexity, and remoteness of collective decision making in our society. This feeling of powerlessness in people who have a fundamental desire for a degree of personal mastery over their lives and environment is greatly aggravated by the unresponsiveness of our political institutions. The desire to be close to government decision making and to have a responsive government has recently been intensified by the many unsolved minority group problems and uncertainties introduced into our private lives by the given political institutions.

Under those conditions the principle of federalism is sound: Have the smallest unit of government that is appropriate for the scale of a problem assume responsibility for that problem. To determine the size and level of government at which a particular public good or service should be produced, we need to weigh and trade off the gains and losses of centralized authority. In this determination the value of the following goods, among others, can be employed: resource allocation efficiency through scale economies and central planning, equity in financing and distributing government services, consumer choice, distance of government from people and the feeling of powerlessness that accompanies large group choice processes.

The financing can be separated from the rendering of public services. Although the rendering of services can be decentralized and accomplished by thousands of units of local government, Federal or state revenues can be used to finance them, preferably under rigorous national minimum standards.

The Constitution contains a prescriptive mandate for a federalized system; yet in the actual distribution of authority and responsibility that has evolved over the centuries the Federal government has become increasingly dominant. The time has come to reconsider a not uncommon assumption that all problems of national concern are to be assigned to departments of the Federal government. State and local governments can be efficient and effective producers of services, although some of the funding and standards for the use of funds will no doubt come from the Federal government. The need is urgent to build new institutions, perhaps on all three levels of government, and to assign to them some of our pressing problems.

Some of the roles presently played by Federal, state, and local governments in providing Americans with various public services are well summarized by Richard Ruggles.[6] Realizing that employment is at best a partial measurement, we can point out that local governments and the Federal government are about equally important employers; states employ only about one-third of the number employed by either local governments or the Federal government. Yet if we exclude defense employment, the Federal government is relatively unimportant as an employer compared with local and state governments.

From the beginning of this century and until World War II, state and local government expenditures were about three-fifths of all government general expenditures. This changed abruptly when the nation mobilized and entered the global conflict; state and local government expenditures dropped to one-fifth of all government expenditures during the war period. Since the postwar recovery period of the late 1940s the state and local share of all government general expenditures has steadily increased; however, Federal expenditures for defense, space exploration, and domestic programs have been so great that the expenditures of state and local governments have not regained their prewar statistical dominance. About twenty years after World War II state and local governments accounted for about 43 percent of all general government expenditures and revenues and for about 36 percent of all taxes.

ACTIVITIES OF STATE AND LOCAL GOVERNMENTS

Some groupings of government services are particularly useful to economists because they illuminate the theoretical aspects of state and local governments that are of interest to them, while other groupings are more policy-oriented. In the past, economists have been concerned mainly with revenue issues and not with expenditure issues. Also, they have paid almost exclusive attention to highly visible and tangible services of state and local governments. Yet there are important intangible services, even though the dividing line between tangible and intangible services is somewhat difficult to draw.[7]

Most of the resources used by state and local governments are applied to produce tangible services, and this volume is mainly concerned with decisions about them. However, in Chapter 10 we will examine highly intangible services that are designed to create an environment and rules for the private sector of the economy.

The activities of state and local governments can also be divided into programmatic and policy missions. Most programmatic missions tend to relate to resource uses in the near future whereas most policy missions tend to relate to the more distant future and emphasize such issues as setting goals and establishing priorities. These categories will be taken up next.

Policy Missions

Governments can and do affect resource allocation, distribution, economic stability, and economic growth. Richard A. Musgrave talks about the allocation, distribution, and stability branches of government.[8] Thus governments must decide about the relative importance they want to assign to each of these missions.

Interest in the performance of state and local governments is heightened by the fact established earlier that they employ far more resources for non-military uses than does the Federal government. Local governments are the most important government producers of tangible civilian services; state and Federal governments rely to a great extent on local governments and on private industry for production. Thus if, for example, we want to improve resource allocation efficiency by government, state and particularly local governments are key places to start.

Income redistribution is principally the mission of the Federal government, the states playing junior parts. Local governments have not consistently pursued income redistribution policies; however, this does not mean that they have not affected relative incomes and the behavior of different income classes. The taxing, expenditure, and service distribution practices of local governments have affected income distribution, but most likely not nearly so greatly as Federal and state governments have.

Similarly, although state and local governments affect business activity they have not in the past and most likely should not assume responsibility for stabilizing the economy. This responsibility has in the recent past been effectively discharged by the Federal government. What has been said above about stabilization of the economy also applies to economic growth, except that state and local government operations contribute directly to economic growth and can create an environment and rules of the game that facilitate regional growth.

Programmatic Missions

Within a program budgeting framework, which underlies major parts of this volume, government in general can be looked upon as facing five great decision areas or missions: maintenance of national security, law and justice, social development and welfare, economic development, and general government operations. Since the Federal government is active in all these areas and monopolizes the maintenance of national security, state and local governments are left with only parts of the other four areas.

In efforts to accomplish the missions of law and justice, social development and welfare, and economic development, most of the actual production is carried out by local governments or by private industry on behalf of all three levels of government. Parts of the important law and justice decision area are judicial and, to some degree, public safety programs. The social development and welfare decision area includes education, health, welfare, housing and community development, and amenities of life programs. The economic development decision area encompasses such programs as natural resources development, transportation, and aid and regulation. General government operations comprise both legislative and administrative authority and fiscal affairs. These programmatic missions and decisions about them are developed in Chapter 11.

PROBLEMS OF STATE AND LOCAL GOVERNMENTS
THAT AWAIT SOLUTIONS

Alvin H. Hansen and Harvey S. Perloff, in their *State and Local Finance in the National Economy*, identified eight basic problems of state and local governments.[9] The problems included lack of better planning, imbalance between local fiscal responsibility and capacity, and lack of cooperation and coordination among governments. Many of the problems recognized in the middle 1940s are still with us, new ones have arisen, and still others can be identified as likely to face us in the near future.

It appears helpful to divide state and local government policy issues that are of interest to economists into five groups. Some of the issues are normative and others are positive. The five groups of policy issues are as follows:

Our first group regards state and local governments as producers of mainly tangible goods and services. "What, how much, where, when, and how to produce?" are the key production issues. Important questions are: "What are the implications for the future of outdated, undermanaged, and undercapitalized production processes of state and local governments?" "Does underinvestment exist and, if so, how important is it, especially by local governments, as a result of interjurisdictional spillovers?" "Does overinvestment exist in some areas as a result, for example, of politicians advocating new programs at election time mainly because of the benefits of the programs, without fully regarding the cost implications of the programs?" "Do the gains outweigh the losses that can accompany government consolidation and, if they do, under what circumstances?" "To what extent do shortages of public employees exist and, if there are shortages, do they result in government inefficiencies and retardation of growth of the private sector?" "What steps can be taken by state and local governments to render better such relatively new services as water and air quality improvement, noise control, transportation, housing, and cultural and recreational activities?"

The second group of public policy issues relates to state and local governments in their capacity as service distributors. The general question is: "Who should get what services?" Specific questions include: "What steps can state and local governments take to develop human capital, especially in minority groups?" "How well can welfare goals be met by cash payments as compared with providing training, health services, and specific welfare services?" "How can state and local governments decide how much fire and police protection, education, recreational service, etc., to offer different income, ethnic, and geographic groups in their jurisdictions?" "What criteria can state and local governments use to 'equitably' distribute services among their constituents?"

The third group focuses on the raising of revenue, specifically on "Who should pay and who does pay how much, in what form, and when?" The following policy questions appear to be significant: "Who should and who does finance primary and secondary education, higher education, police protection, and recreational services?" "How can state and local tax systems be made more productive so as to meet more readily the rapidly increasing service demands?" "What are the implications of business cycles for revenues (and expenditures)?" "What are the special problems associated with raising funds for capital improvements and what are some promising solutions?" "What is the fiscal outlook of state and local governments?" "In the hope of mitigating the fiscal crisis of local governments, should steps be taken to provide them with funds from local or shared income taxes, or should the Federal government assume greater responsibility in the financing of health, education, and welfare services, and should state governments subsidize schools more heavily?"

The last question above directly relates to the fourth group of issues, concerning relations between state, local, and Federal governments. Other questions include: "What benefits accrue to state and local governments from the Federal government's successful pursuit of full employment policies?" "What are the relationships between urban, suburban, and rural America in terms of growth, services, expenditures, and taxes?" "How important are the cost and benefit spillovers that result from services provided by state and local governments and how can they be compensated for by Federal financial aid to state and local governments?" "Which level of government is the most efficient producer of services and which is the most efficient income redistributor?"

Finally, a fifth group of issues involves provision by state and local governments of rather intangible services in the form of an environment and rules of the game in which households, commerce, and governments operate. Some relevant policy questions here are: "To what extent do state and local governments have responsibility to improve the environment in which the private sector functions and how far can they, and should they, go in the discharge of that responsibility?" "What are the effects of government price and other regulation of the transportation-communications network on transportation, transit, and land use (urban sprawl, for example)?" "How do different types of zoning affect resource allocation efficiency and distribution of costs and benefits?" "Which local industries should be encouraged and which should be discouraged by governments concerned with improving the employment, income, and stability of their jurisdictions?" "How can local governments improve their planning function?" "What part can local governments take in mitigating interjurisdictional spillovers through smog control, zoning, etc.?"

THE THRUST OF THIS VOLUME

With the fiscal structure of American government to some extent decentralized, with state and local governments more important users of resources for civilian services than the Federal government, and with state and local government expenditures steadily increasing as a percentage of GNP, economists can no longer neglect subnational governments. These governments are important segments of the American economy.

In the past, those economists who have looked at the problems of state and local governments have been preoccupied with revenue matters. We hope to offer a more balanced approach by probing the expenditure side no less than the revenue side. Thus we will seek to develop methods for investigating the demand, production, cost, and supply of services together with techniques to study different ways of funding government activities. However, we will not be concerned exclusively with the more visible, tangible services; we will also explore such intangible services as planning and zoning and the regulating of certain privately performed services.

In this volume we have singled out for attention the economic dimensions of planning and carrying out state and local government activities. From the different economic approaches we chose the application of neoclassical microeconomic theory to key decision problems of the subnational government sector of the economy—admittedly, a comparative static analysis. Relatively little attention is paid to description of fiscal institutions. We do consider certain aspects of political behavior in our analysis of decisions about state and local government services. For example, in the estimation of demand we look at voters' behavior. Nevertheless, the approach is basically economic and the thrust of the volume is the elucidation and improvement of economic decisions.

Demand, supply, and financing decisions are first considered separately; then a program budgeting framework is developed to integrate the decision-making process. Such a framework provides a systematic way of considering government objectives and of evaluating the gains and losses in achieving those objectives through alternative actions.

Both normative and positive theories are relied upon. For example, a normative theory is applied to an evaluation of the efficiency with which user charges help bring about an efficient allocation of resources under conditions of existing individual preferences for certain government services. On other occasions a positive theory is used to predict how the state and local government sectors will behave; for example, whether city government consolidation will produce scale economies or diseconomies. Some such positive theories are supplemented and enriched by empirical studies which attempt to validate a positive theory.

In this volume one of the great differences in environment between national and subnational governments is explicitly recognized. Unlike the national government, local governments and, to a somewhat lesser extent, state governments cannot close their borders to the citizens or economic activities of other jurisdictions. Subnational governments operate in an open economy, one in which spatial or interjurisdictional spillovers are abundant and governments have little control over them. Such spillovers occur if any portion of the benefits or costs of a government service that is provided in one jurisdiction is realized by residents of another. Specifically, in a highly industrialized and mobile society, benefits and costs tend to spill over from one jurisdiction, in which expenditure and tax policies are decided, to another jurisdiction that can benefit or suffer without, however, having participated in the policy determination. Spillovers can cause serious distortions that lead to inappropriate investments as well as to undesirable distributions of gains and losses among people in different jurisdictions.

Spillovers, as described above, are "external" effects—those imposed or freely given and unearned or unavoided by receivers. Ralph Turvey has defined spillovers in the most general way as "the impacts of the activities of households, public agencies, or enterprises upon the activities of other households, public agencies, or enterprises which are exerted otherwise than through the market. They are, in other words, relationships other than those between buyer and seller." [10]

There are two types of spillovers. A technological spillover affects the physical outputs which others can produce from their physical inputs. It represents a real production gain or loss to the affected party and should be counted as a benefit or cost in efficiency calculations as well as in distribution calculations. A pecuniary spillover is one which does not affect the units of output that can be obtained from given inputs. Instead, gains or losses are the result of changes in the prices of inputs or outputs. These changes to affected parties are distributional aspects—important and often decisive; therefore, they should be counted and evaluated by decision makers. But pecuniary external effects do not enter into production efficiency calculations.

Spillovers are highly visible and more easily calculated, for example, when a person publicly educated in one community migrates to another—an example of interjurisdictional spillover of government benefits. Preventing the outmigration of a nonhuman benefit in the form of direct services also can result in a spillover; for example, a mosquito control program conducted by one jurisdiction in an area can benefit all the other jurisdictions in that area.

When a community expends resources on such a public good or program it will consider its own benefits against the costs of the service. Let us assume that all the costs are borne only by the community that is under consideration. Then the community will tend to increase its production of the service until the marginal costs equal the marginal benefits to the community. From society's viewpoint, production should increase until the marginal costs equal the sum of the marginal benefits to *all* areas. This condition implies aid from a higher level government to the spending government to ensure production consistent with allocative efficiency.[11]

Less obvious but no less important, spillovers occur through economic interaction and fiscal interdependence. When residents of one community buy and sell products or work in another community they are engaged in economic interaction with citizens of the other community; pecuniary external effects are spilled over through the prices of the market transactions. Other spillovers occur when the revenues collected by a government are levied without regard for the residence of or benefits received by the person paying a tax. This is an example of fiscal interdependence, and it can produce spillovers even when revenue collection is restricted by place of collection but not by residence of the payer.

State and local government services differ greatly in likelihood and importance of spillover. For example, spillovers of the benefits and costs of such services as water, air, and noise pollution control, planning, and public instruction are very widespread. But for such services as public utilities and state liquor stores spillovers are minimal.

Spillovers will be uppermost in our minds as we examine the economics of subnational governments, develop methods for analyzing those governments, and seek policy solutions to the problems of improving the quality of their decision processes.

CHAPTER 2
DEMAND FOR STATE AND LOCAL GOVERNMENT SERVICES

In competitive markets where goods and services are traded by private persons, the prices at which sales are made reflect production costs, the marginal value of resources incorporated in the product, and the marginal value of the product to the consumer. Price movements signal producers to increase or decrease their production or to divert resources from one good to another. We seldom find such a competitive market situation in state and local government services. Government services are typically supplied with an explicit pricing policy, at constant, nominal, or zero prices. Officials responsible for producing government services must therefore rely on other means for rationing such services and for estimating the demand for such services. The revenues received from the public, which provide for the purchase of the inputs for public services, are most often independent of consumers' evaluations of benefits received from public services. Some of the demand estimation alternatives will be considered in this chapter, but first we will examine the reasons why state and local governments do not employ the price mechanism.

There are four, often interrelated, characteristics of government outputs that explain why direct money prices are not widely used for state and local government goods and services:

1. Joint consumption
2. Externalities in consumption
3. Costs of exclusion
4. Distributional or welfare considerations

These four characteristics constitute the crux of pricing, i.e., demand information, problems faced by state and local governments. A good that is jointly consumed cannot be readily priced. Each consumer knows that, if the service is provided at all, every unit of production can be consumed by every consumer; additional consumers, at least up to some point, will inflict no costs on other consumers by enjoying the full benefits of all units that have been provided. For example, the government could provide mosquito protection by producing and selling a personal mosquito repellent, an ordinary private good. Or it could set up some jointly consumed abatement program, a public good. The important problem for government is to determine the demand for mosquito protection in the latter case.

The presence of externalities may lead to a public policy of zero pricing. As stated in Chapter 1, by externalities we mean impacts of activities of one economic unit upon another not exerted through the market. Thus these relationships are not those between buyer and seller. Public health measures usually illustrate this characteristic. The incidence of a disease declines when an inoculation program protects not only the person who receives a serum but also those who might contract the disease from him. It would be no problem to exclude people from receiving the serum by pricing, but persons other than the direct user will benefit greatly from the inoculation, and they cannot cheaply be charged by either the doctor or the direct user. Such external benefits make worthwhile giving the inoculations without charging the patient the full marginal social value. Individuals choosing to be inoculated might not place a value on protection of others, and a less-than-optimum number would be inoculated if only those receiving the serum were made to bear the full cost of the service.

The costs of exclusion can lead to zero pricing even though neither joint consumption nor externalities are involved. During peak periods, a beach-front parking lot may be priced. But during off-peak periods the lot may be closed and unattended, so no parking fee will be charged. The private owner finds that the revenues from charging in the off-peak periods are less than the costs of paying an attendant. Likewise, public parks and neighborhood playgrounds can be priced, but usually at a cost that exceeds the revenues.

Finally, and of particular importance, distributional or welfare considerations lead to zero or nominal pricing. Neighborhood parks are often provided to make recreational areas available to specific groups of consumers, for example, the poor, the very young, the aged, or the infirm. Such services are known as merit goods and are priced by government so as to change the allocation from that which would result if a strictly market-clearing price were employed. Merit goods involve interdependencies in utility functions; citizens other than direct users receive pleasure from knowing that the users of certain services consume more of them than they would if the marketplace alone determined distribution.

For the above economic reasons, state and local governments quite often employ zero or nominal prices. (It may also be argued that there are political, philosophical, or other noneconomic reasons for zero pricing.) In so doing, they forgo valuable information regarding the preferences of consumers for government services. To determine the demand for its services, a government unit must answer such questions as: "How much do consumers value alternative rates of use of particular services?" "How much do individual consumers value specific changes in the quality of a service?"

The methods that can be used in determining demand are the individual (economic) preference approach, which attempts to apply market criteria to the choice of public goods; the voters' behavior approach; and benefit-cost analysis.[1] Benefit-cost analysis is perhaps the only one of these three approaches that can be applied if demand signals are weak or absent. Furthermore, the individual preference and benefit-cost approaches are relevant to a normative theory whereas certain voters' behavior approaches, such as the one concerned with legislators' behavior, are relevant to a positive theory. These approaches will be discussed next.

THE INDIVIDUAL (ECONOMIC) PREFERENCE APPROACH

The individual preference approach of microeconomics is used in analyzing the demand for private goods. A large body of theory has been developed over the years which is based on the individual's calculus of the private costs and rewards that are associated with satisfying his desires in private markets. It is easy to understand that economists have therefore been tempted to draw upon this venerable body of theory in analyzing the demand for public goods.

The individual (economic) preference approach to estimation of demand for state and local government services is based on the premise that the individual is aware of his desire for a government service just as he is aware of his desire for a product provided by the open market. This approach is compatible with the notion that the individual may reflect in his scale of preference not only benefits and sacrifices of his own but also those of his neighbors and even of posterity. However, it is difficult to demonstrate that in fact a relationship exists between the taxes by which government services are financed and the demand of any one individual for government services, backed up by his willingness to make tax payments.

The model of the economic man cannot be applied easily and without alteration to estimation of the demand for outputs of public goods or services that are characterized by extensive joint consumption and only to a minor extent by individual consumption. The individual (economic) preference approach is most applicable to state and local government services that are free of significant externalities. We will discuss in this chapter the demand information produced under the condition that consumers must make large expenditures on private goods in order to consume the government output—in other words, consumers are willing to incur large associated private costs as they consume government services. We also recognize that demand estimates are possible if substitute services can be bought privately.

To derive demand functions, we must specify such relevant independent variables as prices and income or wealth and the shape of the function—for example, should it be linear or only linear in logarithm? We must also specify the period to be used and the lags to be introduced. We must account for the reactions of consumers to such special price policies as tie-in sales and price discrimination as well as to elements of monopoly and externalities.

Ideally, dynamic demand shifts might be analyzed and their paths traced with the aid of lags. More often, however, the demand function will be derived in terms of comparative statics, e.g., partial elasticities of demand or measurements of effects of change variables, such as technology.

To begin, we will examine state and local government services that involve major associated private costs. In his use of either public or private services the individual incurs not only costs for the services but costs associated with the services, such as the associated cost of transportation to a school or recreational facility. An individual's preference for a service is efficiently revealed when there is direct pricing, but many services are provided by government at zero or nominal prices. Therefore, information about the demand for a public service may be obtained by estimating the magnitude of the private costs associated with consumption of that public service. Given that the service will be zero priced, the manager still desires to have some information about the quantities demanded by various groups at various times.

The Case of Associated Private Costs

Certain state and local government services to some extent involve associated private costs. Weekend and vacation trips to recreational facilities, for example, involve considerable associated private costs. Marion Clawson has proposed "user-day" as the unit of measurement of the output of recreational facilities and private trip costs as the dominant associated costs and thus as a main component of the "price" of recreation.[2] However, this approach is vulnerable to attack, especially if we measure recreational demand by expenditures of sportsmen and campers.

Empirical efforts to derive a use function for recreational facilities could proceed along the following lines. Monthly or quarterly data could be adjusted to reflect the fact that recreational services are used in different intensities in the fall, winter, and spring-summer seasons. The changing patterns of vacation periods could be reflected in the analysis, as well as the overall increase in leisure time. Effects of changes in technology on the time-and-goods costs of consuming recreation (for example, the reduction in boat and engine prices and the increased provision of public marinas and freeways to reach them) also could be included. Cross-elasticities of these use functions might be calculated.

Associated costs are incurred at the point of origin, when the weekend or vacation recreational activity is planned and as a result capital equipment is procured. Travel to and from the recreational facility involves a time cost, as well as expenditures that would not otherwise be made. At the recreational site, user charges and entrance fees might be incurred.[3]

Recently an empirical study of recreational demand was conducted by Wayne E. Boyet and George S. Tolley.[4] They developed a "state characteristic" approach to recreation, in which facility use is a function of the distance of the state of origin from the recreational facility and in which travel outlay is regarded as the same for all persons who originate in a given state.

These considerations led Boyet and Tolley to the use of the following equation for the estimation of recreational use functions:

$$Y = 10^{\alpha} X_1^{\beta_1} X_2^{\beta_2} X_3^{\beta_3} X_4^{\beta_4} X_5^{\beta_5} X_6^{\beta_6} X_7^{\beta_7} e, \qquad (2.1)$$

where

Y = the dependent variable and is the total number of visits from each state

X_1 = the travel cost as measured by distance

X_2 = population

X_3 = per capita income

X_4 = median age

X_5 = median education

X_6 = percentage of population residing in census-defined urban areas

X_7 = percentage of the population that is white

e = a random variable

Multiple-regression techniques were used to obtain estimates of the parameters of equation 2.1 for each national park for which data on visits by state of origin are available for 1950. Distance and population elasticities are significant at the 1 percent probability level, and their signs are as expected. Although income elasticities have the expected signs, they are not uniformly significant. However, there is no consistency in either the algebraic sign or the level of significance of the elasticity estimates associated with the remaining variables.

Boyet and Tolley estimate the elasticities of the equation and apply them to project facility use for recreation. For example, using the state characteristic approach, they project a 27 percent increase in the use of a certain North Carolina recreational area between 1963 and 1980. Using a disaggregated or individual characteristic approach, they projected a 120 percent increase for the area in the same period.

However, they do not discuss the effects of expected technological changes or of private market alternatives to certain public facilities. The effects of those as well as of improvements in transportation, reduced costs of recreational equipment, and other factors should be considered by using comparative statics. It is not difficult to predict that, for example, as the wages and the participation in the labor force of married women increase, the rate of use of certain parks as child-care centers will tend to increase.

The Case of Private Substitutes Costs

Quite a few of the goods and services provided by state and local governments are free of significant externalities. These range from private goods which the state might sell to raise revenue—for example, liquor sold in state liquor stores—to public utility services where scale economies favor a single large producer, and include goods that involve minor externalities. If for any reason the same good or service becomes privately provided, some demand signals can be observed and estimates of demand become possible.

Hospital services might be looked upon as an example of private substitutes, although little rigorous analysis has thus far been attempted.[5] The demand for hospital care can be analyzed by type of service: outpatient, surgical, etc. Independent variables include the price per unit of service for each category of service in the public hospital; an index of prices in competing private hospitals (and possibly a measurement of substitutability between hospital and at-home care); income (or wealth); technological trends; amount of insurance purchased, independent of income, size, and age distribution of population (for time series); additional demographic features of population; etc.

The Case of Mixed Associated Private Costs and Private Substitutes Costs

A number of state and local government services both involve associated private costs and have substitutes in the private market. Education is a good example: Education is offered in both public and private markets and involves substantial associated private costs. Such costs are expenses other than tuition incurred by individuals in their efforts to benefit from education and include expenses for transportation, books, and additional clothing as well as earnings that students forgo.

Mathematical models of the demand for education can be formulated in various ways. For example, to learn about the demand for higher education, regardless of whether it is offered privately or publicly, we could use as the dependent variable college enrollment as a percentage of the eligible, college-age population. Independent variables could include estimates of tuition and other associated private costs; income level; occupation of father; demographic information on the ethnic composition of the eligible, college-age population; and a dummy variable reflecting private versus public enrollment. On the assumption that associated private costs correlate closely with tuition costs, the associated costs item could be dropped. A somewhat simplified model has been formulated and tested by Robert Campbell and Barry Siegel.[6]

If we estimate the demand only for public higher education, we should use as the dependent variable a percentage figure of enrollment in public institutions to enrollment in private institutions.

Ideally, instead of dealing with all higher education we would look at the problem in terms of relatively small geographic units and consider for them scholastic ratings of institutions of higher learning; types of institutions (junior college, four-year college, institutions with undergraduate and graduate education, etc.) ; and fields of study. Empirical demand functions in these terms could be used by school officials in comparative static analyses to estimate changes in junior college enrollment in relation to four-year college enrollment over a relatively short period of time. If the results of such analyses proved reliable, improved decisions could be made about further investment, pricing, and student aid.

Also, in the analysis of local police services it is possible to identify private market substitutes and associated private costs that can yield information about the demand for government-supplied protection. In particular, insurance premiums are a market indicator of a private service that is to some extent a substitute for police protection. To the extent that police protection fails to prevent losses, insurance will be relied upon for compensation. Insurance is a form of risk shifting whereby the costs of losses are transferred from individuals to second parties who pool risks of a large number of persons. We can assume that the amount an individual pays (his premium) for insurance against each type of potential loss (e.g., theft, burglary, vandalism, personal assault) approximates his individual evaluation of a potential loss from such an occurrence. His premium, or the approximate expected value of potential loss, could be interpreted as equivalent to the individual's valuation of the quantity of police services that would be sufficient to prevent such a loss or, in other words, as his demand for police services. Additional purchases of theft insurance from private insurers imply either increases in theft-susceptible wealth and (or) an increase in the possibility of a loss. His additional premiums for theft insurance would approximate the amount he would be willing to pay for a quantity of police protection sufficient to reduce the size of the potential additional loss. To reduce the possibility of losses citizens can also purchase various services and devices that can prevent unauthorized entrance to premises or facilitate immediate detection of intruders, such as sophisticated locks, private police services, burglar alarms, etc.

In summary, the extent to which individual (economic) preference analysis can be used in the study of the demand for state and local government services is inversely related to the degree of "publicness" of those services. The more important the associated private costs and the more available the private substitutes, the more demand and facility use information that can be obtained. With the use of appropriate data, econometric models can be developed to organize this valuable information about the demand for certain government services.

The econometric estimation of demand functions for state and local government services usually relies on whatever data are available. However, in at least one recent case gaming was used to generate relevant demand data. Robert L. Wilson designed a game to learn the value that representative members of two North Carolina communities attached to certain government services.[7] Wilson played the game with individual representatives of the two communities; he used three schemes to rank their preferences: First he asked the individuals to rank their likes and dislikes; then he presented them with a list of goods and services with hypothetical prices and gave each person a lump sum ($2,000 in one community, $1,800 in the other) with which to choose a preferred bundle; and finally he gave each person an additional $3,000 windfall and asked him to reorder his preferences.

That the game was unrealistic can be seen from the results: The players ranked a bus stop high as a preferred service, even though they had no notion of how frequently a bus would come and pick up passengers. In short, no account was taken of the myriad interacting decisions in the economy.

The main problems with Wilson's approach were: the assumed fixed nature of wealth (a stock, not a flow), so income could not enter as a variable in the analysis; the failure to offer private market alternatives to government provision of goods and services; and the ambiguous dimensions of the goods (What quantity? At what price per unit?). From the standpoint of contributing to economic analysis, the game designed by Wilson has, at best, limited usefulness. However, this critique is not intended as a condemnation of Wilson's effort; a simple and more meaningful extension of Wilson's model would allow some distribution of income over the sample population and introduce income as a flow variable.

VOTERS' BEHAVIOR APPROACH

So far we have considered an approach in which individuals are viewed as economizing on actual purchases of state and local government services. We now turn to the behavior of voters on issues and expenditure packages.

Even if a large group of individuals are able to effectively express their preferences and vote officials into office and programs into being, they have merely initiated actions that must be translated into final outputs by the political process. After the preference of a majority of the voters has been expressed, elected and appointed officials must interpret the vote and act (or not act) on it. Most programs require substantial lead time between the vote and the production of the services.

The voters' behavior approach may supplement and be compatible with the individual (economic) preference approach discussed above. This expanded individual preference approach can provide a better understanding of the entire complex maze in which public decisions are made. The political behavior approach is concerned with the resolution of conflict through private decisions.[8] Thus, our next task will be to present a number of methods by which voters' behavior and the political process can be examined.

Analysis of Voters' Behavior

Political scientists and, more recently, economists have taken an interest in analyzing voting behavior in the hope of gaining insight into collective decision-making processes. Such analyses could yield valuable information regarding demand for government services. Perhaps the most noteworthy effort of this kind has been the revealing statistical analysis carried out by William Birdsall.[9] Birdsall begins his analysis with the individual, proposing the following "demand" function:[10]

$$g_{ij} = d_{ij}(X, C, \mathbf{p}, G, \mathbf{t}, L) \tag{2.2}$$

where

$X =$ a matrix of the personal characteristics of all individuals
$C =$ a matrix of quantities of privately produced goods consumed by all individuals
$\mathbf{p} =$ a vector of prices for private market goods
$G =$ a matrix of all other publicly produced goods partitioned by level of government
$\mathbf{t} =$ a vector of tax rates partitioned in accordance with G
$L =$ a matrix of locational characteristics by political subdivision
$g_{ij} =$ the quantity of public i demanded by the jth individual
$d_{ij} =$ the functional notation

Assuming a stable preference function for individuals, Birdsall performs cross-sectional analysis of 26 voting issues over 55 districts of New York; he tests the percentages of yes votes against some 50 variables by the use of a stepwise regression technique. The data are aggregated by summing over all individuals (with only some of the information desired in the ideal model being observable).

With this analysis, Birdsall is generally able to explain past voting behavior on the basis of income differentials, the structure of relative private and government prices, and demographic variables.

Using independent variables such as percentage residential property (the value of residential property as a percentage of the total value of all taxable property) as a proxy for locally owned wealth and percentage "stable" population as a proxy for "permanent" residents, Birdsall obtains positive results when he is explaining the percentages of yes votes on issues such as housing referenda that have expected "neighborhood effects" on land values. Thus, Birdsall does provide a test of whether people take account of (positive) spillovers—at least of the most overt ones—in their voting behavior.[11]

Birdsall does not claim to be able to predict the outcomes of future voting propositions. He recognizes that there are too many variables (such as "degree of emotionalism") that the economist cannot take into account. However, as indicated above, Birdsall's tests do render some useful results. A positive theory remains to be developed to predict the outcomes of political conflicts that involve voters' expressions of their preferences and to explain how divergent preferences are reconciled in the collective decision-making process.

Groups of voters appear to differ in their voting behavior. John Due concludes that ". . . many persons in middle- and high-income levels support programs that will primarily aid the minority low-income group."[12] James Wilson and Edwin Banfield found that steps to extend and improve government programs are often supported by the higher- and lower-income groups and opposed by middle-income groups.[13]

It must be remembered, furthermore, that voters' participation in the making of decisions on state and local government issues is often small and unpredictable. This is one indication that the linkage between the behavior of voters and that of legislators is uncertain. An officeholder normally has a strong incentive to be reelected. Although his reelection may require a majority of the votes actually cast, the number of voters is usually far less than the majority of eligible voters. For example, the median percentage of adults voting in local elections of cities over 25,000 population in 1961–1962 was estimated to be 44 percent when local elections were held concurrently with national elections and 31 percent when not held concurrently.[14] In the spring of 1967 when the Los Angeles Unified School District held a runoff election for the office of school board member, only about 20 percent of the eligible voters voted.

Not only is the turnout of voters small and unpredictable but the interest groups that will use influence and expend resources cannot always be readily identified. Sometimes the enthusiastic support of only a small minority of all voters is sufficient to produce a win that requires a majority vote. That the problem of predicting voters' behavior is extremely complex will be more fully realized if we add to the factors that have been discussed voters' ignorance of election issues.

The "Voting with One's Feet" Approach

By and large ours is a highly mobile society; therefore, in theory the voter who cannot obtain the kind of service package he desires will reach a point where the disutilities are so great that he moves to another community in which public officials are more responsive to his demands. This phenomenon can affect decisions made by governmental officials as well as by voters.

Outmigration by members of middle- and upper-income groups is especially feared by city officials, who strenuously seek the growth of their cities and even like to boast about it. Outmigration by people of middle and upper incomes often means not only major losses of tax base but a decline in the fiscal health of the community as well. Specifically, middle- and upper-income people tend to "produce" more revenue than is spent to provide them with services. Furthermore, it may be feared that such outmigration can have a snowballing effect by bringing into the community many people of lower incomes, many of whom often are assumed to have certain other "undesirable" characteristics.

Charles M. Tiebout developed a model of individual choice of governments which assumes that individuals can freely move among government jurisdictions.[15] Governments are motivated to attract "desirable" families and activities from other areas while discouraging their own "desirable" residents and activities from outmigrating. Movement can be looked upon as resigning from a social contract. Tiebout's model stipulates an infinite variety of communities, each offering a different package of public services and taxes. On the assumption that all private goods are available at the same price, the individual selects his site in a manner that balances marginal site costs, i.e., housing costs including taxes, with his marginal evaluation of the public services package. However, since the model does not offer explicitly a political process for policy making and for generating the optimal set of packages for itinerant households, it is not clear that an optimal supply of government services will result.

Moving from one community to another is a form of "voting" in which a market decision (site choice) and a political decision (on public services) interact. With this interrelation in mind, Julius Margolis has extended the voting with one's feet approach to the case where community leaders are strongly motivated in their decision making by fiscal health considerations; decisions are evaluated in terms of the effect on the community of tax revenue minus public cost.[16] If officials of a local government mainly pursue the policy of enhancing the community's fiscal health and if individuals make locational decisions on the basis of a differential between value of services and tax cost, land values in such a "fiscally healthy" community should rise. Although current residents would find increases in fiscal health capitalized into land values, inmigrants would be likely to face a relatively low tax rate, yet higher property values, which in turn would mean higher interest and tax payments.

The voting with one's feet models of Tiebout and Margolis emphasize the importance of mobility and of the market for assets, both of which are linked to the fiscal policies of government. The models remain to be further improved, possibly by the incorporation of features of the political process and of outcome optimization.

Analysis of Legislators' Behavior

The voting behavior of legislators as well as that of citizens can be analyzed. Legislators are the representatives of the electorate and yet the linkage between the two is usually remote and extremely complex. Furthermore, each legislator is only a single decision maker and one who must act, taking full account of the powers of executive officials of government and the reactions of civil servants.

Relatively little creative work has been done to explain the voting behavior of legislators, who must bargain not only among themselves but also with special interest groups and program administrators. One view of what drives public officials, and their bargaining mechanism, has been well described by Roland N. McKean, who states:

> Inevitably each person has a separate utility function. . . . In government, if the cost to an official of one action increases, he will take less of it. If the gains that he feels increase, he will take more action of that sort.
>
> If a public official's action will use up someone's property or damage certain interests, he will probably find a cost associated with that action.
>
> He has to bargain with many people who are affected and, in one way or another, encounter costs if he makes decisions that impose sacrifices on others. From those who are benefited, on the other hand, he can bargain for compensation. . . .
>
> Like the price system, this bargaining mechanism has many desirable effects. It might be called the "unseen hand in government." The right kind of bargaining process can make special interests and parochial viewpoints, which one might think would produce chaotic decisions, lead to an orderly and sensible pattern of choices.[17]

The motivation of bureaucrats has been examined by Anthony Downs, who suggests that they are guided by a mixture of self-interest and a desire to further the programs under their jurisdictions.[18] He finds it useful to divide bureaucrats into five categories—climbers, conservers, zealots, advocates, and statesmen. John Due sees bureaucrats exercising disproportionate power over government activities when voters and legislators suffer from a lack of full information.[19]

Albert Breton has attempted to develop a theory of demand for public goods which assumes:

> that governments maximize the probability of their re-election, a probability which is dependent on the policies that are implemented as well as on the degree to which they are implemented. . . . Governments and their electorates

are engaged in a sort of exchange in which policies are traded for votes; to maximize the probability of their re-election, governments endeavor to "produce" those policies which can be exchanged for the largest possible . . . number of votes.[20]

Otto A. Davis and George H. Haines also have built models of municipal government on the assumption that government officials are motivated by a desire to attain and remain in power.[21] In their model, government officials must take action which appeals to a dominant coalition of voters. Thus, they view officials as followers of a perceived "will of the majority" rather than as molders of public opinion. The results of some empirical studies appear to validate such a model.

The "Calculus of Consent" Approach

The recent trend in economics has been to extend modern welfare economics away from notions of social welfare functions or enlightened, centralized computational techniques and toward market analysis of democratic political institutions. For example, James Buchanan and Gordon Tullock offer for the understanding of voting behavior and its implications some theoretical propositions of value and exchange theory.[22] Working in the context of a three-person game, they examine the economic efficiency of different projects under various decision rules, one of which is that the participants are constrained by decision-making costs. The desire for personal gain establishes the rationale for individual and group (coalition) actions. Buchanan and Tullock present an interesting theoretical discussion of collective choice, varieties of decision rules, and the possible efficiency or inefficiency of outcomes from such rules; however, they derive relatively little positive analysis. Their approach does not greatly improve prediction of the outcome of decision-making processes. No specific demand function is created through which the consequences of changes in independent variables can be traced through to changes in the quantities demanded of various government outputs. The calculus of consent approach does yield insight into the rationality of constitutional agreements and the general effect of alterations in constitutional rules of decision making on the extent and overall range of government activities.

Anthony Downs, a forerunner in the modern economic approach to collective decision making, provides us with a pioneering discussion of the behavior of parties and party candidates. Whereas Buchanan and Tullock concentrate on constitutional decision rules and politics in *The Calculus of Consent*, Anthony Downs concentrates on functioning political systems in which parties or coalitions capture government offices and then attempt to perpetuate themselves in office.[23] A political unit in office weighs the effects of all of its acts and tries to gain the votes of at least a majority of the electorate. Voters must compare the utility income derived from the decisions of the office-holders with the estimated utility income they would derive if the politicians who are seeking the offices were to make the decisions. Then voters must evaluate the programs and platforms proposed and the other promises made by the contestants for office in the coming decision-making period. Individual votes depend on the services to be received for the taxes that are anticipated. To capture and hold office each political unit is engaged in the enterprise of estimating the demand schedules of individuals for governmental actions.

Downs's analysis also is quite general and yields no specific demand functions or prescriptions for deriving operational demand formulas. Despite their shortcomings for our purposes, the works of Buchanan, Tullock, and Downs are outstanding examples of particular theoretical approaches to understanding the demand for and the supply of collective actions. The economics of politics has not yet provided us with sufficiently general theorems to convince welfare theorists that collective actions are either "overproduced" or "underproduced." We have at this time only Arrow's General Possibility Theorem which proves the impossibility of devising collective decision processes, based on individual values, that yield total, general social optimums (the avowed purpose of social welfare functions).[24]

BENEFIT-COST APPROACH

Welfare economics, dormant for a number of decades, has in recent years blossomed into an attractive area of economic inquiry. One of its contributions is benefit-cost analysis, which was initially applied to evaluation of investment programs for river basin development. The application of benefit-cost analysis has since been broadened to include virtually all state and local government services. Technical details and examples of benefit-cost analysis will be presented in the chapter on Program Budgeting.

The purpose of benefit-cost analysis is to provide information to decision makers—government officeholders, political rivals, and voters. The detail and quality of the information provided by such studies are of course a function of research cost. A community of decision makers that wishes to remove some uncertainties by increasing its information can do so, but benefit-cost studies are costly. Often we observe each rival in a political dispute advancing his own, often very limited, benefit-cost study, based on assumptions that favor his side. Little uncertainty is removed if so few resources have been devoted to these studies that the information they provide to decision makers is of low quality. Decision makers may, in fact, regard a great quantity of information of low quality as confusing and misleading, and therefore as increasing uncertainty.

The usual situation in collective action is that those individuals who bear the costs of the action are not the only beneficiaries of the action; they may not even be the primary beneficiaries. Thus, since the demanders of a particular service decision will not be the sole bearers of the costs of providing the service, the redistributive consequences must be considered. The separation and identification of differential benefits to various groups made possible by benefit-cost analysis provides decision makers with information on who is likely to gain, who is likely to lose, and in each case by how much. Such information is relevant to all political decision making because it helps to identify bargains that can be made in support of legislation and for the funding of government activities. In other words, such information helps to identify the demand for various government services.

The shortcoming of benefit-cost analysis in the estimation of demand for public goods and services is that such studies often appear to reveal only what the investigator believed demand ought to be—if voters were rational—rather than to reveal effective demand. The nexus between benefit-cost analysis and approximation of a service demand curve may lie in the following sequence: Benefit-cost analysis identifies community benefits, which in turn are the sum of differential benefits to various groups of potential users. For example, we might assume that a group of affected individuals who receive $20 million in real benefits from a good value the good at least by this amount, and that if the quantity of the good produced were offered in the private market the group would be willing to pay up to $20 million to have the good. Thus, in the presentation of an all-or-nothing offer (to provide the good or not to provide the good), we have obtained a point on a community demand function,[25] although we cannot claim to have estimated a schedule of points that would approximate a demand curve. If a series of alternative offers (different quantities or qualities available to the public at different theoretical prices) were incorporated in the benefit-cost analysis we could say that the resulting information for decision makers approximated a demand function for the good.

Formal benefit-cost studies of the quality that would yield detailed information about individual demand schedules are seldom undertaken because of their astronomical costs. In the absence of such studies our notions of demand are based on estimates of benefits to groups of individuals.

In general, each interest group in society is producing cost-benefit "studies" of proposed government policies from its own point of view. And these calculations are widely advertised to the general public and extensively distributed to government officeholders. In general, two types of actors participate in the process of allocation of state and local government services: consumers and public decision makers. Consumers take a variety of steps to formulate and articulate their desires so as to obtain government services. Public decision makers—legislators and administrators—must translate consumers' demands into allocation decisions. The citizen who does not bother to articulate his views on public issues will have less influence than the one who does; usually, an individual acts only on matters that are of direct concern to him, because his participation involves sizable costs. However, because of the high cost of determining with accuracy the present (or prospective) supply of state and local government services and his realized (or expected) benefits and costs, the typical citizen relies on information presented by organized interest groups and government agencies in favor of their positions. A substantial amount of time is required of the citizen merely to collect such cost-benefit information.

The production and dissemination of such information are the costs entailed in the effective articulation of demand. Most state and local government services cannot be purchased by consumers in individual consumption units; instead relevant government decision makers must be persuaded to provide particular quantities and qualities of service. Affected parties must encounter the decision maker with specific proposals regarding specific issues. Yet both the communication effort and the uncertainty of outcomes represent costs to participants.

The existence of these cost considerations has several implications for the political allocation process: The number of persons who aggressively supply benefit information for a given service tends to be less, the greater the costs of obtaining and communicating information. Participation, and therefore demand articulation, will be higher among those having the most to gain or lose on a given issue. Furthermore, because of the "public goodness" of information and because transaction costs are subject to economies of scale, individuals will be motivated to consolidate their efforts to influence the government decision maker on a particular issue. This gives rise to the interest group, i.e., an aggregation of individuals who pursue a perceived common goal.

Behind any group decision, there are elaborate mechanisms for consultation, bargaining, informing and directing, etc. Group decision processes which ultimately lead to the articulation of the group's cost and benefit information tend to be more important in the public than in the private sector, both because there are many more parties involved in each decision and because there is no money market as a coordinating mechanism.

Thus, the absence of coordination through the market mechanism makes it important to understand the reconciliation process among consumers of state and local government services and the formation of interest groups. In the private sector of the economy, according to John Due, ". . . no problem of reconciliation of varying preferences arises, effective demands are summed by the market and production adjusts accordingly. With public goods, summation does not occur automatically since the amounts to be produced must be determined in a single nonmarket decision." [26]

As mentioned above, the "unseen hand in government" can lead to a sensible pattern of choices in the complicated bargaining process among consumers of state and local government services. It can lead to the formation of interest groups and to bargaining between such groups, legislators, and administrators. But the outcomes produce demand information and demand schedules of lesser quality than exchanges in money markets.

There remains the question: What affects the ability of a group to effectively articulate its demand? A group's influence depends first of all on the rules by which public officials are selected and their relative power in different issue areas. The availability and cost of information, the potential for formation of groups, the availability of leaders unsatisfied with the decisions of the elite, the potential ability to influence a decision and consequent incentive to try to do so, the incentives to cooperate or withhold cooperation, and the way in which each of these factors varies in different socioeconomic groups—all will determine the potency of the group's influence network.[27]

SUMMARY

Analysis of consumer preference for state and local government services is similar to demand analysis for private sector outputs. We want to know how individual consumers determine their opinion about state and local government services, reconcile possibly conflicting desires among consumers, and effectively communicate these desires in the light of complicated bargaining among consumers themselves and between consumers, legislators, and administrators.

In the absence of price signals, estimation of the demand for state and local government services is complex and circuitous. Fortunately, for many of the services provided by state and local governments, consumer demand signals can be identified even though some are quite weak.

The individual (economic) preference approach is particularly appropriate where strong price signals are available; an excellent example is a public utility service for which user charges are imposed. Certain public goods provided by state and local governments entail some associated private costs or have substitutes in the private market. The demand for such goods may be estimated with the aid of econometric methods.

Because the chain of interactions between consumer and service producer is long and tenuous and the preferences of consumers are not easily revealed, voting behavior must be studied. The behavior of the electorate as well as that of legislators and office seekers can be studied empirically and useful theories can be built. But citizens vote not only at the polls but every day through pressure groups and "with their feet." Although "voting with one's feet" is an interesting concept, the effects of such movements on decision makers remain to be better understood and quantified.

Political economists have recently attempted to develop theoretical models in which political institutions are substituted for market processes in efforts to link individual preferences to public expenditures. Important theoretical propositions have been advanced but remain to be refined for empirical testing.

Finally, the benefit-cost approach can be applied to analysis of demand for state and local government services, regardless of how weak the demand signals are. In such analysis, we are less interested in overall benefit-cost estimates than in the benefit-cost positions in which different important interest groups find themselves with regard to specific increments in services. This requires understanding of how groups are formed, their characteristics, and how effectively they articulate their demands. Rather than revealing effective demand, this approach helps to indicate what demand ought to be if voters were rational.

CHAPTER 3
USER
CHARGES

In the preceding chapter we pointed out four characteristics—joint consumption, costs of exclusion, externalities in consumption, and welfare or distributional considerations—any one of which would explain why government does not employ prices to ration and finance the production of a particular good or service.

However, since many of the goods and services of state and local governments are not significantly affected by any of these characteristics, user charges can be applied to them. A user charge is defined as the dollars per unit of a good or service produced by government that are collected from the recipient. User charges differ from other government revenues primarily because they involve an exchange.[1] User charges account for a large percentage of state and local revenues; official statistics place general miscellaneous revenues at about 16 percent of total general state and local government revenues (see Table 5.1 of Chapter 5). By a broad measure, user charges accounted for 47 percent of state and 35 percent of local government revenues from own sources in 1965–1966; by a narrower measure, user charges accounted for 15 percent of state and 29 percent of local government revenues from own sources in that fiscal year.[2]

It is ordinarily assumed that government-operated water, gas, and electric utilities offer most of the opportunities for applying user charges and that such utilities produce most of user-charge revenues. In actuality, however, even by a narrow measure such user charges account for only about 43 percent of the user-charge revenues of local governments and for less than 1 percent of the user-charge revenues of state governments. As we will illustrate in this chapter, the opportunities for state and local governments to employ user charges are much broader than those offered by the so-called commercial activities of public utilities.

BROAD AND NARROW MEASURES OF USER CHARGES

By a narrow measure, user charges are those revenues embraced by the census revenue category, "current charges and miscellaneous revenues," *less* special assessments, donations, fines, forfeits, and all other miscellaneous general revenues but *plus* all revenues from government-operated utilities and liquor stores.[3] Estimates of such user charges are presented in Table 3.1.

By a broad measure, user charges include the census revenue category

TABLE 3.1   Estimates of User Charges Levied by State and Local Governments,
1965–1966

	Narrow Measure of User Charges		Broad Measure of User Charges	
	User Charges (millions)	User Charges as a % of Total Revenue from Own Sources	User Charges (billions)	User Charges as a % of Total Revenue from Own Sources
State governments	$ 6,599	15	More than $22	More than 47
Local governments	12,021	29	More than $15	More than 35
Total	$18,620	22		More than 41

"current charges and miscellaneous revenues" and, as defined by the Bureau of the Census: "Amounts received from the public for performance of specific services benefitting the person charged and from sales of commodities and services." Included in such "amounts received" are interest earnings for deposits and securities owned by the governmental unit minus those earnings and assets held in trust funds; also such special assessments as compulsory contributions collected from owners of property benefited by specific public improvements to defray the cost of such improvements, and which are apportioned according to the assumed benefits of the property affected. Thus the estimates in Table 3.1 include items, such as donations, fines, forfeits, and special assessments, that would not ordinarily be considered user charges.

The following are also included in the broad measure: liquor store revenues; local utility receipts and franchise or concession receipts; motor fuel sales taxes; license taxes (including vehicles, drivers, corporations, public utilities, hunting, fishing, general business, occupations, etc.) ; insurance trust revenues (including employee contributions, employer contributions, and earnings on assets held in trust) ; and permits.

CHARACTERISTICS AND RATIONALE OF USER CHARGES

Financing state and local government services through user charges means that government officials levy charges on the users of particular units of output and that the total revenues from these charges closely reflect the cost to the government of supplying the output. The financing of services by user charges depends on the ability of government officials to identify all beneficiaries of particular government outputs. For some outputs the beneficiaries are the direct users and no unusual difficulty arises. But for other outputs the principal beneficiaries are not the direct users and the principal beneficiaries are difficult to identify.

The principal advantage of user charges over other possible levies is that user charges provide government officials with more information about the economic efficiency of government operations. The person who pays a user charge accepts a sacrifice in a voluntary exchange; he prefers what he receives to what he gives up; and he reveals that his expected private benefit from using particular units of output is at least as great as his private sacrifice.

The various functions that user charges can perform for government can be grouped as follows:

1. Provision of revenue
2. Rationing of government output
3. Allocation of burdens
4. Provision of demand signals

Each of these four functions of user charges will be taken up in turn.

Provision of Revenue

State and local government officials see user charges as a source of revenue to cover the expenditure of their agencies; they do not regard user charges as sales receipts directly related to personal wealth, as most private producers do. The principal difference between government and private producers is that government has the power to obtain revenue by taxation, and this difference makes the analysis of user charges especially interesting. We may regard public officials as possessing monopolistic powers; however, they are not allowed to exploit this power to obtain personal pecuniary rewards and therefore do not tend to regard their programs as competitive, profit-making enterprises. Instead, in each budget period their immediate concern is for funds with which to cover planned operating expenses and to service the debt incurred on outlays for capital equipment and facilities. Government officials may have strong personal preferences for obtaining budgeted funds from tax levies rather than from user charges levied on their clients. In any event, government officials tend to view user charges as only one among several possible ways of raising revenues and thus "staying in business."

Rationing of Government Output

User charges help to ration the output of each production period among competing claimants and to eliminate shortages or surpluses of government output. User charges perform a rationing function by excluding those potential users of government output who are not willing to pay as great a price as other potential users and thereby allocating the limited outputs to those individuals who are willing to make greater sacrifices. Because there are always competing demanders for the services of government some rationing scheme will usually be necessary. Historically, a common rationing practice has been to distribute output on a queuing or first-come-first-served basis. However, a legal scheme may provide administrative rules for identifying the government's user priorities by directing that state or local government officials deliver goods and services to specified individuals according to specified formulas.

Economic efficiency requires that government officials produce goods and services in such a manner that the same benefits could not be produced with fewer resources. Government officials would be required by the economic efficiency criterion to adjust output in each production period so that no rearrangement of resources could result in an output mix of higher value or preference to "the community." In a competitive market economy the price system encourages economic efficiency by yielding rewards to or imposing losses on those who cater to the demands of individuals. User charges would have a similar effect on state and local government production if public officials were competitively challenged by producers of substitute goods or services. Thus, the absence of a competitive challenge from close substitutes can prevent user charges from fully performing their function of rationing government resources most efficiently. Other institutional arrangements such as open market bidding for limited time period monopoly rights and marginal cost pricing might effectively compensate for the absence of competitive challenge from substitutes. In some cases the very absence of competitive challenge can be explained by government pricing practices and (or) explicit legal restraints on the behavior of potential competitors.

It must be reemphasized, however, that economic efficiency is only one normative criterion of performance; there are many other norms for determining the "best" rate of output, the "most desirable" quality to supply, and, of course, the "right" distribution of total supply in the community.[4] In a broader context it is probably a misconception to regard economic efficiency in government services as independent of the political forces that mold collective decisions.

Allocation of Burdens

We have described above the allocation of financial burdens among members of the community that is implied by financing through user charges. Those individuals who are the recipients of government output assume such burdens in close relation to the quantity of output that they choose to take. If government officials were to switch to another source of revenue, such as a sales tax, to finance a particular activity it would be quite unlikely that exactly the same individuals would bear the same sacrifices or would bear sacrifices in relation to the amount of output they received. State and local government officials usually seek to redistribute the wealth of individuals in the community by financing output from revenue sources other than user charges; often it is precisely the allocation of burdens implied by financing by user charges that prompts government officials to seek alternative means of financing. According to particular conceptions of desirable wealth redistributions, state and local governments are motivated to levy burdens on the basis of ability to pay and to ration output on some basis of "need."

Provision of Demand Signals

Attaining economic efficiency is essentially a problem of obtaining correct information about demand. The search by state and local government officials for demand information to improve their decisions and to make their tasks easier is facilitated by user charges. User charges yield demand information as an almost costless by-product.[5] These charges shed light on the question: Which recipients value additional units of output as much as or more than the per-unit user charge being levied? When the producers of state or local government services combine this demand information with marginal cost estimates, they are able to make more efficient decisions about what quantity to produce, what changes in services to make, what kinds of capital investments to make, and when to make investments. User charges are thus a valuable source of information with which to improve government decisions. Substitute information of equal quality could be obtained only at great cost, as was shown in Chapter 2. In the present chapter we will attempt to show how this information is useful in making the decisions listed above.

DETERMINING USER CHARGES

We stated earlier that whether state and local governments can rely on conventional user charges for particular outputs depends on the nature of the good being produced. In the case of extensive possibilities for joint consumption and great costs of excluding potential beneficiaries, no effective pricing system can be efficiently employed. A beneficiary will be unwilling to voluntarily assume costs for the good or service—especially if it is realized that the short-run marginal costs of an additional user are zero; i.e., once the good is provided, nonpayers may join in consuming the good at zero social cost. Each potential beneficiary knows that if other individuals pay to obtain the good or service his personal consumption will be increased at no direct sacrifice in consumption on the part of the other individuals. Therefore, each consumer acting in his own interest attempts to avoid personal sacrifices for the good and at the same time encourages others to pay for its provision.

The employment of user charges depends on the costs of excluding nonpayers. The amount that state and local governments are willing to spend for exclusion depends in turn on the benefits expected from exclusion and the forgone benefits of alternative uses of government resources. Thus, government-sponsored parades and fireworks displays are not priced and nonpayers are not excluded; but for government-sponsored sports events, beauty contests, and rodeos, the usual procedure is to incur the costs of excluding nonpayers.

And although user charges are economically feasible in the narrow sense, distributional or welfare considerations may dissuade officials from using them. The distribution of benefits and costs that results from imposing user charges, like the results of other rationing and financing schemes, must pass political tests of acceptability. Such tests are necessarily made to determine the desirability of the changes in distribution that result from imposing user charges instead of employing some other source of revenue. Tests of political acceptability are based on individual preferences expressed through the political process.

For such services as public libraries, school lunches, and public hospitals, distributional considerations appear to dominate considerations of the benefits derivable from pricing. But when such goods and services are provided by private producers they are priced to exclude nonpayers. The benefits of employing user charges for financing and rationing the government supply of these goods are attenuated by significant interdependencies of utility among community members—there is concern about the quantity particular individuals consume of these goods. Therefore full user charges may be applied.

Assuming that user charges are to be applied, what then are some of the considerations and techniques for levying user charges? We believe some of the requirements are:

1. Quantity and quality dimensions of output units must be specified and to some extent quantified.
2. Exclusive ownership or rights to use must be defined and must lend themselves to exchange.
3. Rights to exclusive use must be enforceable at reasonable cost. For example, enforcement costs should not exceed the social cost required to extend production to meet the quantity demanded at a zero price.
4. Total estimated costs of an output program must be less than total expected sales revenue or else sales revenue must be augmented by nonsales revenues (from the government's budget or elsewhere) that have been justified by political tests.

Determination of the feasibility of pricing state and local government outputs must take into account estimates not only of production costs but also of costs of measuring the amount of output desired by any one consumer at alternative prices, costs of levying and collecting specific prices, and costs of excluding nonusers (or of protecting exclusive rights). Consider, for example, the feasibility of financing a specific public service—sidewalks.[6] The costs of excluding all nonpayers from use of sidewalks and of charging users according to quantities consumed are obviously prohibitive. Decisions about how many sidewalks to build, where to locate them, who shall pay for them, and who shall use them may not be economically optimum because demand information from direct users is lacking. Apparently, however, such decisions about sidewalks can be made at lower social production and distribution costs if decisions are made on a special assessment basis or, as in some modern subdivisions, if sidewalks are supplied and charged for by private builders.

Three different techniques to determine charges will now be explored— monopoly pricing, fair pricing, and marginal cost pricing.

Monopoly Pricing

State and local governments can in many cases prevent private firms from entering an industry by applying their police power and can forbid production of many or all close substitutes. The government can, at least in theory, then proceed to exercise its monopoly position to maximize net revenues. Unless citizens are vigilant, the management of such a public enterprise may be less efficient than if the monopoly were a private monopoly. This is because the incomes of government managers are not so directly related to profit as those of private managers. But, within limits, the manager of the public enterprise could be directed to act as a monopolist and to attempt to produce and sell an amount that maximizes the net return to government by equating marginal revenue and marginal cost in each market.[7]

Most likely, few government outputs are monopoly priced because of the political implications of the inequities associated with monopoly pricing. We can imagine situations, however, where the results of a monopoly solution may be sought, e.g., where the purchasers of a government output are a minority of the population. A monopoly pricing solution might be especially attractive if the government service has external diseconomies to nonpurchasers or if the direct user receives other nonpriced benefits from the state or local government.

An example of the first case might be government retailing of alcoholic beverages; the effect of first-order, nondiscriminating monopoly pricing would be similar to that of sumptuary sales taxes on liquor. In the latter case a monopoly price for one public output can act as a tie-in sale for another public service that is received free of charge. For example, a tunnel, bridge, or limited-access highway may be priced to include the services of access roads and other highway services that are free of direct charge.

"Fair" Pricing

State and local government officials, lacking strong incentives to maximize the net revenues of their operations but usually finding themselves constrained by a break-even rule, appear to favor some sort of "fair" price—apparently by far the most popular scheme for levying user charges. If only one price is charged to all purchasers the fair price usually cannot be less and is seldom much more than average cost.[8] Thus purchasers pay a price determined by per unit costs and the manager breaks even, symbolizing that no one has been "taken advantage of." When it is decided that for some customers the fair price is lower than average cost, the average price for other customers must be compensatingly higher. This in one sense is also fair, because the manager must break even. However, once there are two or more classes of consumers, fair pricing will allow a variety of prices. Notions of fairness in addition to average cost equal to price must be employed.

The computation of total costs that are to be averaged is of crucial importance. Total costs of the producing government agency include all operation and maintenance expenses and a "fair" return on the "fair" value of sunk costs and unallocated joint costs. Sunk costs include the part of past facility expenses that is to be recovered in the current production period. A possible measure of capital costs to be recovered may be the amount of debt retirement that must be financed out of sales receipts. Frequently, joint costs are allocated to one output or another where more than one output is produced by the agency. One output may be zero priced; other outputs must then be fair priced so that the entire operation breaks even.

The overriding concern of this pricing scheme is fairness. Strict economic efficiency is disregarded and only by accident do relevant marginal costs equal price for a determined rate of output; this is true for both short- and long-run cost calculations. But fair pricing of user charges is believed simple and relatively inexpensive to the agency. It requires little information that is costly beyond what is yielded by the price system.

Fair pricing techniques do not provide correct information about efficient capital investment in new facilities and replacement of used capital items. Managers tend to pursue investment policies that will reduce shortages and are calculated to make fair rates of return. Thus fair pricing tends to result in overproduction of public goods and to jeopardize efficient factor employment.[9]

Marginal Cost Pricing

Economists have long been interested in marginal cost pricing schemes because such schemes have the advantage of yielding information relevant to social efficiency. Marginal cost pricing schemes can be roughly divided into two categories. One category involves competitive sales: If a government output is sold in a competitive market where the public producer is a "price taker," and if all revenues take the form of sales receipts, we can assume that the public producer acts as if he priced at marginal cost. A good example is the renting of publicly owned property or facilities in a competitive rental market. Another similar example is where a government owns timberland and as trees ripen sells timbering rights in a competitive market. In such cases economically efficient pricing is achieved without imposing an elaborate set of rules on government officials. The results of marginal cost pricing are achieved by assuring that entry is not barred to prospective bidders wishing to purchase government output and there are competitive suppliers of the government output so that government employees must quote market prices. In the case of timber the government manager can gain valuable information about when to harvest trees by imitating efficient private tree growers.

The second category of marginal cost pricing schemes involves cases where government producers are not subject to open market competition. For a number of reasons, the government supplies an output in an industry in which there are restrictions to entry of rival suppliers. The classical case is a natural monopoly due to economies of large-scale production. Quite often these restrictions are legal barriers imposed by the political process. But in all these cases the state and local government officials who want to pursue marginal cost pricing face some difficult questions: What pricing and investment rules would permit officials to imitate the results of open market, competitive industries? How can the forces of open market competition be simulated in the production and distribution activities of public producers? [10]

Certainly, complete uncontroversial answers to these questions have not been developed. Furthermore, limitations of space and interest do not permit an exhaustive discussion in this chapter. We will, however, review some of the more important marginal cost pricing problems and draw some tentative conclusions.[11]

We will consider a one-period pricing rule for an output that is highly perishable (cannot be stored) and for which there are no disposal costs (units of output that are produced but not used merely consume themselves). For an example we may consider the services of a public bridge or road. At first we will take the capacity of the facility as a given, with no regard for whether the government should have built any facility at all or whether the existing capacity of the facility is too large or too small. Furthermore, we will assume that the services of the facility are produced at zero operating and maintenance costs. For this classic case the marginal cost of any unit of output, up to the capacity of the facility, is zero. Therefore, the efficient price would be zero as long as the capacity of the facility were never exceeded—the output quantity demanded at the zero price never exceeds the quantity available at capacity.

However, output quality must be specified for the facility's service. If a greater quantity of output is demanded than is available at capacity, then crowding, or creating a greater quantity of output out of an unchanged capacity, will result in a decreased quality. That is, once capacity is reached, additional users at a zero price will begin to inflict congestion costs on other users without paying compensations. Therefore the social costs of supplying capacity or overcapacity output at the initial quality are not zero. In order to have users of the facility reflect this fact in their private decisions, a price greater than zero may be employed. The efficient pricing rule would instruct the facility manager to set a zero price as long as the quantity demanded was less than capacity and—when quantity demanded exceeded capacity—to set the price of the facility's output at the maximum consistent with maintaining the specified quality of the output but not so high as to reduce the quantity demanded to below capacity.[12]

As long as the total agency costs of a government producer are equal to the social costs of production, the efficient pricing rule is the rule above: The manager of the government program should levy a per unit charge or price on all users equal to the marginal cost of supplying an additional unit of output in the same period.[13] We will endeavor to explain below how this rule holds for the various special cost cases that government managers might face—including the perplexing case of decreasing marginal costs.

However, in addition to deciding which pricing policy will yield marginal efficiency (price equal to marginal cost), governments are frequently confronted with the welfare question—whether to produce a particular output at all. In the above example of a service-yielding facility we discussed the correct pricing policy for an existing facility. At some point in the past the government must have asked whether or not to build the bridge, road, or whatever the facility might be. In order to answer this question, with respect to economic efficiency, the government officials should have determined what might be called the long-run solution, i.e., ascertained that the present value of all future benefits is at least as great as the present value of estimated total costs. Only in the event that the present value of expected total revenues from user charges (resulting from marginal cost pricing in each production period) is greater than the present value of expected total costs will the decision to build the facility be clearly affirmative. Which discount rate is the "correct" one to use in this calculation is discussed in another chapter. In some instances total costs will be greater than total benefits, as measured above, and additional benefits must be found before the government program can be justified.[14] These additional benefits might be found in the consumer surplus of direct users or in the external benefits enjoyed by individuals other than direct users.

Thus, in order to capture additional benefits for the long-run solution, while at the same time preserving marginally efficient pricing in each production period, two types of policies have been suggested:

1. The government may plan to levy an earmarked, lump-sum tax on users— charges unrelated to the quantity of output a user actually purchases. Or the government may plan to subsidize the program out of the general budget.

2. The government may plan to levy dissimilar average prices on different users, e.g., employ some form of price discrimination, while assuring that all marginal user charges are equal to relevant marginal costs.

State and local governments are seldom faced with the long-run question of whether or not to engage in a particular output program. Most often a government is interested in finding a user-charges policy that will efficiently allocate output in each production period, indicate the optimal rate of output, lead to an increase or decrease in physical capacity until the correct investment in durable capital is achieved, and finally, assure efficient utilization of the physical plant.[15] We will assume in the following discussion that the long-run solution referred to above has been satisfied and that any additional revenues required to justify engaging in the program have been obtained by policy 1. Ultimately any problems of satisfying long-run conditions that are not met by employing marginally efficient pricing and efficient investment policies will be solved by the political system.

All real-world applications of marginal cost pricing are performed under conditions of uncertainty. Therefore, given whatever the capacity or size of the physical plant the government manager actually has, the efficient pricing and output policy will always be to increase or decrease the rate of output until short-run marginal cost (SRMC) is just equal to the price that yields neither queues nor unsold surplus output.[16] This price-equal-to-SRMC rule also gives valuable information regarding the efficiency of the physical plant size. For the government manager to determine whether he can produce the same rate of output (for whatever number of periods he believes the prevailing demand conditions will continue) at a lower per unit cost, he must estimate the long-run marginal cost (LRMC) of adjusting his rate of output. If the manager finds that the price he is currently charging (equal to SRMC) is greater than the estimated LRMC of producing the same rate of output in future periods, then additional capital investments should be made. The productivity of such increases in the size of the physical plant—in terms of cost reduction—will exceed the rate of return required to justify expansions in physical plant size.

If the government manager estimates, however, that the user charge he is levying is equal to SRMC but less than the LRMC of supplying the same rate of output in future periods, he would realize that the physical capacity was greater than optimal. Thus, rather than continue underutilizing and maintaining the current plant size the manager should set about to disinvest or reduce the plant size. The optimal capacity or plant size is achieved when the manager is levying a user charge that is equal to both SRMC and LRMC.

Viewed in this manner short-run marginal cost pricing is always the correct pricing policy for any one production period and provides valuable information for an optimal investment policy. Long-run efficient pricing will thus depend upon the ability of government managers to perform at price equal to SRMC in each period and upon the accuracy of managers' estimates of LRMC.

Differences of opinion have existed where a given plant or capacity produces more than one good.[17] In such cases the plant costs are common to all outputs of the government program and cannot, in an unarbitrary way, be allocated to each or any one good being supplied. Other costs are separable, however, in the sense that they are unambiguously attributable to increases in the rate of output of specific services. It has often been suggested that common costs incurred from changes in capacity should be specifically levied on those demanders "who are responsible for" or "who cause" the increment in capacity to be undertaken. For example, an increase in demand for one of the government's outputs from a given plant may be brought about by a specific group of new clients. The argument goes that with the additional demand, the optimal-sized plant is larger than the existing capacity. But once the new plant is constructed, the outputs are all priced at SRMC except for the output that realized the increase in demand and made the larger plant necessary. To this SRMC is added a per-unit capacity charge which is determined by a capital recovery calculation for the increment in capacity. Although this may provide a convenient operational method and will yield the optimal plant size and efficient rates of output under some cost conditions, it is not correct generally and will not always give the same results as strict marginal cost pricing.

The generally efficient pricing policy for cases where two or more outputs have common costs is to levy a price for each output equal to its relevant SRMC. And the quantity supplied of each output would be determined by avoiding shortages or surpluses of any output. If in equilibrium (SRMC equal to price for each output) the sum of the incremental costs that would be incurred to produce an additional unit of each output in future periods is greater than the estimated LRMC of doing the same thing, then the plant size should be increased for the reasons discussed earlier. The optimal capacity is achieved when, following the same rule of SRMC equal to price for each output, the sum of SRMC to produce an additional unit of each output in future periods is just equal to the estimated LRMC of accomplishing the same thing. That is, no conceivable alteration of common plant costs could result in producing the same quantities of output at a lower social cost. This rule remains the same at any point in time, avoids allocating common costs to any particular set of users, and provides valuable information for the calculation of the optimal plant size and utilization.[18]

OTHER PRICING SCHEMES

In some instances bona fide user charges cannot be applied, yet a variety of closely related pricing schemes are possible. Coupon rationing and special benefit tax charges differ only slightly from conventional user charges, mainly in their objectives and legal foundations. Other benefit taxes are quite different from conventional user charges; they can be used when the cost of directly collecting charges at the time of use is too great. In such a case taxes may be levied on privately sold goods whose sales are closely correlated with the intensity with which certain government services are used.

Three other pricing schemes will be discussed: coupons, special charges, and tie-in taxes.

Coupons

We have repeatedly emphasized the desire of state and local government policy makers to alter the distribution of certain goods and services consumed in the community. This goal may be achieved in some instances without major sacrifice of strict economic efficiency; for example, governments sometimes rely on a coupon price schedule to ration particular goods. Coupon pricing systems have been used to ration strategic resources during times of war and at other times to alter the distribution of certain consumer goods. Currently familiar examples are coupon rationing through food stamp plans and rent subsidy schemes.

For a given quantity of government output the money price or user charge is set below the market clearing price, and then coupons are distributed which must be collected in the final exchange, thus effecting a rationing function. As a result, the distribution of the specific output among consumers will differ from what it would have been had only money prices been used. The extent of the difference will depend on to whom the coupons are distributed and on the relative amount of the rationing function performed by coupons. In the extreme case, money prices are altogether disregarded and coupons are accepted completely in lieu of other payment.

The more usual case is where coupons are issued to consumers of privately supplied goods and services. Again, a major purpose of issuing coupons is to affect the distribution of consumption of specific goods. The effect of the coupons on the receiving household is the same as that of an earmarked subsidy, i.e., a subsidy earmarked for specific household expenditures for specific goods. As a result, the price of goods for which the coupons can be used is lowered—to the subsidized households—and hence the quantity demanded is increased.[19] The supplier in turn cashes in the coupons to the government for a fixed money price per coupon.

When government provides such earmarked subsidies, the consumers whose purchasing power is to be increased are selected on the basis of distributional criteria. Recipients may use their earmarked subsidies to bid specific resources away from other consumers and may alter their consumption expenditures, but recipients are generally forbidden to sell their coupons. This implies that there are definite costs and limitations to converting the subsidies into general purchasing power.

Special Charges

State and local governments commonly bestow privileges for which they levy special charges. These privileges can be considered outputs, since the government is exchanging specific rights. One set of privileges derives from the licensing functions of government. Most license fees (such as for building permits, bicycle and animal tags, fishing and hunting permits, and marriage licenses) and most revenues (such as engineering inspection fees and examiners' and auditors' fees) are levied on the basis of legal liability that must be removed to avoid a penalty. Another set of privileges derives from government grants such as those to "explore and deplete" state-owned resources; this set includes the granting of franchises and concessions and the granting of easements on public land. Special charges are similar to benefit taxes but may be regarded as a type of user charge in which the sale constitutes transferral of rights to exercise some privilege granted by the government. User charges of this type provide revenues and result in some rationing just as do other taxes that are levied on the benefit principle.

Tie-in Taxes

Quite a few state and local governments levy taxes on the benefit principle, which means that efforts are made by these governments to allocate tax burdens according to who enjoys specific benefits. Certain of these tax levies act more like prices than do other taxes. For a benefit tax to act like a price, a necessary condition seems to be that the tax revenues are earmarked and the tax levy is an excise on some private good that is commonly consumed in conjunction with a government-supplied good. When the total individual tax payment increases with greater use of the government good the excise performs a rationing function like that performed by a user charge. The fact that the tax revenues are earmarked means that the revenue yields provide an additional investment signal which is usually lacking in nonpriced output programs. Therefore, we have here a case where a private sale can be used to tie in a user charge (excise) for some government output. The excise will act like a price the more complementary the consumption of the private good is to the government output. In the extreme there would be strict joint consumption of the private good together with the public good.

For example, an excise tax on textbooks could be used as an approximate price of attending a specific class in a public adult education program, especially if ownership of new nonreusable textbooks is mandatory. Similarly, an earmarked excise tax on gasoline and diesel fuel is roughly a user charge on public roads.[20] Such a tax neither distinguishes between streets, freeways, mountain roads, etc., nor fluctuates with the time of year, week, or day. Furthermore, the tax does not distinguish between differences in ton-mileage of vehicles. For example, since trucks are more efficient in ton-miles per dollar of tax, truckers tend to be charged lower prices per unit of road service than drivers of private cars. Certain other levies such as earmarked registration fees and special ton-mile levies, however, allow the government to discriminate and make up for some of the inadequacies of the highway rationing system. Furthermore, the earmarking feature provides some of the investment signals that are missing in nonpriced output programs.

OPPORTUNITIES AND PROSPECTS

User charges occupy an important place among the sources of revenue of state and local governments. Especially when we apply a broad definition of user charges we find that state and local governments use them extensively in charging for water, electricity, gas, transportation, roads, streets, parking, higher education, hospital services, cultural activities, and recreational facilities. Mainly welfare considerations have dissuaded governments from reliance on user charges for additional programs where pricing is technically feasible—for example, primary and secondary education, welfare services, library services, and some police and fire protection services. Welfare considerations in conjunction with "public goodness" features of the specific outputs have been important in the pricing of the services of courts of law and government-produced information. Because of widespread belief in agrarian fundamentalism as well as because of farmers' low incomes, many states have for more than a century provided a variety of free services to farmers.[21] However, the continuing urbanization of our society may lessen the political source of agriculture's ability to justify many such special concessions.

What are the prospects that user charges will become more, or less, important in the future financing of government activities? An answer to this question depends on our appraisal of how the public and its elected and appointed officials are likely to act in the light of great technological changes and of how increasing affluence will modify individual values. Let us begin by considering some factors that appear to favor increased reliance on user charges and then turn to some factors that appear to deter acceptance of them.

Technological innovations and inventions promise to greatly reduce the costs of administering a pricing system. Thus, the costs of making the exclusion principle operative appear to be on the decline. For example, electronic devices may be used to monitor and meter the use of streets, roads, and highways by specified users.[22] Unfortunately, the reduction in costs of administering such a pricing system tends to be accompanied by increases in social costs associated with public intrusion into privacy. It is too early to know what the trade-offs are likely to be between reduction of administrative cost and loss of privacy.[23]

A second factor favoring greater reliance on user charges by state and local governments is simply the continual, substantial increase in planned revenue collections as a percentage of private income. Under such a circumstance citizens are likely to be increasingly concerned with efficiency and individual choice in the financing of public services.

Federal subsidies to state and local governments and Federal income tax credits promise to continue to increase—in absolute and relative terms. This will tend to reduce the need for income redistribution on the local level, and local governments may therefore increasingly employ benefit-related levies such as user charges.

Finally on the positive side, user charges provide information that is valuable for rational decision making in state and local government. Efforts are underway to introduce program budgeting, including benefit-cost analysis, and these techniques of improving collective decisions require accurate information. Should further progress be made in this direction, public officials as well as taxpayers may become increasingly conscious of economic efficiency and attempt to advance it through greater reliance on user charges.

However, these positive forces appear to be opposed by major counterforces. For example, increased affluence in the United States is likely to make certain costs virtually negligible; at least they will tend to be treated as negligible. Governments in a wealthy society can increasingly neglect the application of petty charges.

A second negative factor is highly political. Campaign promises to deliver more and better public goods and services lose much of their appeal if financing by user charges is mandatory; if goods are to be purchased virtually at market prices, less benevolence and cost shifting can be promised by the distributor—the politician.

A further counterforce is increased urbanization. It is alleged that increased crowding of city populations results in a pervasiveness of the kind of spillovers for which the employment of user charges would entail too great an amount of transaction costs; such spillovers rule out pricing as a scheme to reduce spillovers. Thus it is argued that programs of noise and other pollution abatement, health improvement, and law enforcement are less amenable to the market solutions. As government expenditure for such programs increases, user charging declines as a source of revenue and as a desirable technique for allocating resources.

Furthermore government employees who are appointed rather than elected might resist user charges in the fear that paying customers can demand "their money's worth." Some government employees might feel that one of the virtues of a public career is that they are removed from the rigors of catering to customers. If the status and perhaps the incomes of government employees were to depend directly on how well they pleased consumers, even to the extent that they worried about competition from suppliers of close substitutes, the preference of some employees for service in government would disappear.

Another alleged impediment to user charges is the fact that there appears to be a trend to denigrate efficiency as a norm for judging the role and conduct of government and to adopt such norms as equality and special merit.

The positive factor mentioned above as favorable to user charges, the promise of more extensive Federal grants to state and local government and of more extensive state grants to local government, will help meet the budget costs of state and local government. If, however, local and state governments turn to user charges they may discourage higher levels of government from broadening their aid, since the amount of government spending then depends more on user demand and less on political budgeting practices.

Governments view their outputs as mechanisms to achieve numerous ends. Many parking meters have been removed from downtown sections of cities to help merchants who find themselves at a disadvantage in competing with suburban shopping centers that offer easy access and ample parking space.

Finally on the negative side, wholesale adoption of user charges would seem a radical change and would therefore be resisted by government officials. The political system is unable to adjust rapidly enough to achieve radical changes. This is of course in contrast to the market system and is a positive feature of user charges. Those seeking political office can often identify the gainers and the losers from some changes in government financing and simply appeal to the self-interests of those people who would be damaged. Politicians tend to believe that changes toward greater employment of user charges will make large numbers of people, including politically powerful people, feel they are among the losers.

It is difficult to foresee whether the forces favoring increased reliance on user charges will tip the scale. It would be easier if we knew more about the nature of the political bargaining process that determines the adoption of user charges, the incentives that persuade public officials to promote efficiency norms, and the exact costs and benefits that would be realized by changing to user charges.[24] Perhaps the poor will oppose user charges and the rich will favor them in some facilities, such as municipal golf courses, where free use would add to congestion and thus annoy the rich.

There are numerous output programs of government that might be considered for user-charges financing. We have previously mentioned such services to farmers and ranchers as free research, advice, and storage. Governments could charge more efficiently for certain services they now render to the public or to other government departments. Consider only one department, health, which could charge prices that fully reimburse the department for the costs of birth registration, marriage examination, laboratory tests, investigation of animal bites, animal quarantine, rabies shots, operation of drug and alcohol rehabilitation centers, immunization for foreign travel, legal abortions, therapy and inpatient care for mental patients, rehabilitation of mental outpatients, prenatal services for expectant parents, and a host of licenses. A community may want to subsidize such activities, but this consideration does not preclude the adoption of user-charge systems; user charges are not only feasible—they may in fact yield efficiency gains.

All too often it is not appreciated that services are just as costly when performed by one department for the employees or clients of another department of government as when they are delivered to the public at large. For example, schools are not often charged for refuse collection, and local public hospitals commonly serve local government employees at nominal fees. Furthermore, although certain curb lanes are priced by the use of parking meters, no prices are charged for taxi parking spaces, bus stops, pickup and delivery areas, or for police and fire department use. Some uses of curb lanes lend themselves to transfer prices which could greatly improve the quality of resource allocation decisions.

We stressed above the difficulties of specifying which goods could be financed by user charges. However, some important state and local programs and many minor services are candidates. We can briefly indicate the variety of programs involved.

The principal state and local expenditure for which user charging has been urged is for schooling: primary, secondary, junior college, and university instruction. Those types of schooling that are typically supplied entirely by private, for-profit producers are user-charged.[25] By and large, schooling supplied by governments has not been user-charged. The most frequently suggested method of user charging for school instruction has been the coupon pricing technique described above.[26] Aside from instruction there are many auxiliary services that are produced by educational institutions that are amenable to user charging. These outputs include bussing, food services, facility rentals,[27] parking, dormitories, cultural events and entertainment, sports events, laboratory services, and health services.

For reasons similar to those used to justify coupon pricing of government schooling, state and local governments could employ vouchers to user-charge for government hospital services. These services include not only bedrooms but first aid, nurses' training, psychiatric care, routine inoculations, medical library and record stores, and ambulance services. In addition to general hospital service, coupon pricing would apply to inpatient care for mental, drug, and alcoholic patients. Even prenatal instruction classes for expectant parents might be handled in this way. This does not imply that many public health services will not be priced.[28]

State and local governments operate athletic stadiums, marinas, golf courses, zoos, art galleries, observatories, museums, convention centers, apartment buildings, and auditoriums. These services are amenable to user charges. As we have mentioned, many neighborhood parks are not priced because of prohibitive exclusion costs as well as merit goods considerations. But some park services can be and often are sold to users: handball and tennis courts, lights for night contests, craft classes, field markings, sports equipment, supervision of youth activities, lifeguard services for private parties, swimming pools, and boats.

We normally think of police services as activities that cannot be user-charged. Interestingly, some county and municipal jails have been financed in the past by levying per day fees on the inmates, related to ability to pay and the length of stay. Other police services need only be pointed out to suggest price applications: embalming and death certification, autopsies, and special security and detective services (services to other departments of government as well as to private consumers). Consider police escorts, searches conducted for lost persons and property and for information from police records, fingerprinting services, and accident reporting.

At present state and local governments do not levy user charges for the services of fire departments, but some opportunities might be explored. Under current practice, service calls are always answered and are not charged, so fire departments are called more often than they would be if calls were priced. Often calls for service do not deserve such costly attention; examples are administering minor first aid, retrieving children and pets, investigating vandalism and family fights, etc. Possibly, appropriate user charges could be devised, as they are, for example, in certain cities in Israel. In Denmark, much of the country's fire protection has been turned over to a private firm with which a very large number of local governments have agreements.[29]

SUMMARY

User charges, broadly defined, are vitally important in the financing of state and local governments. Programs can rely on user charges if joint consumption, externalities in consumption, costs of exclusion, and distribution or welfare considerations do not dominate. Financing by user charges provides a source of revenue, rations government output, allocates burdens, and provides demand signals.

In addition to bona fide user charges, state and local governments can use three other pricing schemes: coupons, special charges, and tie-in taxes. All four user-charges schemes can employ monopoly pricing, "fair" pricing, or marginal cost pricing.

It would be wrong to suggest that governments have overlooked many important user-charge sources. However, technological changes promise to greatly reduce the cost of administering pricing systems, though possibly at the price of intrusion of privacy. On the other hand, increasing affluence is likely to diminish government's desire to employ user charges. No political forces are known to constitute unequivocal opportunities for or impediments to user charges. Important opportunities exist where government departments do not charge either clients or other departments for services rendered (or make only nominal charges). We have stressed not only the economic efficiency promoted by employing marginal cost pricing but also the value of the increased information that governments would reap regarding demand for their services.

CHAPTER 4

TAX
ANALYSIS

Methods for estimating demand and the relative costs of obtaining demand
information were discussed in Chapter 2. Pricing techniques whereby government officials could obtain revenue, ration government output, and also receive
demand information were suggested in Chapter 3. However, we have repeatedly stressed that for many government programs the employment of pricing
techniques is not possible, and often ethically undesirable.

Taxation is the power of public officials to exact compulsory payments
from citizens chiefly on the state and local level for the purpose of raising
revenue. In democratic societies citizens command the power of taxation but
collectively yield taxation authority to elected or appointed government officials. In this view of the nature of taxation, we will define a tax as an obligation that makes some individual(s) liable to the government. A tax payment
is the sum of money that when transferred to the government cancels the
liability imposed by the taxing authority. This payment is distinguished from
user charges in that the tax assessor offers no specific services directly in
return to the taxpayer and therefore tax payment is not an act of exchange in
the usual economic sense. (Special property assessments, license fees, and
earmarked excise "taxes" are included in the discussion on user charges,
Chapter 3.)

In this chapter we will discuss some truly basic issues in taxation: Who
should bear the burden of taxation? Who in fact does bear the burdens of
taxation? And given the tax structure, how many dollars of revenue will be
paid to state and local governments? This discussion will vary from the usual
treatment of tax analysis, particularly in its emphasis on mobility of tax
base—the most significant distinguishing feature of taxation by subnational
governments. Most tax analysis discussions make the assumption that the
costs of avoiding a tax through relocation are sufficiently great to preclude
such behavior as a major factor in tax incidence. Second, it is ordinarily
assumed that the beneficiaries of government activities are the citizens of the
government that supplies the services. The tax analysis in this text will recognize the special problems of incidence and tax avoidance behavior that result
from activity spillovers.[1] State and local tax policy is directly related to the
mobility of the tax base, and therefore not only to the question of who pays
what taxes but also to who benefits from the services financed by these levies.

In this chapter the tax policy issues of burden distribution, efficiency,
growth, and stability will be considered. In the final section the issue of how

much in taxes will be paid, i.e., tax revenue productivity of a given structure, is discussed from the point of view of an income elasticity model.

WHO SHOULD PAY: ABILITY TO PAY
VERSUS BENEFIT PRINCIPLES

The ability-to-pay principle of taxation states generally that the amount of tax burden borne by an individual should be related to his economic ability to bear the burden. Such a general principle raises a number of important questions. First, in order for the principle to be operative, some agreement must be reached on what measure of ability to pay will be used for tax liability assessment. In the Middle Ages land acreage was the principal measure because relatively few resources were exchanged through markets and consequently valuation of other wealth components for purposes of taxation was difficult. As markets developed, however, increasingly larger portions of wealth were valued in exchange and the flow-of-money concept replaced the older stock-of-resources concept as the standard of capacity or ability to pay.

A second question requiring an answer is: What relation should hold between ability to pay and the amount of the tax burden? The above statement of the principle does not make clear whether greater absolute amounts of tax payments and (or) greater proportions of tax burdens relative to ability to pay are implied. If only greater absolute amounts of tax payments were required for greater ability to pay, then the principle could be consistent with "regressive" taxation (measured here as a declining ratio of tax payment to ability to pay).

The benefit principle of taxation rests on the presumption that those who receive benefits from goods and services provided by government should bear tax burdens in proportion to the amount of those benefits. The principle automatically links the expenditure and the receipt sides of government budgets. However, in order to apply the principle one must be able to identify those who benefit and to measure the value of benefits they receive. This requirement results in a paradox: If it is extremely costly to exclude nontaxpayers from benefiting and very costly to estimate the value received by beneficiaries, then it may be economically rational for the community not to attempt to levy tax liabilities according to benefits. But as the costs of exclusion decrease and as the costs of identification of the beneficiaries decline, benefit taxation can be used, less in the form of a tax than of a price. Thus, conditions that permit efficient use of the benefit principle of taxation also lead to opportunities to employ user charges or a price system in place of taxation.

The inherent superiority of user charges over benefit taxation, if the costs of assessing and collecting payments are roughly the same for each revenue source, was described in Chapter 3.[2] Taxation performs for government the functions of providing revenue and allocating burdens among individuals. We stressed that user charges, in addition to performing these two functions, would perform a rationing function for the distribution of government services and would also yield information of high quality that is useful in determination of the demand for government services. In general, benefit taxation will provide some rationing and demand signals. But as pointed out in the section "The Individual (Economic) Preference Approach" in Chapter 2, for the same revenue yield, the quality of performance and thus the value to government of benefit taxation will be less than that of prices.

The normative question, Who should pay? fundamentally relates to an issue of equality. The ability-to-pay notion of taxation asserts that, whatever the measure of ability, the pertinent policy consideration is equality of individual tax burdens relative to individual capacities to bear such tax burdens. The benefit notion of taxation asserts that to be useful for policy a measure of equality cannot consider only tax burdens; therefore, the proper measure of equality among individuals is that the tax burdens borne are in proportion to the individual benefits derived from government services. Thus, all citizens enjoying equal service benefits bear equal cost burdens. Obviously, ability-to-pay notions of taxation will be favored by policy makers who are interested in promoting greater equality of distribution of income or wealth, whereas benefit notions of taxation will be favored by policy makers who are attempting to achieve total resource allocation efficiency.

A sizable body of theory has been produced by economists to describe the optimal tax structure or optimal budgets.[3] Such theories have attempted to answer the normative question, Who should pay? Or, in other words, what tax burden should be borne by each individual? But, as we indicated in Chapter 2, normative theories do little to help us understand how tax structures are actually formed. Nor do they help us predict the outcomes of tax decisions.

WHO PAYS: TAX SHIFTING AND INCIDENCE

The preceding section was strictly normative, since a determination of who should bear tax burdens is always based on value judgments. In this section we consider a positive question: Who do we expect will actually bear the burdens of a given tax change? To answer this question we must first define what we mean by a tax burden and then show a way whereby changes in individual choices and individual wealth can be deduced from alternative tax assessments.

Some Concepts

We will be concerned throughout the analysis with a government that is producing a given amount of services per period. The fixed budget, of the size necessary to provide these services, is financed by the government from both residents and nonresidents.

We will relate changes in revenue collection policies to changes in an individual's income. In particular, we will examine alternative methods of collecting funds for government expenditures. For example, we will describe the effects (on an individual's income) of collecting a given number of dollars of revenue by means of a new set of tax liabilities, but where the rest of the government revenue collection, spending, and production policies remain unchanged. For total government revenue collections to remain at the same dollar level we will always assume an offsetting decrease in old tax liabilities within the jurisdiction and unchanged conditions in other jurisdictions. Musgrave refers to this technique as *differential incidence* determination.[4] The accompanying simultaneous decrease in tax liabilities will always be assumed to be in a per-period head tax that has an equal money yield. We will further assume that while the reductions in head tax liability are always for citizens of the taxing government, the new tax liabilities can affect the income of nonresidents as well as residents of the taxing jurisdiction.

Any *decreases* in individual after-tax income that result from specific changes in government revenue collection policies will be called the burden of the tax change. The amount of burden an individual expects to bear will change with the passage of time; as he adjusts his behavior to the new set of tax liabilities, each individual obtains greater information. The ultimate net decrease in after-tax income realized by each individual for a given period of time will be a measure of the differential incidence of the burden of the change in revenue collection policy.

In a community of given population and other productive resources, an increase in tax burdens will reduce household demand for privately supplied goods and services (either in the present or in a future period) and will therefore reduce the resources engaged in private production for household consumption. Not only do increased taxes discourage private consumption and production, however; increased tax revenues finance additional government expenditures and thus result in an increased supply of government services. Privately owned resources are encouraged to shift into production of those goods that realize a net increase in demand and out of production of those goods that are left with a net decrease in total demand. Complications resulting from alterations in resource employment and from shifts in demands can be minimized by adopting the convention of differential incidence suggested above. In our tax analysis, the government budget remains at the same dollar size, government service levels remain unchanged, and the government continues to purchase the same quantities of resources to produce the service levels.

A further comment on tax analysis must be made with respect to increase in tax liabilities that are not levied directly on specific individuals. Very often the economic unit initially assessed will not be a household. However, all resources are owned ultimately by individuals, through either private property or collective ownership rights. Thus, by the market mechanism the incidence of all taxes will fall upon individuals, and tax burdens can be associated with decreases in individual income. The question of who pays a particular tax can therefore be answered by examining changes in some measure of individual income.

We will assume that the initial level of an individual's income and its prechange tax payments either are known or can be accurately estimated. Then, for each change in tax policy, the "who pays" question can be divided into two parts: First, how will the change in revenue collection policy alter the choices of individuals and thus the expected earnings that can be attained by household resources? In this part, the focus is on how a change in policy leads to changes in household (or class of households) income as a result of alterations in resource employments and payments to various resources.

The second part of the question is: What is the magnitude of tax payments after the change in revenue collection policy? Both parts must be answered to predict how much of the incidence of a tax a particular household or class of households will bear. It does little good to know that the amount paid in the form of a particular tax by a household varies with its income without also knowing how the tax affects the level of that income.

Incidence theory usually commences with the presumption that the economy is at full employment.[5] We shall assume that collecting a given number of dollars of revenue by means of an alternative tax will not induce persistent and long-term underemployment in the regional economy. Changes in tax liabilities will induce changed behavior with respect to resource employment. So-called frictional unemployment, caused by the adjustments of resource owners to the new tax liability assessments, will be discussed. Adjustments in relative wages and prices as well as expectations of resource owners are assumed to yield shifts in employment until a state of full employment is again achieved.

The term "tax shifting" usually refers to the adjustments that occur in response to changes in tax liability assessment. Tax shifting is the result of burden avoidance behavior. As expectations become more certain that a tax change will occur, specific households begin altering their behavior in order to avoid the tax payments they anticipate. Thus the tax burdens are shifted from legally liable taxpayers to other households who alter their behavior but accept part of the tax burden rather than accept the costs implied by complete burden avoidance.

Resource specialization is a concept that will be useful in explaining burden avoidance behavior, and geographic specialization of resources, in particular, will be useful in our discussion of state and local tax changes. We will call a resource "specialized" to a particular employment (such as task, industry, or region) if the wage the resource is receiving in its specialized employment is greater than the wage the resource could earn in its next best alternative employment. The difference between the earnings a factor is currently receiving and the best alternative earnings the factor could receive, for a given period of search, is a rent from the point of view of the resource owner. Factors of production can be specialized to geographic areas as well as to industries and tasks. A factor of production is geographically specialized when there is a discontinuous gap between its highest-valued use inside and outside the region. Obvious examples of geographically specialized resources are land and improvements; a less obvious example is knowledge. For instance, the value of the services of a lawyer with special knowledge of the inhabitants and institutions of a particular area (or the value of the reputation within an area of someone engaged in its retail trade) will be greater in that area than in the next best alternative earnings outside the area.

We assume that owners of resources, when confronted with tax changes or expectations of tax changes, will compare these two alternatives: (1) the estimate of after-tax income that would result from confining tax avoidance behavior to the particular tax jurisdiction and (2) the estimate of after-tax income that would result from taking evasive measures that allow moving— shifting employment and (or) residence—outside the tax jurisdiction. The decision to move activities out of the tax jurisdiction entails estimation of direct moving costs as well as of differences in factor earnings. Obviously, in the long run relatively few resources remain highly specialized geographically.

It follows from our discussion thus far that geographically specialized factors will engage in less shifting out of the jurisdiction and can therefore be made to bear more of the tax burden than resources that are less geographically specialized. Less specialized resources, compared with specialized resources, find that tax avoidance behavior is less costly but not costless.

Although a region may be a single market area,[6] it may be divided into a large number of local government jurisdictions, each with its own structures of taxation and expenditures.[7] And resources may exist that are geographically specialized either because economies can be achieved by locating in close proximity to certain other economic functions or because of favorable intra-metropolitan transportation cost relationships.[8]

Firms as well as factors can have different degrees of geographic specialization. An example of minor geographic specialization is a manufacturing firm using relatively unskilled workers to assemble, in rented space, a product that is sold primarily outside the metropolitan area. Such a firm faces a nearly horizontal supply schedule for inputs and would have to add to its wage costs any increase in a municipal gross personal income tax levied on its payroll. However, the firm can avoid tax liabilities entirely, at the cost of some moving expenses, by locating outside the taxing jurisdiction. By doing so, the firm may reduce its demand for other factors of production, e.g., resources that are specialized to the jurisdiction. In this event, owners of the specialized factors will suffer a tax burden.

For firms that are more geographically specialized, e.g., a wholesale firm located within a particular jurisdiction because of transportation cost advantages, the effects of a change in revenue collection policy may be different. Firms in this category will have to reduce their wages or increase prices in order to shift tax burdens. To the extent that the firm is a price-taker and market wages and prices do not change in the desired direction, the firm will have to bear the tax burden. This loss will be realized by the owners of the firm's assets.

However, one input—land—is always completely specialized and immobile, while durable structures and utilities approximate this situation. The long-run result will depend on whether the number of similarly specialized firms is large enough to affect the demand for space of a given quality within the area. If the firm is unique, the value of a given stock of occupiable space will be determined by the demand from other sources. If geographic specialization is so great that the increase in other costs due to locating outside the jurisdiction is greater than the costs imposed by new tax liabilities, specialized firms rather than landowners will continue to bear the tax burden.

Complementary and substitution relationships exist among specialized and unspecialized factors of production. In the complementary relationship, which is probably the most common, a factor of production leaving the tax jurisdiction lowers the marginal product of the more specialized factors. This drop in marginal productivity causes opportunities outside the jurisdiction to become relatively more attractive for other factors and causes some of them to migrate to avoid tax burdens. Factors that have relatively poor external earnings opportunities will tend to stay, and their wealth will tend to be reduced directly by a fall in their marginal products. In the substitution relationship, if unspecialized factors leave the tax jurisdiction the marginal productivity schedules of the remaining, more specialized, factors will shift upward. This effect will tend to mitigate against outmigration of the less specialized factors.

Taxation Base

To analyze the incidence of specific taxes, one must carefully examine the base of taxation. Tax base determines how liabilities will be assessed. Each tax law will specify a more or less unique measure of taxpayer liability. But for purposes of simplicity and generalization, this text will discuss the three most common groups of state and local tax bases: income, expenditures, and wealth. Chapter 5 discusses tax institutions and groups the various tax instruments into these three categories, since they offer a fruitful organizing device for state and local governments, with the mobility of the tax base playing a principal part.

Income Base

At least two concepts of the income tax base are employed concurrently in the Federal and state income tax structures.[9] The first concept, *factor flow income*, is measured as the money receipts of the supplier of employed resources over a specified period. The use of this concept does not require that money flows be imputed to the owner of employed resources; thus corporations, as well as the stockholders who own the corporate assets, have income.

The second concept, *accrual income*, is measured as the flow of consumption expenditures by a household plus any change in net worth or wealth of the household over a specified period. Under the accrual concept all factor receipts must be imputed to those households that own the rights to factor services and all revaluations of owned assets are considered in determining household wealth. Thus, income becomes the maximum amount of real goods and services, expressed in money terms, that may be consumed during a specified period without changing the value of real capital.

Since the national economy is relatively self-contained, conflict between the two concepts causes few difficulties for income taxation by the Federal government. However, one state may employ the factor flow income concept, and another, the accrual income concept, with the result that some income will be double-taxed and other income not taxed at all, a not uncommon phenomenon.

Income producing resources located in one state are often owned by households that reside in another state. Thus, if the state in which the resources are employed uses the factor flow income concept and the state in which the owning households reside uses the accrual income concept, double taxation will result. Because of this conflict most states provide exclusions and deductions for income taxes paid to other states.

Discrepancies between taxable income and income as defined by the two concepts are created, among other causes, by exemptions of nonmonetary income flows. The most significant exemptions are income in kind, services of housewives, and services of durable goods possessed by an individual or household that yield real income in successive periods. Furthermore, as measured, taxable income does not include the personal consumption derived from government services distributed free of charge and from nonpecuniary advantages of nature and social environment. While such nonpecuniary income differentials as living in a pleasant community perhaps should be added to the income tax base, the benefits of doing so are highly subjective and no ready way can be found to tax them. If the differential is generally recognized it will tend to be capitalized in land values, and in this manner indirectly reflected in the accrual income tax base.

A tax on factor flow income can be avoided by moving the location of the employment of the factor to an area outside the tax jurisdiction. If a tax is levied on the accrual income base, then tax avoidance will require moving the residence of the owner of the factor out of the tax jurisdiction. In the latter case, if no costs result from the physical separation of factors and their owners' residences, factor locations will be nearly invariant to tax changes. In general, taxation of household income under the accrual concept will result in less shifting of resource employment than will a levy of equal yield on factor flow income.

For important classes of factors, the costs of separation can be substantial. For example, the value of a lawyer's services may be greatest in New York but the tax rate on his income may be lowest in Mississippi. However, the high costs of traveling between Mississippi and New York may dictate that his wealth-maximizing decision be to both work and reside in New York. More generally, when a large proportion of household income is derived from the employment receipts of a single resource and when the costs of physical separation of resource employment location from resource owner residence are great, there will be more similarity between the effects of tax liabilities levied on household income from resource ownership and tax liabilities levied on flows of factor receipts.

A tax on personal income discriminates against money income compared with income in kind since the latter is not taxable. A tax on income affects the work-leisure choice of taxable individuals since the tax tends to be viewed as a reduction in returns to market employment of resources. The effect of a wage rate change on leisure demanded and hence on labor supplied is complex, since each change in the wage rate carries with it an income and a substitution effect. The income effect of rate changes on the quantity of leisure demanded is positive; i.e., leisure is not an inferior good. The substitution effect on leisure demanded is negative; for reduced rates of return the opportunity cost of a unit of leisure time is reduced. Thus, the income and substitution effects on labor supply have opposite signs and move in opposite directions.

To assess the effects of changes in personal income tax liabilities, however, we cannot neglect the differential incidence mentioned earlier in this section. For instance, if an increase in personal income tax that yields a given number of dollars is exactly substituted for a decrease in a head tax of specified dollar yield, leaving the total tax take unchanged, then the income effect on work-leisure choices will be neutralized for many individual households, and more completely neutralized in the aggregate. The negative substitution effect on leisure of the increased income tax will remain.[10]

A tax on personal income also affects individual consumption-saving choices. If income tax liabilities are levied on the receipts of an employed resource, the owner will find that his income is taxed regardless of the use of the receipts. Both the portion that may be consumed in the current period and the portion that may be saved are subject to taxation. But payments made to owners of saved income (returns on savings or investments) are also subject to income tax liabilities. This appears to be the central contention of those who have argued that income taxes are a double tax on savings.[11]

A further effect of personal income taxation on the consumption-saving choice derives from tax discouragement of risk taking. Again, income and substitution effects result from changes in the rate of return on risky investments.[12]

Another important shifting feature of income taxes derives from the exemption from taxation of many forms of income which are not realized in money flows. These forms of income tend to be taxed at reduced rates and, to the extent that income changes are not realized in money exchanges, these sources of income are not taxed at all. Income taxes have also discriminated between the sources of income and between who receives the income. Thus the personal income tax laws have allowed different employment activities and specific classes of income recipients to enjoy special treatment. In the light of such discrimination much effort and ingenuity are devoted to exploiting existing loopholes and creating new ones. As a result the income tax laws are complex beyond comprehension. There is much inequality in the collection of taxes from individuals who have equal pretax income, and substantial resources are devoted to creating greater inequalities, violating the principle of horizontal equity.

Personal income taxes are often regarded as the tax instrument which is most neutral—which causes the least tax shifting because fewer tax liabilities can possibly be avoided by given changes in behavior. But as we have suggested above a great variety of tax avoidance behavior is possible. Furthermore, to the extent that income tax liabilities are levied on payment flows to resources that are geographically specialized only in a minor way, personal income taxation can often be completely avoided (except for moving costs) by relocating either residence or employment or both. It is primarily this feature of personal income taxation that makes it unsuitable for small tax jurisdictions to singly levy such liabilities. In general, personal income tax burdens can be shifted to the extent that aggregate tax avoidance behavior changes market rates of payment to services supplied by resource owners.

Most states levy a special version of income taxes on earnings of corporations. The incidence of corporate income tax changes is still an unsettled question.[13] We will stress the effects of corporate income tax changes on factor payments, a feature of the tax that is often ignored in discussions of the Federal corporate income tax but is extremely important to the states.

Many corporations operate in more than one state. States provide legal formulas that corporate accountants can use to determine what percentage of a firm's earnings will be in the tax base of each state in which the corporation operates. The formulas differ from state to state.[14] Such apportionment formulas introduce effects that must be considered with regard to state corporate income taxation, but are not present on the Federal level. The Federal tax is concerned only with the difference between receipts and expenses; it is invariant with respect to kinds and amounts of goods and services purchased by the corporation and for what purpose the expenditures are made. Apportionment formulas link certain classes of expenditures with the amount of taxes that a firm pays to a particular state. Consequently, they can be expected to affect a corporation's demand for factors of production.

State corporate income taxes become an indirect levy on property ownership, wage payments, and expenditures made to increase sales distribution within the state. If one of these factors is weighted relatively heavily in a particular state's formula, corporate decision makers will have an incentive to substitute factors that are weighted less heavily or are not included and to shift expenditures on heavily weighted factors to other states. If the demand for factors of production by interstate corporations is sufficiently great, relative to total demand for factors within the state, one would expect the corporate demand for heavily weighted factors to be relatively lower in the state. The more specialized the factors, the greater the portion of the tax shifted to them.

Expenditure Base

Differences in conclusions regarding the incidence of expenditure taxes arise from divergent views on the analytic assumptions and on the definition of tax burden.[15] No expenditure levy is completely general on all possible expenditures. Therefore, we shall be interested in incidence arguments for less than completely general sales taxation. Suppose that new taxes are levied on receipts of one or more competitive industries producing private consumption goods. The effect of this tax change on firms in the industries taxed will be to increase their expected costs of production. The firms will thus tend to revise downward their planned quantities supplied at the current market price. Thus, in the short run, the price to consumers will tend to increase and the demand for factors of production will fall. Households can therefore expect both increased cost of consuming the newly taxed goods and decreased demand for resources employed in the tax-increased firms. Buyers can avoid paying much higher prices for the goods by substituting non-tax-increased goods in consumption. Owners of resources that have relatively good opportunities elsewhere will alter their employments at some losses in income (not necessarily in the form of lower money wages!), while owners of resources that are more specialized to the taxed industries will experience greater income loss. If the shifting of factors out of the taxed industries is great relative to the total quantities of those factors supplied, then, as the supply of factors is increased to the non-tax-increased sector, the price they can obtain will fall and factors that vacate their original employment cannot escape a reduction in their money income. In addition, factors that are competitive with them in other industries will also suffer reduced money income, while industries that produce commodities that are complementary with the taxed products will also experience a reduction in demand for their goods and a decline in their market prices. Like the taxed industries, they will release factors to the other non-tax-increased productive processes in the region.

As the period becomes longer in which adjustments to the increased expenditure tax liabilities have taken place, the effects described above will be important and total reductions in output and quantities of purchased factors will be larger. This is so because, for longer adjustment periods, demand for the taxed commodities becomes relatively elastic—for both industry output and factors of production. The less specialized the factors of production, the larger the proportion of the tax burdens that households will realize through increases in prices of the tax-increased commodities. As firms attempt to shift the tax burden through increased prices, buyers will have greater incentive to reduce their demand for locally sold commodities and to increase their demand for substitute commodities sold outside the tax jurisdiction.[16]

Since we are concerned with differential incidence, decreases in demand for both products and factors in the area will be offset by the reduced head tax. The owners of factors of production will experience changes, however, and the direction of many of these changes has been indicated in the above discussion. The income reductions due to increased sales taxation in some industries will be split among four classes of factors: those in the taxed industries, those competitive with factors in the taxed industries, those in industries supplying outputs on which consumers choose to economize, and factors competitive with the latter. How much burden each household bears will depend on eventual long-run demand elasticities and specialization of resources employed in each industry.

In all cases, the gross prices of the tax-increased commodities will rise, while the prices of non-tax-increased commodities will rise in some cases and fall in others. Households will ultimately bear the tax burdens even though they consume relatively smaller quantities of commodities whose prices rise and conversely consume relatively larger quantities of commodities whose prices fall. The burdens will be realized by households either through reductions in income from factor employment or reductions in income from increased consumption costs.

The above analysis applies equally to a tax on any number of commodities. However, the larger the proportion of money exchanges that are in the tax jurisdiction's expenditure base, the smaller the sector of the local economy into which the factor can be released. Therefore, if the expenditure levy results in a decrease in market rates of factor payments, factors employed in non-tax-increased industries may experience relatively large declines in income due to the tax change, thus inducing more factor outmigration.

The incidence of general retail sales taxes levied by state and local governments can be analyzed in accordance with the above notions. These taxes are not general because many important consumption goods are excluded, such as government outputs, exchanges occurring outside the tax jurisdiction, leisure, food, medicine (in many states), services of houses and apartments, etc. Therefore, specific excise taxes are merely the least general of all expenditure taxes.

In the special case where the taxed sector is a single industry, resources are shifted out of the taxed commodity, and its price to consumers is increased. The increase in the relative price of the taxed commodity clearly harms its consumers, but only indirectly places a burden on nonconsumers. A portion of the tax burden will be realized by factor owners of the taxed commodity. The relative extent of forward and backward shifting will again depend upon the competitiveness of the industry and upon the long-run cost conditions. The more unspecialized the employed resources, the closer the industry will approach long-run constancy of costs, and thus the more likely greater relative burdens will be borne by those consumers with great and inelastic demand for the taxed commodity. Despite differences in assumptions employed in tax incidence models, there seems to be general agreement among economists on the distribution of burden of specific excise taxes.

Wealth Base

The familiar property levies in the real world are not general wealth taxes but are liabilities levied on the estimated capital value of particular assets in an individual's wealth holdings. Real property levies are assessed on a base defined as the capital value of land and structures, both of which are inputs in the production of an output which we will refer to as "occupiable space" or "floorspace of shelter."

Land services are completely specialized geographically—the geographic mobility is zero. Structures also are highly specialized both geographically and in their employments. Thus, owners of land and structures are unable or find it too costly to avoid taxes by geographically shifting the employment of their assets. For this reason taxation on the base of real property value is an extremely useful tax instrument for state and especially local governments, at a time that the relatively great geographic mobility of the tax base makes their use of income and expenditure taxation difficult.

In contending with the taxing of land value and improvement, owners of taxable assets are restricted to avoidance behavior which shifts property to alternative use at the same location. The quantity and quality of property services engaged in current production can be varied in the short run among various kinds of occupiable space, but the physical stock of structures can be varied only in the longer run. This restricts short-run variance of output quantity (of structure services), but allows for greater elasticity of supply for long-run adjustment. In our analysis of property tax incidence the total land area—within and outside the taxing jurisdiction—will be assumed fixed for both the short and the longer run. We will assume that land services can be shifted among various land uses, one use being to hold land idle for future use. In all cases, the land services relevant to production of occupiable space for the jurisdiction's citizens will include services of land within the tax jurisdiction and of land located outside the tax jurisdiction.

The orthodox treatment of land value taxation is that unexpected increases in tax liabilities cannot be shifted. However, once the new tax liabilities are known, land ownership rights are revalued in the market. The tax liabilities on a particular parcel of land can be transferred to new owners, but the tax burden will be completely capitalized in the price of land.

Land value taxation has been enthusiastically promoted for state and local government policy on the argument that revenue can be raised by a land value tax without decreasing the total amount of land services offered on the market.[17] It can be argued, however, that the effect of land taxation on the behavior of landowners is not completely neutral and that land value taxation also affects the allocation of land between uses. A variety of issues can be raised in this regard, but the most important is the effect of land value taxation on intertemporal allocation of land—the effect on "speculative" behavior. An unexpected increase of tax liabilities on land means that the holding costs of land ownership will be greater, that less acreage will be held idle (conserved for later development), and that the pattern of land development over time will be altered.[18]

The orthodox treatment of tax liability changes based on the value of existing structures distinguishes between the short run and the long run.[19] In the short run, unexpected increases in tax liabilities levied on the owners of structures will diminish the net expected returns per period to the asset owners; thus the present value or current market value of the structures will fall. This fall in value is a wealth loss to owners of structures and occurs when knowledge of the new tax liabilities becomes generally available. The magnitude of fall in value will depend on the prospects of shifting part of the tax; the more limited the ability of improvement owners to successfully raise prices to tenants or to lower wages of inputs, the greater will be the capitalization of their corresponding tax burden. Owners of improvements will be able to raise the price of occupiable space to tenants. But the ability and willingness of owners to raise tenant lease rates will be conditioned by several important factors that condition the supply and demand of occupiable space.

The price of occupiable space will increase more the greater the decrease in the rate of expansion in the stock of improvements. Unexpected increases in tax liabilities on improvements will reduce the amount of planned investment in improvements and cause the services of the existing stock to be relatively more scarce in the future. Owner returns on structures are reduced by such tax levies relative to other investor opportunities; fewer resources will flow into building new structures. Factors of production previously employed in the construction industry will bear some of the tax burdens by reduced wages and (or) by incurring the costs of moving to alternative employment. In this way some of the tax burden will be shifted to less specialized factors of production in industries other than the immediate construction industry.[20]

To the extent that the supply of occupiable space is made relatively more scarce by the reduced rate of growth in the stock of structures, the rental value to tenants can be raised by improvement owners. Investment in new improvements will continue to be postponed until tenant lease rates have increased and (or) input prices have fallen sufficiently to achieve the prevailing market rate of return on such projects. The price of occupiable space to tenants can be increased more the greater the willingness of tenants to bear the higher prices rather than move. Some tenants will be willing to pay a higher price for the same quantity and quality of occupiable space previously enjoyed; but as prices increase more, and the period of adjustment is extended, more tenants will choose to avoid the tax shifting by altering their quantities demanded. Some tenants will opt for less quantity and (or) lower quality of occupiable space. Improvement owners in general may find that their derived demand for maintenance and repair services is reduced, leading to some backward shifting of the tax onto factors supplying such services. Other tenants will opt for relocating completely outside the tax jurisdiction. Some tenants previously planning to locate in the tax jurisdiction will alter their plans and obtain occupiable space outside the tax jurisdiction.

Thus, it can be seen that the smaller the physical area of the tax jurisdiction and the greater the number of surrounding jurisdictions that offer comparable but less costly government services to property, the less will owners of improvements be able to shift the tax burdens forward and the greater will be the reduction of growth in the stock of structures within the jurisdiction. The smaller the jurisdiction that raises its tax liabilities on improvements and the greater the surrounding alternative supplies of occupiable space, the less the costs of moving—tax avoidance—to tenants. And the greater will be the incentive for entrepreneurs who are planning new investments in improvements to merely switch the planned location to an adjacent area rather than to postpone the entire project.[21]

Not all of the various factors of production employed as inputs to the supply of occupiable space possess identical geographic specialization. In particular, the land services of parcels located within the jurisdiction cannot relocate or shift to employments outside the taxing jurisdiction. Therefore the more geographically specialized resources, particularly land, will bear more heavily the tax burdens shifted backward by the owner of improvements.[22] The derived demand for land services within the tax jurisdiction will decline relative to the demand for land services outside the jurisdiction, and the owners of land located within the jurisdiction will suffer decreases in the market value of ownership. Thus, the smaller the tax jurisdiction and the less costly it is for tenants and improvement suppliers to avoid tax liabilities by locating outside the jurisdiction, then the greater will be the tax burden capitalized in the value of landownership.

Some economists have argued that the portion of the tax shifted forward to tenants will have a differential effect on the demand for new and existing supplies of structures. For example, it is argued that the "income elasticity of demand for quality" is high for certain classes of structural investments—notably apartments.[23] Thus a general increase in taxes on the value of structures may lead to a change in the relative prices of structure services of different qualities; the price of low-quality structure services will rise relatively more than the price of higher-quality services. As noted above, owners of structures can, within limits, shift the quality downward by investing less in maintenance. Under such conditions, we can expect changes in property taxes on structures to lead to general as well as relative deterioration in the quality of structures.

In real estate taxation the owner of land, the owner of structures, and the user of the structure will usually be the same individual. Under such conditions, the imposition of new tax liabilities on the value of structures allows almost no shifting or tax avoidance behavior, except for those individuals who are in the stage of planning to obtain occupiable space. When individuals in the planning stage learn that the tax will be introduced, they will plan to substitute other kinds of consumption. The demand schedule for services of housing substitutes will rise and the planned increments to the currently existing stock of structures will decline. Owners of improvements already in operation who are also users or tenants of structures will bear the burdens of increased scarcity, since any increase in prices of services or more intensive use of existing stocks must be paid to themselves. And as stressed above, unexpected increases in property taxes on structures will result in a reduction in the value of land available for current and future use *within* the tax jurisdiction. And thus the owner will bear some of the tax burdens as a landowner.

State and local government wealth taxes also take the form of liabilities levied on selected capital items other than real property—such as consumer durables. The incidence analysis of these taxes is similar to that of real property taxes. When increases in personal property tax liabilities are announced the wealth holder owning taxable capital items will suffer windfall losses. He may reduce the amount of cash tax payments he must make in the future by merely divesting himself of the taxable property items. However, after the tax change becomes generally known, a wealth owner can divest himself of some of his taxable wealth only by accepting a lower price for the capital items than he could previously have received. If the taxable items of personal property were completely geographically specialized, the resulting loss of capital value would constitute an immediate and nonshiftable tax burden. But some of the tax burden can be reduced by selling to buyers who do not reside in the taxing jurisdiction. Over time, wealth holders will allow these stocks of taxable capital items to diminish and they will substitute alternative non-taxed goods that yield similar services. As the mix of household assets changes in response to the tax change, some of the tax burden will fall on productive factors employed in producing new tax-increased capital items. The fall in demand for new tax-increased capital items will thus be accompanied by a fall in the derived factor demands. It is therefore difficult to tell what the effect will be on the production costs and relative prices of other capital items that are produced in the regional economy.

State and local governments also engage in taxation of wealth transfers, i.e., taxation where the base is defined as a gift. Since the largest and most enforceable tax takes can be levied on those gifts transferred at the time when the wealth owner dies, wealth transfer taxes have come to be known and largely treated as death taxes. For purposes of our incidence analysis of wealth transfer taxes we will disregard complexities arising from distinctions between taxes on givers and taxes on wealth received. We will examine the general case where liabilities are levied on wealth transfers—either on the inheritors' receipts or on the giver's bequest. Assuming that both consumption during life and estate transfers are superior goods with respect to changes in wealth, and that a bequest can be regarded as a form of consumption enjoyed by the giver, a proportional tax on death transfers will result in reduced lifetime consumption on the part of the giver. That is, more wealth must be accumulated and more wealth transferred in order to yield the same benefits from bequests. However, the after-tax magnitude of transferred wealth will be reduced by increased tax liabilities on transfers. Since the relative price of consumption from bequests is increased, the giver will choose to substitute toward non-tax-increased forms of consumption. Therefore, both givers and receivers of wealth transfers bear burdens of tax liabilities levied on the size of transfers. The incidence of the tax will be on the individual making the bequest, during his life, in the form of less consumption of commodities and leisure, and on the individuals receiving the inheritances, in the form of reduced wealth.

Wealth transferred to particular institutions, such as colleges and philanthropic foundations, is often exempt from estate taxation. Such exemptions increase the relative price of leaving wealth at death to nonexempt classes of beneficiaries. Given his preferences for leaving wealth, an individual will substitute some exempt for nonexempt transfers when tax liabilities are increased. Exemptions allow the giver to forgo relatively less consumption in making a given amount of net, after-tax payment, transfer. Consequently, if an estate tax has exemptions, the individuals who would have benefited if tax liabilities had not been increased may have their wealth reduced by more than the share that they would have borne under a proportional tax on the entire value of the estate. The reason is that the individual providing the wealth can be expected to give more of it to exempt institutions.

Wealth taxes will elicit relocation behavior. In the case of tax liabilities levied on the value of specific assets, the owner will, all else equal, have a greater incentive to relocate assets outside the tax jurisdiction or, when new assets are created, to locate them outside the tax jurisdiction. Thus, just as in the case of other wealth taxes, relative price and wage changes will be inflicted on resource owners and consumers both within and outside the taxing jurisdiction.

In the case of tax liabilities levied on individual wealth holders where the base is the value of specific assets they might possess, tax avoidance behavior would require that the individual take up residence outside the tax jurisdiction. This would be true for personal property levies. Likewise, wealth taxes levied on the size of wealth transfers can be avoided by a move of residence out of the taxing jurisdiction (by either the giver or receiver, depending upon who must bear the liability). Since wealth transfer taxation typically involves much greater potential burdens, estate taxes will elicit much more relocation behavior.

POLICY ISSUES: EQUITY, EFFICIENCY, GROWTH, AND STABILITY

State and local governments face a number of important policy issues. In a sense these issues are the criteria by which a given tax or tax system should be evaluated. Four key issues will be taken up in this section: equity of tax burden and income distribution (which directly ties into the incidence analysis of the preceding section), economic efficiency, economic growth, and economic stability. A further policy issue of tax productivity will be taken up in the next section. Whatever the tax objectives, they can be pursued with the aid of laws designed to elicit an appropriate tax avoidance behavior. In this sense, properly designed tax changes can take the place of government expenditure and service distribution policies.

Equity of Tax Burden and Income Distribution

Equity relates to the issue, Who should pay? That is, how much of the tax revenue is extracted from each household in relation to the ability of each household to pay its tax liability? Every tax will have distribution effects because revenue is collected in some relation to the household's ability to pay. In some instances, a particular tax change will substitute one set of tax liabilities for another set, with the principal objective of rearranging tax burdens among households so that a more equitable distribution of tax burdens is achieved. As stressed earlier, tax liabilities are in most cases enacted in order to finance increased government expenditures; the criterion of distribution will merely be a subsidiary concern, determining, along with other side effects, how well the new tax conforms to the standards of ethics and good government of the dominant coalition of political organizations and individuals. For deciding on the distribution side effects of a particular tax, state and local governments usually ignore effects of the change in government spending. This procedure disregards some of the more important distributional implications of particular taxes, i.e., those which are levied for the specific purpose of financing government expenditures designed to alter the household's relative ability to pay.

To evaluate the distributional effects of various tax instruments, state and local governments must first conceive of a useful measure of household ability to pay. Historically, among the measures used were jewelry, land, personal property, physical wealth, current consumption, total factor receipts, and leisure. The modern view is that income, defined by the accretion concept, is the most relevant measure of ability to pay. In this section, income is defined as household consumption plus the net change in household wealth. It is understood that all assets are valued at market prices, all communally owned property is ignored, and consumption of government services is ignored except for direct money transfers and to the extent that specific exchange is involved (see chapter on user charges). Again, we wish to stress two important points: First, whichever concept is chosen as a yardstick to assess ability to pay, the choice is always a value judgment; and second, usually only approximate and very rough measures of whichever concept is chosen can be developed at a reasonable cost.

Earlier empirical studies and attempts at evaluating the distributional effects of state and local taxes, particularly of expenditure and property taxes, appear in the light of recent economic analysis to suffer major defects. First, incomplete measures of household income, obtainable from taxable income data, were employed. These measures excluded numerous important sources of consumption and changes in household wealth; [24] as a result, ability to pay was distorted. Second, excessive and divergent assumptions were made concerning shifting. Unwarranted assumption of forward shifting of general sales taxes and of nonresidential property taxes, for example, led to possibly erroneous conclusions that these taxes are quite regressive. If ability to pay is measured with greater regard for wealth changes and consumption and if reasonable assumptions are consistently followed, general sales and property taxes may be found to be less regressive, and net personal income taxes less progressive, than previously thought.

To evaluate the distributional effects of various taxes, state and local governments must also employ a tax incidence theory. This is necessary because controlled experiments where everything else is held constant are not possible. If such controlled experiments were possible, discovering the distribution of tax burdens in relation to income would be a simple matter. The experimenter would merely measure after-tax income in period 1; then announce the tax and begin collecting in period 2; and after the direct and indirect effects of the tax had taken place so that adjustments to the tax were complete, the experimenter could again measure after-tax income. All of the resulting differences in income would be an exact measure of the distribution of tax burdens; the distributional effects of the tax on relative incomes or households' ability to pay would be known with certainty. Because such controlled experiments are not possible, tax incidence theory must be relied on to separate direct and indirect effects of the tax from other changes occurring in the system. It is necessary also to make assumptions about the composition of wealth of households in different income classes, the income levels of owners of various resources, and other matters that will weight the tax effects for each income class.

Detailed knowledge about the distributional effects of the major kinds of state and local taxes is very scarce; however, we have been able to state a few general conclusions in the development of this chapter. Our conclusions were derived from incidence analysis in concert with casual, representative perceptions of the wealth positions of households in different income classes, income elasticities of various types of consumption, and the income classes of suppliers of various productive factors.

Economic Efficiency

Among other things, government must organize decision making on matters of collective action, enforce laws, and supply constitutents certain goods that are financed out of collectively owned resources. We will stipulate that government production is efficient if for any level of expenditure no change in technique of production or factor employment could result in a greater quantity supplied of one government output without some reduction in the quantity supplied of some other government output. We will be solely concerned with changes in tax policy that leave at least one individual or group of individuals better off and no one else worse off. In the process of employing this criterion in tax policy questions, we will have to give thought to potential losers from any change and investigate how potential losers can be compensated for the change so that in the new situation everyone is at least as well off as before.

There are three contexts in which efficiency criteria are most often used with respect to taxation policies:

1. The first context is the relationship between the benefits an individual or household receives from the expenditures of the government and the tax burdens he bears due to the government's taxation policies. Certain aspects of this criterion were discussed above when we briefly considered the benefit principle of taxation as the primary set of efficiency criteria. Revenue instruments that most clearly can relate specific services to individual burdens were discussed in Chapter 3—user charges, special assessments, and earmarked excise levies.

Efficiency criteria in private markets relate to marginal benefits and costs: Households at every location in the local economy are supposed to equate the ratio of the value they associate with consuming small additional amounts of all goods supplied at the location with the ratio of the goods' prices. Each good, in an ideally efficient state of the world, will be supplied in the community until the cost of an additional unit, compared with the added cost of an additional unit of any other good, just equals the willingness of any household to substitute that good for any other in consumption. Because of the nature of collective goods and constitutional restrictions on discriminating among individuals with tax levies, the relations between tax burden and benefits enjoyed are never so ambitious as is the criterion for ideally efficient private markets. Tax policy makers are interested in the more limited objective of building into tax assessment legislation practices that allow individuals to "feel" the relationship between expanded services and individual cost burdens. Taxpayer reactions will then yield information that is useful in the collective decision-making process. Both government employees supplying services and citizens benefiting from the services will derive increased knowledge for deciding whether to expand or contract specific government programs. For state and local governments a primary consideration must be the extent to which their services are enjoyed by nonresidents who bear none, or nearly none, of the costs of providing those services.[25]

2. Tax policies cannot be administered costlessly. A relevant efficiency criterion for taxation policy is administrative costs: assessment of liabilities,

collection of payments, and policing of tax compliance as well as honesty of tax officials. In this connection important issues are: Who evaluates the tax base and how well? How fair is the tax assessment and collection? How well coordinated over time are payment of taxes and receipt of services? Since the tax base can be evaluated by taxpayers or government, we can find different mixes of private and agency costs. For many purposes all costs, regardless of who incurs them, should be taken into consideration. In case of self-assessment, fairness requires that government diligently check quality of tax base evaluation and validity of exemptions claimed. Fairness in tax collection is often extremely expensive.[26]

Policy makers concerned with efficiency of administration will attempt to change taxation policies in a way that, all else the same, will reduce at least some individual's cost and will leave no one's uncompensated costs greater. Policy changes that seem to be gaining adherents are intergovernmental revenue collection and transfer processes that take advantage of superior information or economies of large scale to reduce total tax administration costs.

3. Traditionally, treatments of efficiency criteria with respect to taxation policy have related to the "distorting" effects of tax levies on private decisions, i.e., the effect of altered relative values and wealth distributions on individual choice. It was realized that since tax assessments were not ideally neutral (completely unavoidable), each tax policy change would result in changed penalty avoidance behavior. The following kinds of distortions are possible:

a. Creation of involuntary unemployment by tax policy changes
b. Adjustments in work versus leisure and adjustments in types of employment chosen as a consequence of tax policy changes
c. Changes in aggregate and relative proportions of consumption and investment activities induced by tax policy changes
d. Alterations of location decisions resulting from tax policy changes

Items (*a*), (*b*) and (*c*) are treated in great length by other authors of public finance textbooks.[27] Our discussion has related primarily to item (*d*) and to only those particular aspects of state and local taxation that relate to the first three kinds of distortions.[28]

Economic Growth

Some classes of efficiency criteria for government policy have become so important that they are accorded special treatment; this is true for tax policy changes with respect to the rate of growth of per capita income. A tax change is said to have growth side effects if individuals, in an effort to avoid or postpone tax liabilities, engage in more (or less) saving than they would in the absence of the tax policy change. The rate of capital formation is affected by tax changes in two general ways. First, tax changes alter individual behavior with respect to risk taking, expected rates of return on investment projects, and an individual's estimated costs of consumption out of current income. Second, tax policy changes alter individual behavior with respect to unemployment, location, and leisure, thus indirectly affecting choices for saving and the rate of economic growth.

Tax growth policies are concerned with changes in individual behavior that, all else equal, will either increase or decrease the rate of productive saving or capital formation yielding increased future consumption to residents of the tax jurisdiction. Even though knowledge about the growth effects of various taxes is very limited and imprecise, we can state with confidence the direction of change each tax change will imply for the rate of economic growth, although we can almost never say anything about the magnitude of the policy's effects on growth.

Stability of Economic Activity and Revenue

Stability criteria with respect to state and local taxation policies are usually considered in two contexts:

1. The first context is a class of efficiency criteria which dominates the policy discussions of textbooks interested in central government finance.[29] These criteria concern the fluctuations in aggregate income of residents and in involuntary unemployment induced by changes in taxation policies. A decline in aggregate local income within a region of the United States economy is most often the result of demand and supply shifts exogenous to the particular region. Efforts in the affected region to counter a decline in aggregate income by altering tax liabilities is not likely to be very effective, because state and local governments do not control total money supply, and to the extent that governments in a region can stimulate local demand, there are great leakages from this to other regions. Furthermore, for state and local governments to coordinate efforts to achieve income stability would entail very large administrative costs.

Probably the most important state and local policy consideration with respect to income and employment stability is not in the area of compensatory finance but rather in concern for private expectations. Tax policies should attempt to reduce the number of rapid and unpredictable changes in tax liabilities that might be implied by other policies and to schedule changes over longer periods so that adjustments can be smaller and less costly to citizens. If the government wishes to systematically expand or contract the magnitude of tax liabilities with changes in aggregate resident income, tax policy makers may build into the tax structure predictable, automatic changes. To the extent that government tax policies are made more predictable with respect to fluctuations, they become sources of stability and reduce what can become disastrous effects created by too optimistic or too pessimistic private expectations.

2. The second context of stability criteria relates to the more direct concern of state and local governments—the stability of tax payment revenues to state and local governments when exogenous changes impinge on the state and local economy. Stability of expected revenues, or their steady growth, simplifies planning and reduces the administrative costs of making budgetary commitments. The threat of fiscal insolvency can be reduced. Furthermore, tax policies that produce revenue yields which are insensitive to a downturn of regional income are desirable with respect to this stability criterion since, as we have stressed, state and local governments have little ability to ensure stable income and employment.

HOW MUCH WILL BE PAID: TAX PRODUCTIVITY

A further positive question is: How much in taxes will be paid to state and local governments? This is a key element in the more general question: How much money can such governments expect from all sources, including user charges and intergovernmental aid? An answer to the broader question, as well as an estimate of expenditures, is important to state and local government officials who must be sure that the various revenue sources will produce sufficient money to finance planned services in years to come.

Tax revenue changes from one year to the next are related to the income elasticity of tax revenue, to short-term revenue elasticity, and to the tax base. For these discussions it must be recognized that some of the taxpayers live within and some live outside a given jurisdiction, and the total number must be considered in determining the tax base that generates the jurisdiction's tax revenue.

Income Elasticity of Tax Revenue (Revenue Elasticity)

Revenue elasticity is the responsiveness of revenue to changes in taxpayers' income over time. The magnitude of revenue elasticity is directly related to the jurisdiction's tax system, structure, and rates, which together determine the level of future revenue.[30]

The coefficient of revenue elasticity (N_Y) is defined as the ratio of the percentage change in government revenue to the corresponding percentage change in taxpayers' income. Specifically:

$$N_Y = \frac{\frac{\Delta R}{R^0}}{\frac{\Delta Y}{Y^0}} \tag{4.1}$$

$$\Delta R = (R^1 - R^0) \tag{4.2}$$

$$\Delta Y = (Y^1 - Y^0) \tag{4.3}$$

where

$R^0 =$ quantity of revenue yielded by a given structure of tax bases and rates in some initial fiscal year

$Y^0 =$ income of jurisdiction's taxpayers, i.e., regional taxable income in the initial fiscal year

$R^1 =$ quantity of revenue yielded by the same given structure of bases and rates in a later fiscal year

$Y^1 =$ income of jurisdiction's taxpayers, i.e., regional taxable income in the later fiscal year

The revenue elasticity relates to a supply of revenue and we can conceive of three cases. One case represents levels of Y^1 and R^1 such that $N_Y < 1$; that is, although the percentage changes in revenue and income are both positive, the percentage increase in revenue yield is less than the percentage increase in income, and the government's revenue is inelastic. A second case represents $N_Y = 1$, where the percentage changes in revenue and income are exactly equal; i.e., the government's revenue is unitary elastic. A third case represents $N_Y > 1$; the government's supply of revenue is elastic because the percentage change in revenue take is greater than the percentage change in constitutents' income. This same terminology of inelastic, unitary elastic, and elastic supply functions of revenue will hold for negative changes in income and revenue where $Y^1 < Y^0$ and $R^1 < R^0$.[31]

Using the notion of revenue elasticity we can express total revenue yield in a given year 0 as a function of effective tax rates—r—and tax bases—B.

$$R^0 = f(r_1 B_1^0, r_2 B_2^0, \ldots, r_n B_n^0) \tag{4.4}$$

Subscripts $1, 2, \ldots, n$ refer to different revenue sources.

The effective rates are initially assumed constant, and are dropped later in the analysis. R^0 can change only if one or more of the bases change. The size of the base depends on constituents' income, while the tax-take relationship may involve an adjustment lag of the base behind income. For purposes of simplicity we will assume that the only relevant independent variable is current income. Now n functional relations can be postulated: $B_j^0 = p_j (Y^0)$ for $j = 1, \ldots, n$. Inserting them into equation 4.4, R^0 becomes a function of Y^0.

$$R^0 = F(Y^0) \tag{4.5}$$

To determine the revenue elasticity for a recent fiscal period, one must first estimate the income change (ΔY) for the fiscal period in question so that the percentage change in taxpayer income ($\Delta Y/Y^0$) can be estimated. Then, ΔR and $\Delta R/R^0$ are estimated. The result is an ex post estimate of the income elasticity of each tax revenue source in a recent year.

To estimate revenue elasticity and revenue yield in a future year, one must modify the elasticity coefficient in line with expected changes in tax rate and tax base. Thus, the expected elasticity of revenue supply for the coming fiscal period is:

$$E(N_Y) = \frac{\dfrac{E(\Delta R)}{R^0}}{\dfrac{E(\Delta Y)}{Y^0}} \tag{4.6}$$

Ideally, in case all tax bases closely covary with regional taxable income, by multiplying the expected revenue elasticity coefficient $E(N_Y)$ with the expected income of the future period—$E(Y)$—one should be able to derive an estimate of the expected tax yield. Unfortunately, in reality not all significant tax bases correlate closely with regional taxable income. This holds particularly for expenditure and wealth taxes, which correlate poorly with income.[32]

The revenue elasticity of a particular tax relates the change in total revenue yield to the change in total constituents' income. Total revenue is the sum of the amount paid by households. Total income is the sum of the incomes of all affected households.

Revenue Elasticity, Tax Progressivity, and Tax Yield

To focus on the relationships between revenue elasticity, tax productivity, and tax yield, we must distinguish between different taxes. For convenience, we will use the three categories—income taxes, expenditure taxes, and wealth taxes—and place all other revenue sources in a fourth category.[33] Therefore:

$$\begin{aligned} E(\Delta R) &= r_1 E(\Delta B_1) + r_2 E(\Delta B_2) + r_3 E(\Delta B_3) + r_4 E(\Delta B_4) \\ &= r_1 f_1(E(\Delta Y), \ldots) + r_2 f_2(E(\Delta Y), \ldots) \\ &\quad + r_3 f_3(E(\Delta Y), \ldots) + r_4 f_4(E(\Delta Y), \ldots) \end{aligned} \tag{4.7}$$

where each r represents the average effective rate resulting from the assumption that policy variables are fixed and the subscripts 1, 2, 3, and 4 refer to revenue sources.

Relevant tax base measures are not easily related to regional income measures. The personal income tax is the exception. The value of the services of property might constitute a proper base for the property tax.

In attempting to estimate future tax yields, we tend to make projections that as a first approximation assume continuation of the existing tax rate system and structure and legal as well as administrative definition of their tax base. If we can assume that the tax rate remains unchanged over time, we can replace the concept of income elasticity of tax revenue by a concept of income elasticity of tax base, or base elasticity.[34]

For any given fiscal period, regional taxable income Y can be regarded as the sum of household taxable income y.[35]

$$Y = \sum_{p=1}^{m} y_p \tag{4.9}$$

where $p = 1, 2, \ldots, m$.

To relate productivity to a tax we can examine the necessary conditions for characterizing the "gressivity" of a levy as regressive, progressive, or proportional.[36] First, let us assume that no exemptions are involved in the levies. We can relate the effective rate of revenue take from each of the four revenue sources to individual household income in order to derive the necessary conditions.

Let T_j = effective revenue take from the jth revenue source
where $j = 1, 2, 3, 4$
and y_p = taxable household income of pth household
where $p = 1, 2, \ldots, m$

The following conditions will then define the gressivity characteristics of a levy:

1. If the relationship between T_j and y_p is characterized by a straight line of any slope, i.e., $\dfrac{dT_j}{dy_p} > 0, \dfrac{d^2T_j}{dy_p^2} = 0$, the revenue source is a proportional levy.
2. If, over the range of household income, the relationship is such that the additional revenue take from additional houshould income always increases, i.e., $\dfrac{dT_j}{dy_p} > 0, \dfrac{d^2T_j}{dy_p^2} > 0$, the revenue source is progressive.
3. If the additional take always decreases from increments in household income, i.e., $\dfrac{dT_j}{dy_p} \gtrless 0, \dfrac{d^2T_j}{dy_p^2} < 0$, the revenue source is regressive.

To represent the gressivity with respect to a particular taxing jurisdiction, we may group all households into income classes. Thus, T_j will become the average effective revenue take in each income class for the entire jurisdiction. This assumes explicitly either that the same number of households are in each class or, alternatively, that the income classes can be so chosen that each class contains the same number of households.

We then have the following:

$$R^0 = F(Y^0) \quad \text{or} \tag{4.10}$$

$$r_1 B_1^0 = r_2 B_2^0 + r_3 B_3^0 + r_4 B_4^0 = G(y_1^0, \ldots, y_k^0) \tag{4.11}$$

where there are k income classes. But since each income class has a distinct average effective rate for each revenue source we get:

$$\begin{aligned}
r_{11} B_1^0 + r_{21} B_2^0 + r_{31} B_3^0 + r_{41} B_4^0 &= g_1(y_1^0) \\
r_{21} B_1^0 + r_{22} B_2^0 + r_{23} B_3^0 + r_{24} B_4^0 &= g_2(y_2^0) \\
r_{k1} B_1^0 + r_{k2} B_2^0 + r_{k3} B_3^0 + r_{k4} B_4^0 &= g_k(y_k^0)
\end{aligned} \tag{4.12}$$

that is, $R^0 = g_1(y_i^0) + g_2(y_2^0) + g_3(y_3^0) + \ldots + g_k(y_k^0)$; the total revenue yield in any one fiscal period is the sum of revenue yields for all income classes. The gressivity of any one tax source will be reflected in the r's of any one column in equation 4.12. This is because $T_j^0 = r_{ij} B_j^0$ for the income class and the revenue source. If, as we move up or down any column, $\dfrac{r_{ij} B_j^0}{y_i^0}$ conforms to condition 1 above, the jth revenue source can be considered proportional—or progressive or regressive if it generally conforms to conditions 2 or 3 respectively. The progressivity of total revenue collections R^0 in the fiscal period can be evaluated in the same manner by examining the column of $g_i(y_i^0)$ which indicates the revenue yield from each income class from all four revenue sources.

The expected revenue elasticity equation 4.6 can still be calculated in the same manner except that there will now be k equations—one for each income class—instead of one, in the estimation of $E(\triangle R)$, equation 4.6, if the government official wishes to make explicit the effects of regressivity on revenue elasticity. In the expanded form $E(\triangle Y)$ will also become more complicated since

$$E(\Delta Y) = E(\Delta y_i) + E(\Delta y_2) + \ldots + E(\Delta y_k) \tag{4.13}$$

In short, officials must estimate the household income change in each income class.[37]

Tax Base Growth and Its Estimation

To determine how productive a given tax or tax system is likely to be, we must not only estimate the revenue elasticity, but we must also obtain reliable projections of tax base changes over time. The importance of tax base information is further underscored by the fact that in projecting tax yields under existing tax rate conditions we can replace the concept of income elasticity of government revenue by the simpler concept of income elasticity of the tax base. As will be discussed in the next chapter, our main concern is with personal income, retail sales, excise, and property tax bases, although we have also some lesser interest in the corporate income and estate tax bases.

Tax base projections can start with the assumption of unchanged tax rates and structures, as well as tax base definition. This does not deny the fact that changes in the tax rate structure and tax base are important policy variables to be considered by state and local government officials in order to bring government costs and receipts into better balance.

Two kinds of issues are involved when considering how to project the tax base into the future: What is the proper tax base measure and how reliable must the projection be?

With respect to the first issue, measures of regional personal income, consumer expenditure, and wealth are commonly accepted as appropriate proxies for the tax base. However, in some instances, there is not a direct correspondence between the measures and the actual tax base. For example, some income flows are taxable that are not in the region's personal income estimate and some expenditures are not in the tax base. If the actual taxable components of these proxy measures are expected to move differently from the aggregates, then serious error might result from use of the proxy measures as the tax base.

REGIONAL GROWTH MODELS
EMPHASIZING FINAL DEMAND CHANGES

Some evaluation of whether such error might occur can be provided by consideration of a simplified regional growth model as shown in Figure 4.1. Four flows can be distinguished: the gross value of production, income earned by local residents who work outside the region, income from outside property owned by local residents, and income transferred from outside the region. The last three flows go directly into household personal income, while the first must pass through the region's factor markets. From the gross value of production in the region, one can subtract the value of goods and services purchased from business, including both imported and locally produced goods, to arrive at the value added in the region. The value-added figure might also be empirically approximated by aggregating employee compensation, profits, and capital consumption in the producing industries. Each of these value-added elements can be related to a region's tax base. The value of the services of physical assets, i.e., capital consumption, underlies the value of the assets themselves; thus capital consumption is a component of the property tax base.[38] Net corporate earnings or profits are taxed directly under the state corporate income tax. Earnings distributed to local residents are taxed as part of personal income. State personal income tax laws are written to include all income of residents and income earned in the state by nonresidents; there-

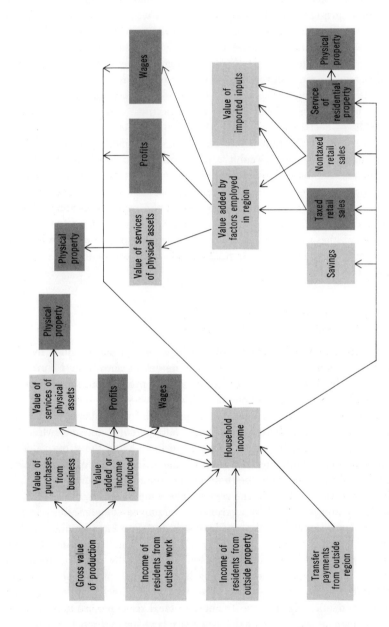

FIGURE 4.1   Simplified regional growth model.

fore, wage payments are taxable whether they are made to residents or non-residents. Thus, depending on the locations of the residences of the individuals who have title to the physical assets (those who own the firms) and of those who work for the firms, a portion of the income produced by the region will flow out of the region and be lost to the personal income tax base.

Next, we turn to household income, which will be either spent or saved. It is convenient to distinguish three classes of consumption: services of residential space, taxed retail goods and services, and nontaxed retail goods and services. The first provides the derived demand on which rests the value of residential property, another portion of the property tax base. The second is the basis for retail sales and excise taxes.

It does not matter to the tax base whether the taxable goods or services are produced in the region. But it does matter whether they are purchased in the region. Thus to the extent that regional residents purchase outside the region, a tax base is lost, while if retail sales are made to nonresidents, the tax base is increased. For this reason a simple relationship between income and personal expenditures is not likely to provide an adequate measure of the expenditure tax base, and even more important, changes in the income distribution will affect the allocation between taxable and nontaxable expenditures and will thereby further complicate the use of expenditures as a proxy for the expenditure tax base.

In this description of income flows, it has been assumed that the income flowing from property ownership is an adequate measure for deriving the amount of wealth that can serve as the property tax base. However, as mentioned earlier there is a considerable lag between assessment of property values and property income flows, which will make this relationship more or less remote.

The answer to the question of how reliable the tax base projections need to be determines what kind of projection model should be used. Figure 4.1 also describes an implied growth model which can provide estimates of the region's tax base. When such a model is extended it can provide consistent estimates of changes in the region's economic base and consumption habits, which are the elements needed for projecting the tax base.

However, it is also possible to project the personal income, expenditures, and wealth in the region on a less consistent basis and still obtain pragmatically useful results.

DIRECT TAX BASE MODELS

Whenever final demand changes can be expected to have only minor effects on the tax base, it is possible to directly project changes in tax bases.

A simple procedure for projecting personal income in a jurisdiction is to project the trend of changes in per capita income in the jurisdiction and compare it with the national trend.[39] Another aggregative approach can be adopted if the jurisdiction's net output projections are available, since the major part of net output produced in a jurisdiction is also part of personal income received. The chief differences between output and income are accounted for by the income earned by commuting workers, the net interregional flows of property income, and transfer payments by the Federal government. The relationship between personal income and net ouput can be projected to obtain a personal income projection.

More reliable projections with greater detail can be made if the industrial sources and components of personal income are analyzed separately. Labor and proprietor income per employee in each industry in a base period can be calculated; allowance can be made for productivity improvements in each industry either by evaluating the regional industry trend or relating it to national productivity projections; then the productivity improvement factor and an industry employment projection can be combined with the estimate of earned income per employee to derive an estimate of the labor component of the income produced. An adjustment for labor commuting would then have to be made in the estimate to arrive at the labor component of income received. Property income (interest, rents, dividends), although a small component of personal income, is most difficult to project because ownership is not geographically distributed in the same way as industrial activity. One might have to use judgment about how the geographic distribution of property income is likely to differ from the geographic distribution of population or labor income.

Retail sales projections can be derived from personal income projections; separate property value projections should be made for unimproved and for improved land.

SUMMARY

A tax is a payment made to cancel a liability imposed by government and for which the government offers the particular taxpayer no specific services directly in return. The analysis of state and local government taxation is directed to a number of key policy questions. The most important normative question is: Who should pay? This issue raises questions about the objectives and criteria of taxes. Two major principles can be applied: The ability-to-pay principle states generally that the amount of tax burden borne by an individual should be related to his economic capability to bear the burden, i.e., the higher his capacity, the higher proportionately the tax take. The benefit principle of taxation rests on the presumption that those who receive benefits from goods and services provided by government should bear the costs for them. The benefit principle automatically links the expenditure and the receipt sides of the government budget.

A second, no less important, question is: Who in fact does pay the tax? In other words, Who bears the ultimate burden? To answer this positive question, one must analyze the shifting and incidence of each tax. Tax incidence theory usually assumes that there will be full employment and that some offsetting modification in an expenditure or other tax must accompany a tax change. As a result total government tax collection remains unchanged. We call this technique differential incidence determination. Tax shifting results from burden avoidance behavior; as expectations of a tax change become more certain and specific, households alter their behavior in order to avoid the tax burden. Tax burdens are thus shifted from legally liable households to other households who alter their behavior in order to accept part of the tax burden rather than accept the costs implied by complete burden avoidance. Resource specialization, especially geographic specialization, has important effects on the shifting of various taxes.

State and local governments must deal with such policy issues as equity of tax burden, economic efficiency, economic growth, and economic stability. These four issues are in a sense criteria by which taxes. can be appraised. Basically different tax objectives can be achieved through laws that result in appropriate tax avoidance behaviors.

Another positive question relates to the productivity of taxes: How much in taxes will be paid to a state or local government? The tax productivity of a given jurisdiction depends on the income elasticity of tax revenue—which is directly related to the jurisdiction's tax system, structure, and rates—as well as to the non-policy-variable tax base. The income elasticity of tax revenue must be examined in the light of the progressivity of the tax (and tax system) and the responsiveness of the tax base. A variety of growth models can be applied to project tax base changes. They fall into two basic categories: regional growth models emphasizing final demand changes, and direct tax base models.

CHAPTER 5
TAX
INSTRUMENTS

The preceding chapter was addressed to some fundamental issues in state and local taxation. The concepts and tools of taxation that were discussed will be applied in this chapter; they will supplement descriptive and institutional information regarding effects of tax laws and performance of tax administrators. Wherever possible empirical studies on incidence and burden distribution of state and local taxation will be presented.

Since the early 1940s state and local taxes have steadily declined as percentages of total general revenue, while the percentages of miscellaneous general revenue and Federal aid have increased. In the late 1960s less than 70 percent of the general revenue of state and local governments came from their own tax collections; the rest was about equally distributed between miscellaneous general revenue and Federal aid (see Table 5.1).[1] Among the various state and local government taxes in the late 1960s, the property tax (although its percentage has been declining) is still the single most important tax, accounting for almost one-half of all tax receipts. It is followed by the sales and gross receipts taxes, which account for a little less than 30 percent, and the income tax, which yields about 15 percent.

It is virtually impossible to find a sole focus around which to build an integrating framework for state and local taxation. In this and the preceding chapter we made use of a conventional scheme that classifies taxes according to the object against which the tax is levied, i.e., the tax base. Emphasizing the tax base of state and local governments that operate in an open economy is a useful organizing device because of the paramount importance of tax base mobility and the problems such mobility poses. Three tax bases have been chosen: income, expenditures, and wealth. We will relate all of the various tax liabilities created by state and local governments to one or more of these bases. Other textbook frameworks distinguish between taxes levied directly on persons and those levied indirectly on activities.[2] This distinction is not irrelevant to our discussion, but will not be used.

In this chapter, we will examine in some detail different income, expenditure, and wealth tax instruments. Then we will briefly discuss borrowing. Both borrowing and taxation are ways to obtain funds for the government's current purchase of resources. However, borrowing, unlike taxation, does not increase an individual taxpayer's payment obligation in the current period. The sum total of individuals incur future repayment liabilities. Finally, some select opportunities (and their prospects) for tax reform will be discussed.

TABLE 5.1 *State and Local Sources of General Revenue, Selected Years, 1942–1967 (in millions of dollars)*

	1942 Amount	1942 % of Total	1948 Amount	1948 % of Total	1957 Amount	1957 % of Total	1960 Amount	1960 % of Total	1963 Amount	1963 % of Total	1965 Amount	1965 % of Total	1967 Amount	1967 % of Total
Federal aid	$ 858	8.2	$ 1,861	10.8	$ 3,843	10.0	$ 6,974	13.8	$ 8,663	13.9	$11,029	14.8	$15,505	16.9
Taxes	8,528	81.9	13,342	77.3	28,817	75.5	36,117	71.5	44,014	70.7	51,578	69.4	61,241	66.8
Individual income	276	2.6	543	3.1	1,753	4.6	2,463	4.9	3,267	5.2	4,090	5.5	5,835	6.4
Corporation income	272	2.6	592	3.4	984	2.6	1,180	2.3	1,505	2.4	1,929	2.6	2,227	2.4
Sales and gross receipts	2,351	22.6	4,442	25.8	9,467	24.8	11,849	23.5	14,446	23.2	17,118	23.0	20,554	22.4
Property	4,537	43.6	6,126	35.5	12,864	33.7	16,407	32.5	19,833	31.8	22,918	30.8	26,280	28.6
Other taxes	1,092	10.5	1,638	9.5	3,733	9.7	4,218	8.3	4,963	8.0	5,523	7.4	6,345	6.9
Miscellaneous general revenue	1,031	9.9	2,047	11.9	5,503	14.4	7,414	14.7	9,593	15.4	11,735	15.8	14,881	16.2
Total general revenue:														
Amount in current prices	$10,418	100.0	$17,250	100.0	$38,163	100.0	$50,504	100.0	$62,269	100.0	$74,341	100.0	$91,627	100.0
Percentage of GNP	6.5%		6.6%		8.6%		10.0%		11.1%		11.0%		11.6%	
Percentage of national income	7.6%		7.7%		10.4%		12.2%		12.9%		13.4%		14.1%	
Per capita in current prices	$77.25		$117.64		$224.09		$280.59		$330.07		$383.61		$463.08	
Per capita in constant prices*	$143.06		$133.83		$226.35		$278.64		$329.08		$374.25		$436.46	

* Deflated by Bureau of Labor Statistics Wholesale Price Index (1957–1959 = 100).

sources: Laszlo Ecker-Racz, "A Foreign Scholar Ponders at the 1957 Census of Governments," *National Tax Journal*, vol. 12 (June, 1959), p. 107; *Statistical Abstract: 1966* (Washington, D.C., 1966), pp. 5 and 423; *Statistical Abstract: 1963* (Washington, D.C., 1963). p. 422; *Economic Report of the President* (Washington, D.C., 1966), pp. 207, 215, 221; U.S. Bureau of the Census, *Statistical Abstract: 1968* (Washington, D.C., 1968), p. 341; Advisory Commission on Intergovernmental Relations, *State and Local Finances: Significant Features: 1966 to 1969* (Washington, D.C., 1968), pp. 17 and 19; U.S. Department of Commerce, *Survey of Current Business*, vol. 49 (February, 1969), p. S-1ff.

INCOME TAXES

Income taxes were initiated in Hawaii before it became a state in 1901; the first state to adopt an income tax was Wisconsin, in 1911. By 1968, the individual income tax was levied in thirty-five states and the corporation income tax was levied in thirty-seven states. State effective tax rates are generally much lower than Federal rates and state personal exemptions are higher than Federal exemptions. Compared with Federal tax laws, state tax brackets are narrower and rate graduation is steeper, but the maximum rate is reached at much lower incomes, usually at incomes between $5,000 and $15,000.

Among states levying income taxes in the late 1960s, the maximum statutory rate applicable to individual income was 14 percent, and to corporate income the rate was 11 percent. However, these rates overstate the impact of state income taxes because such taxes are deductible from taxable income in the computation of Federal taxes. In 1964, twelve states had income tax revenue of less than 1 percent of their constituents' Federal adjusted gross income; another twelve states had revenue of less than 2 percent; and only nine states had revenue of more than 2 percent. The maximum state income tax revenue was 3 percent in Delaware, Oregon, and Wisconsin.[3]

Withholding on wages and salaries for state income tax purposes was introduced in Oregon in 1948; by 1968 withholding was practiced in thirty-five states.[4]

States that do not levy income taxes have, on the average, much lower per capita total state and local revenue collections. Also, total state and local revenue collections per $1,000 of personal income are, on the average, greater in states with income taxation than in states without income taxation.[5] There are wide variations in the amount of state income taxes levied per $1,000 of personal income; for example, Delaware collects almost one hundred times as much as South Dakota.

Personal Income Taxes

Individual income taxes levied by state and local governments increased from $276 million in 1942 to $5,835 million in 1967. Personal income taxation as a percentage of all general revenue sources increased about 2½ times during this period, from 2.6 percent in 1942 to 6.4 percent in 1967. There are two reasons for these increases: More states were levying income taxes in 1967, and the tax rates were higher.

State income taxes are generally patterned after the Federal tax and tend to conform with Federal definitions and practices. By 1968, Alaska, Nebraska, and Vermont based their rates on the Federal income tax liability.[6] Like the Federal tax, most state income taxes allow for personal exemptions and certain deductions to produce a net personal income tax base from which the actual tax liability is computed. The accrual concept of income includes all changes in household wealth. However, since all states do not have income taxes and those which do have employ the factor flow concept of income, wealth changes are taxed less than other sources of purchasing power. This is especially true for states that have adopted provisions similar (if not identical) to those of the Federal law, in the following respects: First, certain wealth increases are entirely excluded from the taxable income of recipients and in some states are not subtractable from the taxable income of givers. These wealth changes include gifts, inheritances, sick pay, insurance payments, certain government subsidies, and unemployment benefits. Second, gains realized on capital (turned to cash through exchange) are in certain circumstances taxed at a lower rate than other income; likewise losses realized on asset devaluation can get full write-off. The major exceptions from capital gains taxation are business inventories, gains unrealized before death, and changes in the value of human capital. Special capital gains treatment is accorded gains realized on personal residences, livestock, natural resources, and patents. Thus one can see that because some states have added the accrual concept of income the generality of personal income tax liability has been increased, though only slightly.

Personal net income taxes allow exemptions of nonmonetary income flows. The most significant exemptions are income in kind, services of housewives, and services of durable goods possessed by an individual or household that yield real income in successive time periods. Furthermore, as measured, taxable income does not include the personal consumption of government services (distributed free of charge) and the nonpecuniary advantages of the natural and social environment.[7]

Although local governments could employ either gross or net personal income taxes, until recently most cities relied mainly on a gross income tax base; these cities are located predominantly in Kentucky, Michigan, Ohio, and Pennsylvania; but New York, St. Louis, and Kansas City levied gross income taxes in the late 1960s. Altogether, more than 3,000 local jurisdictions, most of them in Pennsylvania, levy gross income or payroll taxes.

Local governments have recently shown more interest in basing their personal income taxes on net personal income. For example, as part of its comprehensive tax revision, Maryland authorized its counties to levy local personal income taxes on their residents at rates up to 50 percent of the state tax liability. Thus in 1968 Maryland became the first state to provide state administration of local income taxes. Furthermore, starting in 1970, city income taxes in Michigan can be administered by the state on the basis of mutual agreement.[8]

Despite its many exemptions and deductions, the Federal personal income tax is considered to have great generality; the tax allows the taxpayer relatively few opportunities to shift his tax burden by altering his behavior. However, state and local income taxes are much more easily avoided; the major differences between Federal and state personal income tax laws are derived from the openness of regional economies. State or local personal income tax liabilities can be avoided by changing to a residence outside the taxing jurisdiction. Thus state income taxes will have a greater impact than Federal taxes on location decisions because the state tax can be avoided by choice of residence. Only as all states adopt uniform income provisions and allow for deduction of income taxes paid to other jurisdictions will the incidence of state income taxes become more like that of the Federal tax. Under such a circumstance, trying to avoid paying state income taxes by changing location would be like trying to avoid the Federal tax. Location effects of income taxes are particularly relevant to local governments, which are reluctant to impose income taxes unless local income taxes are uniform throughout the state and, preferably, in adjoining states also.

Most state and local governments that levy personal income taxes claim the right to tax all income no matter where earned. Thus they tax both residents who earned money outside the state and nonresidents who earned money in the state. Difficulties arise when the factor, or tax base, is located in one jurisdiction and its owner resides in another, e.g., when a property located in New Haven, Connecticut, is owned by a resident of New York City. If the jurisdiction where the property is located employs factor flow income taxation but the jurisdiction of residence taxes household accrual income, then the income from the property will, in effect, be taxed twice.

Some states have attempted to alleviate this difficulty by allowing residents to deduct from their tax payments a portion of the taxes paid to other states if those states allow reciprocal privileges; less frequently, nonresidents may be allowed to deduct a portion of the taxes paid on relevant income and in another state if that state has similar provisions in its income tax laws.[9]

Although householders can avoid paying income taxes by moving outside a jurisdiction, actual outmigration rates are not predictable with any great accuracy. Several factors are of primary importance in reducing outmigration. Moving and commuting costs will help prevent a jurisdiction from experiencing sizable population losses. It is extremely costly to separate certain employment areas of factor services, such as labor, from the households that supply them. Outmigration will cause prices of services supplied in the jurisdiction to fall, reflecting reduced demand for the services and the desire of suppliers to "save business" and discourage outmigration.[10]

A tax based on personal or household income is clearly related to equity and ability to pay; income is often regarded as the most reliable measure of ability to pay. It is much more difficult to relate the income tax to the benefit principle. Two conceptual, admittedly minor, links between income taxation and the benefit principle can be imagined for cities that levy payroll taxes on the gross earnings of persons working within their jurisdictions. First, local governments engage in a number of activities that benefit laborers and thus make some labor services more valuable; for example, they establish and protect legal rights, enforce laws regulating child labor and minimum wages, and help mediate labor disputes and police strikes. In general, these activities increase returns to employed workers. Local governments also sometimes provide cooperating inputs that benefit employers, such as public transportation that makes labor services available throughout the market area at lower wages than would otherwise prevail.

A second link between a municipal gross earnings tax and the benefit principle relates to goods and services provided by a local government that are consumed not only by residents within its jurisdiction but also by nonresidents who are employed in the city. While they are working, nonresidents benefit from many services provided by the local government. In addition, if they work in a central city, the nonresident and his family benefit to some extent from certain services usually subsidized by the central city but available to all in the metropolitan area at varying traveling costs, e.g., museums, symphony halls, zoos, etc.

However, the tax base of income provides little or no discrimination between workers on the basis of differences in the services they receive and the amount of taxes they pay. Furthermore, payroll taxes are almost never earmarked for the provision of specific services to wage earners. Certain revenues discussed in Chapter 3 would be exceptions: worker's compensation, health insurance, unemployment relief funds, retirements, etc.

Since the early fifties a number of studies have been made to estimate the income elasticity of state individual income taxes. Harold Groves and Harry Kahn used income and individual tax data for the State of Wisconsin for 1936 to 1950. They estimated the income elasticity by regression of tax collections on income, using logarithms for both variables. They estimated an elasticity of 1.75 for the period.[11] Lee Soltow made a similar study of Wisconsin for 1933 to 1951 and found an income elasticity greater than 2.[12]

Dick Netzer in 1961 estimated the income elasticity of state individual income taxes for all states combined by developing "a pattern of rates and exemptions which is average, when weighted by income or individual tax collections, for the governments using the tax in the base year. These tax provisions were applied to income distribution data in various postwar years to gauge the rise in taxable types of personal income."[13] He concluded that under this characteristic income tax structure, the income elasticity is 1.7.

Robert Harris in the mid-sixties developed a methodology which, seeking to circumvent the problem of rate and base changes, applies sets of effective rates to size distributions of adjusted gross income for 1952 to 1961. The effective rates were calculated, using standard deductions for single taxpayers and married couples with two children. The resulting "synthetic" tax series was regressed on personal income, using logarithms on both variables, as had been done by Groves and Kahn.[14] Harris provided for each state two different estimates, based on different assumptions about the proportion of joint returns per income class, with the difference between the two usually about 0.1 to 0.2. The lowest income elasticity was found in relation to Delaware (1.2) and the highest in relation to Louisiana (2.3).

Neil Singer slightly modified the method used by Harris by introducing dummy variables.[15] His results are quite similar to those of Harris.

Finally, Selma Mushkin and Gabrielle Lupo recommend for the projection of 1970 state personal income taxes an income elasticity coefficient of 1.7 related to gross national product and 1.8 related to personal income. The corporate income tax elasticities recommended are 1.3 and 1.4, respectively.[16]

How well the personal income tax is evaluated by taxpayers depends to no small extent on how many resources the government employs to check the accuracy of taxpayers' returns, especially the validity of the exemptions claimed. Only if substantial resources are employed are equals likely to be treated equally. Municipal gross earnings taxes pose serious problems in connection with the fairness of their collection. Such taxes are much more difficult and costly to collect from individuals receiving income from many sources and on contingency arrangements. As a result, municipal gross income taxes may discriminate against wage earners. The agency cost of administering income taxes is relatively low compared with the cost of other taxes. The income tax liability is levied only once a year; however, the possible burden of year-end illiquidity can be lessened by monthly projections and advance transfers of funds to the government. Withholding increases agency administration costs but is in effect in virtually all states that have income taxes.

Corporate Income Taxes

The corporate income tax treats the corporate form of business enterprise as a legal person whose factor flow income is subject to taxation in much the same manner as the income of an individual. Under the accrual concept of income, corporations per se would not be taxed; instead, the owners of corporations would be taxed on all dividend receipts and all changes in stock value. The entire income generated from corporate activities could be imputed to household personal income tax bases. But since governments mainly tax factor flows, they define the corporate income tax base as receipts of the corporation over and above accounting expenses. Receipts from all assets owned by the corporation are taxable after deductions are made for depreciation and for interest paid on loans. Capital gains on assets owned by corporations are treated the same way under corporate as under personal income taxation.[17]

State corporate income taxes, although they increased from $272 million in 1942 to $2.2 billion in 1967, have not increased as a percentage of states' total general revenue; they have amounted to 2 to 3 percent of such revenue (see Table 5.1).

Both the ability-to-pay and benefit principles are defined for a particular individual or household. There is little reason to expect either principle to apply to corporate income taxes; corporate income taxes do not discriminate between corporations on the basis of the ability to pay of its owners, customers, or workers. As pointed out in the preceding chapter, if the corporate form of organization (especially the rights granted to it to issue stock and limit liability) permits the corporation to realize greater economies of scale and greater specialization of economic activities, then, not only the owners of the corporation but all those who exchange goods and services with it are likely to benefit. Thus the corporate income tax does not constitute a clear benefit levy.

As described in Chapter 4, shareholders bear a large share of the corporate tax burden. The amount and direction of tax shifting that corporate owners can achieve are in doubt. Since we believe most corporate ownership is by upper-middle- and upper-income classes, the distribution of corporate income taxes would seem to be progressive, at least in the higher range. Thus, even though the corporate income tax does not discriminate among owners, corporate customers, or corporate factor suppliers on the basis of ability to pay, the tax, taken as a whole, may be a rough ability-to-pay levy where corporate ownership holdings are a proxy for wealth, or even for income.

The corporate income tax in conjunction with a factor flow personal income tax can and perhaps often does result in double taxation of some incomes. Double taxation is difficult to justify fully on grounds of ability to pay. While many shares of stocks are owned by members of high-income groups, shares are also owned by members of middle- (and even low-) income groups. Rich and poor are subject to identical corporate tax burdens and, as noted above, shifting of the corporate income tax, either forward or backward, will not predictably cause it to fall on members of high-income groups.

If the accrual concept of income were substituted for the factor flow concept, no double taxation could arise. Furthermore, income taxation of returns from corporate ownership could then be related to ability to pay. Thus, while advocates of the flow concept of income emphasize the relatively low collection costs for taxing corporations separately as entities, advocates of the accrual concept stress that the corporation tax relates poorly to benefit principles and fosters inequitable treatment of the individuals who happen to bear the burden of corporate tax changes—both double taxation and special treatment of capital gains.[18]

Just as state and local personal income tax liabilities can be avoided by changing residence, corporate income tax liabilities can be avoided by changing the location of economic activity, although clearly at a cost. Alan Campbell found that because of the larger New York corporate income tax in the late 1950s, which tended to iron out tax differences between locations in that state, moves to less populated areas in New Jersey proved more advantageous than moves to the same sort of locations in New York State.[19]

Much of what has been said about the administration of personal income tax also holds for the administration of the corporate income tax. To this must be added the great difficulty of allocating interstate income.

EXPENDITURE TAXES

Expenditure taxes are liabilities imposed by government on participants in market exchanges and can be imposed on either buyer or seller. We will consider the two most common forms of expenditure taxes employed by state and local governments: general sales taxes and specific excise taxes.

State and local government taxes on sales and gross sales receipts yielded $2.4 billion in 1942 and $20.6 billion in 1967, predominantly collected by states. Interestingly, during this period expenditure tax revenue as a share of all state and local government general revenue has remained rather stable, at about 23 percent (see Table 5.1).[20]

General Sales Taxes

General sales taxes, as their name indicates, are general levies on a great variety of exchanges—in the United States, retail sales of most final consumption goods. State tax liabilities are usually assessed on the basis of gross sales receipts of retail firms.

The retail sales tax emerged as a major source of state revenue in the 1930s and by the late 1960s was in force in forty-four states, plus the District of Columbia, at rates ranging from 2 percent to 6 percent, with 3 percent being the most common rate.[21] Fourteen states exempt food from the retail sales tax, twenty-two states exempt medicine, and three states exempt wearing apparel other than luxury items.

In 1963 Indiana and Wisconsin began to offer tax credit (or refunds) against state personal income taxes for sales and property taxes presumed to have been paid by the poor. The purpose is to relieve any regressiveness of expenditure or property tax levies. By 1967 eight states had adopted such a program. Indiana, for example, provides an $8 tax credit against the personal income tax for the taxpayer and an additional credit for each of his dependents; cash refunds are paid to individuals and families who do not pay enough income tax to cover the entire credit.[22]

Since New York City started collecting general retail sales taxes, in 1934, about 3,000 other local governments, mainly in Illinois and California, have imposed this tax. In quite a few of the states with local general sales taxes, collection is facilitated by coordinated state and local action.[23]

In Chapter 4 it was argued that if an increase in general sales taxation were offset by a reduction in neutral tax liabilities, one of the major results for local governments would be altered retail shopping behavior. Shoppers, it was argued, would more often attempt to purchase goods either by traveling to, or importing from, markets outside the taxing jurisdiction. Both of these activities would reduce the ability of suppliers in the local economy to shift burdens forward. Furthermore, there would be some outmigration of factors of production as a result of the backward shifting local suppliers might engage in.

The extent to which this phenomenon would occur was related to the costs of altering retail shopping behavior and of relocating factor employments to avoid backward shifting. The size of the geographic area of the taxing jurisdiction and the proximity of alternative, untaxed markets are prime determinants of these costs.

William Hamovitch conducted an empirical investigation in which he tried to verify the tax incidence notion described above.[24] The study compares general sales tax changes for the City of New York and the State of Alabama between 1948 and 1965. New York City, a relatively small area, is surrounded by sales tax–free market areas; Alabama, a relatively large area making the same tax rate increase, is surrounded by sales tax market areas.[25] The data indicate that New York City retailers lost customers and sales and that the demand for locally marketed retail goods was much more price elastic than was true of Alabama. Part of the tax effect in New York City can be explained by the altered retail purchase behavior of commuters and of tourists to the city. An earlier study by Harry McAllister also confirms the consumer tax avoidance behavior for state residents who are located near state borders and out-of-state cities.[26]

The effects of backward shifting of sales taxes in terms of reduced factor wages and factor relocation are much more difficult to evaluate. In the current institutional setting, markets for productive factors have important constraints on competitive wage adjustments. Thus, factor prices do not adjust as rapidly and evenly as more competitive market institutions would suggest—especially for wage reductions. Therefore, we expect relatively more unemployment to occur as shifting to the new tax liabilities progresses. A disproportionate share of tax burden is placed on resources which become unemployed both within the retail industries and outside. The temptation to central governments, if state unemployment is widespread, is to relieve unemployment by increasing the money supply and thus the price level. Therefore, in some cases a stabilization policy of the Federal government affects the apparent incidence of sales tax changes.

The estimation of the income elasticity of expenditure taxes requires that tax rates do not change over time. Selma Mushkin and Gabrielle Lupo have estimated expenditure tax elasticities with regard to both gross national product and personal income to project tax receipts in 1970. For all states, the income elasticity of the general sales tax was estimated to be 1 and that of a specific excise tax was estimated to be .7. Of the selected excise taxes, the income elasticities were motor fuel taxes, .6; alcoholic beverage taxes, .6; and tobacco product taxes, .4.[27] No significant differences were found between elasticities with respect to changes in gross national product and elasticities with respect to personal income.

Use Taxes

For analytical purposes, we can include the use tax (employed by some states to supplement sales taxes) in the category of general sales taxes. A use tax is a state levy on commodities purchased outside the state but brought into it for use. Use tax rates are identical to the corresponding sales tax rates; tax coverage is also identical. The growth of use taxes is a natural response of governments to the growing employment of state sales taxes in an increasingly mobile society.

Enforcing a use tax is costly, yet the difficulties are minimized when the article must be registered, as is true of an automobile. Quite a few states have out-of-state sellers collect the use tax for them, guided by Supreme Court decisions in 1941 and 1960.[28] Interstate sales cause problems for state tax collectors similar to those caused by corporate income taxes. One possible solution would be for Congress to prohibit use taxes and declare that only the state in which the seller is located can collect sales taxes, including taxes on interstate sales. While such a prohibition would simplify the situation, states wishing to employ general sales taxation would suffer from both out-of-state purchases and business location avoidance.

Specific Excise Taxes

A specific excise tax is a levy on a narrow range of exchanges, so the tax base is defined as the buying or selling of a *particular* good or service. Even before the general retail sales tax emerged as an important source of state and local government revenue more than thirty years ago, selective excise taxes on entertainment, cigarettes, liquor, and luxury goods had been extensively used in the United States. By 1968 all but one state (North Carolina) imposed a tax on cigarettes. The tax varied from 2½ to 13 cents per pack of twenty cigarettes—8 cents being the modal tax. All states levied gasoline taxes, ranging from 5 cents to 9 cents per gallon.[29]

The overriding initial political motive for assessing specific excise taxes was not to raise revenue; other tax devices are more productive. Most excise taxes were initially imposed for sumptuary or regulatory reasons. Specific excises most commonly levied are on items believed to be true luxury goods, such as jewelry, entertainment, liquor, wines, gasoline, and prestige goods. Such tax burdens are held to be desirable on moral or ethical grounds. To be defensible such a tax should have clearly predictable incidence, since the desire is to reduce specific acts of consumption. In adopting a sumptuary tax, governments express their conviction that the consumption of certain products or services should be discouraged but not completely outlawed. State, local, and Federal governments have seen fit to include tobacco, alcoholic beverages, playing cards, billiard tables, soft drinks, and cabaret admissions among items to be so taxed to discourage consumption of them.

The other main purpose of specific excise taxes is regulatory rather than sumptuary and is not frequently pursued by state or local governments. An example is a tax on the sale of oleomargarine imposed by a number of dairy-producing states; another is a tax levied on the sales of chain stores. In a sense, regulatory taxes skirt the boundaries of constitutionality, and for this reason they have not been widely utilized. In Chapter 4 we emphasized that specific excise taxes on consumption items result merely in a change in the relative prices of consumption goods. Resources are shifted out of the taxed industry.

Specific excise taxes are not easily thought of as relating to a benefit principle of taxation. The gasoline tax, as described in Chapter 3, varies with the amount of gasoline purchased and therefore the mileage traveled; it is a concealed, though admittedly imperfect, user charge.

WEALTH TAXES

Wealth taxation comprises government levies assessed on the value of assets; it can be a personal tax levied on the value of claims owned by a particular individual or it can be an impersonal tax levied on a particular resource yielding future services irrespective of who owns it. In this section we consider the two most important state and local wealth taxes: property taxes and estate taxes.

Real Property Taxes

A property tax is a government levy on certain physical or tangible assets that are claims to future services in kind as opposed to intangible or financial assets that are claims to future receipts of money.[30] The tangible assets most heavily taxed are real property and, to a lesser extent, personal property.[31] Real property is primarily land, structures, fences, irrigation systems, and other long-lived assets attached permanently (or nearly so) to a particular site. Real property taxes are impersonal levies, whereas personal property taxes are personal levies.

Since financial assets, such as common stocks, represent claims to money returns on real corporate assets but do not embody legal title to the real assets themselves, they are exempted from property taxes. Furthermore they are hard to discover and to add to the tax base. Thus, if real property taxes were levied on the real corporate assets, the corporation would be made liable, and if personal property taxes were levied on the owner of common shares, additional liabilities would be created against the incomes flowing from the same real corporate assets.

Real and personal property taxes originated approximately with the origin of government; they are no doubt the most venerable of local taxes. In the middle eighteenth century the physiocrats proposed that only in production of the land, i.e., agriculture, was a genuine net product produced. This net product was received by the owners of agricultural land as rents and, the physiocrats proposed, this net product should be made the source of taxation. Influenced by the physiocrats, Adam Smith and David Ricardo formalized what is often referred to as the classical theory of rent. According to Ricardo, the original and indestructible power of the soil was a genuine surplus received by the landlords and should be taxed.[32] Such wealth taxes have not been popular, however, since in the real world very few tax instruments can identify pure economic rents and capture these rents without affecting future resource supplies. There is no single source (land) of pure economic rents.

Although property taxes have frequently been criticized and their general demise has often been predicted, they have been a major source of state and local revenue for a long time. Property tax revenues rose from $4.5 billion in 1942 to $26.3 billion in 1967. Even though absolute property tax collections increased substantially during this period, their percentage of state and local general revenue declined—from 44 percent of all revenue in 1942 to 29 percent in 1967 (see Table 5.1). Nevertheless the property tax provides about two-thirds of the revenue from all local sources and seven-eighths of local tax revenues.[33]

The predominance of real property taxes as a source of local government revenue is directly related to one of the tax's key features, tax base immobility. Fear of tax avoidance via outmigration or commuting to neighboring communities has significantly deterred local governments from diversifying their tax bases.

Effective rates do not appear to be as high as is often implicitly assumed. The median effective property tax rate among 122 large cities in the United States in 1967 ranged from 0.36 percent to 4.3 percent of assessed value. Half of these cities showed a median rate of at least 1.85 percent.[34] Most effective rates among cities in the Northeastern United States are higher than those in other regions, particularly in the South and West. Effective tax rates tend to be higher in core cities than in suburbs. For example, of 63 large cities (where the city and the large suburban areas adjacent to it employed the same assessing agency in 1967), 39 cities showed a higher, 15 a lower, and 9 about an equal median effective rate for houses in the core city compared with houses in the city's suburbs.

A number of states grant *partial* exemptions from the local general property tax to specific owners (homestead loans, veterans' exemptions, and others). Although most states have a relatively insignificant set of partial exemptions, in the aggregate exemptions amount to one-sixth to one-fourth of gross assessed evaluations. For example, in 1966 partial exemptions amounted to 18 percent in Florida, 19 percent in Georgia, 21 percent in Louisiana, 24 percent in Mississippi, and 16 percent in Oklahoma.[35] Furthermore, much real property is completely exempted; e.g., property belonging to religious and charitable organizations is exempted as is property owned by other governments. Property owned by the Federal government is completely outside the state and local property tax base. The Federal government, however, in some cases makes adjustment payments to local governments in lieu of taxes.

Local governments are the primary users of real property taxation. A majority of local services, financed by property tax revenues, are site-oriented; that is, the value of such public services as fire stations, police precincts, neighborhood parks, neighborhood schools, sewage disposal, and refuse collection is usually capitalized in the surrounding real property values.

Some local government services may be of benefit to some constituents but detrimental to property owners. For example, highway improvements that benefit residents by allowing better and more rapid movements about the city can lead to a decline in the value of certain lands and improvements close to the highways. But, in general, local services tend to be site-oriented and much of the benefit received by citizens can be taxed by levying liabilities on real property.

The link between real property tax burdens and benefits received from local government services holds for commercial, philanthropic, religious, and agricultural property owners as well as residential property owners. Real property taxes on similarly valued real property assets do not ordinarily discriminate between differences in the owners' ability to pay.[36] And, in general, real property holdings are a poor proxy for ability to pay since debt liabilities are ignored.[37]

James Buchanan argues that the property tax, as it is administered, has a great advantage in that it can be broken down into separate rates (mill rates) ; these rates can be applied to each public agency or function for which revenues from the tax are earmarked. Rarely do taxpayers get this sort of information and the opportunity to weigh the relative costs of separate public functions one against the other.[38]

Another feature contributing to the popularity of property taxation in the past has been revenue stability, largely the product of persistent urban growth and of assessment practices. Infrequent and delayed property reassessment prevents the tax base from shrinking when local economic activity declines and from rapidly rising when such activity increases. Thus large revenue fluctuations are uncommon. But the long-run effect of steadily increasing property tax rates may be more destabilizing.[39] It is generally held that in the long run property taxation discourages renewal of urban property and encourages location of improvement investments outside urban tax jurisdictions (especially local school jurisdictions). At the same time, local expenditures on non-property-related services have increased.

Empirical studies have assumed that property taxes on residential property are almost entirely borne by owners. But as we have reasoned in Chapter 4, current owners may have purchased the taxed assets at tax-discounted prices, and thus past owners may have borne much of the burden of tax changes. For nonresidential property, empirical studies have almost always assumed that the entire amount of the tax burden is shifted even though this practice is not supported by the results of theoretical analysis. The owners of nonresidential property at the time of expected tax increases on their assets will suffer decreases in their wealth positions, just as owners of residential property do under the same circumstances. We have some reason to believe that nonresidential asset owners will be more able than residential owners to shift tax burdens.[40] But much of the purported regressiveness in property taxes appears to be due to the assumption that rental property and business property taxes are nearly completely shifted, predominantly forward. It has been reasoned that lower-income classes have higher average and marginal propensities to consume housing services and thus bear a greater proportion of shifted property taxes.

If ability to pay were measured with greater regard for wealth changes, and if consistent assumptions regarding shifting were maintained for all types of property taxes, then, as we have argued, it would seem likely that property taxes would be found to be less regressive than earlier studies concluded. This finding is quite consistent with analyses in the preceding chapter, which stress that property taxes are similar to a benefit levy for financing state and local expenditures of property-oriented services. This result is also quite consistent with our normative judgment that local, and in part state, taxes should be benefit-oriented and the income redistribution objective should be left to the Federal tax structure.

Although governments have employed the property tax base for centuries, they have seldom done so either consistently among jurisdictions or uniformly through time. Tax assessors are poorly informed generally and tax administration is subject to powerful political pressures throughout the states. Prevailing property tax assessment procedures tend to make effective property tax rates proportionately higher for property falling in lower price ranges than for property falling in higher price ranges, higher for newly developed than for old property, and higher for property of business firms, especially large ones, than for property of individual citizens.

In recent years, a number of studies have been made to estimate the income elasticity of the property tax. As Dick Netzer points out:

> The concept of income elasticity . . . is rather more ambiguous for the property tax than for most other taxes. . . . First, the nominal or legal base of the tax—assessed values—and the economic base of the tax—the market value of taxable property—do not necessarily vary proportionately with one another. Second, local government jurisdictions typically can adjust both the legal base [assessments] and nominal tax rates, an option not present with other taxes. Third, actual property tax revenues are residually determined for most local governments: the tax levy equals previously determined expenditures less revenues from other sources, notably state aid. Thus, the elasticity of property tax revenue is really a reflection of the income elasticity of the demand for local government expenditure [or of residual revenue needs].[41]

Jesse Burkhead analyzed fifty-seven New York counties for each year from 1949 to 1959; he used as the dependent variable the ratio of annual increase in property tax collections to annual increase in county personal income.[42] An important explanatory variable was the rate of population increase, a factor that raised local expenditure requirements faster than did personal income. Increases in the ratio of the over-sixty-five population were associated with higher revenue elasticity, perhaps because the outmigration of younger, higher-income families reduced income disproportionately to revenue needs. Average per capita income was negatively associated with income elasticity.

Robert Lampman estimated the income elasticity of the property tax to be 1.2 and concluded that the high elasticity of the recent past might be continued.[43]

Eugene McLoone, using national wealth estimates prepared by Raymond Goldsmith, concentrated on the real property tax base and concluded that the income elasticity has approached 1 over the years, and that a coefficient of .8 is the most reasonable one to use in projections for the years immediately ahead.[44]

McLoone estimated that the income elasticity of property taxes in agricultural taxing districts throughout the nation averages .5, that nonfarm business property taxes have a long-term elasticity of .57 and that the income elasticity of personal property taxes is 1.2. Using early 1960 data, McLoone estimated that state-by-state property tax elasticity coefficients vary from a low of .47 to a high of 1.08.

In the mid-sixties a large-scale effort was undertaken under the direction of Selma Mushkin to project state and local taxes for 1970. Projected changes in the yields of the present tax structure, aggregated geographically for each tax, were related to the assumed changes in gross national product on which the projections were based. These elasticities generally agree with earlier findings, but there are considerable state-to-state variations. Property tax elasticities were estimated on two assumptions: first, that the property tax base grows with the market value of property and that the ratios of assessments to market values of property remain unchanged; and second, that the rate of lag in reassessment observable between 1956 and 1961 will continue. Under the first assumption, property tax elasticity, averaged for all states, turned out to be 1.2 with respect to changes in gross national product and 1.3 with respect to changes in personal income. Under the second assumption, the elasticities turned out to be 1 and 1.1, respectively.[45]

The projected 1970 income elasticity of residential property varied from a low of .7 in South Dakota to a high of 2.2 in Oklahoma. The income elasticity of commercial and industrial property ranged from a low of .6 in North and South Dakota to a high of 1.8 in Oklahoma.[46]

The income elasticity of death and gift taxes for 1970 was estimated to be 1.1 if taxes are related to gross national product and 1.2 if they are related to personal income.[47]

Personal Property Taxes

Personal property taxes are levied by state and local governments on specific personal, tangible assets, e.g., on the assessed value of automobiles, furniture, appliances, jewelry, raw materials inventories, and finished goods inventories. Effective rates on personal property taxes are lower than those on real property taxes, and personal property tax liabilities have been declining since the last quarter of the nineteenth century; they made up 19 percent of total assessment in 1932 and have been about 16 percent since 1937. The explanation for this decline in the relative importance of personalty relates to legal and extralegal exceptions, but not to a secular growth rate of wealth, in the form of privately owned equipment and inventories, which was less than the growth in the form of privately owned real estate. On the contrary, there is evidence that in the period 1900 to 1958, the growth rate of tangible personalty value was half again as rapid as that of realty, i.e., 2,100 percent versus 1,400 percent.[48]

Netzer points out: "The progressive withdrawal of particular classes of personal property from the scope of the general property tax represents a surrender to reality. The process of exception has gone furthest for those classes which pose the greatest difficulties in regard to discovery and valuation of the assets and in regard to the economic consequences of uniform valuation and taxation even where these are possible."[49] In short, the administration of many types of personal property tax base is so difficult and costly that governments have been discouraged from using it.

Likewise, intangible personalty poses many of the same problems and, as a result, is not commonly assessed. For example, where bank deposits have been subject to the general property tax at the areawide rate, very large annual shifts of deposits to other states and into nontaxable United States Treasury securities have occurred on the reassessment date. Cook County, Illinois, is an excellent example of this. As a consequence, total personal holdings of intangible property are included in the legal base for local general property taxation in only nine states; in an additional five states certain types of intangibles are legally subject to local general property taxation. However, in only a single state—West Virginia—are intangibles a significant element of the tax base. Intangibles represented about 4 percent of the total personal property tax assessments for the nation as a whole and about 0.6 percent of the total general property tax assessments in the early 1960s.[50]

Taxation of tangible personal property is much more common than taxation of intangibles. Still, substantially general coverage of tangible personal property exists in only sixteen states, with complete exemption in four states, including New York and Pennsylvania.

Assessment difficulties, loss of privacy, and ease of avoidance are responsible for the limited reliance on the noncommercial, tangible personal property tax base. Household effects are completely exempted in eighteen states and partially exempted in another eighteen. But commercial and industrial personal property is taxed in virtually all states. It was estimated that tangible personalty assessments in the early 1960s were only about 17½ percent of the amount estimated to have been legally taxable.[51] Altogether, in the late 1950s, commercial property amounted to 66 percent, agricultural property to 9 percent, household property to 5 percent, and motor vehicles to 20 percent of all revenue obtained from the taxation of tangible personal property.[52]

Further unhappiness in regard to taxation of commercial and industrial personal property in some jurisdictions results from a tax immunity enjoyed by private property located on land under exclusive Federal jurisdiction. Since many Federal contracts provide for the government to absorb any and all state and local tax increases or new tax enactments, removal of the tax immunity would probably shift the burden of the tax to the Federal government and ultimately to taxpayers throughout the United States. Perhaps more important is the fact that this immunity, related to a somewhat arbitrary jurisdictional status of certain Federal lands, results in discrimination among certain taxpayers as well as among economic activities.[53]

Estate Taxes

Estate and inheritance taxes are the two major types of death taxes. Estate taxes are based on the undivided estate, while inheritance taxes are based on the individual shares transferred to the heirs. The estate tax is simpler and more productive, while the inheritance tax is often more equitable, since it has some correlation with the ability of the heir to pay.

States have been levying estate and inheritance taxes for many years, although such taxes have never been a major source of revenue. For example, in 1967, estate, inheritance, and gift taxes combined amounted to $795 million, i.e., $2\frac{1}{2}$ percent of all state general revenue, or $4 per capita.[54] Except for Nevada, all states levy estate or inheritance taxes. However, tax rates and exemptions vary greatly among states; many states exempt from the first $100,000 in the estate. Virtually no two states have the same inheritance tax rates and exemptions.

Estate taxes levied by states suffer from the drawback that interstate competition tends to reduce such taxes to negligible proportions. This difficulty has been overcome in part by the adoption of a Federal credit under which a considerable portion of Federal taxes can be paid with receipts for state estate taxes. In 1968, twenty-two states and the District of Columbia permitted deductions of Federal estate tax for purposes of state inheritance and estate taxes.[55]

Much effort has been devoted to exploiting and creating methods to transfer wealth before death. A principal method of death tax avoidance is transfer of ownership to heirs through gift allowances, while maintaining control of the wealth by keeping it in trust accounts; gift taxes have been employed to prevent this avoidance of death taxes. However, the integration of death and gift taxes has not made much progress. Gifts of life insurance (with the donor the insured party and the donee the owner of the policy) are a prime technique of reducing death taxes. Also, marital estate splitting makes it possible to fragment an estate and reduce the effectiveness of the progressive rate scale.

Death taxes take advantage of the fact that death dates are uncertain; and even if the death date were known with some certainty, the transaction costs of moving both residence and estate out of the tax jurisdiction are very great. Furthermore, we argued in the incidence section that death taxes tend to discourage total lifetime consumption and encourage estate formation to offset the increased costs of bequests.

The support for estate taxes rests on the claim that they are based on ability to pay, and produce desirable wealth and income redistribution effects. Estate taxes must generally be considered progressive, since it is the higher-income classes that transfer wealth at death and there are large exemptions for gifts at all income levels. Within the upper-income classes the estate taxes may be regressive because of the multitude of trust and charity exemptions that are employed for larger estates. The total income of a person or household—including that income associated with inherited wealth—is the relevant measure of ability to pay. Under the accrual concept of income all wealth increments, including gifts and inheritances, would be counted as income to the recipient. An accrual income measure of income would make greater allowance for changes in income due to inheritances and gifts than does current measured income and would be a preferred indicator of ability to pay. It is likely that large inheritances are systematically associated with relatively high current measured incomes of the recipients, although we would assume that this correlation is far from perfect.

BORROWING

State and local governments raise funds for two main purposes: to meet operating expenses and to fund investment in public facilities. Admittedly the dividing line is not always entirely clear. Basically, governments use bonding as their major means of financing capital facilities.

We define taxes as amounts of money that individuals must pay for the removal of liabilities assessed on them by a government and where the particular taxpayer does not receive specific services directly in return. Clearly taxation involves a certain degree of coercion. This compulsory reduction in individual resources to finance government expenditures is distinctly different from government borrowing. Through borrowing, state and local governments can obtain funds without imposing current-period tax liabilities on individuals. By borrowing, a government obtains funds in the current period on a voluntary exchange basis. Individuals purchase government obligations—a promise that the government will pay future income to the bondholders. Thus, when a government borrows, taxpayers incur future-period tax liabilities while obtaining the benefits of government expenditures, possibly even in the current period. Taxpayers are willing to contract to pay certain amounts of money to creditors in future periods because those individuals who pay taxes in the future may be individuals who benefit from future services produced with the aid of current government expenditures. Such bonds, where obligations are created against future tax revenues, are the most common form of state and local government debt.

There is an important class of debt instruments that do not create general obligations backed by the tax powers of the government. Such debt instruments are called revenue bonds; the obligation of repayment to the lender is limited to the expected revenues from whatever "project" is financed by funds from the bond sale. Use of revenue bonds is thus generally restricted to government production programs involving long-lived capital investment as an input where the output is user-charged. Government-owned utility enterprises are often authorized to sell revenue bonds. An obvious effect of using revenue bonds rather than general obligation bonds is to shift risk. Under general obligation bonds, the risk that returns from invested capital on a government project will be less (or chances that returns will be greater) than the return promised to bondholders must be borne by future taxpayers. Under revenue bonds, bondholders themselves must bear the risk that revenues from a particular government investment will be less than expected. Thus, we would expect under similar circumstances interest rates on revenue bonds to be higher than interest rates on general obligation bonds, and this is the case.

Total annual state and local revenue collections are only about one-half the total value of outstanding debts of these governments. The bonded indebtedness of state and local governments has undergone great changes since the turn of the century. Early in this century, state and local governments accounted for about two-thirds of all public debt. Since then, two world wars, a serious depression, and a new Federal fiscal philosophy have dramatically increased the Federal portion of total public debt. At the same time local debt creation became more and more curtailed so that state and local debt as a percentage of total public debt reached a low of 7 percent in 1948. In postwar years increased demands on existing public facilities led to large capital expenditures for new construction by state and local governments and caused a steady rise in their share of the public debt. In the late 1960s this share was more than 25 percent of the debt of all governments and was in excess of $120 billion (see Table 5.2).

Because of the openness of state and local economies there is an interesting difference between some aspects of Federal and subnational government borrowing. Whereas Federal borrowing results mainly in an internally held public debt, state and local borrowing in many cases results mainly in an externally held debt. This difference makes for some significant economic differential effects that are relevant to state and local debt policy making.

TABLE 5.2 *State and Local Debt as Percentage of Federal, State, and Local Debt, Selected Years, 1902–1967 (in millions of dollars)*

	1902	1913	1922	1932	1942	1948	1957	1960	1963	1965	1967
Debt outstanding, end of year:											
All governments	$3,285	$5,607	$33,072	$38,692	$92,128	$270,948	$323,566	$356,286	$390,916	$416,786	$440,833
State and local:											
Amount	2,107	1,411	10,109	19,205	19,706	18,656	53,039	69,955	85,056	99,512	114,614
Percentage of total	64.1%	78.7%	30.6%	49.6%	21.4%	6.9%	16.4%	19.6%	21.7%	23.9%	26.0%
State and local debt, change from previous period		−696	+8,698	+9,096	+501	−1,050	+34,383	+16,916	+15,101	+14,456	+24,047

SOURCES: Laszlo Ecker-Racz, "A Foreign Scholar Ponders at the 1957 Census of Governments," *National Tax Journal*, vol. 12 (June, 1959), p. 107; *Statistical Abstract: 1966* (Washington, D.C., 1966), pp. 5 and 423; *Statistical Abstract: 1963* (Washington, D.C., 1963), p. 422; *Economic Report of the President* (Washington, D.C., 1966), pp. 207, 215, 221; U.S. Bureau of the Census, *Statistical Abstract: 1968* (Washington, D.C., 1968), p. 341; Advisory Commission on Intergovernmental Relations, *State and Local Finances: Significant Features: 1966 to 1969* (Washington, D.C., 1968), pp. 17 and 19; U.S. Department of Commerce, *Survey of Current Business*, vol. 49 (February, 1969), p. S-1 ff. Figures for 1967 from U.S. Bureau of the Census, *Governmental Finances in 1966–67*, ser. GF67-no. 3 (1968).

Ursula Hicks points out that a responsible citizenry should realize that commitments entered into by a government loan start not in the future but immediately, when the loan is contracted.[56] She advocates a discounted cash flow accounting system to more easily identify commitments created by borrowing. In Europe, particularly on the Continent, the *tutelle* of the provincial government is strong, and in Britain the Ministry for Housing and Local Government keeps a close eye on local borrowing. These techniques do not have an exact counterpart in the United States. However, state governments somewhat police local borrowing practices and set certain regulations, and most state constitutions and local charters impose limitations. Also, the bonds of state and local governments are rated, and borrowing costs vary with the rating. Altogether, the great mobility of Americans can provide an added incentive to local government borrowing.

OPPORTUNITIES AND PROSPECTS

The policy issues of state and local government taxation reform are very numerous and we will consider only a select number of promising changes. We pointed out in Chapter 1 that local governments are the single most important government producers of civilian services, and since the Federal government is responsible for growth and income resdistribution, we consider it desirable for local governments to pursue tax policies that result in more efficient resource allocation and reflect benefit considerations. This objective requires that when conditions discussed in Chapter 3 are met, user charges be employed and taxes consistent with the benefit principle of taxation be developed and promoted for other services. We also mentioned the special merit of property taxes to finance property-related services, perhaps with a greater emphasis on special assessments.

Currently, many local officials are looking for substantially larger revenues and appear convinced that tax bases commonly in use are unlikely to produce them. As a result they are seeking to diversify their tax base and (or) to obtain increased Federal and state aid. A major local revenue source currently under consideration is the progressive personal income tax. Because of mitigating location effects, local personal income taxes are more appropriate for large county and school district governments than for city governments. As we have stressed, this tax does not relate well to efficient resource allocation but it is well designed to redistribute income. If local governments were to levy progressive income taxes, all three levels of government would participate in income redistribution, making it virtually impossible to pursue a unified rational tax policy to redistribute income.

In the hope of minimizing location "distortions" and the associated "growth-impeding" effects, local governments wanting to levy a personal income tax will seek legislation from the state that would impose a uniform income tax on all local jurisdictions. Such a tax, however, would not be dissimilar from a state income tax. Why, therefore, not raise the state income tax and allocate funds to local governments, especially for financing education and health and welfare services with major intercommunity spillovers? This issue will be considered in more detail in the next chapter.

If local school districts fail to obtain substantial aid increases from either the Federal or state government, state governments could increase educational support by levying a statewide property tax on all nonresidential property. As a result commercial and industrial property tax bases would be pooled throughout the state, and a school district's finances would no longer benefit (or suffer) from the absence (or presence) of local commerce and industry.

If local governments pursue tax policies that lead to efficient resource use and income redistribution and if growth is the principal mission of the Federal government, perhaps state taxation should be designed to help provide funds for state and local governments to carry out their activities. Clearly, state taxation could also seek income redistribution and, in certain specific programs, efficiency. If the emphasis is on state tax productivity, a tax structure could be designed to grow in proportion with service demand changes; it could thereby be more income elastic than local income tax systems. As the state tax system becomes more income elastic, state revenues will become more cyclical. To compensate states for tax losses during recessions, the Federal government could commit itself to provide compensatory funds to state (and local) governments in such periods. Thus for the sake of high tax productivity, state governments could rely heavily on income taxes, on sales taxes that exempt food and housing, or perhaps on a value-added tax in combination with credit against the state income tax. Such a value-added tax will be discussed next.

In years to come, serious thought might be given to a value-added tax to be levied by state and (or) local governments. Earlier in this chapter, brief reference was made to multistage sales taxes—turnover and value-added taxes, with the latter having many advantages over the former. Value added is a measure of the contribution that each business firm makes to the total productive activity in the private sector of the country. The value-added tax would have each firm pay for public services in proportion to its own production of valuable goods and services. At least three basic versions of value-added taxes are possible: consumption, gross income, and net income.

Value added in the consumption type of tax can be computed by either the subtraction or the addition method. Under the former, each firm starts with its total receipts from sales and simply subtracts all purchases of goods and services from other business firms. The residual is a gross margin equal to the value of the firm's own productive activity and of the amount of income that it generates in carrying out that activity. The addition method arrives at the residual by adding together all the incomes generated, i.e., wages and salaries of workers and profits of owners. While the consumption type of value-added tax does not impose a tax on the production of capital goods, the gross income type disallows the deduction of all capital goods purchased from other business; and the net income type, while also disallowing the deduction of capital goods purchases, allows the deduction of depreciation on those goods over their lifetimes.

The value-added tax base includes all income originating from factors of production employed within the jurisdiction of the government levying the tax, but its incidence is not too clear. Arnold Harberger argues "The consumer-type value-added tax will in the long run be borne by the consumer; and the income-type tax will be borne proportionately by all factors of production." [57]

Agency administration costs for value-added taxes are relatively low, particularly if small firms (with gross receipts of less than $25,000 per year) are excluded. Difficulties, however, arise in connection with firms that operate in more than one taxing jurisdiction yet keep only one integrated set of accounts. The gross margins tax is much praised for the general neutrality of its impact.[58] Unlike the property tax, it does not discriminate against capital-intensive businesses; unlike the gross receipts tax, it does not favor firms that are vertically integrated; and unlike corporate income taxes, it does not discriminate against the corporate form of enterprise or against equity financing.

The value-added tax can be a productive tax with relatively high income elasticity. The State of Michigan, from 1953 to 1967, used a sort of value-added tax under the name of a business activities tax; its revenue elasticity is estimated to have been 1.49 between 1959 and 1967, and 1.39 from 1965 to 1967.[59]

The value-added tax offers much promise, but its implementation will rely on careful investigation. Henry Aaron, using input-output techniques, estimated that, were the Federal government to replace its corporate income tax by a value-added tax, different industries would incur distinctly differing effects. For example, agriculture would be severely penalized, while utilities, communications, transport equipment, etc., would enjoy major reductions in tax liabilities.[60]

Some promising opportunities to improve tax administration should be considered. In this connection, it is useful to remember that tax administration poses problems related to such questions as: Who submits the first estimate of the tax base? What techniques are used to evaluate tax base estimates? Is equal treatment of equals achieved? What shall be the timing of tax payment and receipt of services?

Of all taxes, property taxation is believed to be in the greatest need of

change. Some have argued that tax assessments should be made profession-
ally, and not by elected assessors; that assessors should be appointed on the
basis of qualifications tests, with more statewide training and with testing
and certification programs. Since some state grant-in-aid programs make it
advantageous for local jurisdictions to understate property values, some believe state assessment review agencies should enforce equalization practices
or central statewide assessment. And to enable assessment review agencies to
work effectively, reliable average assessment ratios for assessment districts
must be provided.

Although the same tax rate is applicable to both developed land and
improvements, unimproved land is commonly subject to a much lower tax
than improved land. Nationally, raw land is assessed at less than 24 percent
of its true market value while single-family homes are assessed at 34 percent.[61] Bringing these two percentages closer to equality could reduce the
incentives of owners of unimproved land to hold it in unimproved uses at the
margin of choice and could induce them to maintain and possibly upgrade
improvements. Under the present system, the disproportionate assessment of
improvements tends to deter urban renewal.

Statistical sampling techniques and correlation analyses aided by computers can be used to improve the speed of making property evaluations and
to keep them up to date. These techniques are particularly applicable to
classes of property that are both reasonably comparable and generate large
numbers of sales. Appraised values have been estimated, using multiple-
regression analysis, involving single-family residences. When applied to
single-family residences, recent sales prices constitute the dependent variable,
and the independent variables are factors that buyers and sellers take into
account when negotiating a sale. Such an effort was undertaken in Orange
County, California, and the results were tested by applying the multiple-
regression equation to the properties whose sales had been used to estimate
the equation. Ratios of estimated selling prices to actual selling prices were
related to coefficients of dispersion of the ratio. It was found that one-half
the appraised values would have been within a range of ± 2.3 percent to
4.8 percent of the actual selling prices in the five test areas,[62] a performance
about twice as good as that of the best assessors in the nation.

Arnold Harberger has proposed that the assessment burden be shifted
from government to the asset holder. He argues that a property owner should
be allowed to declare the taxable value of his property, subject to the condition that he would be forced to sell his property (if he received a bid) that
was a given percentage (perhaps 20 percent) above the value he declared.[63]
Harberger has argued that such a scheme would be self-enforcing and would
provide additional incentives to use resources more efficiently while reducing
agency administrative costs and allowing less scope for corruption. Since the

requirement of forced sale may violate private property rights, a modification has been suggested: The owner would be allowed to keep his property if he increased his declared value by a given percentage greater than the bid. Clearly, strong incentives to stimulate individuals to make bids would be required.[64]

Self-assessment poses additional difficulties. While it may reduce the government's assessment cost, the increased expenditure of resources for assessment by property owners may result in an even greater total allocation of resources to assessment. The social costs of stimulating enough bids to make owner assessment work may be greater than the social gains. Furthermore, owner assessment with forced sales raises issues relative to property that is encumbered. The constitutionality of the plan would also demand that the bidding process be "open" as opposed to the dangerous system employed in some countries where only the government is allowed to bid and claim forced sales.

SUMMARY

Of the major tax instruments used by state and local governments, the property tax—although its relative significance has been declining—is still the single most important tax, followed by the sales and gross receipts tax and income tax in this order. Personal income taxes, used in most states, are much more readily avoided than the Federal personal income tax. State income taxes have a substantial impact on location decisions. A tax based on personal or household income is clearly related to ability to pay, but not to the benefit principle. The state personal income tax has been found to be income elastic, and on the average its income elasticity coefficient appears to be about 1.7.

The corporate income tax treats the corporate form of business as a legal entity whose factor flow income is subject to taxation in much the same way as the income of an individual. Most likely the ability-to-pay principle applies indirectly to the corporate income tax which, however, also often results in double taxation. Just as personal income tax liabilities can be avoided by changing residence, corporate income tax liabilities can be avoided by changing the location of economic activity.

General sales taxes are general levies on a great variety of exchanges. An increase in general sales tax liabilities that is offset by a reduction in neutral tax liabilities tends to alter the geographic pattern of retail shopping: Shoppers tend to make purchases outside the taxing jurisdiction. Some empirical studies appear to bear out this conclusion. The effects of backward shifting of sales taxes are very difficult to ascertain. For all states, the income elasticity of the general sales tax is estimated to be about 1; this is somewhat higher than the .7 estimate of the tax elasticity of specific excise taxes which are levied on exchanges of particular goods or services. Initially the overriding political motives for assessing specific excise taxes have been sumptuary or regulatory, although today revenue production is important.

Wealth taxations are government levies on the values of assets. The tax may be a levy on the value of claims owned by a particular person or an impersonal tax levied on a particular resource that yields future services, regardless of who owns the resource. A property tax is a government levy on certain physical assets that are claims to future services in kind. Real property taxes have been a significant source of local government revenue because of the immobility of the tax base. There appears to be some link between real property tax burdens and benefits received from local government services. While the burden of property taxes on residential property tends to be borne to a large extent by owners, current owners may have purchased the tax assets at tax-discounted prices, shifting some of the burden to past owners. Nonresidential asset owners may have greater ability to shift parts of the tax burden than do residential property owners. If ability to pay is measured with greater regard for these changes and if consistent assumptions regarding shifting are maintained for all types of property taxes, these taxes may be less regressive than earlier studies concluded. Empirical studies of the income elasticity of the property tax appear to indicate that it is slightly higher than 1, i.e., between 1 and 1.3.

The personal property tax is levied on specific personal tangible assets. Yet the administration of the personal property tax base is so difficult and costly that governments have been discouraged from using it.

Estate and inheritance taxes are the major types of death taxes; the former is simpler and more productive and the latter is often more equitable. They are reasonably progressive taxes, since it is the higher-income classes that transfer wealth at death and there are large exemptions for gifts at all income levels. The income elasticity of death and gift taxes has been estimated to be 1.1 to 1.2.

In the future, local governments in particular are likely to attempt to diversify their tax bases, possibly resorting to the progressive personal income tax and the value-added tax. In each case the cooperation of state governments will be needed. However, existing taxes can be made more productive and equitable. Of all taxes, the property tax is probably in greatest need of improvement. Perhaps the most revolutionary proposal to improve property taxation involves self-assessment. Simpler improvements include the use of better-trained and qualified assessors, responsible to effective review agencies; the closer harmonization of tax rates applicable to land and to improvements; and the use of statistical sampling techniques and correlation analyses aided by computers to improve the speed of property evaluation.

CHAPTER 6

INTER-GOVERNMENTAL FISCAL RELATIONS

Federal, state, and local governments relate and interact in numerous ways; some ways are formal or even codified, some are informal, some are institutionalized and continuing, others are ad hoc. Some involve transfers of money, others not. Some are horizontal, between governments on the same level; some are vertical, between levels of government. Most are managed but some are beyond the control, and in part even beyond the knowledge, of governments. Of the many relations between the Federal, state, and local governments we are concerned here with fiscal relations and with only some of them. We are principally concerned with transfers of funds from higher to subordinate governments. Of such transfers attention is devoted primarily to those brought about by the desire of subordinate governments for additional revenues or by the desire of higher levels of government to accomplish certain of their objectives.

Although our emphasis is on fiscal intergovernmental relations, we must recognize that they are only part of a more inclusive set of relationships between local, state, and Federal governments. Many are not fiscal in nature, since they do not involve the transfer of funds. For example, there are direct nonfiscal intergovernmental relations that specify the powers and authority that local governments derive from the state. Direct nonfiscal intergovernmental relations involve specific laws, rulings, directives, and authorizations within the framework of which local governments may operate. For example, the state commonly authorizes schools to levy a limited set of taxes; provides that only licensed teachers be employed; directs the schools to teach specific courses, e.g., physical education; specifies the ages during which young people must attend school, as well as the length of the school year, etc.

But there are also a host of indirect nonfiscal intergovernmental relations which affect local government through the environment in which it operates. For example, a Federal-state highway program can reduce the amount of taxable property and displace businesses and people. A Federal program can train young adults and help them find jobs; as one result, local welfare payments to these persons will decline.

Under fiscal and political federalism, it is not clear which level of government is the prime decision maker. Local government is constrained from completely independent action by both its fiscal and its nonfiscal intergovernmental relations. If one concentrates attention on the law, one is impressed by the limitations that state and Federal governments place on the behavior of certain local governments. If one focuses on the flow of funds from the Federal and state governments to local governments, one can see an intricate pattern of inducements intended to influence local government resource allocations. However, a meeting of a city or county council or of a school board reveals that local government is not a passive body but one that makes important choices about broad policy issues as well as about narrow management issues. At the same time, it would be wrong to assume that local governments merely either respond to such offers of intergovernmental aid or never react to change them altogether. In most instances local governments will actively lobby for intergovernmental transfers of funds.

Under the impetus of increasing urbanization, mobility, and local government "fiscal crises," Federal-state-local government relations have undergone major changes. The year 1932 has been cited by Roscoe Martin as representing a kind of geologic fault line in the development of Federal-local government relations in general and Federal-city relations in particular.[1] The years 1950 and 1965 represent more recent fault lines in Federal assistance, particularly for urban governments. By the end of 1965, the Federal government was administering more than seventy-five grant programs for urban governments, and more than three-quarters of these were authorized after 1950. Congressional enactments in 1965 included grants for basic water and sewer facilities, advance acquisition of land, open space for urban beautification, neighborhood facilities, code enforcement assistance, demolition of unsafe structures, rent supplements, and support for councils of locally elected officials—all as parts of the Housing and Urban Development Act of 1965.

Federal grants to state and local governments have been increasing rapidly: Federal aid as a percentage of state and local sources of general revenue increased from 8 percent in 1942 to 11 percent in 1948, to 15 percent in 1965, and to 20 percent in 1967. The amount of Federal aid in 1967 was about $16 billion.[2] The relative importance of Federal aid is indicated by the fact that in 1967 state receipts from the Federal government amounted to 26 percent of total state general revenue.

The amount of Federal aid varies greatly among the fifty states. In 1967, state and local governments in Delaware received $40 million from the Federal government, while those in California received $2.3 billion. Admittedly, the difference was much smaller on a per capita basis. The percentage of total aid that local governments in various states received directly from the

Federal government ranged from 2 percent to 25 percent of their expenditures.

States have responded, often quite creatively, to the increased Federal interest in state and local governments as well as to the serious fiscal problems of local governments. In addition, Federal legislation in some cases stipulates states as indispensable administrative partners in carrying out programs.[3]

States have in recent years set up state offices or departments of local government, community affairs, or urban affairs, as well as coordinating offices to provide effective liaison for intergovernmental programs.

More important, perhaps, during the twenty-year period from 1948 to 1967 the amount of annual state payments to local government multiplied almost sixfold, from $3.2 billion to $19.1 billion. Throughout this period, however, such payments made up a fairly consistent fraction of the annual nationwide total of state general expenditures. Between 1952 and 1967, for example, this percentage relationship ranged merely between 33 percent and 37 percent.[4]

State governments differ widely in the amounts they pay to local governments. For example, state intergovernmental expenditures in 1967 ranged from $178 per capita in New York to $21 in New Hampshire.[5] Payments to all local governments totaled almost 36 percent of all state government general expenditure in 1967; however, the percentage ranged widely among the states, from less than 10 percent in Hawaii and New Hampshire to more than 54 percent in New York. During the past twenty-five years, state-local fiscal relations have become more uniform. In the 46 states subject to direct comparison, there was an increase in the number whose payments to local governments ranged from 20 percent to 40 percent of state general expenditure: The numbers of such states increased from 22 in 1942 to 26 in 1952, and to 32 in both 1962 and 1967.[6]

Most of state aid is for four local government programs. Thus, in 1967, of all state aid, 62 percent was given to education, 15 percent to public welfare, 10 percent to highways, and 8 percent to general local government support. In terms of types of governments, 50 percent went to school districts, 25 percent went to counties, 21 percent to municipalities, and the rest went to townships and special districts.[7]

In this chapter, we will start by examining some reasons for the transfer of funds from higher to lower levels of government. Thereafter a variety of intergovernmental fiscal instruments will be presented and some expenditure effects of such instruments examined. Next, criteria will be developed for evaluating the relative desirability of different intergovernmental fiscal instruments. Finally, we will speculate about some possible changes in future intergovernmental fiscal relations.

REASONS FOR INTERGOVERNMENTAL TRANSFERS

A variety of explanations for the fiscal difficulties of state and local governments and justifications for the transfer of funds to lower levels of government have been advanced. Some are valid; others are not entirely correct.

As an illustration, the case for lower levels of government receiving subsidies from higher levels of government is often based on the fallacious argument that the Federal government is rich and state and local governments are
poor. The total economic resources of the Federal government equal the sum
of its parts, and those parts are the economic resources either of all the states
or of all the counties. Legally, the tax base of the Federal government differs
from the tax bases of the states in several respects; for example, the Federal
government is enjoined by the Constitution from taxing real property, and
some states are enjoined by their constitutions from taxing income. Further
exceptions include customs duties, which only the Federal government collects, and the leakage that may result from state or local tax laws that permit
a taxpayer who moves to or buys in another jurisdiction to reduce his tax
payments. However, in such respects even the Constitution is subject to
change—witness the passage of the Constitutional Amendment of 1913 which
legally entitles the levying of the Federal income tax. Thus it is not entirely
correct to assert that the Federal government must make grants to state and
local jurisdictions because the Federal government has greater tax resources
or a different tax base. It merely has greater revenues, and only under present
circumstances.

Arguments for aid from higher levels of government can be advanced
that are based on two types of causes of the fiscal difficulties of state and local
governments: factors that are mainly beyond their control, and other factors
that are within their control but are largely not controlled because of political
considerations. Examples of the latter include tax competition, voting procedures on taxes and bonds, and principal reliance on taxes such as property
and sales taxes that tend to have a lower income elasticity than the expenditures they finance. State and local governments having difficulty in financing
their programs have achieved only marginal success in obtaining voter approval of new tax bases or of rate increases on present tax bases.

The principal factors that are largely beyond the control of state and
local governments and that justify aid from higher levels of government are
regional income differences and interjurisdictional spillovers of costs and
benefits.[8] Or to put it differently, transfer of funds to lower levels of government can be justified on the basis that such transfers can help equalize income
distribution throughout the country by reducing interregional service and
income differences (granted that in some respects direct aid to individuals

or households can be a more effective income equalizer). Furthermore, such transfers can be justified on the basis that the nation as a whole can suffer some of the effects of uncontrollable interjurisdictional spillovers of costs and benefits that result in major fiscal difficulties and therefore in underinvestment by state and local governments.

Interjurisdictional Spillovers and Nonoptimal Spending

Interjurisdictional spillover takes place whenever any portion of the costs or benefits of a public service that is provided in one jurisdiction is realized by residents of another jurisdiction. State and local governments cannot close their borders to the citizens or economic activities of other jurisdictions and therefore have little control over spillovers. Since the state or local government that makes a decision to provide a public service cannot completely internalize costs and benefits it may under- or overspend.[9]

If the Federal government suspects underspending it may subsidize part of the costs of the service to encourage the state or local government to produce the socially desired level of output.

As mentioned in the last section of Chapter 1, portions of both costs and benefits of one jurisdiction's public decisions may spill out to another jurisdiction. Likewise portions of both the costs or benefits of a public service provided elsewhere may spill into a jurisdiction. If a particular community has spillout benefits in excess of spillout costs from its own services, these net local costs are an inducement to underspend; the marginal social benefits of local expenditures are greater than the marginal social costs. Likewise, if the particular community is realizing benefit spillins in excess of cost spillins from the service of another community, these net local benefit spillins can act as an inducement to become a lobbyist in its neighbor's deliberative processes.

It is interesting to consider how voters perceive these cost and benefit spillins and spillouts and how their conjectures about spillovers may influence their voting behavior. Before this issue can be examined the temporal concept of community must be clarified. Clarification is particularly important to such services as education, the benefits of which are delayed by a number of years. The community can be viewed as an aggregate of persons identified by location at the time an expenditure or investment decision is made. Where a student or his family will be living in the future is therefore of consequence to the community only if the student's eventual location affects the estimate of benefit magnitudes and the distribution of benefits in the community. An alternative concept of community assigns only those benefits or cost burdens realized by individuals while they are actually residing in the specified location; this alternative concept does not relate residents to an expenditure or investment decision. The electorate's perception of spillovers depends on the view of community.

Some economists, primarily concerned with the great difficulties of estimating cost and benefit spillovers, have assumed that if voters consciously or subconsciously consider spillovers at all, they are likely to consider all four spillovers—cost and benefit spillins and spillouts.[10] Other economists, primarily concerned with the difficulties of assessing the location of tax burdens, assume that voters cannot be readily persuaded that the merit of certain public spending projects will depend on the notion that cost incidence can be spilled out. Consequently, these economists conclude that "cost spillouts are not likely to play an important role in local evaluations of new government programs."[11] Property tax decisions in cities such as St. Louis and Los Angeles, which are located in large metropolitan areas and have commercial centers that serve residents of other local jurisdictions such as Clayton, Missouri, and Beverly Hills, California, appear to indicate that voters in those commercial centers are influenced by the possibility that part of the property tax incidence can be spilled out. The layman's intuitive reaction apparently has not been affected by the inability of economists to agree on the specific mechanisms and amounts spilled out.

Without engaging in elaborate studies, one may categorize services in terms of benefit spillovers. Only minor spatial spillover of benefits can be expected from such public services as electric power and water distribution, libraries, welfare, police and fire protection, and neighborhood parks. Major spatial spillover of benefits can be expected from air and water pollution control, sewage disposal, mass transit, public health services, hospitals, planning, public housing, urban renewal, street maintenance, and education. Such services with major benefit spillovers might be subdivided into those whose benefits spill over only into adjacent jurisdictions and those whose benefits may spill over to the entire nation. Public education and the control of communicable diseases may be examples of national spillover,[12] while fire protection is an example of local spillover.

The benefit spillovers in public education illustrate several of the issues mentioned above. We are concerned here with two classes of education benefits: the increase in the future earnings of the student and the increased productivity of society in general because of the education of the student. If a person moves from the community in which he was educated, his augmented earning potential and his effect on his coworkers and neighbors move with him. Why should a community invest in children who are going to take the benefits away from the community? This is the argument which has led some to expect underinvestment and which in turn provides a stimulus for the policy of Federal participation in local education finance. But all government intervention (Federal, state, and local) is premised on the argument that the benefits of education are greater than the financial returns to the student alone.

We noted a view of the community, however, which relates a person to his residence at the time the investment decision is made. In this view the decision is made to provide the student with added education because he is part of the community now, despite the possibility that he may move in the future. This is the view of the family extended to the community through the ballot box. Still, under this view the spillout of benefits to coworkers and neighbors tends to encourage underinvestment in education and may justify subsidy from a higher level of government.

Resolving the question of community does not complete the discussion of spillovers, since in either view a net benefit to society in general *may* be created by education. Furthermore, an interjurisdictional spillover occurs when parts of the income increment of a former student of another jurisdiction are taxed; the spillover may occur because of migration, fiscal interdependence, or both. Wherever the student lives in the future, his presence will tend to raise the tax base. People with more education and therefore more income pay greater taxes and may demand more public services than people with less education. But to the extent that the additional taxes they pay exceed the marginal cost of the additional public services they consume, some of the benefits of education are thereby transferred to other people in the form of reduced taxation or added benefits as public services other than education are increased.[13] Even though the students educated in a community do not migrate, there will be a benefit spillout from that community because of economic interaction and fiscal interdependence. That spillout will be in proportion to the investment of that community in education. For purposes of analysis education benefit spillout may be considered a tax levied on the community in proportion to its education investment. This form of benefit spillover will also tend to reduce the investment in education and justify a policy of Federal financing.

Endogenous Forces and Underinvestment

State and local governments, although they have little control over cost and benefit spillovers that reduce investment, can make a number of changes in institutional arrangements to reduce their fiscal difficulties. Three such institutional arrangements will be considered: tax competition, voting procedures on tax levies and bonds, and the selection of forms of taxation.

Horizontal tax competition exists between state governments and between local governments. Horizontal tax competition enters into the battle between communities for new industrial and commercial activities: Each competing community avoids making otherwise prudent tax increases for fear of decreasing its attractiveness to new businesses. Vertical tax competition exists between a state government and local governments that rely on the same tax base. More will be said below about the effects of such competition and remedies for them. At this point we merely indicate that state and local governments can institute such taxing procedures as tax supplements to reduce horizontal tax competition and that coordinated or centralized tax administration can reduce vertical tax competition. Coordination can internalize competition and reduce administrative costs.

A second institutional arrangement that can lead to underinvestment is voting and government allocation procedures. In the United States we have a long history and tradition of how different levels of government levy taxes and vote on bonds. On the local level popular vote on tax levies as well as on bonds is common. At the state level the legislature votes on tax levies, but popular vote on bonds is common. In the Federal government the legislature votes on taxes and indirectly on bonding, by establishing a legal debt ceiling, although in fact bonding decisions are made by the Treasury and influenced by the interest rate policy of the Federal Reserve Board.

Funding state or local programs appears to be more difficult for government administrators if a popular referendum is required, particularly if a two-thirds majority is needed, than if the voting of funds is left to the legislature. Local government officials are under the additional constraint of a ceiling on bonded indebtedness that often amounts to about 10 percent of assessed valuation of property—a holdover from the days when reckless financing frequently led to government bankruptcy. To change this situation, state and local electorates could assign more of the taxing and bonding decision responsibilities to their elected officials. It should be pointed out that this change in public decision making would tend to return state and local policy to representative bargaining. Representatives of various constituencies desiring various decisions can negotiate with each other when the legislature debates and passes expenditure and revenue measures with intended logrolling. A referendum is a one-time vote, basically on a one-time measure, which precludes much political bargaining and negotiation, and for this reason the referendum is a device that may unduly constrain public expenditure and revenue decisions.

State and particularly local governments provide services that are usually more income elastic than their tax structures. The reliance of state and particularly of local governments on proportional or at best slightly progressive tax structures, which are rather inflexible and have relatively low income elasticities, has left a continuing budgetary imbalance between the resources of state and local governments and the cost of the services they provide for their constituents.

The situation of the Federal government is quite different. For example, expenditures on national defense and mail delivery appear to be much less income elastic than on such services as education, fire protection, and refuse collection. The demand for services conventionally provided by the Federal government would for this reason seem to be increasing less rapidly than the demand for services expected from state and local governments. In spite of the fact that Federal government expenditures for civilian services appear to be increasing less rapidly than state and local government expenditures, the Federal government, relying on the progressive income tax with its great income elasticity, appears able to collect sufficient revenue without rate increases. As a matter of fact, Walter Heller has argued that, in peacetime, Federal surpluses would result without rate decreases and tend to constitute a fiscal drag on the overall economy.[14]

In short, if state and local governments were to rely more heavily on income elastic revenue sources, including the Federal tax base, they would be in a better position to finance services demanded of them without continually seeking rate increases.

INTERGOVERNMENTAL FISCAL INSTRUMENTS

The techniques of intervention by which higher levels of government provide subordinate governments with greater revenue may be divided into three major categories: direct transfer of funds to subordinate governments, sharing of the tax revenues of higher levels of government with lower levels of government by indirect transfers, and coordination between the three levels of government.

Direct Transfer of Funds to Subordinate Governments

Direct transfer of funds can take the form of loans or of grants-in-aid, which can be categorical or unrestricted.

Loans. Higher-level governments can transfer loan funds to subordinate governments in exchange for contracts held by the lending agencies. The terms of these contracts, although they can vary in detail, state the agreement of the borrowing government to repay principal and interest to the lending government out of future revenue collections.

Loans are especially appropriate if the subordinate government can expect revenues in the future that would justify current expenditures and if the lending government wishes to subsidize particular projects. An example would be borrowing from the Federal government for the building of urban public transportation systems which involve large initial investments and from which only delayed and uninternalized benefit returns can be expected.

In this instance the Federal government would probably provide a categorical loan, stipulating the kinds of expenditures for which loan funds can be used.

Categorical Grants.   Categorical grants are money transfers to subordinate governments made without conditions of repayment but exchanged for stipulated spending commitments that are binding on the subordinate governments. The commitment usually designates expenditures to be made with the transferred money and with other revenues of the subordinate government (the matching provision).

A variety of criteria can be used to classify categorical grants. Most grants can be readily placed in the matrix shown in Table 6.1. The three columns of the matrix distinguish between the restrictions imposed on the use of grant funds: grant funds without restrictions on expenditures, grant funds earmarked for programs and subprograms, and grant funds earmarked for expenditure on specific inputs to programs or subprograms.[15] Only those

TABLE 6.1   Classification of Grants

	Grant Typology: Restrictions on Use of Funds		
Grant Qualification Criteria	Grant Funds without Restrictions on Expenditure	Grant Funds Earmarked for Expenditure on Programs or Subprograms	Grant Funds Earmarked for Expenditure on Specified Inputs to Programs or Subprograms
Grants without Matching Provisions			
General criteria to determine grant level (a) relative to input or need, e.g., population, regional income, unemployment, employee work loads, etc.			
General criteria to determine grant level (b) relative to output or performance, e.g., service levels, expenditure levels, service results, etc.			
Grants with Matching Provisions			
Matching criteria to determine financial obligations of recipient government from its own sources, e.g., fixed percentage, varying percentages, etc.			

grant funds would be placed in the second column whose use is restricted to specified outputs. Grants in this category might be those which are restricted to particular programs, e.g., unemployment compensation, school lunches, research projects, etc., and those restricted to particular departments or agencies, e.g., airports, agriculture, etc. Grants placed in the third column would be those whose use is restricted to certain inputs. Such grants include those which are restricted to particular kinds of expenditures related to a specified program or department: hospital construction, sewage disposal equipment, teachers' salaries, forest fire fighting equipment, etc.

The two principal rows differentiate between the qualification criteria of grants: grants with and grants without matching requirements. Grants without matching requirements can be further subdivided between criteria related to input or need and criteria related to output or performance. Until recently, major reliance has been placed on criteria related to input or need. Now, however, there is much interest in using output or performance standards designed to increase both the efficiency and the freedom with which grants can be used by recipients.

The Federal government can apply different formulas to the distribution of grant funds. For example, the amount of the grant per subsidy unit can be fixed, with the size of the unit varying from the total government unit to any part thereof. Other criteria, such as the number of inhabitants, the number of unemployed, or the road mileage of the unit, can be employed. But the subsidy need not be fixed; instead it can vary inversely with the jurisdiction's financial ability. Such subsidies are consistent with the equality motive. Furthermore, a ceiling might be placed on the maximum grant per subsidy unit.

Matching grant funds which apply only to the portion of expenditure that exceeds a specific minimum expenditure level are mainly designed to encourage subordinate governments to initiate and carry out new programs. In the extreme, a grant for the entire amount of spending with no matching requirement would tend to weaken the responsibility motive. Another frequently used distribution formula offers a fixed percentage up to some specific expenditure level; a varying percentage formula could apply to additional grant funds. In the latter case, the percentage contribution of the granting government could vary directly with per capita income of the receiving jurisdiction and thus be consistent with distributional motives.

In the past, categorical grants have been heavily relied upon and their importance has continued to increase. Spillover and distributive considerations appear to favor Federal aid to specified programs, since national values and goals can be pursued in this manner. Categorical grants enable the higher level of government to maintain control over the expenditures of lower levels of government, greatly increasing the chances that programs considered important to the national interest are initiated and carried out. As will be seen below, categorical grants could theoretically increase economic efficiency by compensating for spatial benefit and cost spillovers and reducing regional inequalities in services and income, even though they inhibit local initiative and responsibility.

Categorical grants have resulted in a bewildering proliferation of subsidy programs, many of which have conflicting objectives. In the period 1964 to 1966, about 400 authorizations of Federal aid programs, grouped into more than 106 major programs, were in force. More than 45 percent of these programs were in the Department of Health, Education and Welfare alone.[16] Nearly 60 percent of the total number of programs involve project grants which are provided on the basis of applications received. However, formula grants, while few in number, accounted for most of the money. Population and per capita personal income were the principal determinants in the distribution of funds under these formulas, the latter measure becoming increasingly popular to equalize fiscal capacity.

Unrestricted Grants and the Heller-Pechman Proposal.   Unrestricted or block grants appeal to local and state governments who fear that categorical grants increase the concentration of power in the national government. By its use of unrestricted grants the higher level of government expresses its confidence that the lower level is competent to decide what services should be provided, and to whom, as well as to render those services effectively and in the most desirable quantities.

We shall summarize briefly the proposal of Walter Heller and Joseph Pechman for unrestricted grants. This proposal has been the subject of debate[17] since the middle sixties. Under the Heller-Pechman plan the Federal government would set aside each year, for distribution to the states, an amount equivalent to about 10 percent of the total amount of personal income taxes it collects. The actual amount set aside would be based on a fixed percentage of total net taxable income rather than of revenue, to make it independent of the level and structure of Federal tax rates and stabilization policy. The amount so derived would be set aside in a trust fund from which periodic distributions would be made to the states. Putting the fund in trust would make it independent of congressional appropriations and the usual budget process. Funds would be disbursed to the states on the basis of population and, since individuals in all states would share equally in the revenue even though they did not contribute equally by the payment of taxes, the plan would involve some redistribution. Funds would be turned over to the states without strings, although consideration has been given to insisting that the states give a major share to local governments, banning the use of such funds for highways, and making some general restrictions on the use of the funds to areas such as health, education, and welfare. If the additional revenue led some states to reduce their own fiscal efforts, a proposed remedy is to reduce the share to such states.

Unconditional grants in general and the Heller-Pechman proposal in particular avoid certain of the shortcomings of categorical grants. But block grants pose some serious problems concerning the redistribution of income between states and individuals, the possible adverse effects on the states' tax efforts, the desire of the states to provide a pass-through of Federal funds to local governments, the efficiency with which funds are spent by state and local governments, and the danger that state and local governments will allocate funds to expenditures that in the view of the central government have low priority. While it is possible to minimize such problems by attaching strings or adding complications to a program of the Heller-Pechman type, such conditions reduce the autonomy of subordinate governments and thus detract from the principal appeal of unconditional grants.

Federal Sharing of the Tax Base

Subordinate governments can use a number of methods to share the tax base with higher levels of government, especially with the Federal government, and thereby bring about an indirect transfer of Federal funds. The more important sharing instruments are revenue source vacating and tax deduction and credits.

Vacating Specific Revenue Sources.   Perhaps the most extreme technique by which the Federal government can share the tax base with subordinate governments is to vacate a specific revenue source and make the source available to subordinate governments. Those who favor separating tax revenue sources argue that state and local governments must have adequate resources of their own with which to finance their projects, keep their autonomy, and enhance their responsibility and efficiency. Extreme separation, which would require that virtually all revenues of a particular level of government come from only one source, could cause difficult problems, especially instability of revenue flow. Furthermore tax separation, even if it were not to change the total amount of revenue, would have differential effects on the states.

Taxes often proposed for vacating by the Federal government include general sales taxes; death and gift taxes; and excise taxes on amusements, cigarettes, club dues, gasoline, local telephone service, safe deposit boxes, etc.[18] Most of these proposals have serious defects—inequality, inefficiency, or both—and would have to overcome strongly entrenched Federal interests.

Tax Supplement.   A second method of sharing the tax base with higher levels of government is the tax supplement. For example, a state government that wishes to participate in the tax supplement plan applies its own tax rate to a tax base defined by the Federal government. The state tax, collected by the Federal government together with the Federal government's own tax on that tax base, is transferred to the state; the state simply pays for the collection service. The state remains free to vary its tax rate each year according to its financial needs. The taxpayer files a single Federal tax return, and perhaps is unaware that he is paying a state tax.

The problems connected with the tax supplement are illustrated by the income tax. First at issue is the Federal government's definition of taxable income; the Federal government changes the income tax law from time to time and the state must then either incorporate these changes in its own laws, or if the state's income tax law provides for automatic changes in conformity with the Federal law and the state does not want to adopt certain Federal changes, the state must pass legislation to exclude those changes. More important, the state can encounter more difficulty in projecting its revenue for a number of years into the future from a tax supplement than from an income tax of its own, the structure of which it controls.

George F. Break aptly summarizes Federal-state coordination of the income tax base as imposing "additional burdens on state legislators and [removing burdens] ... from state tax administrators and state taxpayers."[19]

Tax Allowances: Deductions and Credits. Subordinate government tax allowances are provisions in the tax laws of higher levels of government that give special treatment to persons who paid certain taxes to subordinate governments. These special allowances permit subordinate governments to share indirectly the tax base of the higher level of government. A good example is the Federal income tax; existing laws make it possible for taxpayers to avoid some Federal income tax payments by making payments to subordinate governments. The Federal government determines which kinds of payments to subordinate governments will be sanctioned for special treatment and how much allowance will be made. One form of allowance is termed deductibility and allows Federal (or state) income taxpayers to reduce gross taxable income by the amount of sanctioned payments. A second form of allowance is termed crediting and allows income taxpayers to reduce their Federal (or state) tax liability by the amount of sanctioned payments to subordinate governments.

Existing tax deduction provisions permit taxpayers to reduce taxable income for Federal income tax purposes, with state and local income, property, gasoline, and general sales taxes qualifying for deduction. Tax credit provisions allow certain state and local tax payments to be credited against Federal income tax liability, in part or in full. Tax credits can be proportional or graduated; they can be unlimited, subject to a proportional ceiling, or unlimited, subject to a gradual ceiling, and so on. Tax credits, as well as tax deductions, represent a highly flexible fiscal device which can be used by the Federal government to prevent taxation of the same base by the Federal as well as by state and local governments and thus to increase the fiscal power of state and local governments.

Is the increase in the fiscal power of state and local governments real, or only apparent? In view of the opposition of state and local taxpayers and their representatives to almost any tax increase, will they accept Federal tax deduction as a means of reducing their cost of marginal state or local tax increases?

Although there are no easy answers to these questions, it appears that taxpayers do consider deductibility when making tax decisions. If a given community proposes to gain increased deductibility as an offset for increased local tax rates, at a time when taxpayers resent any tax rate increase, deductibility is likely to have limited effectiveness on state and local revenues. Also, upper-income groups are likely to benefit more from deductibility than lower-income groups, and the former seem to be more aware of the benefits of deductibility than the latter. Yet since much voting power rests with middle- and lower-income groups, reducing indirect taxes through deductibility and replacing the lost Federal revenue with the aid of increased direct taxes has little political appeal.

Because of these considerations, George F. Break voices serious "doubts on the revenue-stimulating powers of all existing Federal deductibility rules except the one applying to state and local income taxes."[20]

There is evidence that, although similar considerations apply, tax credits tend to be more effective than tax deductions. The difference in effectiveness is one of degree. In general and under similar circumstances, tax credits tend to produce greater savings to taxpayers than tax deductions. Tax credits should therefore offer taxpayers and legislators greater incentives to capture Federal income tax savings by instituting and raising state and local taxes that can be offset against the Federal tax.

Of the numerous tax credit proposals, the most discussed is perhaps that of the Advisory Commission on Intergovernmental Relations (ACIR),[21] which would allow a taxpayer a Federal income tax credit against Federal income tax liability amounting to 40 percent of the income tax he paid to the state. For the individual who pays less than a marginal rate of 40 percent to the Federal government, the initiation of this tax credit would result in a tax saving, and it is reasoned that the state, realizing this, could simultaneously increase its own tax rate without causing an additional burden to such a taxpayer.

It is argued that the tax credit will stimulate states that do not currently have an income tax to levy one, since the tax credit will yield additional revenue to a state only if the state introduces a state income tax or increases the rate of an existing one. Thus the tax credit would cause the substitution of progressive income taxes for the less progressive sales and property taxes which are more commonly used. Such a scheme, it is also argued, would counteract the danger of overcentralization of power in the hands of the national government that is associated with categorical grants.

The ACIR and other Federal tax credit plans are criticized because they provide additional revenue to states only if and when the states do take advantage of the tax credit by raising the rate of an existing state income tax or instituting a state income tax. No one can be sure that states would take advantage of a Federal tax credit, even though by doing so they could increase their tax revenue at no increase in total tax liabilities to taxpayers. In 1969 more than one-third of the states did not have an income tax and some had constitutional provisions prohibiting such taxes.

Because of the importance of tax credit proposals as alternatives to a Heller-Pechman type of proposal, we will offer an evaluation.

Tax credits, if successful, can complicate Federal fiscal policy making, since they can be inconsistent with efficiency criteria and regional equality considerations. They do little to compensate local governments for significant spillovers and do not provide for equalization of either services or incomes among subordinate governments. If tax credits return to each state a portion or all of the taxes its citizens formerly paid to the Federal government, wealthy states in which Federal income tax collections are substantial would tend to gain most. The overall effect of Federal tax credits on progressivity of the tax system in the United States is not clear-cut. On the one hand, overall progressivity will be reduced as a result of state income tax structures being much less progressive than the Federal tax structure. On the other hand, however, this is counteracted by a Federal tax deduction or credit plan inducing local governments to substitute income taxes for less progressive sales and property taxes. On balance we would expect that the increased reliance on local income taxes would have less effect on progressivity than the partial replacement of the Federal income tax by a state income tax. Finally, the use of tax credit or deduction devices does little if anything to reduce the inequality in tax resources, and therefore in services, between various units of local government.

Tax Coordination

Tax coordination is the third category of techniques of improving the fiscal position of state and local governments. Tax coordination problems result from horizontal and vertical tax overlapping. Horizontal tax overlapping is typical of a highly industrialized, urbanized, and mobile society where businesses and individuals conduct economic activity in many different taxing jurisdictions, all at the same level of government. Vertical tax overlapping results when two or more levels of government use the same tax base; for example, if both Federal and state governments collect an income tax.

Horizontal and vertical tax overlapping create economic inefficiencies and taxpayer inequities and can seriously handicap the tax effort and the spending powers of state and local governments.[22]

Horizontal tax overlapping reduces the independence with which state and local governments can pursue certain tax policies; it can therefore adversely affect the amount of revenue raised. Many persons, especially in metropolitan areas, live in one jurisdiction and work in another; conflicting claims on income from the governments of the two jurisdictions are not resolved.

The taxation of interstate sales poses similar problems. Two basic principles have been enunciated: One tax policy assigns interstate sales to the state of destination, while the other assigns them to the state of origin. Perhaps more complicated is the taxation of interstate business income. The two basic questions are: Where should interstate business be taxed and which business should be taxed in a given state, and what should be that state's fair share of total taxable interstate income of the business? Here too we must choose between a destination basis and an origin basis of corporate income. While the destination basis would cause many corporations to be taxed in numerous states, the origin basis would in many cases lead to taxation by only a single state.

Solving problems associated with vertical tax overlapping calls for reliance on many of the techniques discussed in connection with sharing the tax base with the Federal government. For example, tax credits, previously discussed, would have the advantage of stimulating tax coordination by requiring eligible state income taxes to be similar in structure to the Federal levy; furthermore residents and nonresidents, and corporations that have plants in many states, would be taxed uniformly.

However, there are two further techniques in the category of tax coordination that are germane to problems of both horizontal and vertical tax overlapping: coordinated tax administration and centralized tax administration. In recent years the Federal and state governments have benefited from some coordinated tax administration. The first agreement on such coordination was signed between the Federal government and the State of Minnesota in 1957, and by now at least thirty-five states have signed such an agreement. As early as 1960 the Internal Revenue Service reported receipts of $10.6 million and costs of only $50,000 from the agreements. In 1959 California reported a net increase in taxes of more than $4 million from its comparison of state with Federal income tax returns.[23] Such coordinated tax administration need not be limited to Federal-state fiscal relations; local governments also can coordinate their taxes.

Gains can also be realized by centralized administration of specified taxes. Taxes are imposed and administered by only one level of government, which returns the net revenue or a portion of it to the various cooperating jurisdictions. For example, states might want to contract with the Federal government for the more efficient administration of a tax. However, Federal administration of an existing state tax requires a high degree of uniformity in the tax from state to state. Good candidates are cigarette taxes, death taxes, and corporate income taxes.

EXPENDITURE EFFECTS OF INTERGOVERNMENTAL FISCAL INSTRUMENTS

When the Federal government provides funds for use by the state or local governments, or the states provide funds for their local governments, what are the effects upon the expenditures of the receiving units? There are several questions subsumed in the general inquiry:

1. Does aid increase expenditures from sources raised by the recipient government?
2. Does aid distort the allocation of resources between the recipient government and the private sector?
3. Does aid distort the allocation of resources among services offered by recipient governments?

In this section we will examine both theoretical approaches to these questions and consider some of the answers suggested by recent research. Our specific attention will be on grants-in-aid, categorical and unrestricted, although the analysis can be extended to other intergovernmental fiscal instruments.

Our first question seeks to discover whether aid stimulates expenditures. To explore this issue consider Figure 6.1, where dollar resources devoted to government activities are on the vertical axis and those devoted to private activities are on the horizontal axis. Let the line AB represent the community's income constraint so that either OA of government activities may be supported or OB of private activities. Following James Wilde,[24] we can consider the preference function of the local government. Given such a function in Figure 6.1, we see that the resources will be divided, with P_1 dollars going to the private sector and LG_1 going to the public sector. Since we have not introduced aid from either the Federal or state government, local resources LG_1 equal total resources for government services TG_1.

Now let a block or unrestricted grant in the amount of AD be made by

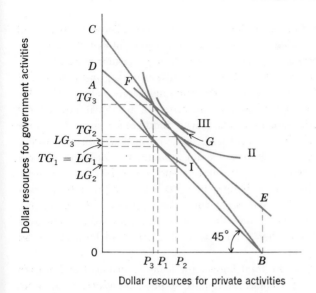

FIGURE 6.1 *Expenditure effects of grants-in-aid.*

a higher level of government; the relevant budget line then becomes *DE*. In this case total dollars allocated for government services in the community rises to TG_2, but the local contribution to government activities falls to LG_2 while dollars for private activities rises to P_2. Thus, we will claim that if block funds are given to lower levels of government to encourage high levels of spending, part of the funds may be used to increase government expenditures in the receiving jurisdiction, but at least part of the gift will be used to decrease the local contribution to government activities. Citizens in the receiving government may be induced to spend more money than they would otherwise wish to spend but at the "cost" (to the granting government) of answering "probably not" to question 1 above.

   If the grant from the higher level of government is made a function of the local government's contribution, as depicted by the budget line *CB* in Figure 6.1, the result is not clear. As shown in the figure, we have an increase in local dollars for government services from LG_1 to LG_3 with a decrease in allocations to the private sector. This is what is referred to in the literature as "stimulation" of local expenditures. But with a different preference pattern wherein the income effect would overcome the substitution effect, there would be a reduction in local support. Hence for conditional grants there is not a clear theoretical answer to question 1.

   Is there a "distortion" that results from the conditional grant? The analysis of this second question can also be made in terms of Figure 6.1. There are two ways to arrive at the same conclusion: Yes, conditional grants cause local governments to favor the aided activity. In Figure 6.1 the aided activity is government services as a whole, but the argument can also be made in terms of two government services rather than government vis-à-vis the private sector. Both the budget constraint *DE* of the block grant and that of the conditional grant *CB* are tangent to the same indifference curve. Thus for a smaller grant by the higher level of government, the local government could be as well off (the tangency of *CB* with indifference curve II is at a point above the line *DE*) if the grant were made on an unconditional rather than a conditional basis. For the same grant amount, the local government could achieve a higher level of utility (indifference curve III), as shown by considering the partially drawn budget line *FG* which represents a grant equal to that made under the conditional offer. The tangency of *FG* and curve III implies that, if given the choice, the local government would substitute grant funds for local funds; hence there is a "distortion" of local choice by use of the conditional grant.

Figure 6.1 shows how the total budget for local government activities is determined when grants are made in support of those activities. If we were to label the axes for two different services, we could answer question 3 in the affirmative: Yes, aid, when it is categorical, tends to "distort" the allocation of funds between the two services from that pattern which would exist if a simple, unrestricted grant were given. This result obtains, we have shown, if the substitution effect outweighs the income effect. David Smith terms this condition a price elastic government service.[25] When the service is price inelastic, the conditional grant will lead to increased consumption of the aided service and other services as well.

What actually happens to expenditures when a higher level of government aids local functions? Here are a few of the findings, each employing an additive regression equation where expenditure by the aided governments is the dependent variable and Federal or state aid is one of the independent variables. No two studies are alike and all may be criticized as using statewide or countywide data so that we are seeing aggregates rather than the behavior of separate government units. This latter point is important, since the theoretical discussions assume a jurisdiction with one decision-making body and the data used combine many governments receiving many different kinds of grants under diverse economic and political conditions.

The effect of grants on recipients' behavior has grown out of the study of the determinants of state and local government expenditures. (The general topic of expenditure functions will be taken up in Chapter 8.) Solomon Fabricant's study[26] set the stage by showing that 72 percent of the variation in these expenditures for the year 1942 could be accounted for by difference in three factors—population density, percentage urban, and per capita income. Glenn Fisher discovered that for 1957 the coefficient of multiple determination or the percentage of variation accounted for by these factors had decreased to .53.[27] Seymour Sacks and Robert Harris felt that a basic fact of life in state and local government financing had occurred in the interval. They therefore introduced aid by higher levels of government which then raised the percentage of variation explained to 87 percent for the year 1960.[28]

Sacks and Harris concluded that ". . . when state and Federal aid are explicitly considered there is strong support for the hypothesis of a positive impact of state aid on the level of expenditures; . . . [for] welfare and highway expenditures, where the Federal government has large programs, Federal aid is by far the most important determinant of expenditures. . . ." [29]

Jack Osman then sought to determine for the same year, 1960, whether, in addition to the positive impact noted by Sacks and Harris, it would be possible to determine the stimulation effect. His analysis indicated that for each dollar of Federal aid the following additional amounts would be spent from state and local sources: [30]

TABLE 6.2 *Rise of Expenditures in Relation to Federal Aid, Selected Services, 1960*

Total general expenditures	$0.94
Education: Total	4.11
Local schools	1.71
Higher education	1.59
Highways	0.37
Public welfare	0.38
Health and hospitals	1.09

Osman went on to show that expenditures for a given function are influenced by aid to other functions. "Each $1.00 increase in Federal aid to all functions other than education was associated with a $0.52 increase in educational expenditures." [31] He concludes that ". . . federal aid has had the effect of stimulating those functions to which it has been directed, and the result has not been merely to substitute federal for state and local funds." [32]

George Bishop studied a different universe and came to a different conclusion. His sample involved the school expenditures of 1,400 towns and cities in New England for the years 1961 and 1962. The result was that ". . . an additional dollar of state aid is associated with an increase in expenditures per pupil ranging from 40 cents to 80 cents." [33] This leads Bishop to conclude that ". . . a town or school district will spend a portion [of state aid to education] on increasing its quality of education (insofar as this is indicated by expenditures per pupil) and it will also use a portion of the aid to reduce its property tax burden."[34] Bishop's conclusions thus stand in marked contrast to those of Osman, with the difference probably resulting from the type of universe employed in the study. But Smith, using a data base similar to that of Osman, comes up with mixed results. He finds Federal grants for highways and welfare stimulative, but other functions show no statistically significant positive association between Federal aid and state and local spending from own funds. He sees ". . . a strong income effect associated with Federal grants that acts to subsidize a wide range of governmental activities." [35] This conclusion is consistent with part of the dual effect explored by Osman.

Robert Adams presents evidence that is also of a mixed nature and leads to a similar conclusion. His study included 1,249 county areas in thirty-four states. In more than half the states, ". . . state aid not only leads to an increase in the consumption of local public services, but also to an increase in activity in terms of the share of local income being diverted through the local public sector." [36] Since this result is not indicated by the theoretical analysis, Adams sought but could not discover an explanation. The results for Federal aid were as expected: ". . . communities absorb only part of the increments of income received as Federal grants into the consumption of public services. Moreover, per dollar Federal aid will lead to a greater reduction in [the recipients'] fiscal effort than state aid. . . ." [37]

Thus we see no clear statistical conclusions about the expenditure effects of these intergovernmental fiscal instruments. There does seem, however, to be some correspondence between the theoretical results that receiving governments will reduce expenditures for government activity, other factors held constant, except for a special case of conditional grants. Of course, conditional grants are a major instrument and this may be the reason that the heavily aggregated data of these studies fail to show a strong direction.

EVALUATION OF INTERGOVERNMENTAL FISCAL INSTRUMENTS

The evaluation of the different intergovernmental fiscal instruments discussed above depends upon the objectives or criteria against which they are measured. In this section, five criteria will be advanced:

1. Equity in income and service distribution
2. Economic efficiency
3. Economic growth
4. Stability of revenue and economic activity
5. Autonomy and pass-through of funds

These five criteria are not necessarily consistent with one another. For example, economic efficiency and growth may have to be sacrificed to some extent to achieve equity in the distribution of income and services. The setting of priorities with respect to these objectives or criteria is a central and difficult task of government.

Equity in Income and Service Distribution

One of the main objectives of the Federal government in the use of intergovernmental fiscal devices is to redistribute income. This may be done on an individual basis, with specific payments made to individuals according to certain personal characteristics such as age or health or income. But income redistribution may be achieved also through intergovernmental transfers by having the Federal or state government pay part of the bill of services usually financed by local governments. This form of redistribution discriminates between geographic areas and different groups of taxpayers.

Often in this context the *local tax effort* criterion is evoked.[38] The concept of tax effort is popular because at its basic level it has a simple intuitive definition: Tax effort is equal to the proportion of taxable resources that actually go to government.[39] The total taxable resources of a state or local government can be roughly measured by the total wealth of all those who reside or function under the government's jurisdiction, where total wealth is adjusted for the legal right of the wealth owner to avoid taxation. For example, wherever General Motors Corporation has a plant it is a component of the total taxable resources of the jurisdiction. But General Motors Corporation can legally avoid one government's taxes by holding assets in another jurisdiction where the tax rate or base is different. Thus, taxable resources is a loose concept dependent upon the legally defined tax base of the community and those forms of wealth and transactions which have yet to enter the defined tax base.

The concept of tax effort is used to measure the burden to a community of its government functions and to measure the local share of expenditures on local government functions. Yet not only is it difficult to give meaning to total taxable resources so that intercommunity comparisons can be made, but the dollar expenditures a community makes upon its government services reflect diverse conditions of production and tastes. That a downtown area and a suburban area spend the same percentage of household income on police protection is relatively uninteresting. What they are buying in terms of services is quite different, partly because of the different problems protection poses in the two areas. While we can admire their administrative simplicity, there is no theoretical or ethical basis for such an effort concept in regard to either individuals or governments.

Discussions of tax effort, however, do point to a central concern: Does a particular transfer of funds increase or decrease the expenditures and revenue collections made by the local receiving government? This issue was discussed in the preceding section and is relevant to questions of service and income distribution.[40] If a Federal grant means that local expenditures and hence local taxes decline, there is a relative shifting of the financing of local government services from local taxes to Federal taxes. The income redistribution that takes place is in terms of consumption as well as in terms of gross personal income. Intergovernmental transfers will redistribute income not only between jurisdictions but also within them. For example, Federal aid to relieve the local property tax may be financed from taxes on income. If the local government reduces property taxes by some fraction of the amount of the grant, a result often assumed by proponents of "tax relief," then income taxpayers including those in the receiving community will be differentially burdened relative to the local property taxpayers. If the receiving government were the only government getting transfers we would expect the receiving citizens to be, on net, better off because the increment in any given individual's Federal income tax liability would be very small.

While income redistribution does occur through grants, neither categorical nor unrestricted grants relate directly to redistribution of regional per capita income. When a receiving government uses grant funds to increase its total expenditures, citizens of its jurisdictions are in effect given income in kind in the form of state or local government services; this is usually the desired effect of a grant program. Major personal income redistribution is not effected by such transfers as much as by specific provisions in the grants to support programs that mainly benefit low-income groups.

Both categorical and unrestricted grants have some distributional shortcomings. The variety and complexity of Federal subsidy programs are such that many state and local governments have hired administrative staffs whose major function is to seek out subsidy programs under which requests for aid can be submitted and to develop skill in project presentation. Governments with the finances to develop such knowledge and ability have been able to get the lion's share of Federal support while less well endowed governments have been left behind. Categorical grant programs with matching provisions have the further disadvantage that the communities that are better able to take advantage of the matching provisions usually obtain more than their proportionate share of the Federal money, leaving the less able areas relatively worse off than before the programs.

For localities of equal per capita income and with identical distributions of income, tax credits and tax deductions will tend to redistribute income toward the area which has the higher state or local taxes per dollar of regional income taxed by the higher level of government. As between wealthier and poorer areas of the country the distributional effects of tax credit and tax deduction provisions are not obvious. And, as stated earlier, tax deductions of equal size are of greater relative aid to those taxpayers with higher tax rates, but it is not obvious that wealthier regions experience higher average effective tax rates or larger deduction allowances on the average. Tax supplements have little direct influence on redistribution of regional per capita income, since these instruments are primarily employed as substitutes for other state or local revenue collections.

A second major objective of Federal intergovernmental fiscal devices is to increase service levels primarily by enabling localities to rise above "substandard" production levels. Financial assistance helps urban centers to service poor inmigrants and thus in part compensates for certain interjurisdictional cost spillovers. This concept implies that a relatively high standard of service is set and all substandard service is discouraged. Clearly, the way funds are raised that are transferred as grants to increase the equality of regional services can also affect how much a grant of given size will alter spending and production decisions.

The various intergovernmental fiscal instruments differ in their usefulness in accomplishing this distributional objective. Achievement of increased if not equal service levels is related to spending and production decisions of state or local governments. Only categorical grants with restrictions and constraints on the use of the grant funds will directly affect specific spending and production decisions. Therefore, categorical grants are the most useful instruments in reducing local service disparities in the sense that compliance with service conditions dictated by the giver can be a determinant of the size of the gift. Unrestricted grants will be less influential in affecting specific service levels. This follows since there is greater incentive, relative to categorical grants, to use block grants as substitutes for the tax of the receiving government, and the aggregate impact on total expenditure levels of block grants will be less than for categorical grants of equal size that have matching provisions.

Tax supplements act as substitutes for state or local revenues and have little direct influence on spending and production decisions. Tax credits and tax deductions are directly related to such decisions only to the extent that the tax provisions apply specifically to earmarked funds. For example, if user charges for toll roads were made tax deductible and if deductions of gasoline taxes were made illegal, then we would expect the quantity and quality of toll roads to increase relative to other highways. Tax credits for revenue collections relating to specific earmarked funds will be even more influential than deductions on service levels.

Economic Efficiency

Alternative employments of intergovernmental fiscal instruments can be judged by efficiency criteria. By efficiency we shall mean a change that could leave at least one individual in the jurisdiction better off and no one worse off. In the process of such efficiency changes, potential losers may have to be compensated by gainers so that in the new situation everyone is at least as well off as previously.

State and local governments face several situations in which employment of various intergovernmental fiscal instruments might, at least theoretically, result in efficient changes. Several changes involving different efficiency aspects will be considered briefly.

1. When the private marginal cost to any individual or individuals for obtaining an additional unit of a particular good does not accurately reflect the marginal social costs of producing that unit of output, then an efficient change may be possible. This source of inefficiency may arise where state or local governments produce goods with the possibility of extensive joint consumption. For these and possibly other types of outputs the benefits spill out of the government's jurisdiction and are enjoyed by individuals who neither participate in the production decisions nor share in the production costs. Since these outside beneficiaries live in other government jurisdictions, are there intergovernmental fiscal instruments which could bring about efficient changes? Such changes would tend to bring social marginal costs into equality with marginal evaluations of the worth of an additional unit of output by all beneficiaries (or the *sum* of marginal evaluations of beneficiaries in cases of joint consumption of the marginal unit).

In a system of independent state and local governments there is a risk that particular goods and services will be either under- or overproduced in the sense that spillover benefits or spillover costs will not be taken into account by decision makers. This first efficiency criterion relates to how nearly a given intergovernmental fiscal arrangement can tax beneficiaries residing outside the tax jurisdiction of the producer and transfer funds to the producer so that under conditions of underproduction the particular output can be expanded. Overproduction can result from the influence of beneficiaries outside the producer's jurisdiction who do not fully pay for benefits received and therefore attempt to get production increased until the marginal benefit to themselves is zero. What is important here is that efficiency relates to charging for benefits so that marginal rates of private costs and benefits can be brought into equality for all beneficiaries. A similar relationship may hold for cost spillovers.

As an example of this issue, consider the relationship between grants to depressed areas and outmigration from those areas. Do these grants tend to interfere with efficient resource allocation? The literature on this subject is extensive.[41] Opponents of such grants have argued that they weaken the incentives of residents to move out of depressed areas and that there are few well-endowed, low-income areas where labor is not in excess supply compared with potential future demand for its services. An efficient allocation of manpower calls for the outmigration of labor from these depressed areas to other sections of the country where employment opportunities are better. Thus, grants that tend to retard the efficient flow of labor would not be consistent with economic efficiency. Massive public works projects in depressed areas would appear to be an inferior alternative.

What kind of aid programs should be encouraged to bring about the desired migration? Do the same programs tend to reduce the unfavorable spillover cost consequences of migration? We have become familiar with the problems faced by the major areas of inmigration, the cities that annually receive thousands of migrants from economically depressed areas. These new city dwellers often become to some extent public charges, placing strains on the welfare rolls as well as on the education and health facilities.

It has been found that "depressed areas tend to lose through outmigration the more productive groups in the labor force: the young, the better educated, the businessman, and the professional. The areas retain a disproportionate number of older people, those who have only a grammar school education, those not in the labor force, and blue-collar workers." [42] Aid to education in depressed areas will raise the achievement level of those in school and thereby tend to increase migration. To increase the numbers in school, "Grant funds used for public health programs and welfare grants to low income families with children may be equally, if not ever more, effective in raising average educational levels and hence in stimulating, sooner or later, the movement of workers out of depressed areas." [43]

In summary, equalization grants for health and education programs may tend to improve resource allocation, even if made to regions that would benefit from labor outmigration. Other grants aimed to achieve higher standards of government service and income redistribution may be implied for poverty cases no matter where they reside.

The essential consideration in the above example was that the efforts of the higher level of government to achieve better services and to redistribute income should not distort the allocation of resources made in either the public or the private sector. While examining the outmigration from depressed areas we are concerned not only with the behavior of potential migrants, but also the behavior of other parties in the private sector. Aid to the depressed area could well have adverse effects on allocative efficiency if it were channeled to, for example, a program that encouraged business investment in the depressed area. Assume that an industrial firm would relocate its plant only with a subsidy from the Federal government. The subsidy would be justified only if the outmigration prevented by the increase in employment opportunities in the depressed areas would cause social costs in the area of inmigration greater than the value of the subsidy. Another example in the same context demonstrates that inefficiencies stimulated by the existing pattern of tax collections can be corrected if that pattern is changed. Let us say that a particular firm would locate in a depressed area if the property tax rate in that area were lower. The Federal government might reallocate its expenditures from welfare in the cities of inmigration to payments to the depressed area so that local property taxes could be lowered while the level of services in the depressed area and total spending by all governments involved remained constant. By substituting a different tax base we achieve an increase in employment in the depressed area, a reduction in the private costs involved with migration, and a reduction in the public costs associated with that migration. Thus tax revenue collections and intergovernmental transfers would be rearranged within a federated government structure so as to promote the greatest private output with a given total government expenditure level.

None of the intergovernmental fiscal instruments discussed in this chapter are specifically designed or well suited to achieve greater efficiency by better handling of the spillover problem. Categorical grants-in-aid are the most promising tools to bring to bear on the spillover problem, but we lack an institutional technique for ascertaining marginal evaluations of incremental units of spillover benefits or costs.

2. Categorical grants restricted to expenditures on particular programs or particular inputs to programs raise some special problems of efficiency. Grant funds that do not require matching appear to the receiving government to be free resources; to the giver the funds appear to be in-kind gifts of inputs to particular programs of the receiving government. First of all, the social value of the resources transferred to state and local governments as calculated by the receivers may exceed the value of increments to particular programs or the value of particular inputs to programs. This means that a lesser amount of wealth in unrestricted form could have been transferred to the same receivers in order to leave them just as well off as they are with the gifts in kind. It also means that for the total benefits from the expenditures to at least equal the total social costs of the gifts, the giver of the grants must derive at least some enjoyment from seeing that the receivers have more of these government services; in addition the giver may have a stake in the direct benefits of these services, and therefore have a demand for the services.

We very often observe that this occurs: Gifts are designed to benefit the giver regardless of who the receiver might be or how much the receiver might be benefited. Often, when a granting government is interested in producing much more with gifts than merely the most well-being for the receiving populations per dollar of gift, the granting government will make the size of gifts depend on "agreeable" behavior of the potential recipients. That is, receiving governments must compete for grant funds by indicating how and to what extent they will gratify the giver. In such competitive situations the receiving governments will expend resources to obtain advantage in the receipt of gifts, and in an extreme case these expenditures may be so great as to equal the value of the gift to the receiver. The chances, therefore, of social waste are greatly increased; some rearrangement of intergovernmental fiscal relations might leave both givers and receivers no worse off and resources could be freed to increase outputs of other goods.

3. In a system of politically independent taxing jurisdictions, the various state and local governments will incur and will inflict on their constituents a

certain sum of collection or compliance costs in order to raise a given amount of revenue. We might therefore ask the question What reduction if any in aggregate collection costs would be realized if each tax jurisdiction received the same amount of revenue but other intergovernmental transfer instruments were substituted for present tax collection instruments? If a given amount of tax revenue could be collected within a federated government structure at a lower social cost, without at the same time changing individual tax liabilities and altering the tax effects realized in the present system, then an efficient change would probably be possible.

Some intergovernmental fiscal instruments might be more efficiently employed in the sense that the same total tax revenue could be raised with a lower sum total of social collection costs. For example, under a tax supplement plan, taxpayers could reduce the number of forms they were required to file and the central collector might be able to take advantage of economies of larger-scale collections. And for some tax collections the social cost may be lowered if subordinate governments collect levies and rebate funds to higher governments. In order to achieve efficiency gains in the ways described above, it would be necessary, in theory, to hold the tax effects and tax incidence unchanged so as to avoid changes in efficiency which would offset gains in efficiency from reduced collection costs. Distributional changes requiring complicated compensation payments would also occur.

4. Alternative intergovernmental fiscal arrangements have different effects on the private economy. Both revenue collection and expenditure acts of governments will affect relative values, the distribution of wealth, and therefore the choices that individuals make. Different methods of rearranging revenue collection responsibilities among governments will have different effects on the efficiency of the private economy. We might therefore ask the question Can tax revenue collections and intergovernmental transfers be rearranged within a federated government structure so as to promote a greater economic efficiency in the private economy (leading to increased total private output) with all potential losers in the rearrangement having been compensated?

The most efficient of these arrangements is that which results in the greatest private output while financing a given level of government expenditures in the federated government system. We assume that each government's expenditures are the same under each arrangement and that if there are losers from a given rearrangement they are compensated for their losses by the gainers. For example, local governments, finding that many tax bases are not productive at reasonable cost or by law are not available to them, have been forced to rely heavily on such tax bases as property. But it appears that extensive use of property taxes causes inefficiencies (misallocations) in the private economy relative to some other set of taxes which could be possible if taxes were levied on different bases through intergovernmental fiscal relations with the result that taxation would be more neutral.[44]

Economic Growth

A principal source of per capita income growth is productive saving or capital formation. Governments compete with private investment opportunities in that, for a given interest rate and limited resources, only the most profitable investments should be carried out. But government investments can be complementary in that they are not independent of the profitability of private investments; certain government investments will make some or possibly all private investments more productive in terms of future consumption returns.

The individual governments in a federated system conceive and carry out numerous investment projects. In an evaluation of intergovernmental fiscal instruments, we would be interested to know what alternative employments of such instruments will produce efficient changes which enhance regional growth. The growth criterion basically relates to efficiency in the intertemporal sense. All the problems raised in the preceding section concerned with an examination of efficient changes are germane, although spillovers, the first problem discussed, seem most significant to regional capital formation.

A state or local government in the making of its own investment decisions will tend to underinvest in a project if it anticipates considerable spillout of benefits. Also, it is unlikely that investments that have a high payoff for the entire population but a low payoff to a particular local or state government will be undertaken by the latter. In such cases a higher level of government might carry out such profitable investments or might encourage subordinate governments to do so by offering categorical grants or loans with matching provisions.

Changes in intergovernmental fiscal arrangements will tend to alter the relative profitability of different kinds of regional investment opportunities. For example, a decreased local property tax offset by an increased income tax, e.g., through a tax supplement, will improve prospects of property-taxed relative to non-property-taxed capital investments.

Categorical grants-in-aid, which we found to be consistent with the first efficiency criterion, appear also to be best designed to advance regional economic growth because they can compensate state and local governments for benefit spillouts and cost spillins.

Stability of Revenue and Economic Activity

Two criteria are germane to the stability of revenue and economic activity. The first relates to the flow of funds over time to state and local governments; the second relates to the effects of the activities of state and local governments on the stability of the private sector.

State and local governments seek predictably constant, if not steadily increasing, revenues to support their activities. Intergovernmental fiscal instruments that tie the revenues of state or local governments to the Federal government's tax base would imply fluctuations in such revenues. To stabilize their total revenue collections, subordinate governments could conceivably engage in countercyclical rate changes or other costly and inconvenient techniques. To the extent that income tax supplement schemes increase the proportion of income tax revenues to the total of all revenues collected by state and local governments, instability of the flow of funds will be increased. During periods of recession and depression, tax deduction and tax credit bases probably shrink. However, while we can visualize the Federal government liberalizing its tax credit or deduction policies for compensatory reasons, state and local governments have historically been unable to raise their tax rates or institute new tax programs during such periods. The intergovernmental fiscal instrument having the most capricious effect on the stability of the revenue of state or local governments can be grants-in-aid, since such grants are almost entirely dependent on the spending decisions of the granting governments. In order to overcome this shortcoming Walter Heller has proposed setting aside a fixed percentage of taxable income and placing it in a trust fund to be used for grants-in-aid.

Effects of intergovernmental fiscal instruments on the stability of private sector activities are extremely difficult to evaluate. In a sense, those intergovernmental fiscal instruments that are likely to stabilize the flow of funds to state and local governments would tend to contribute to the stability of economic activities in the private sector, and vice versa. The Federal government probably finds categorical grants the most efficient of all intergovernmental fiscal instruments in pursuing its discriminatory (nonautomatic) anticyclical policies; unconditional block grants are probably most amenable to automatic stabilizer programs, although, as mentioned above, the Heller plan has attempted to minimize effects of the business cycle on disbursements.

Autonomy and the Pass-through of Funds

If a government is autonomous in the fullest sense of the word its citizens are subject exclusively to that government's own laws and law enforcement; yet this is clearly not the case in a federated system of governments where each citizen is subject to the laws of numerous governments. Furthermore, governments in a federated system are themselves interdependent. The criterion of autonomy relates to the distribution of power among different governments and to effects of alternative intergovernmental fiscal instruments on changes in the distribution of power. It should be emphasized that state or local government autonomy can be regarded as good or bad, depending on whether it is seen from the point of view of the superior or of the subordinate government; but whether it is seen as good or bad it will be costly to retain or change. Attainment of greater autonomy for one government can often damage national values or the regional goals of other governments and many individuals.

Let us remind ourselves of four crucial issues of taxation (and expenditure) decisions:

1. When to tax (or spend)
2. Whom to tax (or what to purchase)
3. How much, for whom to tax (or to purchase)
4. Which tax (or expenditure) effects to attempt

Clearly, intergovernmental fiscal instruments and relations have a bearing on the power of state and local governments to effect these decisions. For example, tax supplements reduce the power of subsidiary governments to make decisions in relation to all four tax issues, especially in relation to when to collect the tax and which tax effects to attempt by way of base redefinition. Since the funds from categorical grants-in-aid are not collected by the receiving governments, these governments give up almost all of their power over the four crucial taxation issues as they relate to specific programs. Matching provisions especially will induce receiving governments to give up autonomy over specific expenditure decisions in order to obtain "free" resources; such provisions induce governments to take actions they otherwise would not take.

One problem of autonomy deserves special notice. Since, in the view of the Federal government, local governments face the most serious fiscal problems, the Federal government would like to deal directly with local governments or be assured of rapid and complete pass-through of the grant funds that are given to state governments for disposal to local governments. A similar pass-through problem arises for state governments that deal with individual citizens through departments of local governments, e.g., state welfare funds administered by county departments. In each case the granting government desires more autonomy in dealing with its ultimate clients, and the intermediate government which handles the pass-through attempts to maintain or increase its own power over spending decisions.

Several techniques have been developed to check encroachments on autonomy or, the reverse, to increase autonomy. Federal categorical and unrestricted grants may have pass-through provisions which would penalize states that give local governments a smaller proportional share of the Federal funds than of state grant-in-aid funds.

Tax credits and to a lesser extent tax deductions also can facilitate pass-through of funds to local governments if, for example, Federal legislation provides that only residents of states with uniform local income tax enabling legislation are eligible to benefit from a Federal tax credit (or deduction) program. However, such a provision would only be permissive. To be sure that Federal funds would pass through to local governments, it would be necessary for the Federal legislation to require state legislation forcing local jurisdictions to impose a minimum local income tax before the state would become eligible for Federal tax credits or deductions.

OPPORTUNITIES AND PROSPECTS

In the United States, there is a long-term cycle in which values that favor centralization alternate with values that favor decentralization.[45] Herbert Kaufman speaks about ". . . a succession of shifts . . . each brought about by a change in emphasis among three values: representativeness, politically neutral competence, and executive leadership."[46] The early post-World War II period saw advocacy of strong central government, in terms of both metropolitan consolidation and emphasis on categorical grants from higher levels of government. In the middle sixties a reversal started to take place, and in the late sixties government decentralization and block grants were advocated. Arguments in favor of decentralization are related to an upsurge of a sense of alienation, powerlessness, and frustration on the part of many people, including a feeling that they as individuals cannot effectively register their own preferences about decisions emanating from government. The feeling of alienation has many sources, including frequent gross discrepancies between the promise and the performance of programs, abundant opportunities for vetoes by opponents of change, and the prevalence of large-scale organizations which do not appear to permit meaningful participation and influence except through huge efforts.

A succession of periods in which a period of centralization of government and heavy reliance on categorical grants is followed by a period of decentralization and noncategorical grants need not be disadvantageous. Wheels turning on their axles can and do advance. New accommodations among the different interests in society are reached and better governing instruments are perfected.

However, decentralization, block grants, and local control, which are wanted now, have built into them forces that tend to generate change. Providing more noncategorical grants and greater local influence on public programs is likely to result in disparities in practice among the numerous small government units, brought on by differences in human and nonhuman resources. These disparities are likely to stimulate calls for central intervention to restore equality and balance, and thus the forces underlying categorical grants and metropolitan consolidation are likely to assert themselves again. According to Herbert Kaufman:

> Decentralization will stand in the way of other goals, such as school integration. . . . It will give rise to competition among the units that will be disastrous for many of them, which will find it more difficult to attract talent and money than others that start from a more advantageous position. In some units, strong factions may well succeed in reviving a new spoils system, thus lowering the quality of some vital services. . . . Economies of scale, which are admittedly overstated very frequently, nevertheless do exist, and the multiplication of overhead costs in local units will divert some resources from substantive programs to administrative housekeeping.[47]

The United States is an exceedingly industrialized, urbanized, and mobile country; as a result, benefit and cost spillovers, particularly in relation to such merit goods as welfare, education, and health services, are widespread. Differences in regional income and public service are quite large. In view of these conditions, a good case can be made for the Federal, and to some extent the state, government assuming in years to come substantially greater responsibility for the financing of welfare, education, and health services. As America's urban problems mount and the fiscal crises of its cities become increasingly serious, Congress is likely to face continuous strong demands for massive Federal aid for many urban programs. If the Federal and state governments respond positively, they will want to have substantial control over the use of "their" funds.

At a time when incentives offered by higher levels of government for the sake of achieving national goals once again become popular, the basis of awards of categorical aid might shift from a need or opportunity basis to a performance or accountability basis. Such a change is particularly promising for education; the rising social costs of school failure, most of which are borne by local governments, together with sharply rising school expenditures unaccompanied by major productivity increases, have resulted in financial crises. On the positive side, recent research is beginning to make it possible for us to know with some accuracy how to achieve specific educational outcomes. For example, knowledge has been increasing about the frequency, duration, and intensity of particular educational activities needed to produce definite types of behavior in students of different ages, aptitudes, and interests. As a result, our analysis is reaching a stage where we can begin to determine cost-effective means to accomplish specific educational objectives.[48]

While state and Federal funds could be used to assure minimum performance, educational improvements could be stimulated with the aid of state and (or) Federal matching grants. The cost of educational improvement should take into consideration the service conditions of the particular district, i.e., whether the same improvements might be more expensive in one district than in another. Grants-in-aid based on performance, which takes into consideration the particular conditions of the specific operating units, might also be applied in an orderly manner to higher education, health services, etc.

SUMMARY

Recent years have seen a substantial, and even increasing, flow of funds from Federal to state and local governments and from state to local governments. Intergovernmental transfers of funds to subordinate governments can be justified for two types of reasons. Fiscal difficulties of state and local governments are caused by some factors that are mainly beyond their control and others that in theory should be under their control but for political considerations are not. Among the factors that justify aid from higher levels of government in the light of the uncontrollable circumstances that face subordinate levels are regional income differences and interjurisdictional spillovers of costs and benefits. Among the controllable factors are tax competition, voting procedures on taxes and bonds, and principal reliance on property and sales taxes that tend to have a lower income elasticity than the expenditures they are called on to finance.

The various intergovernmental fiscal instruments are conveniently categorized into three main groups: direct transfer of funds to subordinate governments; sharing of the tax base by the Federal government with state and local governments, i.e., indirect transfers; and coordination between the three levels of government. Within the first group are such transfer instruments as loans, categorical grants, and unrestricted grants. In the second group are such transfer devices as vacating specific revenue sources, tax supplements, tax deductions, and tax credits.

Intergovernmental transfers can, and often do, affect expenditures of recipient governments. Under certain circumstances, such aid increases expenditures financed by recipient governments, distorts the allocation of resources between the recipient government and the private sector, and distorts the allocation of resources between different government services offered by the recipient government. But there are conditions that lead to opposite effects.

Five criteria, not necessarily consistent with one another or of equal importance, can be applied to evaluate desirability of different intergovernmental fiscal instruments. They are equity in income and service distribution, economic efficiency, economic growth, stability of revenue and economic activity, and autonomy and pass-through of funds. How complex the evaluation of these instruments is can be seen from the fact that there are at least three different types of efficiency considerations—two relating to the public sector and one to the private sector.

In the late sixties there was much interest in decentralization, block grants, and local control. At the same time, because the United States is so highly industrialized, urbanized, and mobile, large-scale interjurisdictional spillovers favored the shifting of more responsibility for the financing of welfare, education, and health services to higher levels of government. At present, categorical grants are awarded on a need or opportunity basis. In the future, at least some of the grants might be based on performance or accountability, and thus would, it is hoped, result in greater efficiency in the use of aid funds.

CHAPTER 7

STATE
AND LOCAL
GOVERNMENT
PRODUCTION

The nature and determinants of outputs of state and local government production have received relatively little attention in the economic literature. Yet, understanding output and the production process is essential if we are to deal, for example, with efficiency problems such as substituting one input factor for another and the presence of scale economies. We will first examine output of state and local governments as to both quantity and quality. Then we will turn to the production process and production function. Finally, some conceptual and empirical issues involved in estimating state and local government production functions will be discussed and a few empirical examples will be presented.

THE OUTPUT OF STATE AND LOCAL GOVERNMENTS: QUANTITY AND QUALITY

Economists have long been concerned with output and its measurement, although few have investigated the public sector and even fewer have studied urban public services. A striking exception is the work of Clarence E. Ridley and Herbert A. Simon, who undertook a major investigation of municipal activities measurements in the late 1930s.[1] They suggested four possible measures: expenditures, effort, results, and performance. Performance is defined as "the effect of the application of effort."[2]

Henry D. Lytton, in a pioneer study in the late 1950s, attempted to measure the output of certain Federal government departments, including the Post Office, Veterans Administration, and Internal Revenue Service.[3] His output measurements were mainly in terms of the number of items handled, e.g., papers and letters. As the author recognizes, these measures neglect quality dimensions. A study by the Bureau of the Budget went somewhat further in measuring the output of the Division of Disbursement of the Treasury Department, the Department of Insurance of the Veterans Administration, the Post Office Department, the Systems Maintenance Service of the Federal Aviation Agency, and the Bureau of Land Management of the Department of the Interior.[4]

All these studies chose relatively simple government services; part of their output clearly defined physical characteristics that could be counted. Under the recent impetus of program budgeting or planning-programming-budgeting efforts on all three levels of government, new output measurements are being undertaken on a wide front and major new contributions can be expected.

Output

State and local government service outputs are those amounts, basically expressed in physical units, that result from, or exit from, the production process. We can visualize the production process in the following manner: Various input factors enter a pipeline in which production converts them into outputs. Since the process takes time, we usually are well advised to assign the production process a time dimension; output is thus measured in the number of units of basic output of specified quality characteristics per unit of time. Output can be produced at a steady or varying rate, which can affect the cost of production as well as the value of the output.

To measure the annual physical output of an urban public service of specified quality, we must first define the basic service unit and estimate the number of units produced per year. We seem to be more comfortable defining basic output units of goods than of services. Goods are more easily defined because their output tends to have clearly identifiable physical characteristics and can be counted. It makes no difference whether the goods are sold privately or by government.

Efforts at defining a basic service unit may involve search for a highly abstract unit to which quality characteristics of concern to producers and (or) users can be attached. The basic government service unit should be defined in such a way as to be a unit of contribution to the successful pursuit of the aims of the government activity. We may have to choose a unit germane to the consumer rather than to the producer, in which case we will deal with the demand side. Another reason a consumer unit may be chosen is that technological changes can greatly modify the production process even though the output continues to satisfy the same desire. For example, the evolution from a horse-drawn streetcar to a cable car, to a bus, and finally to a high-speed electric train involves distinctly different processes, all of which, however, are designed to meet the urbanite's need to move rapidly and conveniently from one part of the metropolis to another. Even good highways, which allow private cars to travel fast and safely, are in a sense substitutes. Thus, to define the basic unit in relation to a specified technological process or type of input is not appropriate, since with the passage of time new processes will appear that have different quality characteristics and that usually defy comparison. However, it is possible that regardless of improvements and changes in production processes, consumer preferences can be judged by the same criteria, and thus quality characteristics on the demand side remain virtually unchanged.

The ideal basic service unit should be flexible and should accommodate the largest possible horizon of existing or potential dimensions of quality. It should be defined in real terms and, if a choice must be made between the demand and cost sides, the former should dominate.

A few services have basic output units with reasonably well-defined physical characteristics. The best example is water, the basic output unit of which is a cubic foot, or acre-foot, of water delivered to the place of use. Another example is refuse collection: a ton, cubic foot, or container of refuse, collected and disposed of, appears to be a useful basic physical service unit. Should this information not be available, we would fall back on the next best position, which might be the number of households or city blocks served. A city block, mile of street, household, or person accorded a specified service usually is a less satisfactory basic service unit, but it often has to be used in an analysis of urban public services.

Keeping in mind the nature of the production process, we can define the basic service unit of street cleaning as a mile or square yard of street cleaned; street lighting, a mile of street illuminated; police protection, a city block protected from crimes; fire protection, a city block protected from fire; urban transportation, the number of cars moved per minute in a rush hour; hospital services, patient-days in the hospital; and schools, the number of pupils who complete a specified grade.

In ease of defining the basic service unit, water is likely to be at one end of the spectrum and hospital services and education at the other. This is particularly so since the number of quality dimensions associated with the unit and the complexity of these dimensions tend to be less for water than for the other two.

But before we consider quality characteristics, let us conclude that defining the basic service unit entails serious conceptual problems and estimating the number of units produced in a given period is complicated by severe empirical difficulties.

Quality [5]

Quality is an extremely difficult and diffused concept. For example, we tend to refer to quality in the sense of a qualitative rather than a quantitative variable, e.g., hot versus cold. Presumably, science transforms such qualitative measures into quantitative measures, e.g., hot and cold are replaced by degrees of temperature. When we are unable to quantify certain items easily, we can set up some dummy variable for each quality.

Sometimes we are tempted to use quality to refer to the quantity of service given per user. Thus, as the number of students in a class increases, the quality of the service to each student tends to decrease. In this case, quality is a sort of quantity measure, the quality characteristics, however, not made too explicit. Even though many people might agree that as quantity of service per user increases, quality goes up, this formulation suffers from the fact that it conceals too many basic issues.

A more useful approach is to view a basic service unit as having numerous quality dimensions, which pose different difficulties in evaluation from either the demand or the supply side. We must pay attention to the fact that quality characteristics are defined and given weights in a subjective manner, which is especially important on the demand side. The question then arises: Whose value judgments should prevail? At least three different judges come to mind: the consumer, society as interpreted by government, and the analyst. Their evaluations may coincide or they may not.

The difficulty of relying on consumer evaluation stems from the fact that people differ in their tastes. Therefore it is important that different qualities be made available.

A city hospital staffed by specialists, i.e., internists, dermatologists, pediatricians, etc., is likely to be a better hospital than one staffed merely by general practitioners. Quality differences here may be correlated with "objective" differences, e.g., longer training of specialists than of general practitioners. However, here too there can be differences that exist only in the eyes of the beholder.

Finally, quality differences may exist mainly in the eyes of the analyst. For example, the analyst may point out differences that most people are unaware of. However, once the difference has been recognized, it may be accepted in the evaluation of many consumers and fit their preferences. For example, the analyst may point out that certain water supplies are contaminated and should not be used, and sooner or later consumers at large may accept a similar view.

On the supply side, the evaluation is in terms of cost (at the margin) associated with quality differences, as well as technologically efficient production.

One point that emerges from these deliberations is that quality differences are often matters of value judgment. The value judgments of those who supply government services can be at odds, to a small or large extent, with those of consumers.

Let us now return to an examination of quality dimensions. For example, if we consider a person served by a library as the basic library service unit, quality dimensions include the library's selection of books, their physical condition and availability, reading room facilities, help to children in selecting books, reference service, location, etc. Such dimensions determine the quality of the service.

Quality identification and determination can involve at least two situations. In the simplest case, the service unit has a single quality characteristic; the service would produce a single direct result, which, however, can assume different values. Perhaps closest to such a situation comes mosquito abatement, in which the sole purpose is to kill mosquitoes. Assuming that there are no indirect effects, different abatement procedures could produce different percentages of mosquito eradication.

A more common and more complex case, such as education, involves numerous quality characteristics—with the possibility of direct and indirect results—each of which can assume different values.

It is important to remember that many government departments are vertically integrated; they produce as well as deliver a service. Under such circumstances, the quality dimensions of both product and delivery service must be considered. For example, a cubic foot of water has important inherent quality characteristics in terms of its physical, chemical, and biological attributes, including hardness, turbidity, temperature, color, taste, odor, mineral content, bacterial count, etc. Quality characteristics of the delivery process include stable water pressure, reliable supply, rapid repair, courteous and correct metering, etc. The situation is simpler in relation to refuse collection, where all quality issues center on the delivery process.

While quality specification is important in defining physical output, quality evaluation is needed to add up different qualities and types of output. Quality evaluations are necessary so that trade-off decisions regarding the quantity and quality of a certain public service can be made and related to budgets.

The existence of different types and qualities of goods and services is commonplace. For example, the California orange industry grows millions of cases of oranges annually. Many varieties are grown, mainly Valencia and Washington Navel oranges, in many different qualities. Likewise, the quality of fire protection differs among communities; and in our public schools a certain number of pupils finish grades 1 through 12 in a given year but with differing educational achievement and performance.

For many purposes it is not meaningful to simply add Valencia and Washington Navel oranges or to list total number of children in our schools. We would often want to separate first graders from high school graduates in measuring the output of schools. When we add up outputs of different types or qualities, we face an index number problem. Each group must be given some weights which reflect, on the demand side, the worth of quality differences at the margin and, on the supply side, their costs. While market prices evaluate relative quality differences, mainly of close substitutes and admittedly not always perfectly, quality evaluation of public services must seek other methods. It is an extremely difficult undertaking.

Proxies

For most purposes, the evaluation of output quality characteristics should be carried out on the supply side in terms of cost at the margin and on the demand side in terms of satisfaction accruing to beneficiaries at the margin. The meaning of benefits at the margin may often be confusing in the public sector. For those public services offered on an all-or-none basis, the concept of the value of a marginal unit of public goods related to a demand function is not useful. Although in the private market at given prices there is a marginal buyer, in the public marketplace all units are offered at the same price, at a zero price, and there is no way to purchase increments in the previous sense. In some cases, however, we may estimate differential output quality characteristics of public goods in terms of the marginal benefit accruing to a representative service user.

Since we are very seldom in a position to obtain such estimates we must rely on various makeshift arrangements, mainly in the form of proxies which more or less approximate what we would actually want to estimate.

We have attempted to present a variety of proxies for output quality, output quality value, and output, respectively. Table 7.1 shows the proxies, by and large in descending order of their appropriateness.

For example, a reasonably good output quality proxy would exist if one or a few output quality characteristics could be estimated. Other proxies are absolute (or relative) input quantities, as well as input performance indicators.[6]

Proxies for output quality values are the value of one or a few output quality characteristics valued in terms of benefits or of costs. Other possibilities are output quality, or any of its proxies, and input costs.

With regard to output, a good proxy on the demand side would be output valued in terms of the benefits of one or a few quality characteristics, and on the supply side in terms of costs of one or more quality characteristics.

Other proxies are output quality value or any of its proxies, output quality or any of its proxies, input costs, physical output performance indicators, and physical output indicators.

Perusal of the literature has uncovered the following proxy applications, most of which are admittedly deficient. Absolute input quantities that have been used to approximate education output quality are average enrollment per secondary school, number of former Woodrow Wilson fellows on faculty, number of American Council of Learned Societies award winners, number of Guggenheim fellows on faculty, number of full-time faculty with doctorates,

TABLE 7.1 Output Quality, Output Quality Value, and Total Output Value Proxies

I. Output Quality

a. Samples of one or a few output quality characteristics
b. Absolute input quantities
c. Relative input quantities
d. Input performance indicators

II. Output Quality Value

a. Value of one or a few output quality characteristics, valued on the demand side in terms of benefits and on the supply side in terms of cost
b. Output quality or any of its proxies (see I)
c. Input costs

III. Total Output Value

a. Output valued on the demand side in terms of the benefits of one or a few quality characteristics or on the supply side in terms of the cost of one or a few quality characteristics
b. Output quality value or any of its proxies (see II)
c. Output quality or any of its proxies (see I)
d. Input costs
e. Physical output performance indicators

number of volumes in library, and full-time enrollment in undergraduate education. Input relationships that have been used as proxies for education quality are annual library acquisitions per full-time graduate student based on a three-year period, members of instructional staff per 1,000 students, percentage of full-time faculty with doctorates, etc.[7]

An example of an input performance indicator applied to education is the number or types of publications of university professors.

A few examples of output quality proxies for fire protection include square miles covered per pumper company, square miles covered per ladder truck company, population covered per pumper company, population covered per ladder company, and average number of building fires per first due pumper company.[8] An output quality proxy for highways is travel time per mile or, better still, user costs per mile (including the costs of users' time).[9]

We will now turn to some examples of total output value proxies. In a few education studies, one or more quality characteristics have been used in benefit terms. Incremental earnings due to education are one example.[10] Below, an example will be presented, using a few output quality proxies in terms of costs.

The first two categories might also include the use of property value increases and the savings and costs of municipal services associated with urban renewal.[11]

Physical output indicators used in relation to education are performance or achievement test scores, school continuation rates, number of doctorates awarded, doctorates awarded per decade and (or) full-time graduate enrollment per year, percentage of baccalaureates who later earn doctorates, ratio of college entrance to high school graduates, number of Woodrow Wilson fellows choosing the school in question, and ability of states to retain their own high school graduates in their institutions of higher learning.[12]

Physical output proxies used in urban renewal evaluation are reduction in crime, disease, fires, and juvenile delinquency, respectively.[13]

Number of subfunctions performed has been used as an output measure by Schmandt and Stephens. For example, they have found sixty-five subfunctions of police protection in Milwaukee, Wisconsin.[14]

In relation to hospital services, beds available per 1,000 population, beds used per 1,000 population, and patient-days have constituted output proxies.[15]

Finally, partial or total input costs have frequently been used as proxies, e.g., wages and salaries and total current expenditures.[16]

An Example

In conclusion, we present an example in which output of a relatively simple urban public service is valued in terms of the costs of a small number of quality characteristics. The service is simple because it is devoid of vertical integration, the basic service unit is reasonably easy to define and quantify, and there appear to be only a few important quality dimensions. The service we have in mind is residential refuse collection.

The output value of refuse collection can be estimated with the aid of the following equation:

$$O = \sum_{i=1}^{n} A_i Q_i \qquad (7.1)$$

where

A_i = number of basic service units of the ith quality per period of time, e.g., number of full refuse containers collected per year

Q_i = dollar value of the ith quality per basic service unit, e.g., in terms of dollar costs

O = output, e.g., in terms of dollar costs

We can consider the basic service unit a container of refuse collected, and there is relatively little difficulty in estimating the number of containers collected per year. Important quality dimensions are collection frequency, pickup location, and nature of pickup, i.e., whether separation of refuse into garbage and trash is required.

For simplicity, we will concern ourselves with only two collection quality dimensions—pickup frequency and location. Specifically we will assume that the choice is between one or two weekly pickups and curb versus rear-of-house pickup. This gives us four different refuse collection qualities:

1. Once-a-week curb collection
2. Once-a-week rear-of-house collection
3. Twice-a-week curb collection
4. Twice-a-week rear-of-house collection

The cost of rendering these different qualities has been estimated with the aid of multiple-regression equations for twenty-four St. Louis City-County municipalities in 1960, with the following results:

$$Q_1 = \$\ 6.13$$
$$Q_2 = \$12.33$$
$$Q_3 = \$\ 9.98$$
$$Q_4 = \$16.28$$

Thus Q_3 is about $1\frac{1}{2}$ times as much as Q_1; Q_2 is about twice as much as Q_1; and Q_4 is about $2\frac{1}{2}$ times as much as Q_1.

If, in a metropolitan area,

$$A_1 = 5 \text{ million}$$
$$A_2 = 10 \text{ million}$$
$$A_3 = \text{zero}$$
$$A_4 = 2 \text{ million}$$

then the total output—*O*—turns out to be about 187 million per year.

PRODUCTION PROCESS AND PRODUCTION FUNCTIONS

Earlier we defined government outputs as those amounts that result from, or exit from, the production process, basically expressed in physical units; since the process takes time, we usually assign the production processes time dimensions; output can be produced at a steady or varying rate which can affect the cost of production as well as the value of the output.

A production function is conveniently expressed by an isoquant map, which relates different combinations of physical inputs with outputs. It represents the relationship between inputs of productive factors and outputs per unit of time, subject to some constraints. More specifically, it shows what each set of physical inputs at different scales of operation, under different service conditions, and with a given state of technology will produce by way of specified service outputs. In more formal terms:

$$O = f(I,S,T) \tag{7.2}$$

where the new notations are

I = input factors
S = service conditions affecting input requirements
T = state of technology

In the preceding section we pointed out that state and local government services have quantity and quality dimensions, which can be traded off against each other. In line with equation 7.1, service output is the product of service quantity and quality, i.e.,

$$O = AQ \tag{7.3}$$

As a matter of fact, since governments in many cases are mandated to serve all constituents, officials tend to vary the quality more often than the quantity of the service.

Earlier we stated that a basic service unit tends to have numerous quality dimensions and that if we are concerned with production, quality should be evaluated in terms of costs at the margin, and if we are concerned with demand, the evaluation should be in terms of benefits at the margin. Usually proxies must be used to evaluate output quality. Admittedly, the introduction of monetary units to reflect costs of quality differences, or for that matter to express inputs and outputs, somewhat contaminates the production function, which, in its purest form, should express physical relations alone.

On a theoretical level, if prices are fixed to the enterprise involved, there is no particular problem in estimation. In effect, one has scaled inputs by prices, and the impact of this is trivial and can be handled through a rescaling of axes by means of a linear transformation.

On a practical level, we often just do not have the opportunity to stay with physical terms. Homogeneous inputs so common in textbooks are rare in the real world. The solution to the problem of nonhomogeneous inputs, as in the case of outputs, requires some sort of aggregation by way of a weighting procedure, e.g., use of index numbers.

Some of the variables on the right side of equation 7.1 will now be considered in detail. Basically, input factors are divided into labor, capital, and resources or material. In addition there is the management factor, which could be included under labor, or considered a separate category, or separated into managerial services—akin to the labor input factor—and entrepreneurial capacity. Let us briefly pursue this third approach, since it may offer us an opportunity to examine whether the public sector has a tendency to be both technologically and economically efficient. The management factor can be divided into two separate parts: managerial services, which may be treated as an input, and entrepreneurial capacity, which is a residual claimant in the production process.[17] This separation allows managerial services to enter into the production function as "rates-of-services" variables and entrepreneurial capacity as services of a fixed factor. In this view, a city manager, police chief, or superintendent of schools furnishes managerial services in terms of internal coordination, supervision of external services, direction, supervision, and task assignment of other resources.

These managerial services are distinctly different from entrepreneurial capacity, which involves decisions by an owner of resources. In the private sector, the owner, e.g., the stockholder of a corporation, seeks to determine the value of his owned resources, when hired out to the highest uses, and the highest value his owned resources have when retained by him and combined with hired resources. The expected returns contain both pecuniary and non-pecuniary yields. The difference between the expected value of owned resources in own use and those rented out yields a residual income, usually called entrepreneurial returns. Entrepreneurial capacity is that complex of factors which is specific to this economic unit and not capable of being rented or hired because it has no value to any other economic unit.

In some broad sense the entrepreneurial function is carried out in the public sector by voters who may act through the legislature and appointed commissions. The voter's success as an entrepreneur expresses itself in good services and relatively low taxes, which also are reflected in land values. If dissatisfied, the voter can move away from the community or vote officials and programs out of office. In certain respects, the voter has a stronger interest in the operations of his government than does the stockholder in his corporation. The latter is merely concerned with the return on his investment, while the voter in his capacity as consumer of services also has an interest in what is produced and how efficiently. At the same time, in the public sector the ownership of resources is not of the relatively simple private type assumed above, and therefore there is less assurance that resources will move to the highest values in use. Vigilant voters and able and devoted commissioners and legislators can exert pressures on government officials to be technologically and possibly even economically efficient.

There are circumstances when this tendency to seek efficient solutions is circumvented. One example is the existence of subsidies and matching funds which can make it attractive to the local or state government not to seek the lowest cost function and possibly to build excess capacity.

Managerial talent in government is subject to some rather unique constraints as well as incentives bearing on the type and skill of the person drawn from the general pool of labor. Among the constraints are those stipulated by law, the rough and tough of politics, and usually relatively low salaries. These constraints are counteracted by nonpecuniary incentives— political power and the ability to move up the political ladder, possibly to national prominence and more power.

Let us now turn to labor and capital and considerations of their rather unique characteristics in terms of their use by government. Markets in which services of policemen, firemen, teachers, etc., are purchased are generally not competitive; instead, government tends to be the predominant, if not often the sole, purchaser of these skills.

The short-run substitution possibilities between capital and labor, especially in the production of local government services, are unusually restricted. These restrictions are not merely technological; they stem from the nature of local public services, which seem to have consistently small capital-labor ratios, and also from severe financial constraints on local governments, i.e., their difficulty in obtaining voter approval for buildings and other capital investments.

Service conditions (S) affect input requirements in several ways. In a sense they are input factors (I), with negative effects. Perhaps a more useful distinction between I and S is that, by and large, I factors can be influenced, and perhaps even controlled, by the decision maker; this is not true for S factors. The importance of S factors is more related to service than public good characteristics.

In considering service conditions affecting input requirements, we can point to a variety of physical, human, financial, legal, and political factors which can make it easier (or more difficult) for governments to provide services of a specified quantity and (or) quality. It is easier for a fire department to provide homes with a specified fire protection quality if the homes are close to a firehouse or a fire hydrant (with constant high water pressure), if they are built of brick rather than wood, and if they are not surrounded by dry brush, etc.

Likewise, the ease of collecting refuse depends on density factors; the closer the various pickup locations are to each other, the less time it takes collection crews and trucks to move from location to location. The average distance to disposal sites also affects input requirements.

In relation to education, a child's native ability as well as his motivation and desire to learn can be looked upon as conditions affecting the ease or difficulty with which a given achievement can be attained. Population density is a factor, since it bears on the need to bus children to school. School crowding and teacher-pupil ratios, the availability of able, well-trained teachers, etc., can also impede or advance the educational process. However, some of these variables tend to reflect quality differences and have been used for that purpose.

Finally, while technological changes generate a new production function, it seems that such changes seldom lead to sudden rapid changes in the production function of state and local government services. Yet, police departments in cities are beginning to use helicopters, and fire departments of some urban counties have begun to acquire aerial tankers designed to help fight brush and forest fires. Refuse is increasingly disposed of by incinerators in place of landfills. And computers are beginning to play an increasingly important role in police and fire departments as well as in administrative offices.

In state and local government services, as in private production, three output concepts have analytic value: total, average, and marginal output or product. They are well discussed in the literature and need not be detailed here.[18]

We are now ready to return to the equations given above. Integrating equation 7.2 into equation 7.1, we have

$$AQ = f(I,S,T) \tag{7.4}$$

Equation 7.4 could be used, for example, if we measured public school output in terms of the number of graduating seniors times their achievement test scores.[19] But in some instances it is not feasible to combine output with quality measures, and then equation 7.4 can be rewritten in the following manner:

$$A = g(Q,I,S,T) \tag{7.5}$$

where $\frac{\partial g}{\partial Q} < 0$

By giving explicit recognition to the fact that public service output is a combination of quantity and quality, which can be traded off and is determined by inputs, service conditions, and technology, we have a formulation of the state and local government production function which lends itself to empirical studies.

SOME CONSIDERATIONS IN ESTIMATING PRODUCTION FUNCTIONS

There are two major ways to provide estimates of public service production functions. One method relies on technical information supplied by engineers, based on their day-to-day operations or upon specially designed experiments. The other method uses ex post statistical information—either cross-section or time series data.

Production functions estimated from technical information benefit from the fact that the range of applicability is known and results of technical progress can be incorporated with relative ease.[20] A further advantage is that production functions can be estimated from engineering data over a wider range than ex post statistical data would permit. Since such production investigations do not depend on the pattern of investment in a plant, engineering production functions conform closely to the production functions of economic theory.

Engineering production functions, however, cannot incorporate managerial capacity as an input variable. As a result, they are mainly applicable to narrowly defined processes, e.g., the cleaning of a particular street, the activities of a refuse collection crew, the operation of a fire fighting unit, etc. In short, engineering data are best used to estimate process functions and, if managerial service (and entrepreneurial capacity) is relatively unimportant, to estimate plant production functions (e.g., a fire station, a school, a refuse incinerator, etc.).

Engineering data must make some assumptions about managerial service (and entrepreneurial capacity), since they may represent the most efficiently managed process of public service or, perhaps, some normal or average condition. As a result, engineering production functions are useful for deriving process and plant cost functions used to estimate manpower, capital, and material requirements. But they are less appropriate for the study of scale economies of government units.[21] While there may be increased returns in the process of a plant function, they may be more than offset by diseconomies of scale in administration.

The production function of a single city is distinct from that of all cities. For example, factors which a given government unit considers fixed, e.g., managerial ability, need not be so for all government units. Furthermore, even if a specific government enjoys decreasing costs, the "industry of governments" might not do so because of limited input supplies, which can result in diseconomies.[22]

Important applications have been found for process engineering data in cooperation with linear programming models. In the linear programming model, technological opportunities of the government unit are expressed in terms of a finite number of activities, and fixed capacities of certain inputs are specified as technical limitations. Computing methods have been developed which permit determination of the most efficient combination of activities in light of specified prices.[23] It must be remembered that linear programming methods are applicable to short-run conditions only and are not a description of existing conditions but a prescription of what governments ought to do with a specified objective in mind. [24]

Only in a very few instances have engineering data been used to derive state and local government production functions. Walter Isard and Robert Coughlin made use of engineering data to estimate sewer, school, road, land, etc., requirements and their carrying capacity.[25] A sanitary engineering research project of the University of California in the early 1950s relied on engineering data which were mainly obtained through time and motion studies. The project addressed itself to the question not only of refuse collection but also of haul disposal.[26]

In addition to engineering information and models, ex post data can be subjected to statistical methods to estimate production functions. The statistical approach describes past operations of production units and is inherently aggregate in character. Whether we use cross-section or time series data, four statistical methods can apply: single equation least squares analysis, covariance matrix method, factor shares method, and instrumental variables. The most commonly used method relies on single equation least squares. In the opinion of A. A. Walters, its attractive properties are "the simplicity of computations, the small standard errors of the coefficients, and the high level of efficiency in predicting output for given inputs, and . . . if the purpose of the model is to predict output for given quantities of input, the single equation approach will be best." [27]

Indeed most empirical production functions, including those pertaining to state and local government services, have been derived by using single equation least squares methods. Because of data difficulties, most public service functions have used cross-section data, either from the Census of Government or from special surveys. Unlike time series data, cross-section data do not need to be deflated; deflation poses almost insurmountable problems. Still, data must often be adjusted and normalized. For example, even if cross-section data are used for labor force functions, labor inputs need to be standardized to allow for adjustment for differences in age, sex, race, and education composition.

Measuring capital is another serious problem, though it is less difficult if cross-section data are used. Most likely, utilization of capital varies less between different government units at any one moment of time than it does over a longer period of time. Nevertheless, estimates of cross-section capital stock need to be adjusted for the percentage of capacity employed. For example, Lawrence Klein made such an adjustment by using the number of train-hours as a measure of the input of capital services on the railways.[28]

Difficult methodological and data problems are raised by the use of time series data. Standardizing labor input over time into "equivalent man-hours" is no mean task; and the measurement of public services output over time, in terms of homogeneous physical units, is virtually impossible. Ways must be found to measure use of capital over time. The ideal measure of capital for a production function is the volume of capital services, but there is no way to measure capital services.[29] Net capital does not measure it well. To some extent, gross capital might be more appropriate, particularly if it can be adjusted to reflect such items as the decline in efficiency of a piece of equipment as it ages. But the capital stock of most governments is a conglomeration of equipment and buildings at different stages in their life, and there seems to be no way to disentangle this bundle. Fortunately, capital plays a relatively small role in many local public services, and errors from inappropriate handling of capital are therefore smaller than they would be in private industry.

SOME EMPIRICAL PRODUCTION FUNCTIONS

Not all the variables mentioned earlier are needed in certain empirical production functions. For example, there are many short-run situations where technology (T) and service conditions affecting input requirements (S) remain unchanged and therefore the T and S variables can be dropped. Also, if cross-section data of government units in a reasonably homogeneous metropolitan area are analyzed, it is often possible to drop the input variable from the equation.

Now we will present a few examples of statistical studies which attempt to estimate urban public service production functions. Herbert J. Kiesling has derived an education production function (primary and secondary) for school districts in New York State.[30] Data from the Quality Measurement Project of New York State's Department of Education pertain to ninety-seven participating school districts over a three-year period in the late 1950s and were applied to derive a single least squares multiple-regression equation.

Kiesling's output proxy was average pupil achievement test score. Inputs were represented by per pupil expenditures during the first year of the three-year study; quantity was represented by school district size, i.e., number of pupils in average daily attendance (ADA); and service conditions affecting input requirements were represented by an intelligence score, i.e., results of the Lorge-Thorndike Intelligence Examination. This analysis was carried out for all pupils as well as for six separate socioeconomic groups in terms of the occupation of the family breadwinner; inclusion of the breadwinner's occupation was designed to reflect the child's motivation and desire to learn.[31]

The regression equation for grades 4, 5, and 6, covering all pupils, was found to be[32]

$$X_1 = -12.78 - \underline{1.269}X_2 + \underline{4.362}X_3 + \underline{0.174}X_4 \qquad (7.6)$$

where

X_1 = average achievement test score
X_2 = size, i.e., number of pupils in ADA (natural logarithm)
X_3 = expenditure per pupil (natural logarithm)
X_4 = intelligence score

All three net regression coefficients are statistically significant at a probability level of 0.05. The adjusted coefficient of multiple determination is

.343, and is also statistically significant at a 0.05 probability level.[33] Thus about 34 percent in the variation of the achievement test score can on the average be explained by changes in size, expenditure, and intelligence score, and there is only a 5 percent probability that the difference between 0 and .343 is due to chance variation.

The statistically significant net regression coefficient of -1.269 can be interpreted in the following manner. In New York State in the late 1950s a 1 percent increase in the number of pupils in ADA on the average was associated with a 1.269 point decrease in the average achievement test score of pupils (and vice versa), holding constant the effects on achievement of expenditures and intelligence.

Production functions for elementary education in Boston were estimated by Martin T. Katzman.[34] Katzman estimated two separate production functions; the first uses percentage of annual continuation rate—the converse of the dropout rate—as an output proxy, and the second uses reading score.

The two production functions are as follows:

$$O_6 = 43.8 + \underline{2.047S_{16}} - 0.047E_1 + 0.138E_2 + 0.049E_3 + \underline{0.190E_4} - 0.006E_5 + 0.035E_6 + \underline{0.097E_8} \tag{7.7}$$

$$O_3 = 174.5 + \underline{8.657S_{16}} - \underline{0.889E_1} + \underline{2.291E_2} - 0.033E_3 - \underline{1.230E_4} - 1.048E_5 - 0.654E_6 + 0.393E_8 \tag{7.8}$$

where

O_6 = percentage annual continuation (in school) rate
O_3 = median change in reading scores between second and sixth grades
S_{16} = index of cultural advantage
E_1 = percentage of school crowding
E_2 = student-staff ratio
E_3 = percentage of teachers with master's degree
E_4 = percentage of teachers with one to ten years of experience
E_5 = percentage of annual teacher turnover
E_6 = percentage of teachers with permanent status
E_8 = number of students in district

In both cases statistically significant regression coefficients—at a probability level of 0.05—are underlined. The coefficients of multiple determination (adjusted for degrees of freedom lost) are .936 and .711, respectively, and are highly significant at a probability level of 0.05.[35]

In summary, output of education in these studies has been approximated by achievement test scores, reading scores, and annual school continuation rates. In place of input factors, Kiesling used expenditure figures, while

Katzman omitted information on this item. From a long list of variables reflecting service conditions that have an effect on input requirements, Kiesling was able to quantify two truly important ones, intelligence score and occupation of breadwinner, likely to affect a child's motivation and desire to learn. Katzman introduced six variables: E_1 through E_6—all of which reflect service conditions and, to some extent, quality characteristics of the school.

The state of technology was not explicitly introduced by either study. Both used the number of students as an additional variable, which is not the most appropriate way of measuring the scale of operation in relation to a production function.[36]

A further statistical production study was carried out in relation to electricity generation, by Phoebus Dhrymes and Mordecai Kurz, who used 1937 to 1959 time series data to estimate long-run electricity generation functions.[37]

SUMMARY

An understanding and measurement of the production of state and local governments require insight into issues associated with defining and measuring output and service quality. Service outputs are those amounts, basically expressed in physical units, that result from the production process. Output is measured in terms of the number of basic output units of specified quality characteristics per unit of time. But very few services have basic output units with reasonably well-defined physical characteristics, as water delivery and refuse collection have.

Defining and measuring quality are extremely difficult. In the abstract, we could view a basic service unit as having numerous quality dimensions that preferably are evaluated from the demand side. Because of great empirical difficulties we often have to rely on proxies for output, output quality, and output quantity value.

Production is best realized in terms of a production function expressed by an isoquant map that relates different combinations of physical inputs with outputs. Input factors can be divided into labor, capital, resources or material, and management. The management factor can be divided into managerial services—an input—and entrepreneurial capacities—a residual claimant in the production process. In this view, a city manager, police chief, or superintendent of schools furnishes managerial services in terms of internal coordination, supervision of external services, etc. The entrepreneurial function is carried out in the public sector by voters who in part choose to act through elected and appointed officials. The voter's success as an entrepreneur expresses itself in good services and relatively low taxes, which also are reflected in land values.

In addition to input factors, output is affected by service conditions and technology. While input factors by and large can be influenced if not controlled by public officials, service conditions affecting input requirements are by and large given and cannot be changed. Finally, although technological changes take place slowly in the state and local government sector, if they do take place they lead to a new production function.

State and local government production functions can be estimated with the help of technical information provided by engineers or ex post statistical data. So far relatively few empirical production functions have been estimated for state or local government services. They mainly pertain to primary and secondary education and measure output in terms of either achievement test scores or annual school continuation rates.

CHAPTER 8

STATE AND LOCAL GOVERNMENT COSTS

Governments, not unlike private enterprise, incur costs in building and operating facilities with which to supply their constituents. Costs incurred by state and local governments are not conceptually different from those of activities in the private sector of the economy. Thus it is possible to draw heavily on established economic theory and apply it to the state and local government sector.

COST AND COST FUNCTION CONCEPTS

Costs may be divided into four components based on the distinction between the nature of the resources employed (operating and capital) and the nature of the payments made (direct and indirect) for a public service. A further useful distinction is between agency and social costs. The actual payments made by governments to secure the services of resources and the value of services rendered by resources owned by governments for the production of current agency services will be called agency costs. Agency payments to labor and the vendors of materials and services usually appear in the budget of the agency. To the extent that such resources are used in the production of current services they are assignable to the current year's costs; if such resources are capital goods (for use in future years) they must be prorated. In current production, a government agency employs goods secured by payments both in the present period and in preceding periods. Where no payment is made for the use of current services, as in capital utilization of a building constructed in a previous period, we speak of indirect agency costs; they represent the value of resources (the building's services) in their next best alternative use in the year for which we are attempting to establish current agency costs.

Social costs entail all the resources required for the activity, in terms of the value in their best alternative use. But they may not equal the costs borne by the government unit that provides the service. Agency costs and social costs may not be equal because other parties, public and private, may incur costs that are neither explicitly charged to the agency in question nor considered in that agency's efficiency and financing deliberations. The same four-part division of costs is applicable. For example, the fire department requires services from the police department in controlling traffic and crowds around a major disaster scene. The police department's costs are direct operating costs, but are not part of the fire department's costs. In its inspection and prevention program, the fire department may require that certain types of fire extinguishers be installed in factories and offices. The owners of these facilities incur direct capital costs when they install the extinguishers. The sprinkler systems of major buildings are part of the private capital costs incurred to meet fire department standards, and the services of such systems may be imputed annually as part of the total social cost of fire protection in the community. Fire drills detain workers from engaging in other productive exercises and may be considered indirect operating costs generated but not incurred by the fire department.

In examining the social costs of public services, we must also distinguish between technological and pecuniary spillovers (or externalities) as discussed in Chapter 1. The first entail actions by one unit, in this case a state or local government agency, that affect the physical outputs other units are able to derive from their physical inputs. An example is refuse collection, where the location of the disposal site may cause a reduction in the utility gained by nearby residents from their homes because of the sights, sounds, and odors of the dump. We would expect such a reduction in the satisfaction attainable from the residential property to result in a decrease in the market value of that property. This decrease would be a pecuniary manifestation of the technological spillover (externality). A purely technological spillover without some associated pecuniary manifestation is hard to find in a market economy.

On the other hand, pecuniary spillovers may exist without a corresponding technological aspect. Pecuniary spillovers do not affect technical productive relationships, but rather raise or lower prices other units pay for certain goods and services. For example, if the city sanitation department greatly increased its employment of skilled laborers to collect refuse, private firms seeking such labor services would, at least temporarily, pay higher wages than they would if the department had hired fewer laborers. The higher wages that private firms must pay are a pecuniary spillover. They do not affect the technical relations of the private operators, although higher labor costs may result in some substitution of other factors and modes of operation.

We should also note that other standard cost concepts are applicable to urban government services. The distinction between fixed and variable costs, while applicable, is likely to be of relatively little consequence in empirical efforts to estimate local government costs of those local government services that are highly labor intensive.

In developing state and local government cost functions, we will concern ourselves with an agency's costs, not with social costs of their activities. In line with state and local government production function 7.4, corresponding agency average unit cost functions can be defined. Long-run average unit cost of a given service is affected by the service quality, quantity, prices of factor inputs, service conditions affecting input requirements, and state of technology. In formal terms:

$$AUC = h \ (Q, \ A, \ I, \ F, \ S, \ T) \tag{8.1}$$

where new notations are
AUC = average unit cost
F = input factor prices

We can be brief since input factors were discussed in Chapter 7 and some manpower problems will be discussed in the following chapter on the supply of services. Because most state and local government services are labor intensive, salaries and wages tend to overshadow all other factor prices. Wages usually tend to vary over time, as well as between regions within the United States. However, we would not expect major differences within any one given metropolitan area. Important differences, if any, would tend to be reflected to a major extent in manpower quality.

SOME EMPIRICAL COST FUNCTIONS

Estimation of public service cost functions is made difficult by conceptual as well as data problems. We will cite only a few of the conceptual problems: For example, in regard to average unit cost, we must know both costs of inputs (which must be totaled) and output (as denominator). For those services for which either input costs or outputs are hard to define, great difficulties are encountered in defining the dependent variable.

On the other hand, independent variables present a difficulty in separation: Should they be part of a cost function or a demand function? To illustrate, in both police and fire protection, the value of the property to be protected has a direct bearing on the cost of the service. At the same time, property values also reflect an ability to pay for the service or, at least, to demand it.

Furthermore, public officials have many reasons for not operating along the lowest unit cost function. Matching grants, preservation of positions, and inertia—among other considerations—can encourage government officials to operate above minimum cost.

The empirical difficulties are no less numerous and grave, whether we use Census of Government data or rely on survey techniques. Separation between operating and capital costs is often impossible. One government finances the acquisition of certain equipment out of taxes, while another one does so by floating bonds. Further, the issue of renting versus buying equipment and facilities introduces empirical difficulties. Even the same government might not be consistent over time. As Charlotte DeMonte Phelps has pointed out, "Capital cost varies over time depending upon the effects of tightening credit conditions."[1] Information on the effects of these credit conditions is hard to detect and ascertain.

Because of great conceptual and empirical difficulties, relatively few empirical public cost studies have been carried out. With the use of 1960 cross-section data for twenty-four St. Louis City-County cities and municipalities, an attempt was made to derive a cost function of residential refuse collection.[2] A multiple-regression equation with the following values was estimated:

$$X_1 = 6.16 + 0.000\ 089X_2 - 0.000\ 000\ 000\ 436X_2^2 + \underline{3.61X_3}$$
$$+ \underline{3.97X_4} - 0.000\ 611X_5 - 1.87X_6 + \underline{3.43X_7} \qquad (8.2)$$

where

$X_1 =$ 1960 average annual residential refuse collection and disposal cost per pickup in dollars

$X_2 =$ number of pickup units, which appears to be a good proxy of the annual amount of refuse collected[3]

$X_3 =$ weekly collection frequency

$X_4 =$ pickup location

$X_5 =$ pickup density

$X_6 =$ nature of contractual arrangements

$X_7 =$ type of financing

The multiple correlation coefficient adjusted for degrees of freedom is .874. It is statistically significant at a probability level of 0.05, as are the underlined net regression coefficients.

The statistically significant net regression coefficient 3.61 can be interpreted in the following manner: In St. Louis County in 1960, increasing the weekly collection frequency by one pickup on the average is associated with a $3.61 increase in refuse collection and disposal cost (and vice versa), holding constant cost effects of number of pickup units, pickup location, pickup density, nature of contractual arrangements, and type of financing.

A second example pertains to sixty-four St. Louis City-County police departments for 1955–1956, for which the following multiple-regression equation was estimated:

$$X_1 = 3.14 - 0.000\ 0103X_2 + 0.000\ 000\ 000\ 00351X_2^2 + 0.000\ 550X_3$$
$$+ 0.000\ 00946X_4 + \underline{0.00315X_5} + \underline{0.00949X_6} - 0.000\ 00212X_7$$
$$+ 0.000\ 946X_8 + \underline{0.107X_9} + \underline{0.000\ 219X_{10}} \qquad (8.3)$$

where

X_1 = per capita total costs of police protection
X_2 = nighttime population
X_3 = total miles of streets
X_4 = nighttime population density per square mile
X_5 = percentage of nonwhite population
X_6 = percentage of nighttime population under 25 years of age
X_7 = combined receipts of wholesale, retail, and service establishments
X_8 = number of whoelsale, retail, and service establishements
X_9 = index of scope and quality of police protection
X_{10} = average per capita assessed valuation of real property

In this equation, X_2 and X_3 are service quantity proxies; X_9 is a quality proxy, and the other variables reflect the service conditions affecting input requirements. The coefficient of multiple determination adjusted for degrees of freedom is .90, which is statistically significant at a probability level of 0.05, as are the underlined net regression coefficients.

The following average unit cost function was estimated for fire protection of the St. Louis City-County area in 1955–1956:

$$X_1 = 0.63 - 0.000\ 0235 X_2 + \underline{0.000\ 000\ 000\ 109 X_2{}^2} - \underline{0.0866 X_3}$$
$$+ 0.000\ 00170 X_4 - 0.00206 X_5 - \underline{0.000\ 0108 X_7} + \underline{1.889 X_9}$$
$$+ \underline{0.00231 X_{10}} \tag{8.4}$$

where the following are notations not found in equation 8.3
X_1 = per capita total current costs for fire protection
X_3 = area in square miles
X_4 = density of dwelling units per square mile
X_5 = 1950–1955 nighttime population increases
X_9 = index of scope and quality of fire protection

In this equation X_2 is a proxy variable for quantity and X_9 for quality. X_3, X_4, and X_5 are indicative of service conditions affecting input requirements; in a sense this holds true for X_7 and X_{10}, which, however, also reflect quantity. The coefficient of multiple determination adjusted for degrees of freedom was .82 and is statistically significant at a probability level of 0.05, as are the underlined net regression coefficients.

Finally, we present the average unit cost function of hospital services which was estimated by Kong Ro for sixty-eight hospitals in western Pennsylvania over an eleven-year period from 1952 to 1963, 1956 excluded.

$$X_1 = 29.64 - 0.0145 X_2 - \underline{0.0721 X_3} + \underline{0.1291 X_4} - \underline{0.0356 X_5} \tag{8.5}$$

where

$X_1 =$ inpatient costs per patient-day
$X_2 =$ number of admissions
$X_3 =$ occupancy rate
$X_4 =$ patient care expenses per inpatient operating expenditures
$X_5 =$ patient-days per personnel

In this equation X_2 is a proxy variable for quantity; X_4 for quality; and X_5 for the state of technology. The coefficient of multiple determination adjusted for degrees of freedom was .89 and is statistically significant at a probability level of 0.05, as are the underlined net regression coefficients. Although in this equation no statistically significant scale economies were found, i.e., 0.0145 had a negative sign but was found to be not statistically significant, Kong Ro noted that if he related these four independent variables to inpatient expenditures per admission—instead of per patient-day—statistically significant scale economies were found.[4]

There are other public service cost functions, but many of them do not concern urban public services; some pertain to expenditure functions, which will be discussed below. Some bona fide cost studies will be referred to when scale economies are examined.

EMPIRICAL EXPENDITURE DETERMINANT STUDIES

During the last thirty years a substantial number of studies have been designed to determine factors affecting expenditures of state and local governments in general and municipal governments in particular. Some have been concerned with general spending, while others have analyzed specific services.

In terms of methodology, simple scatter diagrams were used at first. Thereafter, and until very recently, virtually all expenditure studies relied on single equation, simple- and multiple-regression analyses. In the late 1960s simultaneous-equation techniques, as well as multiple-regression analysis of per capita cross-section data, using two equations derived from explicit optimizing behavior of local governments, were employed.[5]

Multiple-regression Analysis

One of the earliest studies of local government expenditures was that of Gerhard Colm, who used scatter diagrams to find the impact on different categories of state-local spending of income, urbanization, industrialization, and population density.[6]

Solomon Fabricant used cross-section data for 1942 and found current expenditures of local governments strongly related to population density, urbanization, and income. Significant correlations were also found when these three variables were related to school, highway, public welfare, health and hospital, police, fire protection, and general control expenditures.[7] Glenn W. Fisher repeated the Fabricant analysis with 1957 data and found that the same variables no longer accounted for as much of the variation in spending.[8]

Seymour Sacks and Robert Harris modified the Fabricant approach by adding Federal and state aid, respectively, as additional independent variables. They found that, particularly for the more recent data, level of income and aid payments explained a large part of the variation in spending and that the effect of other variables was insignificant.[9]

In 1964 Glenn Fisher categorized the determinants under three major headings: economic variables (percentage of families with less than $2,000 income, and yield of representative tax system as percentage of United States average); demographic variables (population density, urbanization, and percentage population increase); and sociopolitical variables (index of two-party competition, and percentage of population over twenty-five with less than five years' schooling).[10] Ernest Kurnow, using the same data, showed that a joint rather than an additive regression model is more appropriate for the study of expenditure determinants.[11]

In addition, there are a number of more specialized studies, mainly concerned with education.[12] The most comprehensive nationwide study on city expenditures was undertaken by Harvey Brazer, who employed five different samples of 1951 data: a large sample containing 462 cities, three smaller statewide groups, and a smaller number of very large cities including the overlying government unit. The analysis was made not only for total general operating expenses, but also for police protection, fire protection, highways, recreation, sanitation, general control, etc. Among the independent variables tested were population density; median family income; intergovernmental revenues; population size; population growth rate; and manufacturing, trades, and services employment. Mainly the first three were found to be statistically significant.[13]

Stanley Scott and Edward Feder made a multiple-regression analysis of per capita municipal expenditures of 196 California cities with over 25,000 population. As independent variables they used per capita property valuation, per capita retail sales, percentage population increase, and median number of occupants in dwelling units. The first two variables, basically reflecting fiscal capacity, accounted for almost all the explained variations in expenditures.[14]

More recently, George B. Pidot undertook a study of eighty Standard Metropolitan Statistical Areas. He found that government expenditures in core areas were significantly related to the level of personal income, size and commercial nature of property base, amount of state aid, population size and density, presence of rented-occupied housing, and, for capital projects, population growth.[15] The study is enriched by a principal component analysis which rests on the assumption that observed data are the work of a small group of independent underlying factors. The study identified the following components: degree of metropolitization, wealth level, size, commercial-industrial nature of the economy, presence of old people, receipt of redistributive state aid, and receipt of Federal monies.[16]

Brief mention should be made of multiple-regression cross-section studies of governments within a particular metropolitan area. They include studies of the New York region by Robert Wood, of the Cleveland region by Seymour Sacks and William Hellmuth, and of the St. Louis region by the author of this volume.[17]

At least one recent study applies multiple-regression techniques to time series data of a specific community's expenditures. W. Whitelaw studied capital and current expenditure patterns of the city government of Worcester, Massachusetts, during the period from 1920 to 1965. Education, streets, welfare, police, and health were studied. The best statistical results were obtained from applying multiple-regression analysis to education, welfare, and general health current expenditures, which together accounted for about one-half of total general expenditures from 1960 to 1965.[18]

Simultaneous-equation Analysis

Ann Horowitz has used a simultaneous-equation approach to explain interstate differences in state and local government expenditures and employment.[19] She argues that this approach is appropriate because many explanatory variables are themselves affected by the level of state and local government expenditures and (or) employment and because Federal aid should not be treated as an exogenous variable but be explained within the context of the model. Federal aid, in her view, represents a sizable proportion of expenditures and is itself affected by many of the variables hypothesized to affect state and local expenditures as well as employment.

Ann Horowitz found that when the effects of other variables are held constant, income is more important in explaining variation in expenditures than in explaining employment. The distribution of income is a less important determinant of government expenditures than a variable that can also explain interstate differences in employment. A positive relationship is found between tax effort and public expenditures and employment. When the effects of Federal aid are held constant, no significant relations are found between per capita expenditures and population size. Population per square mile is found of little value in explaining interstate differences in overall public expenditures or public employment, other variables held constant, though it is useful in explaining interstate differences in expenditures for particular government services. Finally, it is estimated that for states with the same per capita income, tax effort, and income distribution, state and local expenditures per capita will differ by $1.26 for each difference of $1 in per capita Federal grants-in-aid, and by $1.01 for each difference of $1 in per capita revenue from the Federal government. The corresponding differences in the number of state and local government employees per 100,000 population are ten and eight employees, respectively.

Two-equation, Welfare Optimizing Analysis

James Henderson, relying on multiple regression of per capita cross-section data, has used two equations derived from explicit optimizing behavior of local governments.[20] Henderson assumes that local expenditure and tax decisions can be explained as if local representatives maximized a specific local welfare function subject to local budget constraints. Henderson selects a "logex" local welfare function, where a community's ordinal collective welfare is expressed as a function of its per capita public and private expenditure levels, and explicit recognition is given to personal income, intergovernmental aid, and population size.

Henderson uses 1957 county data, separated into metropolitan and non-metropolitan counties. A marginal income dollar generated a tax increase for the nonmetropolitan counties twice as large as a similar increase for the metropolitan counties—7.9 cents contrasted with 4 cents. The expenditures differential is somewhat smaller than the tax differential, most likely because of the greater expansion of debt by the metropolitan counties—8.2 cents versus 4.4 cents. A marginal dollar of intergovernmental revenue led to more than $1 of new local expenditures for both types of counties—$1.42 for metropolitan counties and $1.04 for nonmetropolitan counties.

Finally, Henderson found that population increments, with per capita personal income and grants held constant, have opposite effects upon the two sets of counties: Metropolitan counties increase per capita local expenditures, taxes, and debt, while nonmetropolitan counties reduce local expenditures, taxes, and debt.

State Expenditure Studies

There are numerous local government expenditure studies but relatively few state expenditure studies. One state study was carried out by Robert Harlow, who used 1957 data. Employing conventional multiple-regression techniques, he found that changes in current expenditures were on the average associated with government structure, i.e., the extent to which local governments in a given state handle most of the activities, income, and Federal aid. Urbanization, industrialization, population growth, and population density were found to have no significant relation to per capita state expenditures.[21]

All these expenditure determinants studies have serious shortcomings, the single most important one being the absence of a rigorous, logical, underlying theory. Expenditure functions are usually related to factors affecting cost as well as demand. In some cases, cost considerations are more strongly emphasized, and in others, demand considerations are more important. Examples of the latter are the Fabricant and the Scott and Feder studies.

Nevertheless, expenditure determinants studies, while not yielding bona fide cost functions, can advance our understanding of why expenditure levels differ among communities and services. In some cases, predictions based upon them can turn out to be reasonably correct.

SOME THEORETICAL CONSIDERATIONS
ABOUT SCALE ECONOMIES AND DISECONOMIES

Our analysis and evaluation of the cost implications of growth or consolidation and decentralization pertain to local governments. We will rely on a quasi-dynamic model in which growth and consolidation can take the form of horizontal, circular, or vertical integration.

A horizontally integrated government controls a number of units furnishing a single service (e.g., police protection) and pursues a unified policy with regard to these units.

If a government unit (or plant) renders a number of services that complement one another, circularity (or complementarity) exists; city hall is a good example. A circular horizontally integrated government controls a number of units that furnish complementary services and pursues a unified policy with regard to these services and units.

A vertically integrated government controls a number of different operations in the production of ingredients that enter into rendering a service and pursues a unified policy. An example is electricity generation and distribution.[22]

In a small community, virtually all services tend to be centralized in a single plant, i.e., city hall, which for maximum efficiency should be centrally located. As the community grows, a number of location-oriented services will require additional plants. Among the first will be fire protection, which is strongly affected by the time-distance between fire station and property to be protected. Growth usually takes the form of more horizontally integrated service plants.

Consolidation can follow and can permit control over more already existing units, i.e., further horizontal integration.[23] However, except for centralization of administrative offices, relatively few changes can be made in the short run with regard to school buildings, police stations, fire houses, libraries, sewage and water treatment plants, etc. The consolidated government will tend to use much of the existing plant, some of which may already have over-capacity use. Only when replacements are built can plant size reflect the needs of the consolidated government; such a government will seldom operate under genuine long-run conditions. Instead, quasi-long-run conditions are usually encountered.

With these considerations in mind, let us speculate about the shape of quasi-long-run cost functions of some horizontally integrated services. For example, police protection in a small community will tend to face a short-run cost function until it reaches a size where an additional station is needed. Deductive reasoning suggests that this short-run cost function should have a flat-bottomed U shape. Its left-hand portion declines, on the assumption that a community needs, on the average, one police officer per 1,000 residents to provide good police protection; around-the-clock service can thus be rendered by a department of no less than four full-time officers. Once these four men are effectively deployed and serve up to 4,000 residents, the addition of officers will tend to change per capita costs relatively little until territory and distances increase substantially. The end of the flat bottom will occur when there are some tens of thousands of inhabitants. Yet the police department may seldom operate in the rising expenditure phase, since location considerations produce diseconomies of scale and can lead to the opening of branch stations. Libraries, schools, and parks also have indivisible but highly adaptable fixed plants. The law of diminishing returns applies and leads to a U-shaped short-run cost function. Since all four service units are basically flexible, their average cost functions tend to have substantial flatness.[24]

Let us assume that services of equal quality are rendered regardless of the scale of operation; that plants are of about equal size, have about equal service functions, tend to be operated at about optimum capacity, and can be readily added to or closed; that factor prices are fixed; and that the long-run average unit cost function tends to be horizontal.[25] There is some evidence that by and large these assumptions tend to be met.

The conditions that help private industry to benefit from scale economies —lower factor costs, larger and more efficient plants, and induced circular and vertical integration—often do not appear to exist when local governments grow or consolidate. Except for labor, cities, counties, and school districts purchase a highly diversified array of factors; few of them are in large enough quantities to obtain major price concessions. Unionization of public servants, however, can produce diseconomies. Also, the nature of local government services, particularly location considerations, tends to keep plants relatively small. Legal restrictions on salary levels of top officials and on permissible debt interfere with good administration and retard technological economies. At the same time, serious diseconomies can accompany a large local government that loses efficiency because of political patronage and administrative top-heaviness.

On a priori grounds, consolidating or decentralizing local governments can approximate conditions under which long-run cost functions for horizontally integrated services (which account for 80 percent to 85 percent of total metropolitan area government expenditures) will be horizontal. Since, however, some plants (and the caliber of their officials) are of fixed size, the quasi-long-run cost functions will resemble a U with a flat bottom over a very wide range. Furthermore, since most horizontally integrated services incur relatively little overhead, the short-run and long-run functions will tend to approximate one another. They coincide in their flat-bottom portion. Net economies are responsible for a negative slope to the left of this area and net diseconomies for a positive slope to the right of it. The more units are horizontally integrated, the flatter the short-run function.

In a similar way we could speculate about the shape of the cost functions of circularly integrated services, which seem to account for 3 percent to 6 percent of total metropolitan area government expenditures. This has been done in another place,[26] and it was concluded that on a priori grounds, short-run average unit cost functions for such multipurpose single-plant services could be expected to be U-shaped, with the trough in communities of medium size.

A similar analysis of vertically integrated services concluded on a priori grounds that the quasi-long-run average unit cost function for water services and sewage services tends to decline until a very large scale of operation is reached.

SOME EMPIRICAL STUDIES OF ECONOMY OF SCALE

Three main approaches have been used to measure economies of scale in individual industries in the private sector of the economy. First, since the 1930s, most estimates of industry average cost functions have been made with the aid of cross-section data. The second approach, taken by Joe Bain, has canvassed managerial estimates of "optimum" scale of plants and interplant scale economies.[27] Since the late 1950s, a third approach, the survivor technique, has been applied, based on an analysis of what plant size over time has gained most in terms of its relative contribution to the industry's value added.[28]

The survivor technique is not applicable to the public sector, since scale of operations does not depend directly on whether a government unit survives in the light of competition; instead, its survival is determined by people's decisions to reside, work, and invest in a given jurisdiction. Canvassing managerial estimates of optimum scale of plants is possible in relation to state and local governments, but has not been employed so far. We will rely on the first approach, and in order to test hypotheses deduced in the preceding section we will examine an empirical study of the average unit cost of governments of different size that are performing similar services. Specifically we will consider how average unit costs vary in relation to the size of senior high schools.

John Riew analyzed 109 Wisconsin senior high schools (92 four-year and 17 three-year high schools) using 1960–1961 data.[29] Per pupil in average daily attendance (ADA) operating costs were correlated with the number of pupils in ADA as a scale measure. Three quality proxies were used (average teacher salary, number of credit units offered, and number of courses taught by average teacher), and two growth variables (growth in the number of pupils and percentage growth in classrooms). A significant parabolic relationship was found between the pupil cost and enrollment. The trough of the cost function was found to be at an enrollment level of 1,675 students. Riew attributed the economies of scale mainly to the fact that senior high schools require a high degree of specialization with regard to teaching staff and facilities—much higher than that of primary schools.

Jesse Burkhead studied Chicago high schools having an average enrollment of 2,200 students and found no scale effects.[30] Although the Riew and Burkhead results appear inconsistent, a high school with about 2,000 students (and about eighty teachers) may prove to be of efficient size.

A hospital cost study by Kong Ro covered sixty-eight hospitals in western Pennsylvania over the eleven-year period from 1952 to 1963, 1956 excluded. Ro considered a number of different quality variables, e.g., amount of usage, per 100 patient-days of anesthesia, X ray, laboratory, operating room, or delivery room; ancillary services as a ratio to patient care expenditures; number of facilities as a ratio to the maximum number listed for the year; average length of stay; and patient care expenditures as a ratio to inpatient operating expenditures. Using the stepwise method to select variables to be inserted into the regression analysis, Ro found patient care expenditures as a ratio to inpatient operating expenditures to be the most appropriate quality proxy. The hospitals studied ranged in size from 36 to 794 beds, and over this range a significant net relationship between inpatient expenditures per admission and number of admissions prevailed. There was no evidence of a turning point, i.e., that over the specified range the average unit cost function was U-shaped. But Ro points out that "this is not to rule out a U-shaped cost curve for hospitals of all sizes. As size increases beyond 800 beds, managerial diseconomies and decreasing labor efficiency will sooner or later outweigh the economies of further specialization and efficient techniques."[31]

Harold Cohen studied eighty-two hospitals in six Northeastern states— New York, New Jersey, Connecticut, Massachusetts, Delaware, and Vermont. He found average unit hospital costs to be about horizontal over a range of 150 to 350 beds.[32]

Consolidation or decentralization involves services controlled by a single government yet possibly carried out in a number of plants.[33] While it is difficult empirically to develop bona fide quasi-long-run average unit cost functions, those developed in case studies for police protection and refuse collection, discussed earlier in this chapter, might be considered reasonable approximations.[34] Each of these cost studies used proxies in an attempt to introduce quality as independent variables. For these horizontally integrated services no significant scale economies were found for communities from 200 to 865,000 residents (and 200 to 225,000 pickup units). Similar results were found for education, while fire protection showed some small economies of scale up to a nighttime population of about 110,000.

A study by Schmandt and Stephens can also be used to test hypotheses about the quasi-long-run average unit cost function of city police departments, whether they have one or more police stations. Schmandt and Stephens analyzed nineteen cities and villages of Milwaukee County, Wisconsin, and correlated 1959 per capita police protection expenditures with service level and population; no significant scale economies were revealed.[35]

Herbert J. Kiesling checked for economies of scale in primary and secondary New York State schools. He found no economies of scale in school district performance and, indeed, had to fall back on geographic differences between school districts to avoid finding diseconomies.[36]

A distinctly different approach to the study of scale economies has been developed by Robert E. Will.[37] Will's approach relies on a set of "engineering specifications," which in some manner are related to service level and service requirements.[38] Specifically, Will starts by identifying relevant standard units of efforts for particular services. The unit of effort used for the measurement of any given service is some physical unit, or combination of inputs comprising a work unit, such as a street sweeper and its crew. Ideally, a measurable output of service can be associated with the effort unit, and the output can be stated in terms that permit it to be related to a need index. Once standard units of effort have been identified and described, their costs are estimated.

Professional expertise is also used to estimate service requirements in terms of standard units of effort. Will relies on the work of professional associations and students of public administration to identify the need determinants of urban services. The need indicators are then translated directly into standard service requirements through professional application of the rules established by experts. Finally cost estimates are made for the total service requirements; these estimates can also be translated into per capita terms.

Specifically, Will estimated annual per capita standard service requirements for fire protection in dollars for thirty-eight cities varying in size from

50,000 to 1 million. He found per capita standard service requirements for fire protection to vary from $23 to $72.[39] These dollar figures were regressed against city population with the conclusion: ". . . there are significant economies of scale associated with the provision of municipal fire protection services, at standard levels of service, for central cities ranging from 50,000 to nearly one million in population."[40] The statistically significant geometrical relationship was that of a hyperbola eventually becoming asymptotic to the horizontal axis. Major economies of scale were realized for populations up to 300,000; little evidence of such economies was found for larger populations.

Will mentions some basic shortcomings of his method. "The major weakness discovered was that the most significant standards, those set by the National Board of Fire Underwriters for aggregate recommended service levels, had economies of scale already built into them."[41] Furthermore, the engineering standards used did not reflect the possibility that large cities might suffer from top-heavy management, political patronage, etc.

So far we have been concerned with horizontally integrated services. Empirical tests of the quasi-long-run average unit cost functions of circularly integrated services are scarce. However, in one case study of the administration of school districts with 500 to 48,000 pupils in ADA, a U-shaped cost function was discovered that had a trough at an average daily attendance of about 44,000 pupils.[42]

Finally, we can point to a few empirical studies testing the hypothesis about the shape of the quasi-long-run average unit cost function of vertically integrated services. For example, Isard and Coughlin have produced 1953 operating cost data for secondary treatment sewage plants in Massachusetts.[43] A correlation analysis of these data reveals a statistically significant negatively sloping unit cost function.

Marc Nerlove has examined returns to scale in electricity supply, using public utility, not government, data. He correlated production costs with physical output, labor, capital, and fuel prices on a firm basis. The coefficient of multiple determination for 145 privately owned utilities in 1955 was .93 and statistically significant increasing returns to scale were indicated.[44]

A number of gas and electricity cost studies were also made in the United Kingdom. K. S. Lomax found long-run average cost functions declining in relation to gas supply.[45] Likewise, J. Johnston found long-run average cost of electricity supply declining.[46]

These empirical studies come reasonably close to approximating bona fide average unit cost functions. In addition, a larger number of expenditure determinant studies claim conclusions with regard to the existence or absence of economies of scale. Most of them claim that they were unable to detect significant scale economies,[47] although two studies claim to have detected some economies of scale. Nels W. Hanson uses 1958–1959 data for 577 school districts in nine states, with school district enrollment ranging from 1,500 to 847,000. He applies a simple regression analysis of the school district's size with residuals of current expenditures per pupil, adjusted for relationships between school expenditures and characteristics of the adult population of the community. This simple correlation analysis does not adjust for the many crucial factors (especially service quality) that can affect unit cost.[48]

Harvey Shapiro, using 1957 government and 1960 census data, more or less by inspection, concludes that "local governments in the smallest and the largest county areas within different states tend to have highest per capita revenue and expenditures."[49]

Although expenditure studies are inadequate to shed light on the complicated question of economies of scale in rendering urban public services, the cost studies summarized in Table 8.1 offer some insight.

SUMMARY

All costs, including those incurred by state and local governments, can be divided, according to the nature of the resources employed, into operating and capital costs and, according to the nature of the payments made, into direct and indirect costs. Furthermore, we can distinguish between agency and social costs. Agency costs, with which this chapter is concerned, are actual payments made by state and local governments to obtain the services of resources. Social costs entail all the resources required for the government activity, according to their values in their best alternative uses.

Long-run average unit costs of a given service are affected by service quality and quantity, prices of factor inputs, service conditions that affect input requirements, and state of technology. Relatively few empirical state and local government cost functions have been estimated; some examples are presented relative to police protection, refuse collection, fire protection, and hospital services.

Although empirical state and local government cost functions are relatively few, empirical expenditure determinant studies are numerous. The overwhelming majority have employed multiple-regression analysis of cross-section data. Recently, simultaneous-equation techniques have been used as well as multiple-regression analysis of per capita cross-section data, using two equations derived from explicit optimizing behavior of governments. Expenditure determinant studies, although they do not yield bona fide cost functions, can aid in explaining why expenditure levels differ among jurisdictions and services.

TABLE 8.1   Cost Curve Studies of Scale Economies

Name and Year	Service	Type*	Result
Horizontally Integrated Services			
Riew (1966)	High schools	S	AUC is U-shaped with trough at about 1,700 pupils
Kiesling (1966)	Primary and secondary education	S	AUC is about horizontal
Hirsch (1959)	Primary and secondary education	S	AUC is about horizontal
Schmandt-Stephens (1960)	Police protection	S & Q	AUC is about horizontal
Hirsch (1960)	Police protection	S & Q	AUC is about horizontal
Will (1965)	Fire protection	E	AUC is declining with major economies reached at 300,000 population
Hirsch (1959)	Fire protection	S	AUC is U-shaped with trough at about 110,000 population
Hirsch (1965)	Refuse collection	S	AUC is about horizontal
Ro (1952–1963)	Hospitals	S	AUC is declining over the range of 36–794 beds
Cohen (1963–1964)	Hospitals	S	AUC is about horizontal between 150 and 350 beds
Circularly Integrated Services			
Hirsch (1959)	School administration	S	AUC is U-shaped with trough at about 44,000 pupils
Vertically Integrated Services			
Nerlove (1961)	Electricity	S	AUC is declining
Isard-Coughlin (1957)	Sewage plants	S	AUC is declining
Lomax (1951)	Gas	S	AUC is declining
Johnston (1960)	Electricity	S	AUC is declining

* S = statistical data, Q = questionnaire data, E = engineering data, AUC = average unit cost.

An important issue that can be analyzed with the aid of cost functions, as well as production functions, is the presence of scale economies and diseconomies. Consolidation of local government services often results in control over more already existing units, i.e., further horizontal integration. Under conditions not uncommon among local governments, the average quasi-long-run cost function of horizontally integrated services tends to be reasonably horizontal over a wide range of operations. This condition is favored by the fact that, because labor is the major input of local governments, few inputs are bought to secure major price concessions; moreover, location considerations tend to keep plants relatively small.

Local governments also provide vertically integrated services, e.g., electricity and water generation and distribution, which appear to benefit from scale economies, at least over a substantial range of operations. Although empirical investigations have not produced entirely uniform results, some have produced results that are consistent with these theoretical propositions.

CHAPTER 9

SUPPLY
OF STATE
AND LOCAL
GOVERNMENT
SERVICES

The literature reveals that few inquiries have been made into either the conceptual or the empirical aspects of supplying public services. Not much can be learned from the theoretical inquiries that have been made into private sector supply functions, as will be shown below. Thus, several intriguing questions remain to be answered: What is the nature of public service supply functions? Who should supply the public with what services? How well, in the absence of a market price, are persons of different income, race, and location supplied with services?

THE NATURE OF PUBLIC SERVICE SUPPLY AND SUPPLY FUNCTIONS

The supply of state and local government service is related to about the same factors that affect its costs. The supply also depends on the government unit's goals, a fact that greatly complicates the derivation of a public service supply function. A supply function relates service costs to output. There is no theory that explains the precise goals of governments in general and of state and local governments in particular. It appears that most governments have a large number of goals, many of them rather intangible and even conflicting.[1] Then, too, the chain of causality between individual and collective decisions and eventual service procurement is long and complex. In very few cases, if any, would government agencies have the strong profit incentive that is common in private firms.

Marginal cost is an optimality concept that can be used when it can be assumed that some rational maximization (e.g., of profits) on the part of decision makers is pursued. This cannot be done in relation to the suppliers of public services as we have no assurance that the least cost combination of resource inputs, i.e., the lowest cost function of an infinite number of such functions, will be selected by the government unit to produce an additional increment of output.

There is a second reason why we cannot readily derive a government service supply function from its marginal cost function. It relates to the fact that most state and local government services are offered in a market with monopolistic characteristics. Marginal cost is not a supply curve for a monopolist, because it does not portray quantities offered at respective alternative prices.[2]

Having recognized the extreme difficulty of deriving a state and local government supply function from producer marginal cost functions, we would like to seek an alternative formulation. A public official charged with the responsibility of supplying the public with services usually is aware of his rather fixed budget, which can be spent differently depending on what quantities and qualities of the service he decides to offer the public. Thus, in contemplating the supply question, the public official will tend to estimate the cost of providing specified quantity and quality sets of services feasible under a given budget. Not only financial, but legal and political constraints or costs will affect his selection of the quantity-quality package of services to be supplied to the public.

An important legal constraint is the mandate charging governments to provide services for everyone: All children must be given an education, all homes must be protected against fire, all citizens must have access to courts, etc. State and local officials thus frequently find the size of their budgets and the number of people to be served more or less fixed and they make adjustments mainly by varying the quality of the service they supply. For example, whenever budget and population changes are dissimilar, officials must make both quantity and quality adjustments to stay within their budgets. Then, instead of moving along a supply schedule reflecting the net relation between dollars and quantities supplied, they tend to "jump" from one service quantity associated with a given service quality to a second service quantity associated with another quality. One of the most demanding tasks facing public officials, who are forced to serve everybody within a given budget, is to offer different client groups different service qualities in such a manner that future budget increases will receive a majority vote and, given that, the official's survival in government employment is maintained.

How much of a given service is supplied depends also on the production characteristics of the service, specifically, on the presence or absence of technological scale economies. In addition, the government unit's effect on factor prices is important. Government units that purchase relatively large amounts of labor inputs often have some monopsony power and tend to face a positively sloping supply function. In this connection it is less important in the short run that the government buys an absolutely large amount of personnel than that it buys a relatively large amount in terms of resources available in the area.

For example, if the City of Los Angeles were to attempt to double its police force in a few months' time, it would have to bid scarce resources away from other places or from other pursuits, and as a result police salaries would tend to rise substantially. This tendency for salaries to increase is less the result of the very large number of policemen hired than of the fact that in the short run at prevailing salaries only a given number of candidates are available. In relation to this available pool of policemen, demand increases substantially. A similar wage increase might result if Iowa City, Iowa, a much smaller and isolated town, were to double its police force. On the other hand, if a city the same size as Iowa City, but located within the Los Angeles metropolitan area, were to double its police force, it could tap a rather large supply of policemen to fill the relatively small number of positions opened, and we would expect that wages and salaries would barely be affected.

Let us now turn to some aspects of the labor supply functions. While it is useful to look upon the labor supply function of governments that furnish public services in a given area as an aggregate, greater insight can often be obtained by breaking it down. For example, teachers may be drawn from at least five groups at the beginning of a school year: credentialed teachers who return after teaching the previous year, newly trained credentialed teachers, credentialed teachers returning to teaching after an absence, teachers who return to a state with permanent teaching credentials, and teachers with provisional credentials. The supply functions of these five groups can differ. For example, the supply of returning credentialed teachers is likely to be related to the number of teachers teaching in a given state during the previous year, number of retirements and deaths in this group, teachers' salaries in the state generally and in the school district in particular, teachers' salaries in other areas, and alternative pursuits to teaching. On the other hand, the supply of teachers with provisional credentials is related to the number of persons who meet minimum teaching qualifications, ease with which they can obtain provisional credentials, teachers' salaries in the state in general and in the school district in particular, teachers' salaries in other areas, and salaries in alternative pursuits.

It is not uncommon to hear reports of shortages in certain classes of public employees, such as teachers or nurses.[3] What is usually meant by such statements is that the number of employees of a certain type is less than the author of the statement would like it to be, even though there may be no shortage in the economic sense. However, not all reported shortages are of this nature. A shortage may be said to exist in the economic sense when quantity demanded exceeds quantity supplied at the prevailing price. In labor markets, this situation is often manifested by job vacancies. We do observe local governments attempting to hire, for example, additional nurses who possess the same qualifications as those already employed, at the wage paid to those currently employed, and finding no more available at that wage.

Several shortage concepts have been advanced in the literature to explain job vacancies. The most widely used concept of shortage relies on price or wage controls; quantity demanded will exceed quantity supplied when a price ceiling is imposed at a level below the market-clearing price. A variant of this, widely utilized by local governments, is the single salary schedule. Employees working under such a schedule may perform different tasks (such as policemen and firemen), or have different alternative opportunities (such as high school physics teachers and physical education teachers), but are paid according to the same salary schedule. Joseph Kershaw and Roland McKean found that the single salary schedule was a significant factor in the current shortage of high school teachers in several subjects.[4] It can also result in job vacancies when a school district is prevented from paying differential salaries for teaching on different grade levels or at different locations within a city.

The concept of a dynamic shortage was applied to the market for engineers and scientists in the 1950s.[5] This concept is based upon a lag in the response of salaries to a shift in demand.

A firm's demand shifts first when it recognizes that it wants to hire more personnel at prevailing wages, but cannot do so. Vacancies will exist until salaries are raised above the current levels and will persist if the demand keeps increasing.

Job vacancies may also exist if the economic unit is a monopsonist (which we define here as an employer facing an upward-sloping factor supply curve) and is unable, for some reason, to engage in wage discrimination.[6] Local governments are typically constrained from discriminating in the payment of wages. The existence of monopsony power is also implicit in the two shortage concepts discussed above. If a school district with a single salary schedule faced a perfectly elastic supply curve for, say, physics teachers having certain qualifications, and the wage was set below the equilibrium wage, the district would obtain no qualified physics teachers. However, we observe that school districts do obtain some qualified physics teachers at the prevailing wage, but not as many as they would like; this implies that these districts face an upward-sloping supply curve. The dynamic shortage concept is similarly applicable only to an economic unit facing an upward-sloping supply curve. If the unit faced a perfectly elastic supply curve, and its demand curve shifted to the right, it would be able to secure all the additional personnel it wanted at the prevailing wage.

Eugene Devine found that in 1967 the Los Angeles County Department of Hospitals had a registered nurse vacancy rate of 27 percent, both the City Police Department and the County Sheriff's Office had a police vacancy rate of 5 percent, and the Watts area of Los Angeles had a high school teachers shortage of about 17 percent.

WHICH GOVERNMENT SHOULD SUPPLY WHAT SERVICES?

Under fiscal federalism, it is conceivable that Federal, state, and local governments could all be actively engaged in supplying people with services. But in line with American tradition, the Federal government has taken a back seat, leaving the production and supply of nonmilitary services mainly up to local governments (i.e., counties, cities, and districts) and, to a lesser extent, state governments.

In this examination of local government services, it should be kept in mind that spillovers can be adjusted for by intergovernmental fiscal measures. In most cases cities cover smaller territories than do districts and counties. Most districts are parts of one county, although a few districts are larger than a single county. The decision about which of these three local governments might best supply citizens with services can be made mainly in terms of efficiency considerations. Specifically, it is important to decide whether local or areawide governments perform certain services more efficiently. Income redistribution considerations can be handled with the aid of intergovernmental instruments. Whether a given government's service is more efficiently supplied by a small municipality or a large county or district can be determined in terms of three criteria: scale economy, people-government proximity, and multiprogrammatic jurisdictions.

Benefiting from scale economies leads to unit cost reduction. In part, on the basis of a number of economic studies, it appears that the following government services are likely to enjoy major economies of scale: air pollution control, sewage disposal, public transportation, power, water, public health services, hospitals, and planning.[7]

Most of the other government units serving more than about 50,000 inhabitants are unlikely to enjoy major economies of scale, if any.

This does not deny that certain specialized services, e.g., crime laboratories, information on criminals, rare book collections, etc., can incur scale economies. Sometimes, these highly specialized services can be assigned to higher levels of government without consolidating all elements of the service or program.

Proximity of people to government is favored because it can exert pressures on government officials and induce them to operate on relatively low average unit cost functions. Furthermore, in a democracy we believe in active participation of citizens in their government (see Chapter 6). Services for which close citizen participation appears particularly important include education, libraries, public housing, welfare services, police protection, and fire protection. In relation to transportation, planning, parks and recreation, and urban renewal, proximity appears to have mixed benefits, as citizen participation enriches democratic procedure but, at the same time, tends to delay decisive socially desirable action.

The importance of multiprogrammatic jurisdictions is pointed out by the Advisory Commission on Intergovernmental Relations: Every unit of government should be responsible for a sufficient number of functions so that its governing processes involve a resolution of conflicting interests, with significant responsibility for balancing government needs and resources.[8] This view can readily be related to organization theory. In addition, the advantages and disadvantages of multiprogrammatic jurisdictions can be analyzed with the aid of microeconomic theory. Specifically, functions can be examined in terms of their complementary versus competitive relationships, which in turn bear on costs.

Next is the question of which services should be supplied by local governments and which by the state government. Using the same three criteria mentioned above, i.e., scale economy, people-government proximity, and multiprogrammatic jurisdictions, we can point to some services as candidates for state governments. Some of these services involve a need to maintain uniform performance, which is difficult and often costly when many small units must be coordinated. One example is welfare payments; they should be administered uniformly and involve the distribution branch of government, which is more appropriate to state than local governments. Other examples are highway and freeway patrol and possibly air and water pollution control.

On the basis of these criteria, and granting that income redistribution objectives can be met by a variety of Federal and state intergovernmental fiscal instruments, the following conclusions suggest themselves: Local governments, particularly if they serve 50,000 to 100,000 citizens, are likely to effectively provide education, library service, public housing, public welfare services, fire and police protection, refuse collection, parks and recreation, urban renewal, and street maintenance programs. Services which appear to be best provided on a district or countywide basis are air pollution control, sewage disposal, transportation, water, electric power, public health services, planning, and hospitals.[9] State governments can best render welfare payment service, patrol highways, and, possibly, control air and water pollution.

In considering the positive question of who does supply services, we find substantial discrepancies between our ideal and the actual situation. Tradition, it can be argued, is one of the many reasons for the existing pattern of service delivery. We have discussed some of the supply forces that encourage retention of the current system or allow only small changes in it. The foundation of today's primary and secondary public school system was laid by Thomas Jefferson, who insisted on locally controlled and financed education.

While such an arrangement suited an agrarian early nineteenth-century economy, it is inappropriate, we believe, for a highly urbanized, industrialized, and mobile twentieth-century economy. As yet, major reorganization of our education system has not taken place.

SERVICE DISTRIBUTION

Earlier we argued that local governments should concentrate on a policy of allocating resources efficiently and that, in the redistribution of income, state governments should at best play a role secondary to that of the Federal government (see "Policy Missions" in Chapter 1). This view is especially relevant to revenue raising. However, it is quite clear that no government that makes allocative decisions and distributes services can do so without to some extent affecting people's welfare.

Governments that supply services at zero or nominal charges must make important distributive decisions. They must deal with the normative question: Who should receive what quantities and qualities of what services—households or businesses, persons or property, rich or poor, blacks or whites, young or old, residents of A or B, etc? Since most state and local government services are not pure public goods, some degree of exclusion can be practiced, but normative questions of equity and efficiency must be answered. In addition to the normative issue of who should be served, there is the positive issue of who indeed is served. Each question will be taken up in turn.

Who Should Receive Services?

State and local government services can be supplied in line with one of three major distribution rules. First, service distribution based on an input equality rule requires that resource *inputs* per service recipient be equalized among all service areas. Second, distribution based on an output equality rule requires that service *output* per recipient be equalized among all service areas. Third, there is what might be called the efficiency rule, which requires that the marginal product of resource inputs be equal in all uses or, stated equivalently, that the marginal cost per unit of output be equal in all uses. The efficiency rule corresponds to the goal of maximum *total* output, using given resources. Thus, in considering service distribution we have the same conflict between equity and efficiency criteria that arises in discussions of income distribution. In addition, with government service distribution we lack good measures of units of output.

Normative issues of service distribution can be considered in relation to police protection, which involves complicated policy considerations.[10] Local police protection, unlike national defense, is not automatically provided in about equal amounts to all citizens of a police jurisdiction. In national defense, essentially the same protection from foreign aggression is provided to all citizens of the nation, and though different persons may value differently the protection thus afforded, they all receive the same amount of protection. However, even within the jurisdiction of a single local police department the quantity and quality of police service given different groups often vary significantly. We are constrained to organize distribution of police protection according to geographic area or division instead of specific recipients such as income class or race. But in many cases geographic location is a good proxy for the socioeconomic characteristics of its residents, and information on a geographic breakdown can be very illuminating.[11]

There are no easy ways to measure police output. The rate of crime against persons or property, per 1,000 residents per year, signifies the probability that any person in a given division will become the victim of a crime in a given year; such a rate might be a rough indication of police output. The lower the probability of victimization, the greater the output of the police department.

The population of each geographic division is a most important factor affecting the crime rate, and the basic crime-inducing characteristics of our society are largely beyond the control of the police.[12] The police have little influence on such crimes as homicide committed by a member of the victim's own family, and thus a crime rate purporting to indicate the level of protective service achieved by the police should exclude those crimes found least susceptible to police control. Furthermore, not all crimes are of equal importance, and it is quite likely that a crime rate obtained by simply adding together different types of crimes will give a misleading picture. Thus, although the number of major felony offenses per 1,000 residents is a rough indicator of exposure to crime in each division, such a rate is defective as a measure of the relative protection from crime that persons in each division receive, for at least four reasons: (1) the police can have relatively little effect on the commission of such crimes as homicide within a family, (2) not all felonies are of equal seriousness, (3) crimes other than major felonies should also be considered, and (4) the proportion of total crimes that are reported to the police may vary among divisions.

Once we have devised a good measure of the crime rate, one that accurately measures the probability of a person's becoming a victim of crime, weighted by the importance of the crime, in each division, we have made progress in relation to a rational distribution of police protection.

The potential conflict between our first two distribution criteria, input equality and output equality, is illustrated in Figure 9.1.[13]

Consider two police divisions, 1 and 2, within a city. Assume that because of social forces, e.g., lack of employment opportunities, in division 1, for any

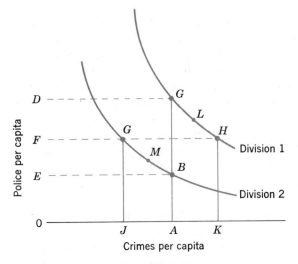

FIGURE 9.1 Police-crime relationship.

given number of police per capita the crime rate is higher in 1 than in 2. Given the total number of police resources (including policemen and equipment), an allocation of police officers that would result in an equal crime rate per capita in divisions 1 and 2 would necessarily involve a much higher ratio of police per capita in 1 than in 2. Such a situation is illustrated in the diagram, where each division has the same crime rate A, while division 1 has D and division 2 has E police per capita. If instead each division were allocated the same number of police per capita (equality in an input rather than an output sense) division 1 would have a much higher crime rate than division 2.

Carl Shoup has demonstrated the conflict between the goal of output equality in terms of equal crime rates among divisions and the goal of minimizing the total number of crimes in the city.[14] Minimization of the total number of crimes occurs when, with an allocation of police that produces equality among all divisions in terms of the crime rate, the marginal product of a police officer is higher in one area than in another. This corresponds to our third distribution rule, that of efficiency. In terms of Figure 9.1, suppose police resources are allocated to produce equal output per capita, so that the crime rate in each division is A; i.e., there are D police per capita in division 1, and E police per capita in division 2. Also suppose that an additional police officer in division 1 reduces the number of crimes per year by 5, and that an additional policeman in division 2 reduces the number of crimes per year by 10. In this situation, the total number of crimes in the city would be reduced by 5 if one officer were removed from division 1 (increasing the number of crimes there by 5) and assigned to division 2 (decreasing the number of crimes there by 10). In general, the total number of crimes in the city will be minimized only when the marginal effect of an additional policeman on the number of crimes is the same in each division. Otherwise, it would always be possible to reallocate police resources from a division in which the marginal product of police resources was lower to one in which the marginal product was higher and thereby reduce the total number of crimes in the city. However, this would then lead to a departure from the criterion of equal output distribution and to a conflict between the output equality and efficiency rules of distribution, in addition to the previously mentioned conflict between the input equality and output equality rules.

Who Does in Fact Receive Services?

Both because of a desire to reconcile conflicting guidelines, as discussed above, and because of the political process by which distribution decisions are reached, it is not clear that actual service distribution can be much elucidated by the above normative inquiries. Just as state and local officials have no clear-cut incentive to be efficient, they have no such incentive to be distributively neutral.

The nature and structure of the government have a direct bearing on the extent to which officials are responsive to the desires of their constituents and supply them with the services they want or should have. For example, a nonelective board, responsible only to a very narrow interest group, can—virtually with impunity—ignore the desires of the great majority of the community. It can become a strong power center in its own area because its dependence on such centralized powers as the mayor, governor, or a political party is slight. At the same time, the authority of a mayor or governor can be reduced by historical precedent in budget allocation and by lesser government agencies' control over patronage and access to supporting organizations.

Service distribution is also affected by the degree of intra- or interparty competition, the level of individual political participation, and the extent of general public interest in specific issues. For example, with less competition, less participation, and less general interest in an issue, public officials' responsiveness to constituents' desires will diminish accordingly. Although public officials may have a difficult task in identifying consumer demand, they tend to be sensitive to the desires of groups whose votes may go either way and thus turn elections against them. Lack of information and high costs of political activity can result in a bias against lower socioeconomic groups and against individuals not represented by strong interest groups.[15] Or a bias can be formed against the general public if a small group which stands to benefit from a decision strongly articulates its demands while most of the community expresses no opinion.

The inadequacy of bargaining mechanisms and of incentives to cooperate in seeking a solution is a determining factor in political allocational decisions. A bias may be created in favor of the small interest group that with-holds its support and scuttles a decision if the mayor or governor does not have the power and (or) the desire to actively seek an integration of the demands of various groups. Such an environment creates a tendency to hold out for more, to appeal all decisions, etc., with resulting inactions and delays imposed on the majority.

In summary, service distribution is influenced by officials who trade off the costs and benefits they are likely to incur as a result of their favoring one or another service distribution pattern.

Relatively little is known about the actual distribution of state and local government services by location, race, religion, income class, or other cate-gories—mainly because records are not kept in those terms. Furthermore, there are occasions when discrimination is practiced which officials do not want known to the public.

Education is one of the few services for which attempts have been made to provide some measurements of service distribution. For example, in rela-tion to social class, a study was carried out in the aftermath of the Watts riots in Los Angeles. Kenneth Martyn compared certain key characteristics of four districts of the Los Angeles school system that mainly serve socially and economically "underprivileged" children—the Watts, East Los Angeles, Boyle Heights, and Avalon school districts—with those of "privileged" school dis-tricts.[16] He found substantial inequality in the supply of education to "privi-leged" and "underprivileged" districts, often in favor of the "underprivileged" districts. For example, the pupil-teacher ratio in the four "underprivileged" districts ranged from 27.8 to 29.7, while the ratio in the "privileged" districts averaged 31.9.

Although one would expect that a higher proportion of portable class-rooms were used in the disadvantaged areas because they have higher growth rates, this proved not to be the case. Average annual expenditures per average daily attendance (ADA) for maintenance were $30.75 in the "underprivi-leged" and $28.24 in the "privileged" school districts. Also, expenditures on textbook funds, both per junior and per senior high school pupil, were higher in the "underprivileged" districts. The picture was the same in relation to expenses for instructional supplies. Finally, while per pupil in ADA annual expenditure for elementary schools was about the same in the "underprivi-leged" and "privileged" districts, junior and senior high schools in the "underprivileged" school districts spent substantially more than did those in the "privileged" districts. For example, for junior high schools the figure was $384 in "underprivileged" districts compared with $365 in "privileged" dis-tricts. And for senior high schools, the figure was $447 in "underprivileged" districts compared with $385 in "privileged" districts.

Not all figures favored the "underprivileged" districts. If the quality of teachers is measured in terms of permanent versus probationary or conditional teaching certificates, or formal education, or the length of experience, etc., the figures favored the "privileged" districts.

Some of the distribution characteristics of public education in the Boston public schools were examined by Martin Katzman. He found that in different Boston schools, costs per pupil do not vary significantly with race or with median family income.[17]

Early in the 1960s, in a study of the distribution of input measures, e.g., teacher training, guidance facilities, etc., in a large city high school system, Patricia C. Sexton found a systematic bias against lower-income groups.[18]

While Katzman found no significant statistical relationship between race and income, on the one hand, and costs per pupil, on the other, he found the two variables strongly related to such output measures as changes in reading score and percentage continuation rate attributed to school inputs, i.e., education quality. He estimated the following multiple-regression equations:

$$O_3 = 74.0 + \underline{0.663S_4} + \underline{0.008S_6} - 0.479S_{12} - 0.127P + 0.982S_{13} \quad (9.1)$$

$$O_6 = 4.5 + \underline{0.169S_4} + \underline{0.002S_6} - 0.006S_{12} + \underline{0.238P} + \underline{0.532S_{13}} \quad (9.2)$$

where

O_3 = median change in reading scores attributable to school inputs
O_6 = percentage annual continuation (in school) rate
S_4 = percentage of white population
S_6 = median family income
S_{12} = percentage of Irish
P = percentage of public elementary school participation
S_{13} = percentage of voter participation

The coefficient of multiple determination adjusted for degrees of freedom in the first equation is .6320 and in the second is .8838, and in both cases the coefficients are statistically significant at a probability level of 0.05. Statistically significant regression coefficients at a 0.05 level of significance are underlined.[19]

On the basis of these partial empirical results, it appears that, under the impetus of Federal programs, culturally and economically deprived schools probably tend to have per pupil expenditures equal to, or even larger than, those of schools in advantaged areas. However, the latter tend to enjoy teachers who are better prepared and more able—possibly the result of the sensitivity of advantaged schools to the electorate, as well as the preference of teachers for such schools. This may indicate another tendency to reach a compromise between input and output equality in our schools, the Federal government providing compensatory fiscal arrangements that are designed to bring schools closer to output equality.

Finally, we turn briefly to some empirical evidence about the distribution of police services. When police costs and output indicators are examined on a geographic breakdown, it is possible to approximate who is receiving how much service at what cost. For instance, in 1967 Los Angeles was divided into sixteen police divisions for purposes of administration. If we take police expenditure per capita in each division as a measure of service to residents, we get one ranking of service in the divisions. We find that, excluding the central business district division, the highest per capita expenditure is 3.4 times the lowest per capita expenditure. An alternative measure of police protective service is the crime rate reported in each division. The division crime rate, reported offenses per 1,000 residents per year, is an indicator of the likelihood that a division resident will be a crime victim. Since reduction in crime is an output of a police department, a low crime rate corresponds to a high level of service, and a high crime rate corresponds to a low level of service. If we take the crime rate in terms of major felony offenses per 1,000 residents in each division as the measure of police service, the ranking is almost a perfect inverse of the previous ranking: Those divisions that score high in terms of police expenditure per capita also have the highest crime rates (i.e., lowest service) and, again excluding the central division, the highest reported crime rate is 2.8 times the lowest.[20]

In view of the conflict between the two equality goals, there appears to be a tendency to compromise between input and output equality. As a result more police per capita are allocated to high crime areas than to low crime areas, but the concentration of police in the higher crime areas is not carried so far as to produce an equal crime rate in all divisions.[21]

SUMMARY

The supply of state and local government services is related to the various factors that affect the cost of services as well as to the goals of the particular government unit. A supply function relates service costs to output. Unlike private firms that have in common a strong profit incentive, state and local governments appear to pursue a variety of goals, many of them conflicting. Marginal costs, an optimality concept useful only when decision makers pursue some rational maximization, e.g., of profits, does not readily apply to state and local governments. There is no assurance that the least cost combination of resource inputs and therefore the lowest cost function will be selected by the government. A second reason why a government service supply function cannot readily be derived from its marginal cost function relates to the monopolistic characteristics of markets in which state and local government services are offered. Thus, marginal cost is not a supply curve for a monopolist because it does not portray quantities offered at respective alternative prices.

Since state and local government supply functions cannot readily be derived from marginal cost functions, alternative formulations of supply are explored. State and local officials usually face a more or less fixed size of budget and number of people to be served and they make adjustments mainly by varying the quality of the service they supply. Therefore, instead of moving along a line reflecting the net relation between dollars and quantity supply, they tend to jump from one line associated with one service quality to a second line associated with another quality.

A common complaint of state and local governments is a shortage in certain classes of public employees. A government's demand for public employees shifts first when it recognizes that it wants to hire more personnel at prevailing wages, but cannot do so. Vacancies will exist until salaries are raised above the current levels and will persist if the demand keeps increasing. Job vacancies may also exist if the economic unit is a monopsonist, i.e., faces an upward-sloping factor supply curve, and is unable to engage in wage discrimination.

Important questions are: Who should supply the public with what services? What considerations should enter into this decision? For example, the decision whether a small municipality or a large county or district should offer specified services relates to the unit's ability to perform the services efficiently. Useful criteria are scale economy, people-government proximity, and multiprogrammatic jurisdictions. About the same criteria can be applied to the decision whether a local government or the state should supply a specified service.

Finally, there is the question: In the absence of a market price, how well should persons of different income, race, age, and location be supplied with specified services, and indeed how well are they supplied? Three major distribution rules are examined: input equality, which requires that resource inputs per recipient be equalized among all areas; output equality, which requires that equal service output per recipient be equalized among areas; and output maximization, which requires that marginal cost per unit of output be equal in all uses. The first two rules relate to equity, and the third relates to resource allocation efficiency. These three rules are in conflict.

In addition to the normative issue of who should receive services, there is the positive issue of who indeed receives services. The need to reconcile conflicting guidelines, as well as the political process by which distribution decisions are reached, makes us wonder whether actual service distribution is much elucidated by normative inquiries. The nature and structure of the government, the degree of intra- and interparty competition, the level of political participation, and the extent of general public interest in the specific issue— all influence officials who distribute state and local government services. Basically, officials trade off the costs and benefits they are likely to incur as a result of favoring one or another service distribution pattern. That officials do so is indicated in the few empirical studies that have been made of the distribution of education and police protection services.

CHAPTER 10
REGULATION

State and local governments impose various regulations to provide an environment and "rules of the game" within which households, industry, commerce, and governments can well perform their activities. Regulation—although it does not produce as tangible a product as does transportation, water delivery, or refuse collection—can have a major effect on production, costs, and supply and demand for the private as well as the public sector. As a result, it can change benefit-cost relations as perceived by private and public decision makers and thus affect welfare. We will concentrate on regulation of the transportation-communications network and of land uses, since these are the main regulatory functions of state and local governments.

The importance of regulation can be demonstrated in relation to its impact on decentralization and urban sprawl. For example, Irving Hoch identifies four government activities that can lead to decentralization; three of the activities are regulatory in nature. They are zoning of building height limits, zoning prohibition of mixed land uses, and pricing of the infrastructure.[1]

The transportation-communications network, when considered in its broadest context, encompasses all those means whereby goods and services are distributed. A narrower concept reduces it to include only those operations that are directly related to spatial movements, and to exclude interregional movements as well as movements within the confines of a single property. In brief, the transportation-communications network comprises modes of transportation (i.e., highways and streets for vehicles and pedestrians, and railways and other specialized constructions including pneumatic delivery systems); communications (i.e., telephone and telegraph services, radio and television transmissions, postal and other message delivery services, and, with an eye to the future, computer utilities); and power and water (i.e., electricity and gas transmission, water distribution, and sewage collection, processing, and disposal).

Land can be put to different uses, some public and some private; among the important private uses are agricultural, residential, recreational, commercial, and industrial, and many subdivisions are possible in each group.

The transportation-communications network and land uses are regulated by different governments. For example, the Federal government has been regulating radio and television services, as well as utilities that for technological and historical reasons cross state boundaries. Both state and local governments engage in major regulation of the transportation network, while local governments dominate the regulation of land uses.

REGULATION INSTRUMENTS

Government can use certain legal instruments to regulate the transportation-communications network and land uses. There are at least four instruments that apply to network regulations; they differ mainly in their comprehensiveness and definiteness. The most comprehensive instrument of regulation is outright government ownership of the transportation-communications network operation; the government either operates the system itself or leases the system, as an input, to private utility firms. Examples of elements of the network owned by government are water supplies, transit systems, and electric utilities.

The second instrument is the legislative directive, which can take the form of a law that applies specifically to the operation or performance of privately owned networks (e.g., utility lines must be underground) or which is general but bears most heavily on the network (e.g., a pollution control law prohibiting the burning of certain types of fuel). Still another form of legislative directive is the franchise for a privately owned network, a contract between the government and a network operator that stipulates performance requirements, pricing policies, service quantity and quality requirements, etc.

The third approach to regulation of the transportation-communications network is through a commission, a quasi legislative-judicial-administrative body, the members of which are given some discretion in establishing and changing rules. Commissioners are usually appointed, often for long and staggered terms of office to make them independent of the executive and legislative authorities. The commission approach is intended to bring the public interest to bear on the transportation-communications network without involving the government in the ownership or management of the operation. This approach usually is supplementary to the initial legislative authority.

Finally, a government can use a variety of indirect or informal controls, e.g., taxation, subsidies, depreciation allowances, and master planning.

Considering instruments used to regulate land uses, we can begin with a master plan which is implemented with the aid of a city zoning ordinance. By zoning, we mean:

> ... The division of land into districts having different regulations .... such regulations shall be made in accordance with a comprehensive plan and designed to lessen congestion in the streets; to secure safety from fire, panic, and other dangers; to promote health and the general welfare; to provide adequate light and air; to prevent the overcrowding of land; to avoid undue concentration of population; to facilitate the adequate provision of transportation, water, sewage, schools, parks and other public requirements. Such regulations shall be made with reasonable consideration, among other things, of the character of the district and its peculiar suitability for particular uses, and with a view to conserving the value of buildings and encouraging the most appropriate use of land throughout such municipalities.[2]

It is apparent from the above definition that zoning can amount to far more than defining the homogeneity of land use with respect to the ouput of improvements. Zoning can be used for such diverse purposes as enforcement of building codes, regulation of factory operations, restriction of floor space relative to site area, and control of population density. The unique feature of zoning, compared with other municipal regulations, is its discriminatory nature. Different zoning regulations apply in different parts or districts of a community.

Zoning originated in the early days of the Industrial Revolution in Germany and Sweden. The first American zoning ordinance was enacted in New York City in 1916 to keep glue factories and other dirty, noisy, or bustling plants away from residential areas and retailing centers. The zone or district approach of the United States is based on two notions: (1) like users belong together and such groupings are "natural" and reasonable, and (2) certain areas of the community, because of terrain or location within the community, are most appropriate to a particular land use.[3] Municipal zoning is the joint product of a commission, mayor, and city council, culminating, after public hearings, in an alteration of a city zoning ordinance and master plan, should such a plan exist. A similar process takes place on the county level. To increase flexibility, three zoning instruments are common among municipalities—zone change, zone variance, and conditional use permit.[4]

ECONOMICS OF REGULATION

In functional terms, regulation by state and local governments is designed to promote what is often loosely referred to as the general welfare. This applies equally to the transportation-communications network and to land uses. Authorization for this function is provided by the 1928 Standard City Planning Enabling Act of the U.S. Department of Commerce. The act states: "The plan shall be made with the general purpose of guiding and accomplishing a coordinated, adjusted, and harmonious development of the municipality and its environs which will ... best promote health, safety, morals, order, convenience, prosperity, and general welfare, as well as efficiency and economy in the process of development. ..."[5]

Goals and Welfare Dimensions

What is meant by promoting an area's general welfare? Seeking to attain a resource allocation efficiency criterion is not the same as promoting the general welfare, for it promotes only one aspect of the general welfare. To illustrate this point: It might be highly efficient to allow the old or disabled members of our society to starve to death or to endow 1 percent of the population with 99 percent of the wealth of the economy, but neither would promote the general welfare. Equitable distribution of income, economic stability, and economic growth are objectives to be considered as well as efficiency.

The four objectives mentioned will conflict when an economy attempts their simultaneous achievement. The widespread conflict between efficiency and equity goals is dominant in any economic consideration of regulation in general, and land use planning in particular.

The main concern of regulation at the state and local levels—particularly at the local level—should, we believe, be economic efficiency, with the state government only somewhat concerned with regulation for equitable distribution of income. As was mentioned earlier, the Federal government holds major, if not exclusive, responsibility for the attainment of distributional, growth, and stability objectives. Given ideal assumptions and definitions, the attainment of economic efficiency would be tantamount to the maximization of aggregate income with a given set of resources and distribution of income. Aggregate income would include items that are intangible in their financial value, since by their nature they do not pass through the market. For example, freedom from air pollution is generally thought to have financial value, but there are few feasible methods of purchasing this good in an air market.

External Effects and Efficiency

There are several defects in our economy that prevent the attainment of efficiency—most noticeably, external effects or spillovers, which were defined earlier.[6] Roland McKean has given us some vivid spillover examples.[7]

Coping with spillovers is of particular concern to land use regulation. It is important to find institutional devices by which the impact of the externalities will be compensated for or prevented. In the case of noisy trucks, compensation or prevention could be ensured by assigning the property right of quiet to the offended person, thereby necessitating purchase, lease, or silence by the noisy truck. Another somewhat older line of thought on coping with externalities is government intervention in the process. It has often been proposed that the government tax the culprit and compensate the victim or that the government take over the ownership of rights so that the external effects are internalized to the political process, since the costs and rewards accrue to a single government enterprise.

Thus, land use planning and zoning are founded on the necessity of correcting for spillover effects that are not handled adequately in any marketplace. Were a marketplace able to accomplish the appropriate corrections for spillover effects, there would be no need for land use regulations. It is the externality problem, perhaps more than any other, that brings the land use regulator into the allocative process. Land use planning and zoning must be designed to ensure that private and public decision makers act in such a manner that the spillover effects produce the largest net social benefits for the community. Or, in negative terms, the land use regulator primarily seeks to prevent potentially harmful steps that would reduce the income (broadly construed) of the community. In short, zoning can be looked upon as a government intervention to correct a market defect.

The land use regulator can adjust spillover effects in various ways. One method is to intervene in the ongoing interplay of market forces in order to try to create an environment in which efficiency can be attained. Zoning ordinances, compulsory dedication requirements, and urban renewal are examples of this method.

Zoning in the United States derives its legal basis from the police powers of state government. Unlike laws based on the right of eminent domain, zoning regulations do not require compensation for losses in property value or income to private individuals. Since zoning can make one person better off at the expense of another person, without the latter being compensated, zoning therefore tends to defy Pareto optimality conditions.

Forms of Regulation

Taking different forms, regulation can relate to output, production relationships, and pricing and market conditions. The three forms will be briefly considered.

In attempting to regulate output policy of the transportation-communications network, government can concern itself with the quantity and (or) quality of the service by specifying the service conditions that the operator must meet. In many instances, highly technical specifications are furnished; e.g., a regulatory commission might specify that water pressure or electric voltage must not fall below a specified minimum level within a city. Technical specifications for transportation can include time and frequency of service, availability of service, safety, and area of service as well as location of stops. In a few instances, government regulates input policy or the use of techniques in the transportation-communications network, e.g., the maximum ratio of capital to labor.

There are also various policies for regulation of pricing and market entry conditions. For such operations as water, electricity, gas, and telephone service a single firm is given exclusive rights to a market. In other cases, notably taxicab service and other for-hire transportation, there may not be an exclusive geographic division of the market, but the entry of new firms is controlled. Potential monopoly rents may be reduced by taxation, stipulation of service requirements, or regulatory attempts to equate price to marginal or average cost. Where discriminatory pricing might be the profit maximizing policy for the transportation-communications network operator, government regulation may require that a single price be charged to all consumers. Where different price schedules are permitted, the rates and bases for differentiation may be regulated.

Land use regulation can take the form of an output policy or a production relationship policy, but not of a pricing policy. An output policy type of control is, for example, a zoning ordinance stipulating the location in which a certain type of activity or establishment is permitted and from which other types are excluded. On the other hand, land use regulation concerned with production relationships entails zoning ordinances that stipulate the location in which a certain level of population density and floor space, or of bulk and spacing of structures, is permitted.

A FRAMEWORK FOR IMPACT ANALYSIS

An analytic structure is needed within which the impact of regulation can be better understood, traced, and—as conceptual and empirical methods improve—measured. The area interaction model offers such a framework; it is composed of four major elements which can be visualized with the aid of a flow chart in which each element is represented by a box (see Figure 10.1). Box 1 represents external forces and is wired directly to boxes 2 and 3, internal area-government sector environment (e.g., regulating transportation-communications network or land use), and internal private sector environment, respectively. Boxes 2 and 3 are also wired to each other. All three boxes, in turn, are wired to box 4, denoting the region's welfare, or health and well-being. Boxes 1, 2, and 3 are the inputs and jointly affect box 4, the outputs. Clearly, there are numerous feedbacks. Activities of area government in box 2 interact with activities represented in boxes 1 and 3, with a resultant flow to box 4, where the impact on the area's welfare is registered. Often there is a feedback from box 4.

Let us see how the area interaction model facilitates our understanding, for example, of the effects of planning and zoning. Zoning changes produce modifications in the environment or "rules of the game" of the private sector, which result in a change of the supply of factor inputs and (or) a change in how factor inputs can be combined in the production function of the private sector. The changed private sector environment brought about by planning and zoning affects the area's welfare and can be traced. If the full information required within this model were given, then it would be possible to identify and measure the product of regulation, i.e., the difference between the area's aggregate income and income distribution prior to and after regulation. Finally, the model makes explicit allowances for reverse flows and feedbacks.

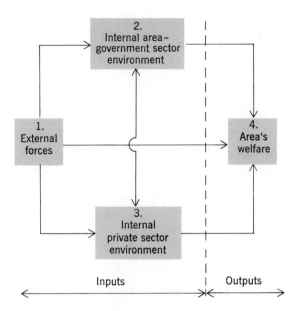

FIGURE 10.1   Area interaction model.

We now are ready to introduce into the area interaction model some network and land use detail. Figure 10.2 concentrates on sectors 2 and 3, and particularly on transportation and land use regulation in sector 2. We should note that insofar as the transportation-communications network is concerned, fields to be regulated are transportation (T), communications (C), and power and water (P), and that the regulation can take the form of an output policy, production relationship, or pricing policies. In short, there are nine "dials" altogether in box 2, designed to help regulate the transportation-communications network. Each of these dials directly affects box 3 and, to a lesser extent, boxes 1 and 2.

Turning to land uses, government regulates: (a) industrial-commercial-agricultural land uses; (b) recreational land uses; (c) residential land uses; and (d) land taken up by the transportation-communications network. Specifically, it regulates output and production relationships. Thus, there are eight land use regulation dials in box 2. Those referring to the output policy and production relationships of industrial-commercial-agricultural land uses and of residential land uses directly affect box 3. Two sets of dials, referring to output policy and production relationships of recreational land uses, basically affect other parts of box 2 and, in turn, box 3. Finally, the two sets of dials referring to output policy and production relationships, of land put to the uses of the transportation-communications network, directly affect both boxes 2 and 3.

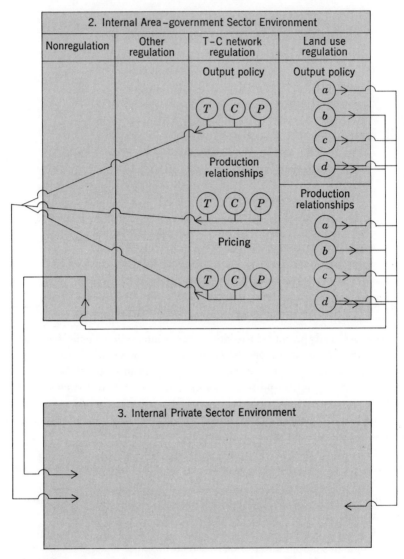

Legend:

T = transportation
C = communications
P = power and water
a = industrial–commercial–agricultural land use
b = recreational land use
c = residential land use
d = transportation–communications network

FIGURE 10.2   *Two amplified sectors of the area interaction model.*

Activities taking place on parcels of land assigned to these four land uses ultimately produce the area's output. The activities on the different parcels can be looked upon as parts of an activity vector which makes up a home and a business enterprise, with the business enterprise constituting an activity of the final area output vector—homes. Thus, home and business enterprises are each multidimensional activity vectors. In this setting, government, developer, owner and (or) user of home or business enterprise, and neighbor are prime transactors. These transactors engage in activities which convert residential (or commercial-industrial-agricultural) land parcels into a house (or business activity), i.e., the physical shell, and finally into a home (or business enterprise).

Government often plans, zones, and provides certain social overhead, which helps prepare parcels of land for development. The developer, particularly in the city, builds residential or industrial-commercial property. Both government and developer take steps to start the conversion of a physical facility into a home or business enterprise. But mainly under the initiative of owner and (or) user, the conversion into home or business enterprise proceeds, with government and neighbors interacting to various degrees.

Thus, government participates virtually continuously in the creation of house, business activity, recreation facility, and transportation-communications network, and the conversion into business enterprise and home. State and local government participation takes the form of regulation and outright rendering of services in the form of final tangible products.

NETWORK REGULATION ANALYSIS

We will now consider some effects of network regulation on spatial arrangements, especially cities. In a certain sense, a city owes its existence largely to the positive costs of using space in the production and exchange of goods and services.[8] The fundamental advantages of the marketplace are the opportunities to economize on the cost of transporting goods, people, information, and ideas. These advantages are at the heart of the growth of cities.

In a world in which transportation and information were not costly, goods and services could be produced and exchanged at any distance, and separate markets or cities would not need to arise. If transportation and congestion imposed no costs, but information was a costly good, markets for production and exchange would have reason to exist but there would be no constraint on market size. Accordingly, the spatial dimensions of a market, and therefore a city, are a function of the costs of transportation and information to those who use it. The lower the cost of transporting goods and people and of obtaining information, the less constraining the use of space will be in the market. Where the costs of vertical transportation are relatively greater than those of horizontal transportation, less of the former and more of the latter dimension will be used. Alternatively, relatively higher costs of horizontal movement may encourage smaller lot sizes with people living and working in closer proximity to each other in the horizontal plane.[9] Thus, other things equal, costs of transporting people and goods and of obtaining information provide a constraint on the spatial dimensions of the marketplace or the city.

Regulation and Location Decisions

Location decisions are made for homes, business enterprises (be they private or public), recreational facilities, and the transportation-communications network. These owner decisions can be analyzed in terms of the demand for and the supply of sites, i.e., specific locations. In such an analysis, it is important to distinguish between the determinants of shifts of demand and supply functions, on the one hand, and movements along them, on the other. Main determinants of demand function shifts are income, prices of competing goods, and taste. On the supply side, technology plays the important role in schedule shifts. For example, technological improvements in transportation shift the supply curves downward, i.e., to the right.

Consider a few cases. Relations between homes may be expressed in "visits" between families and friends who live in the same or different neighborhoods. The more costly the visit (for example, across the city), the fewer such visits take place and the closer to relatives and friends a family will tend to locate. A more important relation exists between home and business enterprise, where the home supplies labor to business, which in turn sells goods and services to the home. Transportation or communication costs are consequential in the location decisions and trip decisions (length and frequency) for business firms as well as for households.

In 1960–1961, utilities and local transportation accounted for 18.6 percent of urban families' expenditures on current consumption.[10] Local transportation accounted for 13.8 percent of such expenditures, and utilities for the remaining 4.8 percent. For over 60 percent of urban families, the transportation-communications expenditures were an even higher ratio of current consumption expenditures, approaching 20 percent. In 90 percent of the families, local transportation accounted for over half of the transportation-communications expenditures.[11] In short, these expenditures are significant and are likely to have an effect on home location, in the context of other land uses, and on moving from home to home and to places of work, shopping, and recreation.

Location decisions of business enterprises are also affected by other factors in the transportation-communications network. Unique demand and supply considerations include density of nearby labor skills and customers, as well as relationships between business enterprises. Two types of economies are germane. The first are localization economies which result when plants are in close proximity. The second are economies associated with urbanization or agglomeration, resulting from the overall size of the community in terms of population, income, wealth, etc.

An example of localization economy would be lower delivery costs when similar customer firms are located in close proximity. An example of urbanization would be a lower peak load of the transportation-communications network due to a diversity of firms with different time patterns for using the network. Thus, density and diversity are central to business enterprises in their decisions on sites for their activities and to the transportation-communications network in its costs of providing services.

Uniform Pricing Cases

As mentioned earlier, the pricing of certain services is commonly regulated by state and local governments. We will now examine the regulation requiring uniform pricing by producers in every market when rates are not permitted to vary with market differences in demand or differences in cost conditions facing the network system operator. Such a case is presented in Figure 10.3: A monopolist operates in only two markets, A and B, which in fact can be separated, and no exchanges can be made between them. Each market has different demand and cost functions and if there were freedom to charge the maximizing price in each market, rates would be p_a and p_b, respectively $(p_b > p_a)$, with quantities q_a and q_b, respectively, being sold.

Such markets are not uncommon. For example, the demand schedule for taxicab service downtown is different from that in outlying sections, where there are relatively few customers per square mile. Similarly, different degrees of congestion in the two areas produce different cost functions. Government

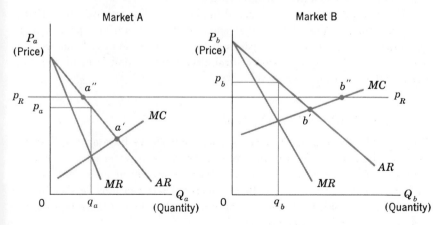

FIGURE 10.3 *Uniform pricing.*

services also offer many examples. If a city has both hilly and flat sections, costs of delivering water or disposing of sewage tend to differ in the two sections. Also, if population density, tastes, and incomes differ in two sections of the city, demand functions for water will tend to differ. As described in the marginal cost pricing section of Chapter 3, a highly perishable good or a service supplied at distinctly different times of the day may be treated as a substitute good; a supplier will face distinctly different cost and demand schedules at different times of the day, week, month, or year.

In general, enforcement of uniform pricing will not yield efficient results —marginal cost equal to p_R. Suppose that the uniform, regulated price is set at p_R in both markets. The efficient price in market A would occur at a' which indicates that p_a was already too high. If the allowable price is set at p_R then p_a must be increased, and thus p_a is forced away from the efficient price, and output q_a is reduced even further. In market B, p_R is set below the profit maximizing price, and thus p_b must be reduced toward the efficient price b'. But the efficient solution b'' cannot be obtained because the level of demand is insufficient.

Thus, the price regulators may be successful in reducing the (monopoly) profits enjoyed by a firm that would otherwise be left free to charge p_a and p_b. But the uniform price constraint moves the rate of output in the right direction in only one market and does not yield the efficient solution of $p_a = MC$ and $p_b = MC$ in either market.

If faced with this type of uniform price constraint, an operator of a transportation-communications network may attempt to lower the quality of services in market B, hoping to shift the marginal cost schedule downward until marginal costs equal marginal revenue at price p_R. Quality reductions will also lead to demand shifts to the right that will in part frustrate the firm's adjustment to a profit maximizing position.

Uniform pricing generates spatial implications. For example, if market A is farther than market B from the center of the city, uniform pricing at p_R encourages relatively higher densities at the center of the city. If market B is a relatively high-cost, congested central city, centralization is further encouraged by the uniform pricing policy.

LAND USE REGULATION ANALYSIS

Why would private property owners want zoning? We have argued that it is because of external effects in the property market, i.e., external economies or spillovers. A property can create an external economy or a diseconomy for, or have a neutral effect on, another property. There can thus be six different types of relationships between two properties. Only two of these types create a desire for zoning.[12] They are the following:

1. If property A creates an external economy for B, but B creates an

external diseconomy for A, then as A makes a location decision, B is attracted to locate on an adjacent site. B's location decision would tend to decrease the property value of A. However, given a location decision by B, A would not be motivated by spillover considerations to locate next to B. A good example is offered by individuals who are attracted to build inexpensive houses near existing expensive ones; but in the reverse situation (i.e., if the existing homes were inexpensive) the motivation would be exactly the opposite.

2. If property A has a neutral effect on B while B creates an external diseconomy for A, then given a location decision by A, B might decide to locate near A because of internal considerations. On the other hand, given a location decision by B, A would not be motivated by externality considerations to locate next to B. Good examples of A and B are a single-family residence and a gasoline service station.

The other four relationships between properties do not create a desire for zoning. Two properties which mutually create external economies would tend to be attracted to each other. For example, retail stores locate in a shopping center so that customers are attracted by the pull of the whole shopping center; each store is thus offered an enhanced business opportunity. A second case is where property A creates an external economy for property B, but B is neutral in its effect on A. In this case, once A makes a location decision, B is attracted to locate nearby, although B does not affect the decision of A. For example, the numerous hotels that locate on the periphery of major airports are benefited by the airport, although the airport does not necessarily benefit from the hotels. Another relationship is where two properties mutually create external diseconomies and are not attracted to locate next to one another. Finally, two properties with neutral effects are neither attracted nor repelled by one another.

Effects of Zone Changes

Various land use regulations can leave different imprints on an area. As one example, let us assume that a local government rezones a large parcel of land from residential to industrial use. Applying this assumption to the area interaction model (Figure 10.2), a dial in box 2 would be turned on and the flow from box 2 to box 3 would be modified. Private decision-making units throughout the country might then reexamine, in the light of their specific demand and supply conditions, the desirability of locating in the particular region. For example, an automobile manufacturer might decide to build a large assembly plant on this rezoned land. Building and operating this assembly plant would be the direct outcome of the new local environment. Valves in box 3 would be turned and the flow from box 3 to box 4 would be modified. The direct effects on the region's economy would take the form of local inputs to the plant. The automobile manufacturer would purchase raw material, labor, and public services from the local economy. Local decision units, as a result of the action of the plant, would visualize certain new business opportunities that (if they materialized) would greatly change the region's welfare, recorded in box 4. To the extent that we can quantify this model, we can play through it a variety of city plans and zoning ordinances and select the one which is likely to result in the greatest net addition to the region's welfare.

Now to consider some of the effects of rezoning a district from business-residential to exclusively residential use. In this connection it should be remembered that zoning ordinances can control the location in which specified activities or establishments are permitted (and from which others are excluded), the location in which specified population densities and floor space are permitted, and the location in which a certain level of bulk and spacing of structures is permitted.[13]

However, zoning regulations cannot be retroactive: A land use existing prior to the enactment of the regulation cannot be changed. Businesses located in the area prior to the rezoning remain there, on a "nonconforming use" basis. Therefore, if the nonconforming uses (e.g., businesses) are functionally related to the dominant activity (e.g., residences), zoning does not eliminate the scattered use. Instead, zoning gives monopoly status to the existing scattered businesses because additional similar activities are not allowed to locate in the same zone. Thus, the nonconforming uses (e.g., businesses) tend to be perpetuated, and the monopoly tends to reduce the welfare of the area.

Increasing the minimum lot size per dwelling unit or reducing the maximum number of families per dwelling unit for a residential zone has similar effects on an area. A short-run shortage in residential land as well as urban decentralization could result from either measure.

Limiting the number of stories and amount of floor space for an office building, relative to site area, in a business zone might turn out to be inconsistent with economic efficiency and could adversely affect the area's welfare. The same result could come from limiting the level of smoke, noise, and vibration of factories in an industrial zone. Increasing the regulation of "nuisances" could increase the cost of factory production and make the area less attractive to industry. This in turn could reduce per capita income and decrease employment and economic growth. On the other hand, the amenities of life might be enhanced, and this might outweigh the other effects.

Finally, let us consider zoning vacant land for future industrial use. This is frequently done by designating an area an industrial park. City planners argue for industrial parks on the grounds that the city will run out of land suitable for industrial use in the future. However, this type of ordinance can constrain the land market's choices for use of the land, and the planners' argument assumes a major imperfection in the price mechanism of the land market. Without zoning constraints and market imperfections, land with a higher value in an industrial use than in its present use will be bid away from the existing use.

Thus, zoning as a resource allocator has advantages and disadvantages. The great advantage of zoning is its ability to correct market defects that result from spillovers. It is on the basis of this feature that zoning has been advocated.

However, zoning can also interfere with efficiency. For example, since zoning regulations cannot be retroactive, zoning gives rise to geographic monopoly of existing businesses. By limitation of the number of stories and total floor space relative to site area, constraints are imposed upon the production function of builders, possibly preventing them from building the most efficient buildings. By segregating into one geographic area industries that create external diseconomies, zoning can increase the overall cost of external diseconomies. Zoning ordinances, by allowing zone variances, tend to have associated with them bribery and graft, which in turn reduce respect for local government officials and laws.[14] Finally, there are administrative costs of creating and enforcing zoning ordinances and there are time costs of property owners who have to wait for zone variance permits.

Political Process and Zoning

We have established that the existence of external diseconomies or spillovers induces property owners to seek aid through zoning ordinances. Still, the question remains: How can these property owners change the internal area-government sector environment, i.e., box 2 in the area interaction model (Figure 10.1)? While private citizens can make proposals concerning zoning restrictions, only authorized officials can enact and enforce these regulations. Thus, in order to understand the flow from box 3 to box 2 in the area interaction model, we would need to introduce a political decision-making process.

There are numerous decision-making models, some of which were discussed in Chapter 2, regarding a legislator's behavior concerning demand for public services. For example, a model can postulate that in making zoning decisions the individual politician seeks to maximize his personal utility. Thus, if one zoning decision becomes more expensive to the decision maker than another, i.e., costs him more votes and (or) side payments, he will make that zoning decision which, all other things being equal, maximizes his personal utility.

Now consider some examples of how the internal private sector affects the internal area-government sector, i.e., how box 3 affects box 2 in the area interaction model. Let us first take the case of a single-family residential district in which some property owners seek to buy out residences and construct commercial improvements.[15] This requires a zone change that is likely to result in external diseconomies for those property owners who retain residential housing in the area. Facing the conflict of interests, the public official can vote for or against granting variances or completely rezoning the district. The greater the number of property owners who resist a zone change and the more political power they can bring to bear, the more costly it is for the public official to vote for the zone change.

If, for example, the area had multifamily apartment buildings instead of single-family residences, and all property owners favored replacing apartment houses with business buildings, the official might face a more difficult decision. The owners are few in number and might not even be living in the district. However, the renters might take a very negative view, if for no other reason than that moving is costly. The more renters with a negative view, the less rewarding a zone change will be for the public official.

Finally, consider the case in which a land developer has constructed and sold single-family residences on half of his land, while an identical second half has not yet been developed. Suddenly, the undeveloped part is facing a zone change as part of the adoption of a new master plan. The land developer may tend to favor keeping the second half zoned for the same use as the developed half. However, residents of the developed half will tend to favor upgrading, by stricter restrictions than those imposed on their property, so that they will benefit from higher-quality residences adjacent to their own. The votes of residents who would benefit from external economies will outnumber the vote of the developer by far, and unless the public official can visualize other rewards such as campaign contributions, he will tend to "overzone" the undeveloped half of the parcel, i.e., give it a higher zoning classification than is warranted. The issue would be more complicated if the developed half had multifamily apartments instead of single-family residences. Tenants would not be so directly concerned about property value effects, but instead would be concerned about the possibility that overzoning might result in higher rents but not necessarily in nicer future neighbors, since tenants will tend to be shorter-term residents of the neighborhood.[16]

OPPORTUNITIES AND PROSPECTS

Today, we hear more dissatisfaction with land use regulation than we have heard in any period since 1916, when New York enacted the first American zoning ordinance. Some city planners (and other nonelected officials) have become disenchanted with zoning, contending that it has proved an inadequate tool to cope with such metropolitan area problems as physical deterioration of downtown areas, the spread of slums, or the unsightly sprawl of subdivisions into rural areas. Also, zoning litigation has been rapidly increasing. More than 300 cases now reach the courts each year, six times the number of the late 1940s when the nation's building boom started.

A more specific complaint is that current zoning laws cannot do the job, and a more powerful, well-defined, up-to-date master plan must be obtained. Yet, some argue convincingly that no city is ever likely to have an up-to-date master plan, especially a city that is growing rapidly and where, perhaps, a master plan would have the greatest impact.

A very common complaint is that rezoning can produce large increases in some property values while creating losses in others. Therefore, it is argued, a planning commission and board of zoning adjustment should become spillover adjusters. Specific proposals have been made that a city sell permits for zone changes, with the difference between the existing land use value and the development value going to local neighborhood property owners (in this way, the "losers," or those inflicted with external costs, would be compensated) or that the city tax a fixed percentage of this "windfall." Those who make such proposals are greatly concerned with a particular distribution aspect of land use regulation, an aspect which we suggested earlier is best handled by the Federal and, to a lesser extent, state governments by the levy of ability-to-pay taxes and by redistribution policies per se.

Finally, there is much unhappiness about procedure. Most planning commissions spend too much of their time on minute rezoning matters, leaving very little time and energy to deal with master planning and development. Moreover, planning commissions and boards of zoning adjustment are composed of volunteer laymen, who at best are paid a token per diem and are thus very often responsible for corruption and political or merely naïve decisions. It has been suggested that members of planning commissions and boards of zoning adjustment be trained in law and planning and be appointed to long-term, properly remunerated positions in many respects similar to those of the judiciary.

Regulation might be extended to cover the quality of the environment and other public goods that have thus far not been explicitly regulated. It could be argued, however, that the quality of the environment was the exact issue which persuaded the United States to borrow zoning from Germany and Sweden. Just as New York City was anxious to keep glue factories out of residential areas in 1916, the entire country is becoming increasingly concerned with the pollution of water, air, and airwaves. Noise pollution is, perhaps, the most recent area of concern. This concern goes beyond the noise that will emanate from the supersonic transport once it becomes operational. The mounting racket of planes, cars, trucks, buses, radio and television sets, etc., promises to produce a noise level of about 80 decibels on an average downtown street corner on a "quiet" afternoon. This may be as much as average human beings can stand for any length of time without suffering physical torment and psychotic symptoms. A critical appraisal of the production of depollution as a public good is currently a lively endeavor.[17]

SUMMARY

In addition to supplying households, industry, and other governments with services in the form of final, tangible products and financial transfers from one household to another, state and local governments perform a regulatory service. They regulate, among other things, the transportation-communications network and land uses.

Network regulation instruments, differing mainly in comprehensiveness and definiteness, include legislative directives, commissions, and indirect control. Land use can be regulated through zoning ordinance, zone change, zone variance, and conditional use permit. Coping with externalities is the main concern of land use regulation. Regulation can be in the form of stipulating output policies, production relationships, and pricing and market conditions. All three are germane to network regulation, while output policies and production relationships are applicable to land use control.

Regulation by state and local governments is designed to modify the area's environment and "rules of the game" so as to promote the general welfare. While promotion of the general welfare can have such dimensions as efficiency, income redistribution, growth, and economic stability, the main concern should be resource allocation efficiency. This concern is particularly important at the local level, since the Federal government holds major, if not exclusive, responsibility for the other dimensions of the general welfare. The achievement of efficiency, especially by local governments, is often impeded by problems posed by external effects or spillovers. Through regulation, the impact of spillovers can be compensated for or prevented. Thus, land use planning and zoning are founded on the necessity of correcting those spillovers that are not handled adequately in the marketplace. The land use regulator can adjust spillovers through zoning ordinances, compulsory dedication requirements, urban renewal, etc.

The impact of network and land use regulation can be analyzed with the aid of an area interaction model in which external-internal area-government sector forces and internal private sector forces are interacting inputs which to different extents affect the system's output, i.e., the area's welfare. Moreover, the effect of regulation on the spatial distribution of economic activity can thus be examined.

Network regulation analysis is carried out in relation to location decisions, and uniform pricing is analyzed. Land use regulation analysis is carried out in relation to zone changes and their effects. Better insight into zoning is obtained by analyzing land use regulation in relation to the political process within which it takes place.

Finally, some concerns for the future are examined, particularly how regulation can be improved and what new aspects of the quality of the environment might be considered for future regulation.

CHAPTER 11
PROGRAM BUDGETING

What and how public services at the state and local levels are rendered and financed, and by and for whom, are matters of tradition, sometimes almost of mythology, but not necessarily of rational planning by governments. Direct government participation in providing constituents with products commonly involves building and operating public facilities and requires public decisions of major complexity and consequence. Among the investment decisions are what plants to build; how, when, and where to build them; and how to finance them. Operating decisions include the quantity and quality of services to render; how, where, when and for whom services should be rendered; and what, if any, charges to make to whom for rendering services. In earlier chapters we considered these issues in isolation. In this chapter we look at demand, supply, and financing matters as a totality. An approach that facilitates making this synthesis in a complete, rational manner is program budgeting.

Public decision theory in the United States is based on two major schools of thought: economic and political. In its extreme, the economic approach argues that a government first identifies its goals; then it collects information about the various courses of action that seem to be open and the consequences of choosing alternative paths. The total effects of each alternative are estimated and a preferred solution is selected. As the preferred solution is planned, budgeted, and implemented, the problem is resolved.

The political school argues that a rational means-end calculus is impossible and unrealistic. Charles Lindblom represents this second school well by arguing that man cannot neatly separate goals from means, or values from facts; the realistic limits of time and cost prevent man from acquiring the needed information to judge rationally among alternatives. Instead, Lindblom says, budget makers pursue "disjointed incrementalism," and decision makers do not pursue goals but move away from a problem by following a policy that is only marginally different from the existing one. If one thing doesn't work they try something else.[1] Perhaps an even more forceful spokesman for this school is Aaron Wildavsky, who suggests that "if the present budgetary process is . . . unsatisfactory, then one must alter . . . the political system of which the budget is but an expression."[2]

Although this volume in general and this chapter in particular are more or less in agreement with the economic rationality school, they reflect an acute awareness of the institutional environment within which policy makers plan and act. The system presented here views program budgeting as a planning and management process which departs from the more conventional government budgeting process. There is a growing dissatisfaction with the latter, which was shaped mainly by a desire to safeguard appropriations against careless or malfeasant government employees. The new system promises to assist in measuring, comparing, inventing, and offering programs to state and local officials for their approval. In so doing, it should provide decision makers with pertinent information needed to allocate scarce resources efficiently among an ever-increasing number of competing activities; it should also help to resolve conflicts between different interest groups.

Program budgeting was adopted by the U.S. Department of Defense in 1961 as an alternative to the then current system. Broad approval was registered on the national level by the Presidential directive of August 25, 1965. It requires a new planning-programming-budgeting system for most Federal agencies. State and local governments will have to understand the new system if they are to anticipate Federal decisions and thus benefit from them— especially in relation to Federal grants-in-aid. Thus, it is a most appropriate time to consider the design and implementation of program budgeting at subnational levels. There is great virtue in having a program budget system that provides for uniformity among all levels of government to permit comparability and understanding of interrelationships between their activities; however, too high a price must not be paid for uniformity. Different types of decisions can have varying significance for each government unit. We should aim at a program budget structure that can identify and elucidate the most significant decisions at each level.

Program budgeting is a complex process covering problems ranging from current evaluations, reporting, and progress control to effects on the future environment of government resource allocation and income distribution decisions. It provides a framework for analysis, discourse, and possible conflict resolution so that issues and goals can be brought into clear focus and a decision maker's intuition can be checked and sharpened. A number of states, counties, cities, and school districts in the United States have taken initial steps to incorporate program budgeting in their decision-making processes.[3] In the late sixties a State-Local Finances Project was initiated at the George Washington University to develop some operational methods that could be readily applied by city, state, and county governments throughout the country.[4]

In this chapter, state and local program budgeting is viewed as a planning-management process with structural, analytic, and administrative-organizational dimensions. Work on these three dimensions, particularly the first two, should proceed simultaneously, since the budget structure is influenced by the analytic parts of the system and vice versa; both of these aspects rely on the administrative-organizational dimension for implementation. After examining conceptual and empirical aspects of program budgeting structure and analysis, we shall take up administrative-organizational issues. Thereafter, multiyear aspects of program budgeting will be discussed.

SOME PROGRAM BUDGET STRUCTURE CONCEPTS

The format in program budgeting helps to structure and organize funding information. It is differentiated from a conventional administrative budget format by its output orientation. That is, the activities and expenditures of several agencies or departments are aggregated in terms of specific output packages, clearly delineated, and composed of elements in close competition with each other (i.e., programs, subprograms, and sub-subprograms). For example, one of the goals of a state is to develop human resources within its borders. To achieve this broad goal, the state must make allocation decisions between vocational retraining programs to develop new skills for segments of the labor force and college education programs to broaden and improve the level of scholarly, technological, and artistic contributions. These two sub-programs compete with each other for resources. Each of them is in turn composed of alternative sub-subprograms which also compete for resources as inputs for achieving the objectives of the subprogram of which they are a part. Thus, instruction in operating a turret lathe or training in physical therapy can be viewed as alternative forms of vocational training and are more competitive with each other than they are with studies in political science, economics, or philosophy.

The program budget format requires that outputs be quantifiable to some extent, so that expenditure data can be meaningfully related to projected performance. And ideally, for certain purposes, as much social cost data as possible should be included in the budget.

It must be recognized that the constituency that must be served by state and local programs is far from homogeneous. Therefore, it is useful to separate recipients of government services by age (infants, children, young adults, adults, senior citizens, etc.) ; by special socioeconomic handicaps (low-income minorities, migrants, refugees, etc.) ; by special physical, psychological, and intellectual needs (mentally gifted, mentally retarded or disturbed, blind, deaf, speech-impaired, physically sick or crippled, etc.) ; by location, etc. Ideally, each sub-subprogram should be related to as many of these target groups as possible. Also, insight could be gained by aggregating expenditures by target groups and learning how much is spent, for example, to help culturally deprived children or low-income senior citizens.

Programmatic outputs, especially on the sub-subprogram level, can be composed of a number of activities: research and planning, training, information dissemination, prevention and detection, treatment (and protection), control and conservation, custodial and long-term care (and support), rehabilitation, retraining and restoration, hardship mitigation, regulation (including inspection and review) and adjudication, and construction of plant and facilities. Ultimately the program budget identifies elements down to the input level of basic building blocks of various required resources: manpower, materials, equipment, buildings, land, etc. These elements can be combined and recombined into various packages to produce desired outputs.

With data arranged in these convenient building blocks, a program budget can be reconstructed at any level of responsibility, according to previously stated goals or objectives. This flexibility allows for convenient reformulation of activities to accommodate changes in perspective and objectives of local and state governments.

To define programs, we must first identify purposeful missions. We will demonstrate this issue in relation to police protection. At the most general level, police objectives have a unique relationship to the objectives of the state. The most fundamental objective of police, therefore, is the preservation of the existing order as stated in the body of law. Yet while the overall goal of the legal system is social order, the mission of the police within this system is a much more limited one—to ensure the public peace and security envisioned by the law.[5] For the police, an operational, more quantifiable, part of this goal—security—is minimizing the costs to society of criminal actions. "Minimizing" means reducing the extent of crime to some "optimal" level below which the cost of reducing crime further is greater than the resulting benefit.

In the development of programs and a program structure that, one hopes, will lend themselves to quantification, it is useful to divide crimes into violations of property and individuals' rights, violations of moral conduct regulations, collective civil violations, and traffic violations. Within each of these categories, police carry out activities designed to deter criminal activity and potential criminals, investigate crimes, and apprehend criminals. An appropriate police program format is presented in Table 11.1, composed of five subprograms consistent with the missions identified above, plus a sixth subprogram, planning, research, and development, designed to support the other five. The proposed police program budget could have such dimensions or target groups as geographic districts or race.

In a similar manner, five major missions of recreation services can be identified:

Improvement in mental health

Improvement in physical health and physical development

Increased attainment of creative leisure skills

Improvement in the quality of the physical environment

Attainment of a more stable community by keeping youngsters off the streets

Admittedly, many of these objectives are highly intangible and difficult to quantify.

The program budget is structured to allow for an extended time horizon; this is one of its most important contributions. It should provide the decision maker with a profile of future obligations incurred by today's decisions. Data found in traditional budgets seldom give him such a view. But, if he is to make rational choices, the decision maker should know something about the implications his decisions will have for the future. Understanding the full costs would help minimize "foot-in-the-door" financing, which often proves

TABLE 11.1   Program Budget Categories of Police Services

I. Minimize injuries, deaths, and property damage due to criminal behavior

  A. Prevention programs
    1. Youth programs
    2. School visitation

  B. Deterrence programs
    1. Patrol
    2. Crime task force

  C. Investigation and apprehension
    1. Personal injury violations
    2. Property violations
    3. Incarceration and trial

II. Minimize damages due to moral code violations

  A. Prevention programs
    1. Narcotics information
    2. School visitation

  B. Deterrence programs

  C. Investigation and apprehension
    1. Narcotics violations
    2. Gambling violations
    3. Pre-trial incarceration and conviction

III. Minimize damages to persons and property due to collective violations

  A. Riot prevention programs
    1. Community relations programs
    2. Minority youth programs

  B. Riot control programs
    1. Special equipment and training
    2. Advance planning

  C. Control of minor disorders
    1. Public events
    2. Family disputes
    3. Other disorderly conduct

TABLE 11.1   Program Budget Categories of Police Services—Continued

IV. Minimize cost of traffic movement and traffic accidents

    A. Accident prevention programs
        1. Driver training
        2. Accident data reporting and analysis

    B. Accident deterrence programs
        1. General patrol
        2. Specialized traffic law enforcement patrol

    C. Accident investigation and conviction

    D. Reduction in traffic congestion
        1. Traffic direction
        2. Parking regulation enforcement
        3. Hazard removal
        4. Initiate traffic advisories

    E. Miscellaneous services
        1. Special events
        2. Assistance to motorists
        3. Abandoned vehicles

V. Provide general public services

    A. Emergency services

    B. Informational services

    C. Missing persons

    D. Others

VI. Planning, research, and development

SOURCE: Stephen Mehay and Donald Shoup, "Missions and Outputs of Police Agencies" (Los Angeles: University of California, Institute of Government and Public Affairs, 1969), OR-143, pp. 25–26.

costly to state and local governments. More will be said about this in the section on multiyear program budgeting.

Program budgets of various government levels differ according to the different kinds of problems each one must deal with and the methods it uses to finance its programs. For example, national security would be included in a national system as one of its programs but would be an inappropriate program for a state or local system. Or the Federal government may view recreation as an alternative use of natural resources, and thus make it part of the economic development program concerned with physical facilities available to present and future generations. Local governments, however, may regard recreation as a means and end of a social development program, in many respects similar to education, health, and welfare programs. The issue may be: How do the people spend their leisure hours? rather than: Will this land be devoted to recreational or other purposes? Thus, through its association with leisure, recreation would be placed in the local program budget under the heading of amenities of life.

In a state or local government program budget, it is important to keep in mind that under fiscal federalism a program may by funded by one government and administered by another. Although the Federal government spends only its own funds on such programs as national security and space exploration, many of the most expensive state and local programs involve Federal funds. Health, welfare, roads, water, and education are outstanding examples.

We pointed out in Chapter 6 that there are many variations in the degree of freedom lower levels of government have in spending specified funds. Frequently Federal or state governments earmark funds which can be used by cities, counties, or special districts only for narrowly specified purposes. Sometimes, local governments are required by law to provide certain services such as health programs. In all such instances, freedom of action is circumscribed, and this should be made explicit in the program budget.

Furthermore, many government services are rendered by more than a single government unit, and often by private units as well. Even within a given geographic area, education is frequently offered not only by local school districts, but also by private institutions; and while basic police protection is provided by the local police department, supplementary services are rendered by the FBI, the state police or highway patrol, private detective agencies, and sometimes by private police patrols. Ideally, each decision-making unit should have information on the activities and expenditures of all other units involved.

Therefore, whenever possible, the program budget would be structured to include information not only on the sources of funds and who operates the program with what discretion, but also to provide separate columns for expenditures incurred by the various decision makers in servicing the area. Admittedly, we have great conceptual and empirical difficulties in allocating subprogram funds to specific sources unless they are earmarked unequivocally for specified subprograms.

SOME EMPIRICAL EXAMPLES OF STATE AND LOCAL PROGRAM BUDGETS

Illustrations of state and local program budgets, for the State of California and Los Angeles County, respectively, were constructed from information contained in the Governor's Budget for fiscal 1963 and from a report prepared by the state controller for the same period (see Tables 11.2 and 11.3). It is important to note that information on the state budget represents requested appropriations, while the local data are actual expenditures.

TABLE 11.2   State Program Budget for California, Fiscal Year 1963 (appropriations in millions of dollars)

	Current	Capital	Local Assistance	Total*
Total All Programs	$1,316.4	$776.0	$1,230.9	$3,323.3
I. Social Development	846.8	121.5	1,183.7	2,151.9
A. Education	258.0	116.0	857.1	1,231.1
General programs	255.7	116.0	857.1	1,228.8
Child-care				
Primary and secondary	19.2	.2	857.1	876.5
Higher education	236.5	115.8		352.4
Special groups	.1			.1
Adult education	.1			.1
Physically handicapped	n†	n	n	n
Mentally retarded	n	n	n	n
Juvenile offenders	n	n	n	n
Libraries	1.2			1.2
Research				
Unallocated	1.0			1.0
B. Health	232.0	5.2	55.8	293.0
General programs	159.0	5.2	11.1	175.2
General health services	8.6	.2	7.6	16.6
Mental health	147.0	4.9	3.3	155.2
Environmental health	3.4		.2	3.6
Special groups	59.1	a	33.7	92.8
Aged	39.8		18.8	58.6
Public assistance cases	n	n	n	n
School children	14.4		5.9	20.3
Blind	.6	a		.6
Handicapped	3.4		9.0	12.4
Alcoholic and narcotic	.9			.9
Unallocated	13.9		11.1	25.0
C. Welfare	356.1	.2	270.8	627.1
Aged	172.5		154.6	327.1
Children	98.3		84.6	182.9
Handicapped	8.1		11.6	19.8
Indigent	15.3		18.9	34.2
Unemployed	48.1			48.1
Veterans	8.8	.2	.4	9.3
Unallocated	5.0		.7	5.7
D. Housing and Community Development	.1			.1
E. Amenities of Life	.6	.1		.6
Recreation (consumer oriented)				
Cultural affairs	.6	.1		.6

TABLE 11.2   State Program Budget for California, Fiscal Year 1963 (appropriations in millions of dollars)—Continued

	Current	Capital	Local Assistance	Total*
II. Economic Development	187.7	628.8	39.4	856.0
F. Natural Resources	73.9	82.1	26.7	182.8
Agriculture	16.7	1.4	2.7	20.9
Pests and diseases	7.5			7.5
Fairs	5.5	1.4	2.6	9.5
Soil conservation	1.9		.1	2.0
Unallocated	1.8	.1		1.9
Water	13.7	65.7	23.5	102.9
Procurement, processing, and distribution	1.4		8.1	9.5
Storm drains and flood control			15.4	15.4
Unallocated	12.3	65.7		78.0
Forest	21.1	3.0		24.1
Recreation (resource oriented)	6.2	9.9	.5	16.6
Beaches and parks	5.5	9.5	.4	15.3
Small craft harbors		.4		.4
Unallocated	.7		.2	.9
Fish and wildlife	10.5	2.0		12.5
Oceanic	1.0			1.0
Mineral	1.7			1.7
Unallocated	3.1			3.1
G. Transportation	63.5	546.6	11.0	621.1
Interurban area	63.5	537.4		600.8
Air	.1			.1
Highway	63.3	537.4		600.7
Water				
Intraurban area		9.2	11.0	20.2
Streets and highways		9.2	11.0	20.2
Local transit systems				
Parking facilities				
H. Aid and Regulation	50.3	.1	1.7	52.1
Aid	6.1			6.2
Inspection and standards	35.9		1.7	37.6
Public utility regulation	6.9			6.9
Unallocated	1.4			1.4
III. Law and Justice	135.2	23.6	7.8	166.6
I. Judicial	11.9		4.3	16.2
J. Public Safety	123.3	23.6	3.6	150.5
Police	39.0	.7	.3	40.1
Detention and correction	78.5	22.1	3.2	103.8
Fire	.6			.6

TABLE 11.2   State Program Budget for California, Fiscal Year 1963 (appropriations in millions of dollars)—Continued

	Current	Capital	Local Assistance	Total*
Disaster control	1.0		.1	1.1
Military affairs	4.1	.9		5.0
IV. Administration	146.7	2.1		148.8
K. Legislative and Administrative Authority	82.1	2.1		84.2
Legislative and executive offices	11.2	1.1		12.4
Licensing and registration	34.1	1.0		35.1
Personnel‡	7.3			7.3
Unallocated§	29.4			29.4
L. Fiscal Affairs	64.6			64.6
Revenue collection	25.2			25.2
Monitoring expenditures	8.8			8.8
Bond issues‖	24.1			24.1
Unallocated	6.5			6.5

* Details may not add to total because of rounding.
† a designates sums less than $50,000; n designates items not separately available.
‡ Civil service functions; employee benefits are allocated by subprogram.
§ Includes special fund credits to general fund, estimated unidentified savings, reserves for salary increases and department contingencies.
‖ Exclusive of school building bonds.
SOURCE: State of California Budget, 1962/1963 (Sacramento: State Printing Office).

Estimates are made for programs and subprograms only. We would have liked to make further divisions into sub-subprograms and extend the program budgets over a five-year time dimension, but limited resources did not allow this. We do not offer detailed information on what funds were received by the State of California from the Federal government, for what purposes, or how these funds were divided between specific state and local programs. However, information is furnished on total programmatic expenditures and on the portion made available by the state in the form of local assistance. Expenditures are separated into current and capital expenditures.

In Tables 11.2 and 11.3, we have identified twelve major programs (A through L), arranged into four broad program areas (I through IV): social development, economic development, law and justice, and general government operation or administration. Since programs often have multiple objectives, other program areas could serve just as well as those we have chosen. In addition, decisions to place various programs in one area instead of another

	Current	Capital	Total[a]
Total All Programs	$1,853.8	$247.2	$2,101.0
I. Social Development	1,126.0	119.4	1,245.5
A. Education	653.7	91.2	744.9
General programs	626.3	86.7	713.1
Child-care	4.4	a[b]	4.4
Primary and secondary	580.0	77.7	657.8
Higher education[c]	42.0	8.9	50.9
Special groups	10.6	a	10.6
Adult education	8.0	a	8.0
Physically handicapped	a	a	a
Mentally retarded	.5	a	.5
Juvenile offenders	2.1	a	2.1
Libraries[d]	16.8	4.5	21.3
Research			
B. Health	189.7	14.9	204.7
General programs	128.4	14.9	143.3
General health services	92.2	1.2	93.4
Mental health	2.3	a	2.3
Environmental health	33.9	13.7	47.6
Special groups	61.4	a	61.4
Aged	18.8	a	18.8
Public assistance cases	26.4	a	26.4
School children	16.2	a	16.2
Blind	n	n	n
Handicapped	n	n	n
Alcoholic and narcotic	n	n	n
Unallocated	n	n	n
C. Welfare	234.7	.3	234.9
Aged	117.1	a	117.1
Children	61.6	a	61.6
Handicapped	16.3	a	16.3
Indigent	12.3	a	12.3
Veterans	.1	a	.1
Unallocated	27.3	.2	27.6
D. Housing and Community Development			
E. Amenities of Life	47.9	13.0	61.0
Recreation (consumer oriented)	45.4	13.0	58.4
Cultural affairs	2.5	a	2.6
II. Economic Development	152.9	80.3	233.2
F. Natural Resources	31.7	29.1	60.8
Agriculture	.9	a	.9
Water	30.8	29.1	59.9
Procurement, processing, and distribution	23.4	14.1	37.4
Storm drains and flood control	7.4	15.0	22.5

	Current	Capital	Total[a]
Recreation (resource oriented)	n	n	n
Beaches and parks	n	n	n
Small craft harbors	n	n	n
G. Transportation	98.3	51.1	149.4
Interurban area	6.3	30.4	36.7
Air	.2	3.4	3.5
Highway			
Water	6.1	27.0	33.1
Intraurban area	92.1	20.6	112.7
Streets and highways	91.5	19.1	110.5
Local transit systems	a	a	a
Parking facilities	.6	1.6	2.2
H. Aid and Regulation	22.9	.2	23.1
Aid	2.6	a	2.6
Inspection and standards	17.0	.2	17.2
Public utility regulation	3.3	a	3.3
III. Law and Justice	240.9	13.0	253.8
I. Judicial	19.9	.1	20.0
J. Public Safety	221.0	12.9	233.8
Police	112.6	4.9	117.5
Detention and correction	31.8	.2	32.0
Fire	75.8	7.7	83.5
Disaster control	.7	.1	.8
IV. Administration	334.0	34.5	368.5
K. Legislative and Administrative Authority	176.3	34.4	210.7
Legislative and executive offices[e]	108.4	34.3	142.8
Licensing and registration	1.1	a	1.1
Personnel[f]	66.8	a	66.8
L. Fiscal Affairs	157.1	.1	157.8
Revenue collection	11.1	.1	11.2
Monitoring expenditures[g]	6.9	.1	7.0
Bond issues[h]	139.6		139.6

[a] Details may not add to totals because of rounding.
[b] a designates sums less than $50,000; n designates items not separately available.
[c] Junior college districts only.
[d] Public libraries only; school libraries included in general programs.
[e] Includes accounting, elections, and attorney.
[f] Includes civil service functions and retirement and employee benefits.
[g] Includes auditors' and controllers' offices.
[h] Includes repayment and debt service.
SOURCES: Alan Cranston, State Controller, *Annual Report of Financial Transactions concerning Cities of California*
———————, *Counties of California*
———————, *Irrigation Districts of California*
———————, *School Districts of California*
———————, *Special Districts of California*, fiscal year 1962–1963, with the exception of Irrigation Districts for which the period is the calendar year 1963.

are somewhat arbitrary. For example, education may contribute as much to social as to economic development. This flexibility is important to the whole concept of program budgeting.

Programs are further broken down into subprograms. For example, we identify six education subprograms in the California State system: preschool child care, primary and secondary education, higher education, adult education, research, and libraries. Research and libraries have been designated separate subprograms in education simply because it appears almost impossible to allocate their contribution to each of the other four subprograms.

The various subprograms could be broken down still further into meaningful sub-subprograms; e.g., adult education could be broken down into refresher and retraining courses for professionals, education for late bloomers, education for greater intellectual participation in social and cultural affairs, etc. Furthermore, each of these sub-subprograms could be regrouped in terms of who the direct beneficiaries are: age groups; special socioeconomic handicapped groups; groups needing special physical, psychological, or intellectual care; location of homes, etc. In addition, the more significant sub-subprograms could be related to any or all of the activities identified above.

Clearly, in many cases very few target groups and activities are relevant. With this in mind, we have developed state and local government program budget formats that incorporate a number of compromises. For example, in education and health, we separate subprograms that are mainly general (i.e., benefit the population at large) from those that benefit special, clearly identifiable groups. In welfare, which we define as providing general income supplements to the current income of the needy, the subprogram breakdown is mainly in terms of target groups.

From Table 11.2 we can see that in 1963 the State of California spent $3.3 billion on social development, economic development, law and justice, and administration, in that order. In money terms, the education, welfare, transportation, health, and natural resources programs dominated all others. About $0.86 billion was spent on primary and secondary education, and $0.35 billion on higher education, but virtually nothing was spent on preschool child care or research.

Table 11.3 pertains to all local governments in Los Angeles County in the fiscal year 1963. It represents 527 separate units that provided services to over 6 million people: One county government is joined by 74 cities, 108 school districts, and 344 districts concerned with a wide range of functions including recreation, transportation, fire protection, sewage and sanitation, flood control, etc. It is really a program budget for an urban region that has no parallel decision-making unit. In money terms, Los Angeles County, the Los Angeles City School District, and the City of Los Angeles are the most important units.

This program budget contains expenditure data (net of user charges where applicable) for a single year.[6] In order to be consistent with Table 11.2, we also separate current and capital expenditures and neglect to indicate the sources of funds expended by local governments on specific programs.

For many purposes, the information in Table 11.3 would have to be supplemented by information on what portion of the funds is raised locally and what portion is obtained from other levels of government. Furthermore, where only parts of the program are carried out by governments, it would be important to supplement the government information with expenditures by the private sector.

PROGRAM BUDGET ANALYSIS AND EVALUATION

Analysis and evaluation by state and local government is an integral part of the program budgeting process and includes the study of objectives and of alternative ways of achieving them, of future environments, and of contingencies and how to respond to them. Often decisions are made by different governments and for different reasons. For instance, the decision could be made by local officials to begin a new education sub-subprogram, or to commit additional funds to an existing welfare subprogram, or to maintain a certain level of health services. Or, perhaps, the decision of state officials could be to reduce the budget by cutting back funds for certain efforts; or to cancel a specific recreation subprogram or to reduce manpower in it; or to alter the salary structure in state colleges. Each decision implies an obligation for some activity or organization to fulfill.

Inherent in each obligation is the requirement to adapt or convert personnel, facilities, equipment, and other resources. Within the structure of these programs and subprograms are numerous components which are interrelated and interdependent. Consequently, once a decision is made, a variety of subprograms can be affected through a chain of interactions. Again some of these subprograms may require new commitments, e.g., the construction of new parks or libraries or the development of new testing procedures. Clearly, planner and policy maker benefit from having a fairly good advance understanding of major implications of the decision. The state and local government official would want to ask himself: Are these preferred programs? Are the resources available? What additional requirements are involved? Given an already committed work load, can a further burden be placed on the organization; e.g., can junior colleges absorb a major additional influx of students?

Planning and policy making by state and local government officials depend on an understanding of implications of a decision to commit, allocate, or reduce resources to a particular program. The additional resource requirements and work loads must be considered in relation to the incremental costs involved and their time phasing, on the one hand, and must be related to the incremental benefits that can be expected, on the other.

Systematic analysis of alternatives available to a state or local government requires an orderly effort of dealing rationally and explicitly with:

1. The objectives or missions that the program is to achieve
2. The criteria in terms of which such achievement is to be measured
3. The spectrum of alternatives worthy of consideration toward these ends
4. The costs and benefits incurred under each of the alternatives

Not infrequently, great difficulties are encountered in fully implementing these steps, as has been shown above in relation to steps 1 and 2.

Step 4, in the narrow sense, involves benefit-cost analysis, referred to by some as cost-utility analysis or cost-effectiveness analysis.[7] The status of benefit-cost analysis is well summarized by Julius Margolis:

> In recent years developments in economic theory have tended to confound the economic adviser to the government, while developments in applied economic analysis have excited the public officials to seek out the economist for guidance on public programming and planning. The theorist has deepened the problem of public goods, asserted the impossibility of a democratic social welfare function, denied the existence of a general theory of the second best, and strengthened the arguments against judging a situation that is allocationally superior independent of distributional effects. Despite these admonitions by theorists, the applied analyst has persisted in developing analytical schemes by which to evaluate the design and scale of public services. His philosophical foundations are weak, bureaucratic and political resistances are strong, but his techniques are being rapidly extended to many areas of the urban public services.[8]

The program budget does not furnish all the information needed for benefit-cost analysis. It itemizes proposed expenditures but does not give information on social benefits, social costs, or spillovers. Social benefits include the total value of added output or satisfaction resulting from choosing one activity over another. Social costs include all resources required for the activity, in terms of their value in their best alternative use. As discussed in Chapters 1 and 6, spillovers are uncompensated effects on the costs or benefits of some external unit or organization.[9]

Social costs concepts have been examined in Chapter 8 and social benefit concepts in Chapter 2. Here we would like to make one additional point. Until recently, benefit-cost analysis has mainly been applied to compare total resource costs with total benefits of a particular program. Although resource allocation efficiency is of prime importance, policy makers are also interested in knowing the distribution implications of their decisions. They want to know who benefits how much from a given program, and how the losses are distributed. In fact, their political survival depends on who benefits and who loses as a result of their decisions. This leads to a detailed breakdown of the benefit-cost distribution by major target and interest groups. Thus, the initial goal of benefit-cost analysis for efficiency in resource allocations is often redirected by the political realities of life, and the results are often inconsistent with efficiency.

Program budgeting analysis can facilitate decision making by state and local government officials on three different levels:

1. On the highest level, possibly that of a governor or mayor, it can be applied to select the proper budget mix between the four program areas or twelve different programs given in Tables 11.2 and 11.3.
2. On the second level, it can help to determine the best mix of subprograms and sub-subprograms regardless of whether they are parts of one or more programs.
3. And, finally, there is the relatively low decision level which is concerned with the determination of the most efficient way of attaining a given program objective.

The first two levels involve output trade-offs, and the third involves input trade-offs. It is seldom possible to evaluate trade-off decisions on the highest level because of the difficulty of defining, quantifying, and comparing such things as social development, economic development, or law and justice. This is also true, though to a lesser extent, on the second level. These output trade-offs can be illustrated by the standard production possibility curve, labeled *PPC*, in Figure 11.1.[10] This curve shows the various combinations of two outputs which can be produced with one input, or, more accurately, with an undefined bundle of resource inputs. Such a curve can be drawn if the outputs are quantifiable, even though they are not measurable in the same unit. An output must be on the production possibility curve to be efficient; i.e., it is impossible, with the given input bundle, to get more of one output without taking less of the other, or, for any given quantity of one output, the quantity of the other is at a maximum. Trade-offs in this context refer to the marginal rates of substitution of output A for B at any point along the curve, represented graphically by the slope of the curve at any given point. The production possibility curve delineates a set of efficient solutions, but it does not indicate which of these efficient solutions is optimal. Any interior point such as X represents an inefficient solution because it is possible to obtain more of one output without taking less of the other. If the outputs are not expressible in a common unit, an optimum solution can be specified only if society's order of preference for the various combinations of outputs is known. A

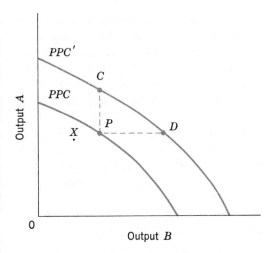

FIGURE 11.1   Production   possibility   curve   (one
input, two outputs).

hypothetical set of social preferences is indicated by the indifference curves
in Figure 11.2. The optimum output mix for the given input of resources is
indicated by the coordinates of point P (the highest attainable level of
utility).

A budget increase (i.e., an increase in the bundle of resource inputs)
may be represented by shifting the production possibility curve outward, as
in Figure 11.1, where it is shifted from PPC to PPC'. Assume that the output
combination represented by point P was being produced with the original
budget. Point C can now be attained by spending the entire budget increment
on output A, and point D by spending the increment entirely on output B.
The points on the segment of PPC' between C and D represent more of both
outputs than formerly, and the slope of the segment at any point indicates the
trade-offs for the budget increase. Budget decrease could be similarly represented by shifting the production possibility curve inward from PPC.

Sometimes it is possible to quantify outputs, though not necessarily in
commensurate units, at the subprogram and sub-subprogram levels. This
means that trade-off analyses of the type just described can be undertaken.
One of the main advantages of the program budgeting approach, as contrasted with the conventional budget, is that it clarifies some of the output
implications of budgetary decisions. In some cases it may be possible to go
somewhat beyond this type of trade-off analysis. When one output can be
valued in monetary terms and the second cannot, it is possible to show the
minimum dollar valuation which must be assigned to incremental units of
the second output in order to prefer them to the first. In other cases it will

be possible to design or redesign the problem so that outputs of different subprograms can be expressed in the same units, even though they differ from the units in which the inputs are measured. This is illustrated in the discussion of trade-offs within a health program, presented below. In these cases, we may either fix the gain and seek a way of achieving it at the least cost, or fix the budget and seek a way of spending it which would yield the greatest gain.

On the highest trade-off level, we might consider the program budget for the State of California, and ask: Is this the right mix between the state's programs in social development, economic development, law and justice, and administration? Specifically, in line with Table 11.2, is California wise to spend about 65 percent on social development, 26 percent on economic development, 5 percent on law and justice, and 4 percent on administration? Or we may move to specific programs and ask why California spends so much on education and so little on the judiciary.

Further questions come to mind in connection with Table 11.3. In Los Angeles County, is the following mix optimum: social development, 59 percent; administration, 18 percent; law and justice, 12 percent; and economic development, 11 percent? Are the governments of the county wise to spend $2.1 billion in the following way: 36 percent on education, 11 percent each on welfare and public safety, but only 3 percent on amenities of life—and virtually nothing on housing and community development?

Answers to such complex questions are likely to be determined more by current policy and the judgment of a governor or mayor and his legislative

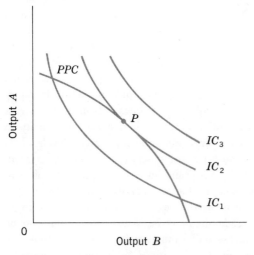

FIGURE 11.2   *Production possibility curve and indifference curves (one input, two outputs).*

leaders than by a quantitative analysis. Their decisions would probably be better, however, if results of analyses at lower levels (where benefits and costs can be defined) could be taken into account.

At a lower output trade-off level, a county government might face a decision on whether to allocate an additional million dollars to fight communicable diseases or use it to improve maternal and child care, or, perhaps, on how to allocate the additional dollars between the two. It might be possible to reveal that a given amount of money allocated to maternal and child care is likely to save the lives of X number of babies and Y number of mothers; if allocated to communicable disease control, the same amount of money is likely to cure Z number of men, age twenty-five, from a disease from which they would otherwise die within thirty years. While this analysis could not provide local decision makers with sufficient information to make an unequivocally correct choice, it would provide them with useful insight to improve their judgment.

It may be possible to go somewhat further by restructuring the problem so that the outputs of both subprograms could be expressed in the same units. Thus, we could consider a sub-subprogram of communicable disease control which also affects mothers and babies, such as control of measles. In this case, we could compare the number of mothers and babies who could be saved if the additional million dollars were allocated to maternal and child care or to communicable disease control. Of course, if one allocation resulted in more mothers being saved and the other in more babies being saved, we would again be able only to indicate the trade-offs.

The third decision level involves trade-offs among inputs, usually conducted on a lower level and easier for economists to handle. This type of decision can be illustrated by Figure 11.3, which shows a production isoquant diagram with two inputs and one output. Efficiency requires the tangency of an isoquant and a price line, i.e., that any given quantity of output (represented by an isoquant) be attained at the least cost, or that for a given budget (represented by a price line), output be maximized (the highest possible isoquant be attained). Thus, in Figure 11.3 the tangency at E indicates that with the budget represented by the price line PP, 200 is the largest attainable output. Furthermore, this output is only attainable, with the given budget, by using the combination of inputs indicated by the coordinates of point E. In this context, trade-off can refer either to the marginal rate of substitution in buying the inputs, as represented by the slope of the price line, or to the marginal rate of substitution in using the inputs, as represented by the slope of an isoquant at any point.

One example of an input trade-off pertains to vocational retraining, which bridges the education and welfare fields. There are two ways to implement vocational retraining, i.e., through on-the-job training and through the

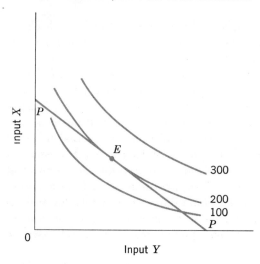

FIGURE 11.3   Isoquants and price line (two inputs, one output).

formal educational establishment of the community, including training in classrooms and (or) in shops and other special facilities. An empirical example will be presented below.

SOME EMPIRICAL BENEFIT-COST ANALYSES

Since benefit-cost analysis is a key tool in the analysis and evaluation of program budgeting, we present some empirical studies of water, outdoor recreation, transport, housing and urban renewal, education, health, and welfare. All these case studies pertain to second- and third-level decisions as defined in the immediately preceding section. No benefit-cost analysis will be presented in great detail, particularly since one partial example will be given in Chapter 12. Instead, we will focus on some special characteristics of specific program analyses and their results.

Water

The supply of water was one of the first to be studied in a benefit-cost framework, and more recently water pollution also has been examined. An early benefit-cost analysis of water supply was carried out by Roland N. McKean, and other contributions have been made by Jack Hirshleifer, Joe Bain, John Krutilla, and Otto Eckstein.[11] These analyses have included various water control structures, irrigation ditches, hydroelectric power generators, and flood control structures. California and other Western states have had to make significant decisions concerning water.

Not necessarily because of its importance, but because of its illustrative value, we present a recent partial benefit-cost analysis by Alan Carlin and William Hoehn.[12] The study analyzes alternative power sources in relation to two dams in the Colorado River Basin Project. Two separate locations for power plants were considered at subsidized interest rates of $3\frac{1}{8}$ percent and 5 percent. Table 11.4 presents the results of the analysis, evaluating power, fish and wildlife, recreation, and area redevelopment benefits, as well as capital costs, operating costs, power purchases, and additional water evaporation. In spite of favorable interest rate assumptions, the benefit-cost ratio of site 1

TABLE 11.4   Benefits and Costs of Grand Canyon Dams (in millions of dollars)

	Site I (Hualapai Canyon) Interest Rates of		Site II (Marble Canyon) Interest Rates of	
	$3\frac{1}{8}\%$ (1)	5% (2)	$3\frac{1}{8}\%$ (3)	5% (4)
1. Benefits				
a. Power	17.00	20.56	9.67	11.45
b. Fish and wildlife	.66	.66	.18	.18
c. Recreation	.33	.33	.16	.16
d. Area development	.36	.36	.15	.15
e. Total	18.35	21.91	10.16	11.94
2. Costs				
a. Capital costs	20.23	32.21	10.42	16.72
b. Operating costs	4.49	4.49	1.94	1.94
c. Power purchases	.91	.91	.39	.39
d. Additional water evaporation	4.59	4.59	.54	.54
e. Total	30.22	42.20	13.29	19.59
3. Benefit-cost ratio (ratio to one)	0.61	0.52	0.76	0.61

IMPORTANT NOTE: Line 3 overstates the benefit-cost ratios in that Carlin and Hoehn make the following assumptions favorable to the projects: (1) use of overstated costs, (2) exclusion of other Site I benefits, (3) use of Bureau of Reclamation cost indexes, (4) exclusion of value of water in bank storage at Site II, (5) exclusion of effects on aesthetic and other park values, (6) exclusion of possible effect of Site II on boating expeditions, (7) use of stream flows assumed in project reports, and (8) use of heavily subsidized interest rates.

NOTES ON LINES: 1a, columns 1 and 2: from line 9, table 1 of source (see below). Columns 3 and 4: line 9, table 1 minus $0.19 million representing the annual loss of revenue resulting from the reduction in energy generation from the Glen Canyon Power Plant if the Marble Gorge Project is built.

SOURCE: Alan P. Carlin and William E. Hoehn, *The Grand Canyon Controversy—1967: Further Economic Comparisons of Nuclear Alternatives* (Santa Monica, Calif.: RAND, March, 1967), P-3546, p. 17.

is 0.61 and that of site 2 is 0.76, indicating that both are poor investments.[13] If a 5 percent interest rate is assumed, the benefit-cost ratios decline to 0.52 and 0.61, respectively.[14]

In the late fifties a number of water quality management studies were initiated. Robert Davis undertook a large study of the Potomac estuary, with the aid of computer simulation, and produced a listing and cost ranking of some 300 different systems.[15]

The Federal Water Pollution Control Administration engaged in an analysis of different plans for eliminating or reducing the pollution of interstate waters and their tributaries and for improving the sanitary condition of surface and underground waters in the Delaware estuary.[16] This study analyzed water quality objectives, defining four objective sets. Objective set 1, the highest objective set, makes provision for large increases in water-contact recreation in the estuary, and for levels of 6.5 parts per million of dissolved oxygen to provide safe passage for anadromous fish during the spring and fall migration periods. At the other extreme is objective set 4, which generally provides slight improvement in water quality over 1964 conditions. For all four objective sets separately, capital costs and operating and maintenance costs were estimated. Benefit estimates include those from swimming, boating, and sport fishing. The benefit and cost estimates of water quality improvement are summarized in Table 11.5, and it is interesting to note that the Delaware River Basin Commission adopted an objective set falling between sets 2 and 3.

TABLE 11.5   Benefits and Costs of Water Quality Improvement in the Delaware Estuary Area* (in millions of dollars)

Objective Set	Estimated Total Cost	Estimated Recreation Benefits	Estimated Incremental Cost Minimum†	Estimated Incremental Cost Maximum‡	Estimated Incremental Benefits Minimum†	Estimated Incremental Benefits Maximum‡
1	460	160–350				
			245	145	20	30
2	215–315	140–320				
			130	160	10	10
3	85–155	130–310				
			20	25	10	30
4	65–130	120–280				

* All costs and benefits are present values calculated with 3 percent discount rate and twenty-year time horizon.

† Difference between adjacent minima.

‡ Difference between adjacent maxima.

SOURCE: Allen V. Kneese and Blair T. Bower, *Managing Water Quality: Economics, Technology, Institutions* (Baltimore: Johns Hopkins, 1968), p. 233.

Recreation

Many benefit-cost analyses of outdoor recreation are carried out in conjunction with studies of multiple-purpose water development projects or multiple-use land management projects. Therefore many of the studies cited in connection with water resources also contain outdoor recreation analyses. When recreation is part of a multiple-purpose water development project, especially difficult problems arise in assigning costs. Direct costs required for recreation, which would not have been incurred if recreation had been omitted as a project activity, should obviously be charged against recreation.[17] Other problems arise because often there are no readily available market values for outdoor recreation. Persons who do not directly use recreation facilities also benefit from such facilities, and estimating benefits to such nonusers poses a serious estimation problem. Finally, as in the case of all investments with an extended time horizon, outdoor recreation involves uneven distribution of costs and returns over time, and the selection of an appropriate interest rate can affect the conclusion as to whether the investment is justified on economic grounds.[18]

While the recreation issues referred to above mainly relate to state and regional government units, local governments make decisions about neighborhood parks. For example, the City of Los Angeles in the late 1960s constructed two vest-pocket parks, one of about 10,000 square feet and the other of about 3,600 square feet. Both were in almost entirely white areas with relatively few children. Michael Kavanagh undertook a benefit-cost study of these parks.[19] He considered both agency and private cost streams, where agency costs include development and equipment costs, the rental value of the park site, plus the tax stream implicit in the present value of the sites over the life of the park. The private costs include travel and time costs, baby-sitting costs, street congestion costs, property damage, and noise costs. Of the costs, the agency costs and the private travel and time costs appear to make up the greatest part of the project costs. The primary benefits are the valuation of "tot-lot" consumption and the value of time that would be allocated to non-tot-lot uses. Additional benefits include the reduction of property damage and noise, the removal of litter strewn in vacant lots, and the benefits of closer community interaction. Only relatively few cost and benefit elements could in fact be estimated, and their magnitudes are summarized for the Howard Street and McKinley Street parks, assuming 4 percent, 6 percent, and 10 percent discount rates (see Table 11.6). The net present value calculated for a fifteen-year stream turned out to be negative in all cases.

Transport

Usually the movement of persons and goods from point of origin to point of destination makes use of a transport vehicle and roadbed. Benefit-cost analyses of various transport systems under differing conditions have been

TABLE 11.6   Benefits and Costs of Two Vest-pocket Parks, in Los Angeles, California

	Howard Street Park Interest Rates of			McKinley Street Park Interest Rates of		
	4%	6%	10%	4%	6%	10%
Benefits	$89,500	$77,300	$58,300	$58,800	$50,400	$38,100
Costs	97,400	85,900	68,800	60,700	53,100	41,900
Net present value*	−7,900	−8,600	−10,500	−1,900	−2,700	−3,800

* Fifteen-year stream.
SOURCE: J. Michael Kavanagh, "Programmatic Benefit-Cost Analysis of Local Youth Recreation Programs" (Los Angeles: University of California, Institute of Government and Public Affairs, 1968), OR-142.

made. One of the unique challenges facing the analyst relates to the quantification of the value of time savings, convenience, and safety of different transport systems.

We will present a transport benefit-cost study in relation to the Victoria Line (VL), a London Transport Underground railway from Victoria at its southern end to Walthamstow in northeast London.[20] It is assumed that 5½ years will be required to build VL, and that it will be in operation for 50 years. For the calculations a 6 percent discount rate was assumed. Costs were divided into initial capital investments and operating expenses. They were estimated to amount to £1.413 billion. Annual costs at a 6 percent discount rate were £55 million.

Benefits are grouped in terms of beneficiaries: diverted traffic benefits of all those who will use VL in place of other means of transportation; undiverted traffic benefits of those will not divert to VL, but will benefit indirectly through faster, better, and more comfortable transit; and generated traffic benefits that relate to new traffic which will result from the fall in cost of transport, not only on the VL, but because of the VL. Discounting at 6 percent, benefits to undiverted traffic are about 52 percent of the whole, and benefits to diverted traffic about 34 percent of the whole.

Under these three benefit categories, we find benefits due to time savings, fare and cost savings, and comfort and convenience. The most important single benefit, amounting to about 25 percent of the total, is found to be time savings from reducing congestion in London streets. If the other effect of decongestion—savings in vehicle operating costs—is added, the two make 35 percent of total benefits. Further major benefits are savings in bus costs (9 percent), time savings of VL traffic diverting from buses (8 percent), savings in vehicle operating costs to motorists diverting to VL (9 percent), and the value to undiverted passengers on the Underground of the increased probability of getting a seat, i.e., a comfort and convenience item (6 percent).

A feature that distinguishes this study from previous efforts (for example, by T. Coburn et al.)[21] is an attempt to measure comfort and convenience and savings accruing to people not directly connected with, using, or operating the Underground system, i.e., road users benefiting from decongestion. Interestingly, these two categories account for 46 percent of all benefits.

The empirical findings can be summarized as follows: Discounted at 6 percent, the present value of benefits is £86 million, the present value of costs is £55 million, and the present value of net benefits is £31 million. The benefit-cost ratio is 1.57. The rate of return that allows for the effect of time is obtained by calculating the surplus of benefits over current cost of the VL for each year of its life separately. Discounting these back to the present, and expressing the total as a level annual rate of return over the period of construction and operation on the present value of the capital invested turns out to be 11.6 percent at a 4 percent discount rate, 11.3 percent at a 6 percent discount rate, and 10.9 percent at an 8 percent discount rate. The internal rate of return, which equates the rate of interest with the present values of benefits and costs, is approximately 10.5 percent.

Many other important studies of transport benefit-cost have been made, but lack of space prevents us from discussing them.[22]

Housing and Urban Renewal

A variety of empirical studies have been carried out, designed to quantify gains and losses associated with specific housing and redevelopment proposals. They include analyses about the preservation of a historic building,[23] studies of the value of government housing programs to tenants,[24] and comprehensive analyses of urban renewal projects.[25]

A careful study of urban renewal has been carried out by Jerome Rothenberg, which includes a case study that in many respects is illustrative.[26] Rothenberg undertakes a benefit-cost analysis of five renewal projects in Chicago: Michael Reese, Hyde Park A, Hyde Park B, Blue Island, and Lake Meadows. Michael Reese, Hyde Park A, and Lake Meadows are large projects, while the other two are small. Most of these projects were started in the mid-fifties and the postproject situation was assumed to be that in 1962–1963.

On the cost side, gross project costs were estimated, and from them the initial value of land was deducted. Three types of benefits were estimated: internalization of externalties in neighborhood land use and their resulting neighborhood spillovers; income redistribution effect through changes in the structure of the housing stock; and changes in the social costs generated by slums. For example, it was estimated that in the Michael Reese–Lake

Meadows complex in 1955–1963, spillovers accounted for a 28 percent benefit increase; such a finding points to the importance of including spillover estimates.

Income redistribution effects concern transfers of real income through the price changes attendant on changes in the structure of the housing stock. Here the question is: To what extent do dislocatees lose, on balance, and the people who subsequently move into the redeveloped area gain, on balance? For example, it was found that in the Hyde Park B area, 98.3 percent of the housing was substandard, yet 82 percent of the relocatees from this section subsequently obtained residence in standard dwellings.

With regard to social costs of slums, four types of benefits have been identified, each connected with the amelioration of a slum-generated social cost: decreased fire hazards, decreased illness, decreased crime, and decreased damage to personality development. The benefit-cost estimates of the five projects are summarized in Table 11.7. The Lake Meadows project turned out to promise a net benefit of $4.7 million, while at the other end of the spectrum the Michael Reese project promised a $2.9 million net loss.

Education

In the post-World War II period, economists have shown great interest in analyzing education.[27] They have been unable to separate investment and consumption in future production capabilities for the sake of allocating these costs. A second unsolved problem is how to distinguish precisely between those benefits of education which accrue to the student and those which are captured by others; the estimation of indirect benefits, especially, poses extremely grave difficulties. (Some of these issues are discussed in Chapter 12.) Among the direct benefits are incremental earnings, the value of baby sitting, and the value of the education-associated reduction in services of police, judiciary, and welfare agencies.

A partial benefit-cost analysis was undertaken in relation to the efficiency of providing either an additional year· of junior college or its equivalent in summer school sessions during the last five years of secondary education to students who would ordinarily end their education at high school graduation. The costs and benefits of these programs have been calculated in terms of (1) capital costs, operating costs, forgone earnings of the student, and other selected costs and (2) benefits in terms of added income that can be expected as a result of the additional education.

The resulting benefit-cost ratios, tentative estimates only, were: (1) one additional year of junior college—male students, 1.66, and female students, 0.64; five additional years of summer school—male students, 3.23, and female students, 1.47.[28] These benefit estimates are only partial and do not

TABLE 11.7 *Benefit-Cost Evaluation of Urban Renewal (in thousands of dollars)*

Benefit and Cost Categories	Blue Island	Hyde Park B	Hyde Park A	Michael Reese	Lake Meadows
1. Resource cost of project					
a. Gross project costs (GPC)	396	638	10,534	6,235	16,761
b. Less initial value of land (L_0), equals	46	49	6,449	1,596	8,777
c. Total resource costs (TC)	350	589	4,085	4,639	7,984
2. Benefits produced by project					
a. Increased productivity of site land ($L_1 - L_0$)	29	30	5,016	1,719	12,711
b. Increased productivity of neighboring real estate (spillover)	+	+	+	+	+
c. Decreased social costs associated with slums (ΔSC)	+	+	+	+	+
3. Total costs not offset by site land benefit (1c–2a)	321	559	−931 (gain)	2,920	−4,727 (gain)

SOURCE: Jerome Rothenberg, *Economic Evaluation of Urban Renewal* (Washington, D.C.: Brookings, 1967), p. 196.

consider such benefits as a decline in demands for public services that might result from fewer social and personal disorders, traceable to more adequate schooling, etc.

Burton Weisbrod made a benefit-cost study of dropout prevention. He worked with a sample of about 800 St. Louis high school students, sixteen years of age and over, and with an IQ of at least 80.[29] A control group received normal school services, while an experimental group received additional special counseling services, assistance in getting placed on jobs and remaining on jobs, and special assistance on the job from employer and school personnel. By the end of two years, 44.1 percent of the experimental group and 52 percent of the control group had dropped out.

Weisbrod estimated two resource costs per dropout prevented—direct prevention costs of $5,815 and additional instruction costs of $725. He divided benefits between internal and external benefits per dropout prevented, and was able to estimate only one internal benefit, i.e., increased present value of lifetime income of $2,750 per dropout prevented. For such external benefits as increased productivity of cooperating resources, increased social and political consciousness and participation, decreased social costs of crime and delinquency, and decreased social costs of administering transfer payments, Weisbrod could make no empirical estimate, although he considered all of them to have positive values.

The quantifiable items add up to a total net cost of $3,800 per dropout prevented. After discussing some of the shortcomings of the analysis, Weisbrod concluded, "Subject to the many qualifications . . . the particular prevention program . . . was found to be 'unprofitable'—in terms of measured benefits and costs—even before benefits were deflated for the effect of such noneducation factors as ability and ambition. . . ."[30]

A number of empirical studies of higher education have been carried out, emphasizing monetary returns to educational investment and factors affecting it. Examples are works by Herman Miller, Shane Hunt, Orley Ashenfelter, and Burton Weisbrod.[31]

Health

Health and medical services, not unlike education, represent an investment in human capital and also constitute final consumption. The direct costs are the medical care expenditures associated with a disease, and the indirect costs are the lost output, attributable to the disease, that results from premature death or disability. Calculation of indirect costs of a disease or injury presents several problems: the treatment of transfer payments, taxes, and consumption; the work of housewives; the appropriate measure of output loss; the choice of assumptions regarding employment; and the discount rate.[32]

A number of empirical benefit-cost analyses of health services have been carried out and we will refer to some of the more significant ones. A team of physicians and economists undertook, in the mid-sixties, a benefit-cost analysis of different motor vehicle accident control programs.[33] The programs ranged from improving driver training and licensing to improving emergency medical services and increasing seat belt use. Benefits were divided into direct and indirect morbidity savings as well as mortality savings. Amazingly great differences in benefit-cost ratios were found in relation to nine programs summarized in Table 11.8. Increased seat belt use had a benefit-cost ratio in excess of 1,300, while at the other extreme improved driver training had a benefit-cost ratio of less than 2.

Steps also have been taken to analyze air pollution control measures in a benefit-cost framework. For example, Ronald Ridker has attempted to measure some benefits of air pollution control in general, and Hugh Nourse has estimated the effect of air pollution on house values.[34]

Welfare Services

Until Bryan Conley recently concluded a benefit-cost study of a set of local welfare programs, little work had been carried out on such programs. He has analyzed on-the-job training and prevocational training as means of enhancing the opportunities and future earnings capacity of certain underprivileged groups.[35] The on-the-job training program analyzed by Conley is an activity of the Los Angeles United Community Efforts whereby some recruits, mainly those with higher educational achievements and higher motivation and with some previous work experience, are trained in an employer's plant or office. Prevocational training of youths is conducted in the quarters of the United Community Efforts, which allows personnel to use more permissive methods of training and to offer more orientation counseling. Prevocational training under such conditions allows greater economic security for the trainee during the training period, as every trainee is eligible for six months of allowances, as well as companionship with his own social-ethnic group. However, the prevocational student is less well prepared for work experience than a student in the on-the-job training program.

Conley found gross benefits of the on-the-job training program to range from $1.7 million to $3.7 million in terms of additional earning power of trainees and found the costs of the program to be $82,000, resulting in benefit-cost ratios of between 21 and 45. Furthermore it was estimated that a reduction in delinquency of about 16 percent would result. Gross benefits of prevocational training were estimated to range from $3.6 million to $9.2 million, and costs were estimated at $345,000, resulting in benefit-cost ratios ranging from 11 to 27; the reduction in crime was estimated to amount to 15 percent.

Conley also examined, in a benefit-cost framework, the efficiency of

TABLE 11.8 *Benefits and Costs of Accident Control Program, 1968–1972 (in thousands of dollars)*

Unit Number	Program	Program Costs	Estimated Benefits					Benefit-Cost Ratio[a]	
			Total	Morbidity Savings			Mortality Savings[d]	Amount	Rank
				Total	Direct[b]	Indirect[c]			
1	Improve driver licensing	$ 6,113	$ 22,938	$ 7,733	$ 4,278	$ 3,455	$ 15,205	3.8	7
2	Improve driver training	750,550	1,287,022	213,471	117,593	95,878	1,073,551	1.7	9
3	Reduce driver drinking	28,545	612,970	144,323	79,673	64,650	468,647	21.5	6
4	Reduce pedestrian injury	1,061	153,110	46,327	25,574	20,753	106,783	144.3	3
5	Increase seat belt use	2,019	2,728,374	617,610	341,207	276,403	2,110,764	1,351.4	1
6	Improve driving environment[e]	28,545	1,409,891	331,730	183,077	148,653	1,078,161	49.4	5
7	Use of improved restraint systems	610	681,452	152,993	84,223	68,770	528,459	1,117.1	2
8	Increase use of protective devices by motorcyclists	7,419	412,754				412,754	55.6	4
9	Improve emergency medical services[f]	721,478	1,726,384	320,080	131,851	188,229	1,406,304	2.4	8

[a] Represents the ratio of benefits to program costs.

[b] Direct costs include amounts spent for hospital care, physicians' services, nursing home care, other professional services, drugs, and medical supplies.

[c] Indirect costs represent losses in earnings for those whose injury and resulting disability prevent them from working. Included is an imputed value for services of housewives prevented from housekeeping as a result of a motor vehicle accident.

[d] Represents present value of expected lifetime earnings for projected motor vehicle fatalities in each year, calculated for each 5-year age and sex group on the basis of 1964 life tables, 1964 labor force participation rates adjusted for full employment (an average 4 percent unemployment rate), 1964 housekeeping rates, imputed value of housewives' services, 1964 mean earnings, and an annual net effective discount rate of 3 percent.

[e] This program unit would also involve the efforts of other government agencies. The benefits assume such cooperation; however, the costs of the program represent only the Dept. of Health, Education and Welfare effort.

[f] This cost figure should, for the purpose of this benefit-cost analysis, be interpreted in light of the fact that one-third of all emergency medical service is for injury resulting from vehicular accident.

SOURCE: U.S. Dept. of Health, Education and Welfare, *Application of Benefit-Cost Analysis to Motor Vehicle Accidents* (Washington, D.C., August, 1966), p. 11.

in-kind contributions. In some cases the Office of Economic Opportunity requires that local welfare agencies must obtain from local charitable sources 20 percent of their expenditures. This contribution usually is solicited in the form of in-kind contributions, which benefit from partial state and Federal government tax exemptions. Conley demonstrates in relation to in-kind contributions not only that governments at different levels have conflicting interests, but also that from society's point of view in-kind contributions are not an efficient use of society's resources.[36]

In summary, recent years have seen greatly increased and improved state and local government benefit-cost analyses. Only a sampling of the numerous state, local, and regional benefit-cost analyses known to us has been presented in this chapter. Such investigations carried out by researchers in universities, government agencies, research institutes, business firms, and other organizations can move us toward more informed and perhaps more rational decisions.

In addition to the conceptual and measurement problems unique to specific programs, a number of general problems are unresolved. They include finding proper methods of handling benefits and costs not priced in competitive markets, determining proper interest rates to use for discounting, and finding ways for the proper handling of redistributions. Most of the benefit-cost studies have much in common, although some express their results in net benefits, others in benefit-cost ratios, and still others in internal rates of return. In general the benefit-cost ratios provide less information than is needed for the decisions. Ultimately, the decision maker who wants to be helped by the study must evaluate much of the information that the benefit-cost study organizes before he can make a judicious choice. His final decision is likely to be facilitated by looking at benefits and costs in terms of increments.

PROGRAM BUDGET ADMINISTRATION AND ORGANIZATION

The first and second dimensions of program budgeting were structural and analytical. Now we turn to the third dimension, which pertains to the process for implementing and controlling allocative decisions. Program budgeting involves much more than the technical aspects of planning and programming. Even in the design of this system one must grapple with the basis of government goals and objectives and with government decision processes. Goals and objectives are not "solved" through program budgeting, but at least they may be sharpened by it. Administrative-organizational aspects are not just operational problems. They strongly influence and mold the realities of program budgeting.

Organizational and administrative issues of program budgeting, although not a major domain of economists, were recognized and examined in relation to the Federal establishment by Roland N. McKean, Melvin Anshen, and George A. Steiner.[37] While initially the issues of program budgeting appear to have been deemphasized, in the late sixties they received increased attention, mainly because of the administrative difficulties that are encountered.[38]

Time is an available resource, and often a constraint, in budget making. To begin with, budgets and funding decisions must be compatible with long-range planning and programming decisions. The customary budget cycle involves scrutiny of detailed resource requirements during a specific budgeting period, but any decision made at this stage should normally be compatible with approved programs for future periods.

The annual or biennial budget cycle is likely to be continued by state and local governments and has some salutary effects on program budgeting. However, government planning should not be rigidly tied to any arbitrary calendar period, since that would increase the time required to respond to changing demands and would result in an unnecessary concentration of decision making within a short time span. Therefore, the state and local government program budgeting system must provide a means for continuous monitoring and review of program decisions and a mechanism for altering planned resource allocations. Preferably provision for the monitoring and control of approved programs is made through a system of timely progress reports or other information sources. In such a system, significant deviations from expected performance and (or) approved plans can be detected at an early date and any necessary corrective action can be taken. For example, if altering a program would require more than a specified dollar amount, central permission for the change would be required. Dollar thresholds would have to be designated, and methods for reprogramming, evaluation, approval, and enforcement would have to be designed.[39] Most likely, such steps would be facilitated by linking the program budgeting process with the prevailing annual budget cycle.

The identification of informational requirements and the quality of the information obtained are critical for successful operation of the system. Integrated state and local government information schemes should be developed to provide planning and programmatic information for both ex ante decision making and ex post evaluation and control. An additional task is the collection of information for the analytic processes. As program budgets develop, the basic bits of information obtainable from program operation should be provided on a routine basis to program analysts. For example, typical state and local government accounting systems do not provide a basis for estimating incremental costs of various programs, which would be needed in program analysis. The basic information system should contain costing methodologies and relevant data for making such costs accurate enough for use in cost-benefit studies.

State and local governments seek reliable methods by which subprograms and sub-subprograms can be assigned to lower levels of decision making. Such subdivision of programs implies suboptimization analysis and the necessity of a feedback system so that officials at higher levels may evaluate and reevaluate the division of expenditures. It makes a difference whether the central or high-level decision is to set subprogram and sub-subprogram budgets with instructions to achieve the highest obtainable level of output, or to specify targets for subprograms and sub-subprograms with instructions to favor the lowest cost method of attaining the target. Each subprogram and sub-subprogram decision implies that new information is now available and may be used in revising the high-level expenditure division. It is important that organizational arrangements and information systems be provided that tend to bring subprograms and sub-subprograms into harmony with the high-level overall performance of the entire program.

For the sake of implementing agreed-upon plans, an effective system to monitor and evaluate operations is essential. Such a system evaluates not only the efficiency with which programs are administered but also their appropriateness. The design of a monitoring and evaluation system entails the development of tests and measures of effectiveness and a systematic and consistent method to apply these tests. With the aid of such tests, subprograms and sub-subprograms can be continually assessed, not only individually but in relation to other programs. Thus, reasonable criteria, i.e., standards of judging, must be agreed upon in order to determine the extent to which objectives are achieved. A proper application of the test criteria takes into consideration the conditions under which programs are carried out. In the case of primary education, for equal inputs one may not expect the same level of achievement from pupils of differing socioeconomic backgrounds or widely differing intelligence, and criteria must be adjusted for such factors.

When program budgeting is introduced into an organizational setting it creates the need for all sorts of organizational changes, particularly for changes in the relationships between staff and line managers. Little is known about the types of organizational and managerial changes that should follow the introduction of program budgeting or how to prevent or correct resistance to them. The economist has relatively little to offer in this field and must rely on organizational theory, political science, operations management theory, and social psychology. Such disciplines might shed light on the impact of program budgeting on organizations and on useful ways to overcome internal resistance to program budgeting. If officials are to be motivated to use program budgeting, organizational arrangements must be made accordingly. Organizational changes must be developed so that functionaries will respond creatively to program budgeting, and the techniques and information flows from program budgeting staffs must serve the demands of top management.

MULTIYEAR PROGRAM BUDGETING

It was pointed out earlier that to be useful a program budget must have an adequately long time horizon. A simple projection of the most recent budget is insufficient. As stated by Charles Schultze, there are two quite different approaches to multiyear planning and budgeting.[40] In one approach, multi-year program budgeting includes only future consequences of current proposed decisions. In this manner a five-year plan accompanying the budget submission would propose decisions for the first year and show output and money costs of proposed and prior decisions for the subsequent four years. Such an approach is particularly helpful to prevent "foot-in-the-door" financing and helps cope with built-in misinformation and unwarranted expenditure increases. Program budgeting information that provides a measure of yearly program costs and identifies future consequences in the context of net present values reveals the extent to which current decisions will impinge on future options. The shortcoming of this approach is that it does not set multiyear objectives insofar as their attainment requires budgetary commitments beyond the immediate year. Yet many program starts make sense only if there is a reasonable chance of expanding them in subsequent years, and decisions about the desirability of such long-term projects must be made within the context of long-range planning. As Charles Schultze puts it:

> . . . We are dealing with . . . efficiency and effectiveness commitments. Certain programs launched today take priority in the use of budgetary resources over other programs only if, at some future time, they can reach a certain minimum level. If, at that level, they would absorb too large a proportion of available budget resources, relative to other priority needs, then a different pattern of resource allocations should be considered which may exclude these programs altogether.[41]

Just as the program budget for this year should reflect current commitments resulting from a careful consideration of present alternatives, a budget for future years requires a view of the world of tomorrow, an evaluation of the pros and cons of future alternative programs and activities. The selection of the most desirable set of programs and assessment of implications of each year's decisions on future resource use is the crux of multiyear program budgeting. The ideal program budget for a given year assumes that major analytic studies have been carried out and used to determine the detailed budget. A multiyear program budget assumes furthermore that such analytic studies have been made for a sequence of years and that on the basis of these studies a set of preferred programs has been selected and their annual cost implications have been projected into the future.

These analytic studies are incorporated in a program memorandum, which provides the analytic backup for the subprograms and the sub-

subprograms incorporated in the multiyear program budget, ideally stated in terms of resource and monetary cost as well as output. Program memoranda should serve as basic planning documents not only for top management but throughout the government agency. Moreover, they should be regularly updated to provide current statements of objectives, programs, costs, and output.

We are interested in monetary figures in a multiyear program budget and would like to have not only agency cost data but some information on social costs. However, social cost data are very seldom available, and we rarely can have agency cost data, but must use instead either expenditure or obligational authority data. Capital and current cost or expenditure data should be given separately, whenever possible, for better understanding of the timing or implications of decisions and guidance in such policies as bond issuance and taxation. In addition to this, which we call the multiyear financial program, we would like to have a physical program: separate tables prepared to include information on the projected resource requirements. In the case of education, such information would include number of personnel required for each year of the plan and classroom and other space requirements. A specific example of the use that can be made of a multiyear education program is in planning the advance acquisition of land necessary for future school sites. For instance, Donald Shoup and Ruth Mack found that advance land acquisition for school sites in Montgomery County, Maryland, resulted in a saving of $50,200 per advance acquisition when all benefits and costs were discounted at the county's borrowing rate.[42]

Finally, we would like to point to the need for a multiyear output statement, which should give some indication of the products implied by the decisions. Since measurement of many government outputs is extremely difficult, proxies will be required.

This brings us to a discussion of multiyear program budget projection models. The options open to education, particularly in a period of an intermediate length, such as the next five years, are not as many or as great as one would sometimes like. All too often merely small changes are possible. The model should include the following parameters, among others: staff, wages and salaries, facilities and their construction costs, physical plant and the costs of maintaining and operating it, library books and their prices, etc. These parameters are basically related to the number of students to be educated, quality of education, nature of the staff needed, subject matters to be taught, scheduling and size of classes, scheduling of students in other facilities, book requirements, nature of the education process, etc.

A simplified multiyear program budget projection model assumes that decision makers have agreed on a set of desirable programs and that reasonably stable coefficients are known. Such a model has been constructed and in part implemented for the University of California.[43] The model assumes that key policy decisions are made, preferably on the basis of analytic studies about future student-staff ratios, space requirements per student, etc. The basic point of departure of this projection model is enrollments (1) on four levels of the university: lower division, upper division, master's and first-stage doctoral, and second-stage doctoral and (2) by schools and disciplines. Fourteen programs, such as instruction and departmental research, summer sessions, teaching hospitals, and organized research, are identified. Virtually all projected resource and money requirements are derived—directly or indirectly—from projected enrollment figures. All program costs are stated in current prices and salaries and may be updated each year. Faculty requirements are derived directly from student-faculty ratios. Space requirements are derived from numbers of students and faculty-space ratios. Requirements for maintenance and operation of plant are derived from the projected space requirements. Research requirements of organized research institutes, centers, and bureaus are based on the 1966–1967 average expenditure per full-time equivalent (FTE) faculty. Requirements of University Extension are based on projected enrollments and fee income, and those of libraries are related to weighted enrollment and staff; work-load relationships on each campus are based on current university experience.

Ideally we would want to transform this simplified model into a dynamic model, preferably in equation form, which would permit policy variables and coefficients to be varied explicitly and simultaneously over time and their appropriateness to be judged in terms of overall performance criteria. Policy variables could then be manipulated to determine the effects of any set of programs and to estimate their budget implications for any future period. Such a model would give expression to the interdependence of policy variables and would help to estimate policy trade-off costs, which in turn would be compared with separately estimated benefits. Trade-off analyses could be made in relation to such variables as different class sizes, changes in the existing single salary schedule, alternative frequencies of the use of facilities during the day and the week, and different policies to reduce dropouts and increase the speed with which students gain degrees. Such trade-off analyses could be made assuming alternative salary and price levels in future periods. Work along these lines has only begun, and how successful and fruitful it will be remains to be seen.[44]

SUMMARY

Program budgeting is a planning and management process which applies notions of economic efficiency to public decision making. It involves choice among alternatives in order to achieve the most cost-effective use of resources, involving achievement of the greatest effectiveness for given costs or given effectiveness at minimum cost.

It is useful to look at this planning-management process as having structural, analytic, and administrative-organizational dimensions. Work on these three dimensions, particularly the first two, should proceed simultaneously, since the budget structure is influenced by the analytic parts of the system and vice versa.

The format in program budgeting helps to structure and organize funding information. The program budget is output-oriented and composed of convenient, flexible building blocks. This flexibility allows for reformulation of activities to accommodate changes in perspective and objectives of local and state governments. Delineating programs requires careful definition of purposeful missions. The program budget is structured to allow for an extended time horizon so that the future implications of decisions can be better evaluated. Under federalism, a program budget should reflect the sources of funds, who operates the program and with what discretion.

Analysis and evaluation is an integral part of state and local program budgeting and includes the study of objectives and of alternative ways of achieving them, of future environments, and of contingencies and how to respond to them. In this connection, benefit-cost analysis is an important analytical tool. By this method, we attempt to compare social benefits and social costs. Social benefits include the total value of added output or satisfaction resulting from choosing one activity over another. Social costs include all resources required for the activity, in terms of the value in their best alternative use.

Program budgeting analysis can facilitate decision making by state and local government officials on three different levels. On the highest level it can be applied to select the proper budget mix; on the second level it can help determine the best mix of subprograms and sub-subprograms; and on the lowest level it can help determine the most efficient way of obtaining a given program objective. Empirical benefit-cost studies have been carried out in connection with water, outdoor recreation, transport, housing and urban renewal, health, welfare, and other programs. Most of these empirical studies are plagued by difficulties in estimating indirect benefits and in handling intangible and incommensurate costs and benefits. Furthermore, no agreement exists on the proper interest rate.

The third dimension of program budgeting is a process for implementing and controlling allocative decisions. Unless administrative problems are solved, program budgeting is unlikely to be introduced effectively into state and local government, and if it is introduced, it is unlikely to produce productive results. Identification of informational requirements and the quality of the information obtained are critical for successful operation of program budgeting. Operational methods are needed by which subprograms and sub-subprograms can be assigned to lower-level decision making. It is essential that organizational arrangements and information systems are provided which tend to bring subprograms and sub-subprograms into harmony with the high-level overall performance of the entire program. For the sake of implementing agreed-upon plans, an effective system to monitor and evaluate operations is essential.

Finally, program budgeting must have an adequately extended time horizon. Just as the program budget for this year should reflect commitments resulting from a careful consideration of alternatives, a budget for future years requires a view of the world of tomorrow, evaluation of the pros and cons of alternative programs and activities, the selection of the most desirable ones, and assessment of implications of each year's decisions on future resource use. A multiyear program budget assumes that analytic studies have been made for a sequence of years and that on the basis of these studies a set of programs has been selected and their annual cost implications have been projected into the future. Ideally, we would like to take the multiyear program budgeting model as constituting a rigorous general equilibrium model. This would permit policy variables to be varied explicitly and simultaneously and their appropriateness to be judged in terms of overall performance criteria. Policy variables could then be manipulated to determine a preferred set of programs and to estimate their budget implications for a future period. Such a model would give expression to the interdependence of crucial variables and would help to estimate costs, which in turn would be compared with separately estimated benefits.

CHAPTER 12

APPLICATION OF SOME ANALYTIC TOOLS TO MAJOR POLICY CONCERNS

In Chapter 1 we pointed to some problem areas that await solution by state and local governments. For the sake of convenience, we grouped these problem areas into five main categories: service producer, service distributor, revenue raiser, Federal government partnership, and environment provider.

We will take four specific significant policy concerns, propose an analytic framework for their examination, present some empirical results, and in some cases offer policy suggestions.

The first example probes the effect of local industrialization on an area's employment and income as well as on its school district's net fiscal resources. While the emphasis is on revenue raising and production issues, ways by which government can change the environment are also explored.

Next, a question is posed about the significance of intercommunity spillovers associated with primary and secondary public education and the relation of such spillovers to distributional equity of other jurisdictions. The spillover example relates to the questions: Who pays? Who benefits? What financial partnership arrangements between the Federal and state governments can offset, and possibly neutralize, intercommunity spillovers that are considered inconsistent with distributional objectives?

The third example considers some of the advantages and disadvantages of local government consolidation. While it is chiefly concerned with how local governments can efficiently produce, it is also involved with how to raise funds and how to distribute services equitably.

Finally, an attempt will be made to identify and measure possible effects of alternative public policy decisions on the fiscal outlook of state and local governments. An analytic framework for assessing the fiscal resources of state and local governments is developed to help appraise the fiscal outlook and evaluate the nature and scope of alternatives open to governments. A model is built and applied to the Los Angeles Unified School District and the State of New York.

It is hoped that the following pages will demonstrate how some of the concepts and analytic tools developed in earlier chapters can be applied to policy problems of state and local governments.

EFFECT OF LOCAL INDUSTRIALIZATION ON EMPLOYMENT, INCOME, AND NET FISCAL RESOURCES

Local governments are concerned with attracting industries that help attain socially desirable objectives, and to this end governments attempt to provide a conducive environment. The specific issues we wish to elucidate here are: What is the impact of local industrialization on an area's employment and income and particularly on a school district's net fiscal resources? What can local government do through its taxation, bonding, service regulation, and zoning policies to change the environment in which the local private sector helps bring about desirable results?

It is ordinarily assumed that industrialization contributes more in local revenue than it requires in public expenditures; therefore local government officials have frequently called for rapid economic expansion as a means of improving the fiscal health of the jurisdiction. Is this assumption correct, and, if it is, which industries have the most positive effect and how great is the effect? Matters are complicated when the actions of one local government, which is mainly responsible for changing the environment, e.g., a municipal government, have a dominating effect on another local government, e.g., a school district. Furthermore, there is much interest in which types of industries have particularly strong positive effects on employment and local per capita income and in whether either or both variables are closely correlated with the jurisdiction's fiscal health.

We will attempt to present an analytic framework within which it becomes possible to relate different types of local industrial development to a region's level of employment and per capita income, as well as to its fiscal health in general and that of its public schools in particular. The specific question for which we need an analytic framework is: How much employment and per capita income will a given local industrial development add, and how much will it add to or take away from the net fiscal resources available to the public schools of the region? A positive answer will mean, for example, that local industrial development permits the reduction of local school tax rates, while services are maintained at their existing quality per unit serviced and the price level remains unchanged.

There are at least two extensions of this question, each of which is important but at the moment most likely not empirically researchable. The first is: Does industrial development within the city limits increase or decrease the ultimate money burden of taxes for people in the region, while services rendered by their public officials remain at the existing level? The second is: Does such a development increase or decrease the net benefits accruing to the people in the jurisdiction, while services remain at the existing level? The conceptual and empirical difficulties associated with tax incidence theory discussed in Chapter 4 appear to prevent ready answers to the first question, and similar difficulties associated with state and local government benefit-cost analysis discussed in Chapter 11 inhibit us from finding easy answers to the second question. Therefore, we will build a model that has net fiscal health as its criterion and requires, in line with discussions in Chapter 11, estimation of the impact of exogenous and local private sector forces on local government expenditures as well as revenues.

Our model employs a regional input-output analysis together with major side calculations.[1] Such a model does not fully integrate local government services into regional input-output tables, but relates services expenditures and revenues to input-output information, in two stages, with the help of an array of subsidiary and supporting computations. In stage 1, a regional input-output model is built that yields information on regional output and income multipliers. With their aid, the impact of changes in final demand on output and income is estimated. In stage 2 of the analysis, revenue and expenditure implications are estimated from stage 1 information, using a variety of side calculations.

In stage 2 of the analysis we look on the revenue side of the model at sources of local government revenue such as property tax base, sales and gross receipts tax bases, income tax base, various user charges, and receipts from other governments. Assuming that local government output programs financed by user charges are self-supporting or yield only insignificant surpluses or losses to the general revenue budget, we can ignore user-charges revenue in an inquiry into net fiscal health, since expansions and contractions of service levels will be appropriately offset by changes in revenue. In relation to income taxes we can use an input-output matrix to directly estimate income effects. From this income information we then can estimate sales implications and sales tax receipts. For analyses made for some purposes, state and Federal aid might be ignored.

However, a special model must be constructed to determine the effects of various activities on the property tax base and hence on the net fiscal health of the community. Local government's property tax receipts are affected by an extremely complicated maze of interactions which can bring about changes in industrial and commercial as well as in residential property tax bases. The direct output and the indirect and income-induced output (which is obtained with the aid of the inverse regional input-output matrix) are multiplied by capital-output coefficients to yield estimates of changes in the industrial and commercial property tax base of each sector. At the same time, the direct output and the indirect and income-induced output for each sector are multiplied by the sector output-employment ratios to yield sector employment estimates. The worker-family ratio is used to convert the employment figure into number of family figures for each sector. With the aid of data on family income by sector and an income–residential-property value coefficient, residential property value per family per sector is obtained. Each of these values, multiplied by the number of families per sector, yields an estimate of residential property values per sector. Finally, estimates of sector industrial and commercial property value changes, on the one hand, and of residential property changes, on the other, are multiplied by the property tax rate to yield an estimate of the locally raised property tax. Estimating the impact of nonlocal government activities on local government tax receipts in this manner is likely to be superior to direct estimation from the input-output matrix. In the short run, particularly because of business cycles, total output of the area tends to be poorly correlated with the property tax base and tax rate.

Let us next turn to the expenditure side. The expenditure impact model must facilitate estimation of the impact of exogenous and private internal sector activities on the area's population and property to estimate the services demand of these activities. Again we can start by tracing the initial stimulus that generates the direct and the indirect and income-induced sector output changes. Individual public output programs must be described in physical quantities and in dollar values whenever possible. The factors affecting the production of these services are identified, analyzed, and related to the information generated in stage 1. With the aid of sector output-employment ratios, we can translate output into sector employment, which in turn can be translated into population figures from which we can make estimates of school enrollment, patients, welfare recipients, etc. Furthermore, from the employment or population figures, we can obtain estimates of residential, commercial, industrial, and recreational acreages as well as of property values, street mileage, etc.

Since a regional input-output table for the St. Louis Standard Metropolitan Statistical Area (SMSA) in 1955 is available, the net fiscal health planning model has been implemented in relation to the 16 major industrial sectors of St. Louis, assuming a $1 million increase in final demand in each of them. Instead of estimating the effect of final demand changes on net fiscal health in relation to all local urban government services sectors, this case study concentrates on the primary and secondary public education services subsectors. The results are summarized in Table 12.1 on pages 260 and 261.

A $1 million final demand increase of the St. Louis food and kindred products industry is estimated to lead to direct, indirect, and income-induced employment increases of 75 employees. Two industries, motors and generators and lumber and furniture, topped the list with 194 new employees. (See column 1 of Table 12.1.) At the bottom of the list are the products of the petroleum and coal industry, known for highly capital intensive production methods. New employment generated by the first group of industries is almost five times as high as that generated by the latter. The average is 144 employees.

The per family income that is generated directly, indirectly, and through induced income by a $1 million final demand change is presented in column 2. As can readily be seen, the industry which has the smallest employment impact (products of petroleum and coal) has the largest per family impact, about $6,050. As expected, such low-wage industries as textiles and apparel and leather and leather products have the smallest income impacts, $4,230 and $4,510, respectively.[2] However, income impacts appear to differ much less than employment impacts.

Columns 3 and 4 of Table 12.1 represent the residential and the industrial and commercial property impacts, respectively. Principally because of its employment characteristics, the motors and generators industry also produced the largest increase in residential property values, $1.96 million. The products of the petroleum and coal industry, with $0.55 million, are at the other end of the spectrum. The average is $1.47 million.

Increases in industrial and commercial property values varied relatively little among the different industries. The high was $1.1 million for the plumbing and heating supply, paper and allied products, iron and steel, and chemical industries. The low was the food and kindred products industry, with $0.49 million. The average was $0.88 million.

Columns 5 and 6 show the school tax revenue generated from residential property and industrial and commercial property, respectively. The former varied from a high of $11,346 to a low of $3,188, and the latter from $6,457 to $2,859.

A comparison of columns 5 and 6 is most revealing. There can be no doubt that if full employment and full plant utilization are assumed, a given final demand increase tends to bring about a greater variation in newly generated residential than in industrial and commercial property tax receipts. The standardized range of the residential property tax increases is almost 60 percent larger than the industrial and commercial property tax increases.

Furthermore, and this is even more significant, the increased revenue from new residential property values exceeded that from industrial and commercial property by a substantial margin. In all but one case, the increased residential property tax revenue exceeded the industrial and commercial revenue. The exception was the products of the petroleum and coal industry.

TABLE 12.1   Impact of $1 Million Final Demand Changes on Selected Industrial

	(1)	(2)	(3)	(4)
			Property Value Impact	
Industrial Sector	Employ-ment Impact (no. of em-ployees)	Per Family Income Impact	Residential Use (× 1,000)	Industrial and Com-mercial Uses (× 1,000)
Food and kindred products	75	$5,860	$ 833	$ 493
Textiles and apparel	182	4,230	1,594	646
Lumber and furniture	194	5,120	1,882	1,044
Paper and allied products	148	5,290	1,523	1,101
Printing and publishing	185	5,840	1,939	931
Chemicals	101	5,710	1,156	1,064
Products of petroleum and coal	42	6,050	550	802
Leather and leather products	174	4,510	1,559	632
Iron and steel	145	5,480	1,545	1,090
Nonferrous metals	126	5,410	1,324	1,045
Plumbing, heating supply	189	5,250	1,931	1,113
Machinery (nonelectric)	178	5,530	1,827	865
Motors and generators	194	5,500	1,956	794
Motor vehicles	81	5,550	869	601
Other transport equipment	123	5,740	1,300	754
Miscellaneous	171	5,140	1,731	1,028
Average	144	5,388	1,470	875

SOURCE: Werner Z. Hirsch, "Local Impact of Industrialization on Local Schools,"

The ratio was more than 2 to 1 in favor of the residential property tax in five cases: textiles and apparel, printing and publishing, leather and leather products, nonelectric machinery, and motors and generators. The average revenue increase from new residential property was $8,525, and that from industrial and commercial property was $5,076. The first figure is almost 70 percent larger than the second.

These two findings point to the severe shortcomings of fiscal impact studies that consider exclusively the direct commercial and industrial revenue implications of industrialization.

Column 7 presents the total increased property tax revenue generated by a $1 million final demand increase. The plumbing and heating supply industry tops the list with $17,654, and the food and kindred products industry shows a low of $7,688.

Turning now to annual school costs, we find the motors and generators

Sectors, St. Louis, Missouri, 1955

(5)	(6)	(7)	(8)	(9)	(10)
				School District Net Fiscal Resources Impact	
	School Tax Revenue Impact				
Residential Property	Industrial and Commercial Property	Total	Annual School Cost Impact	Without State Aid	With State Aid
$ 4,829	$2,859	$ 7,688	$ 8,364	$— 676	$ 975
9,243	3,748	12,991	20,347	−7,356	−3,361
10,917	6,056	16,973	21,623	−4,650	− 404
8,833	6,388	15,221	16,541	−1,320	1,928
11,244	5,399	16,643	20,605	−3,962	100
6,706	6,173	12,879	11,291	1,588	3,808
3,188	4,649	7,837	4,704	3,133	4,063
9,040	3,666	12,706	19,436	−6,730	−2,899
8,961	6,323	15,284	16,183	− 899	2,284
7,682	6,059	13,741	14,024	− 283	2,470
11,197	6,457	17,654	21,094	−3,440	710
10,595	5,016	15,611	19,900	−4,289	− 375
11,346	4,605	15,951	21,623	−5,672	−1,426
5,040	3,483	8,523	7,775	748	2,525
7,540	4,373	11,913	13,663	−1,750	938
10,039	5,963	16,002	19,088	−3,086	662
8,525	5,076	13,601	16,016	−2,415	750

Review of Economics and Statistics, vol. 46 (May, 1964), p. 196.

and the lumber and furniture industries on one end of the spectrum, with an annual cost increase of $21,623, and the products of the petroleum and coal industry at the other end, with $4,704. The average was $16,016.

The last two columns of Table 12.1 are perhaps the most interesting. Column 9 represents the net fiscal resources status change of public schools exclusive of state aid as a result of a $1 million final demand increase. Thus, 13 out of 16 types of industrialization led to losses. (See Table 12.2.) The greatest loss in the net fiscal resources status was incurred when industrialization took the form of textile and apparel manufacturing. In that case a $1 million final demand increase resulted in a $7,356 deterioration of the net fiscal resources status of the district. Industrialization also led to major losses when it took the form of leather and leather products, motors and generators, and lumber and furniture industries. Net gains of $3,133, $1,588, and $748, respectively, resulted from the products of petroleum and coal, chemicals, and motor vehicles industries. Not only were there few industries that produced gains, but the gains were small. On the average, $2,415 would have been lost per $1 million final demand.

To reflect more fully the fiscal position of the school district, one must add intergovernmental transfer payments, that is, state subsidies to the locally raised revenue. (See column 10 of Table 12.1.) If adjustments are made for state aid, the picture changes, and 10 of the 16 industries produce improvements in the net fiscal resources status of the school district, 5 continue to lead to a deterioration, and 1 is about neutral, in that it leads to a change of a mere $100, not enough to warrant placing it in either of the other two groups. (See Table 12.2.) Even after adjusting for state aid, one finds that the net fiscal resources status of the district would have deteriorated most if the textiles and apparel industry had expanded ($3,361 per $1 million final demand) and improved most if the products of the petroleum and coal industry had expanded ($4,063 per $1 million final demand). Other industries contributing net fiscal losses are leather and leather products, motors and generators, lumber and furniture, and nonelectrical machinery. It can be concluded furthermore that, under the stipulated assumptions and after adjusting for state aid, a $1 million final demand increase in each of the 16 major St. Louis industries would have led to a $750 improvement in the 1955 net fiscal resources of the school district.

What can we say about the relative order of magnitude of the net fiscal resources? The 1955 St. Louis final demand of these 16 industries amounted to about $3.3 billion. For example, a major industrial expansion of 10 percent, equally distributed among the 16 industries, would have improved the schools' net fiscal resources status by $2.5 million, which is about 4 percent of 1955 public school expenditures.

TABLE 12.2   *Effect of Given Final Demand Increase on Resources Status of Selected Industrial Sectors, St. Louis, Missouri, 1955*

	Without State Aid	With State Aid
Positive net fiscal resources status change	3	10
Negative net fiscal resources status change	13	5
No net fiscal resources status change	0	1

SOURCE: Table 12.1.

Let us summarize the results. The case study confirms the claim that industrialization, on the average, improves the fiscal health of a school district, but only if state aid is included as a revenue source. Yet is also calls for a rejection of the hypothesis that local industrialization in all cases improves the net fiscal resources status of the district. Let us hasten to state that even in those cases in which the fiscal results are negative, increased benefits from education may exceed the cost increases.

Why do some industries affect the net fiscal resources status of a school district positively and others negatively? Apparently, on the one hand, low-wage industries have many employees with school-age children, and yet their plants and the homes of their employees have a relatively low assessed valuation. About the opposite appears to hold for high-wage, capital intensive industries, such as products of coal and petroleum. But even here the gains are perhaps smaller than expected, since parents with high incomes tend to insist on high-quality education, which is costly to the school district unless the parents prefer private schools.

It is interesting that the 8 St. Louis industries which generated an employment increase in excess of 170 employees led either to net fiscal resources losses or to very small gains. There was a reasonably high negative correlation between the number of new employees generated by an industry and the school district's net fiscal resources change, excluding state aid. The rank correlation coefficient is $-.805$, which for 16 observations is statistically significant at a probability level of 0.05.

Can we estimate the net fiscal resources impact of a given type of industrialization if we have only employment and income impact estimates? In other words, is there perhaps a shortcut which can give us good estimates without complicated cost and revenue side calculations? Our hypothesis would be that the net fiscal resources impact is correlated negatively with the employment impact and positively with the family income impact; that is,

$$X_1 = a_{1.23} - b_{12.3}X_2 + b_{13.2}X_3 \qquad (12.1)$$

where

X_1 = net fiscal resources impact after adjustment for state aid
X_2 = employment impact
X_3 = family income impact

Using the data in columns 1, 2, and 10 of Table 12.1, we obtain the following values for 1955:

$$X_1' = 7,676.486 - 20.325X_2 + 21.080X_3 \qquad (12.2)$$
$$(.5540) \qquad (.5661)$$

The values in parentheses are partial correlation coefficients. With 13 degrees of freedom, these coefficients are statistically significant at a probability level of 0.05, if they are larger than .514. Thus, both are significant. The coefficient of multiple determination adjusted for degrees of freedom lost ($R_{1.23}{}^2$) is .6363. It, too, is statistically significant at a probability level of 0.05.

In general, it appears that the net fiscal resources status improves most if expansion occurs in an industry that has major income and only minor employment effects.

By what means can the local environment be modified so as to induce "desirable" private industry to expand or to locate in the area? Inducements usually take the form of advantageous taxes, services, and zoning decisions and other regulations. Few of these means are available to the school district, and for this reason it must cooperate closely with the municipal government. They can jointly decide to provide select tax incentives to those industries they seek most. Municipal government can also provide such industries with preferential regulatory treatment as well as services. While it can help industry directly through favorable zoning decisions, local government can also do so indirectly by zoning that tends to keep out large families with low incomes and, as a result, provides for a desirable relationship between services and taxes. In practice, this means zoning for single-family dwellings on large lots; however, such zoning is likely to be self-defeating in areas close to industrial plants. Clearly, the social justice of such a step is, at best, questionable.

INTERCOMMUNITY SPILLOVERS AND DISTRIBUTIONAL INEQUITIES

Public services are provided in the United States within a federated political structure in such a way that, except for defense and space exploration, local and state governments make important decisions. This political structure was generally formulated almost two centuries ago when our present complex and highly interdependent industrial economy was only beginning to emerge. In those days of physical isolation, individualism, and self-determination, each community raised funds to finance its services, and virtually all cost burdens and benefits stayed within its boundaries. However, in a modern nation which enjoys a federated political and fiscal system and is distinguished by great specialization of economic activity—and therefore economic interdependence—by rapid mobility, and by advanced industrialization and urbanization, local government decisions become much more complex.

In the context of today's industrial economy, people, as well as their commercial activities and products, continuously cross political boundaries, so a wide diffusion of effects can be expected from many government decisions. These effects will be felt in varying degrees in other jurisdictions. For example, parts of both the costs and the benefits generated by the provision of such public services as education in a particular local jurisdiction will utimately be realized by individuals elsewhere. This occurs, for example, when part of the cost of education is shifted outside the school district's political boundary by being included in the prices of goods and services its residents produce and "export." The benefits of education are shifted out of the district by the migration of individuals who initially received education in the district and because of fiscal interdependence.[3]

As a result of intercommunity spillovers, local decisions can be inconsistent with the nation's goals. In Chapter 6 we stated that if any portion of the costs or benefits resulting from a public service provided in one jurisdiction is ultimately realized by residents of another, we speak of intercommunity cost or benefit spillover. The flow can move in both directions—into the jurisdiction and out of it. In the first case we have spillins, and in the second, spillouts.

The general policy problems we would like to raise are: How significant are benefit and cost spillovers? What are their implications for distributional equity? What policies are available to counteract these spillovers? The more specific questions that will be subjected to an empirical analysis are: To what extent do the benefits and costs of primary and secondary public education spill over the boundaries of the Clayton, Missouri, school district? To what extent do education financing decisions of Clayton affect people in other areas (and vice versa), particularly in terms of distributional equity? What policies are available to counteract these effects?

We have chosen for our analysis a local decision-making framework. Within this framework, the political unit that is decisive in evaluating the effects of cost and benefit spillovers is that in which the beneficiary resides when the decision is made. Just as all future events are discounted to their present values, so too are the future places of residence of people related to their present places of residence.

Some of the cost and benefit components of public education, except for the consumption aspects, differ in their time horizons. While most of the costs are incurred during the year in which education is provided, few of the benefits are realized at that time. To the extent that education benefits are measurable, a lifetime investment approach can be taken, discounting the stream of future benefits back to the year for which the cost analysis is made. This technique provides comparability in that costs associated with the education provided during a single year—the budgetary period for school district expenditure decisions—can be examined and compared with benefits related to the same period.

A basic analytic tool is the annual benefit-burden statement of a school district, as discussed in a general way in Chapter 11. It is composed of two columns, cost burdens and benefits for a given year. The entries represent not only the burdens and benefits realized by residents of a given school district from the education it provides and finances but also those benefits or burdens that the district realizes as a result of education provided throughout the country.

Cost entries represent the values in alternative employments of resources allocated to education. Some are direct; i.e., they appear with specific reference to education in the accounting statements of public or private units. Other costs are imputed. The imputed costs can involve operating or capital resources; some are financed out of taxes, and others are not. Among the more interesting imputed operating costs that are not tax-financed are the earnings forgone by students and the various expenses incurred by students and parents while students are attending school. Imputed operating costs financed by taxes are, among others, annual interest on direct operating costs and services rendered by municipalities. All these, together with the largest single cost item, the direct operating costs associated with teaching and non-teaching manpower and materials, constitute the overall cost of operating resources.

There are four major capital costs: the annual principal repayment and the annual interest on outstanding debt, which are direct costs; and the excess of annual capital consumption over annual principal repayment and the interest on school district equity, which constitute the imputed portions of the costs.

On the benefit side, we regard total or social benefits of education as the outward extension of the utility possibility function of society, just as costs are defined as a contraction of that function. The difference between total benefits and costs is the net benefit (or cost) to society associated with a particular education decision.

What are the major forces that can push outward the utility possibility function? First, there are those aspects of education which increase production potential, such as improved skills and capabilities of students, and those which make possible the reallocation, total or partial, of resources. For example, it appears that the presence of educated individuals in a community can reduce the need for such services as law enforcement, fire protection, and public health, and thereby free resources for other uses. However, to the extent that education merely alters relative prices, without affecting total utility opportunities for a particular group, it is omitted from the list of social benefits (or costs). Most education benefits add to long-run satisfaction, i.e., incremental productivity and earnings of students (and their families) attributable to education. Furthermore, some short-run or current benefits are direct and accrue to the student's family while he attends school. Children who are in school do not require the daytime attention of their mothers, who are therefore free to seek employment outside their homes. A partial increment in the output of society results as resources are reallocated.

In addition to these direct benefits to the student and his family, education benefits many other persons. Nonstudent families may receive indirect long-run benefits in the form of lower taxes or increased services or both. If the level of a person's consumption of public services is independent of his education and income, then the additional taxes generally paid by persons with more education and income tend to decrease tax burdens and (or) increase the services to other taxpayers.

Other possible indirect benefits, partly financial and partly nonfinancial, are schooling that can increase the productivity and income of the former student's coworkers and schooling that benefits the student's future children, who will receive from him informal education in the home. Increased education may result in a decline in service needs through a reduction of police, judicial, and other costs of crime as well as of welfare payments; neighborhood living conditions may improve by the application of positive social values developed in children by the schools; employers may be helped by having available a well-trained and skilled labor force; and society at large may be favorably affected by the fact that education furnishes the basis of an informed and literate electorate.

Let us turn to the spillover mechanism. Public education cost spillovers result from both tax and expenditure decisions. The major costs are entered into the burden-benefit statement as a result of analyses of school district revenues. For each revenue source a separate analysis must be made because of different spatial tax incidence patterns. Analysis of these patterns helps to place the ultimate cost burden. The net amount of a district's resources apportioned to its public schools is determined by the level of local taxes, their spatial burden pattern, and the proportion of local tax revenue spent on public education provided within the local community. Together these factors determine the net balance between the ultimate resource cost or tax burden of a community and the amount of resources ultimately utilized for public education. The latter is the expenditure incidence. In a local government decision framework, all costs, except those costs to parents and students that are not related to taxation, can spill in and spill out.

As was mentioned above, it is the school district where the beneficiary resides when an education decision is made that is the decisive factor in evaluating effects of cost and benefit spillovers. Insofar as benefits that come about in the market are concerned, disposable income—which accrues directly to students and their (present) families—does not spill over. This is true for both short- and long-run direct benefits. However, indirect benefits— disposable income and tax benefits which accrue to nonstudent households— can spill over. The reasons are two: migration and fiscal interdependence.

The tax burden considerations include the location of the taxpayer's residence and the geographic jurisdiction of the tax-levying unit. Tax savings of nonstudent families are likely to be realized at all levels of government. To the extent that the additional taxes paid by people with more education exceed the marginal cost of any additional public services they consume because of their additional education—and, therefore, income—some of the benefits of education are thereby transferred to other people within the fiscal units. As a result of education, all nonstudent families in the country benefit from additional taxes paid to the Federal government; all nonstudent families in the state benefit from additional payments to the state; and all nonstudent families in the school district benefit from additional taxes paid to the local government. In short, existing fiscal arrangements are such that part of the benefits appear as tax savings in other districts; i.e., they lead to a sharing of benefits with residents of other districts.

Further benefit sharing comes about because students migrate. Thus, as educational capital moves from one district to another, tax savings are transferred with it. The loss of future tax base, and the consequent tax rate reduction, as a result of student outmigration is a benefit spillout, not a cost of providing local education.

Examining some other benefit elements, we find that within a local government decision framework benefits resulting from incremental productivity and net private earnings of students and of mothers for whom schools provide custodial child care will not spill over. On the other hand, benefits in the form of declining service needs for protection and for social and welfare services readily spill over, if only because of fiscal interdependence.

A key fiscal objective is fiscal progressivity, which requires that some appropriate relationship be. established between those who receive services and benefits and those who ultimately pay for them, specifically that the benefit-cost ratio varies inversely with per capita income.

Empirical Findings

This basic model was applied to Clayton, Missouri, a suburb of St. Louis that had a population of 15,000 in 1960.[4] Only resource opportunity costs and tangible benefits of public education have been estimated; intangible costs and benefits are not included. The spatial distribution of costs is based on estimated average tax shifting patterns; these are assumed to reflect the spatial shifting of a marginal tax increase. Migration patterns and rates for 1959–1960 are assumed to continue for all future periods. Benefits are discounted at an annual compound rate of 5 percent; they are identified geographically with the beneficiary's area of residence during the period the education is provided—not with the area in which the beneficiary lives when the benefit is actually realized.

Figure 12.1 presents a summary of the public education benefits and costs generated and realized by Clayton for 1959–1960 and relates them to five other areas. The dollar benefits (+), costs (−), and net (+ or −) entries in each cell of the first row are the discounted present values of

FIGURE 12.1 Benefits and costs of public education generated and realized by Clayton, Missouri, by area, 1959–1960 (in thousands of dollars). Source: Werner Z. Hirsch, Elbert W. Segelhorst, and Morton J. Marcus, Spillover of Public Education Cost and Benefits (Los Angeles: University of California, Institute of Government and Public Affairs, 1964), p. 385.

Generating area / Realizing area	1	2	3	4	5	6	Total spillouts	Total Clayton education
1. Clayton School District	+2,979 / −1,647 / +1,332	+24 / −568 / −544	+21 / −84 / −63	+7 / −57 / −50	+44 / −115 / −71	+738 / −409 / +329	+834 / −1,233 / −399	+3,813 / −2,880 / +933
2. Rest of St. Louis County	+38 / −574 / −536	+8 (0.57)* / −389 (4.17)						
3. City of St. Louis	+29 / −481 / −452	−177 (1.71)	−874 (4.75)					
4. Rest of SMSA	+18 / −245 / −227		−1,013 (2.73)	−2,445 (1.93)				
5. Rest of Missouri	+86 / −1,031 / −945			−2,445	−2,445			
6. Rest of United States	+1,353 / −2,037 / −684							
Total spillins	+1,524 / −4,368 / −2,844							
Total education, all areas	+4,503 / −6,015 / −1,512							

* Figures in parentheses are spillover ratios, i.e., the ratio of the spillout ratio (benefits spilled out over costs spilled out) to the spillin ratio (benefits spilled in over costs spilled in).

Clayton-provided education. From its own education Clayton realized a net benefit in excess of $1.3 million, while society as a whole realized a net benefit of $945,000. The difference between these net figures was the net cost spillout of $389,000. Of the five other areas, only the rest of the United States realized net benefit from Clayton's education; all of Clayton's neighboring areas realized net costs, ranging from $50,000 to over $500,000.

The dollar entries in each cell of the first column in Figure 12.1 represent the present values of benefits, costs, and nets realized by Clayton as a result of education provided in all areas, and the bracketed entries are spillover ratios. Although Clayton realized a net benefit of $1.3 million from its own education, the net cost spillin of $2.8 million from other areas left Clayton with a net cost from public education of nearly $1.5 million. Clayton realized net cost spillins from each of the five other areas ranging from approximately $250,000 to $1 million.

The diagonal entries of Figure 12.1 indicate the net spillover position of Clayton with respect to other areas. Only with respect to one area, St. Louis County, did Clayton realize a relative gain—a small one of $8,000. In total, Clayton realized a net cost or loss in wealth of $2.4 million as the result of spillovers. Because of spillovers the $933,000 net benefit Clayton would have realized from its own education in a closed, migrationless economy was turned into a net cost of $1.5 million.

In Table 12.3 the net spillover magnitudes between Clayton and other areas, shown on the diagonal in Figure 12.1, are related to per capita income of the various areas. In the center of the table are the magnitudes of spillovers between Clayton and each area. On the left these magnitudes are shown in relation to Clayton, first on a per capita basis and then as a percentage of per capita income in Clayton for 1959. All spillovers decrease per capita wealth in Clayton by $163 or nearly 2 percent of 1959 per capita income. To the right the consequences of these spillovers are shown for the areas interacting with Clayton. Both on a per capita and increase in per capita income basis, St. Louis City gained most.

Are spillover relations between Clayton and other areas operating in the direction of equity? If per capita income is selected as the index of wealth, then the criterion of equity in relation to intercommunity spillovers is that spillovers should benefit the poorer areas relative to the wealthier. Table 12.3 shows that Clayton has a higher per capita income than the other five areas. If the spillover relations between Clayton and the other areas are to satisfy the equity criterion, then Clayton should be a net loser. Figure 12.2 indicates that this is true for Clayton's relations with four of the five areas, since negative dollar figures are entered in the diagonals of the chart. Only in relation to the rest of St. Louis County is Clayton a net gainer, and there the magnitude is small ($8,000).

TABLE 12.3   Relation of Clayton Net Spillovers to 1959 Per Capita Income, by Area (in dollars and percentages) *

In Relation to Clayton			In Relation to Other Areas	
Dollars Per Capita	% of Per Capita Income	Net Spillovers with	Dollars Per Capita	% of Per Capita Income
+ 0.53	+0.0063	2. Rest of St. Louis County		
		$8,000	−0.012	−0.0002
− 25.93	−0.3090	3. City of St. Louis		
		$389,000	+0.510	+0.0155
− 11.80	−0.1406	4. Rest of Standard Metropolitan Statistical Area		
		$177,000	+0.303	+0.0077
− 58.27	−0.6944	5. Rest of Missouri		
		$874,000	+0.318	+0.0109
− 67.53	−0.8048	6. Rest of United States		
		$1,013,000	+0.006	+0.0002
−163.00	−1.9426	Total net spillovers		
		$2,445,000	+0.014	+0.0003

* Per capita income by area: Clayton School District, $8,391; rest of St. Louis County, $5,317; City of St. Louis, $3,289; rest of Standard Metropolitan Statistical Area, $3,888; rest of Missouri, $2,912; rest of United States, $3,667.

SOURCE: Werner Z. Hirsch, Elbert W. Segelhorst, and Morton J. Marcus, *Spillover of Public Education Costs and Benefits* (Los Angeles: University of California, Institute of Government and Public Affairs, 1964), p. 389.

We can apply a still stronger equity criterion, namely, that the lower the per capita income in an area relative to the subject area (Clayton), the greater should be the transfer of wealth from rich to poor through the spillover process. To test this criterion we will divide the gains to Clayton (benefit spillins and cost spillouts) by the losses to Clayton (benefit spillouts and cost spillins). The resultant ratio will be greater than 1 if Clayton is gaining and will be less than 1 if Clayton is losing. (This ratio removes the size of the economic areas from consideration, whereas using only the net differences of Figure 12.1 would lead us astray.) As the per capita income of an area rises (and it should be remembered that all areas are poorer than Clayton in this example), the ratio should rise. Ideally, if Clayton and another area had the same per capita income, this strong equity criterion would say that the ratio of Clayton's gains and losses through spillover interaction should be equal to 1. In Figure 12.2 the 45° line indicates the points that would perfectly satisfy this equity criterion. Points above the 45° line indicate that the strong equity criterion is violated in Clayton's favor, while points below that line represent violations of the criterion in favor of other areas. We see in

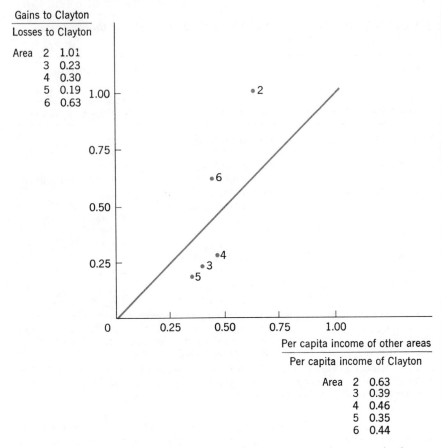

FIGURE 12.2   *Clayton gain and loss ratios relative to comparative per capita income.*

Figure 12.2 that the ideal is not met but that in three of the five observations spillovers operate to favor areas poorer than Clayton more strongly than our criterion suggests, while in the two remaining areas spillovers operate less strongly than the criterion suggests.

In summary, the case study indicates that spillovers are of major magnitude for the Clayton school district. The existing patterns of economic interaction and fiscal interdependence, aided by the progressive features of the Federal income tax, provide for net transfers from Clayton to four of the five other areas. Since each of these areas is less wealthy than Clayton, distributional equity is being satisfied. There is also some evidence that the poorer an area is, in relation to Clayton, the more spillovers operate to diminish the wealth differential, but this factor is not firmly established.

IMPLICATIONS OF LOCAL GOVERNMENT CONSOLIDATION

The United States is a country of many governments, although in recent years the number has been declining appreciably. Local government units numbered more than 81,000 in 1967 compared with more than 91,000 in 1962, 117,000 in 1952, and 155,000 in 1942. As can be seen from Table 12.4, during the last twenty-five years the most remarkable changes have taken place in the number of school districts, which declined by almost 50 percent, and in the number of special (other than school) districts, which increased more than $2\frac{1}{2}$ times.

Since World War II, there has been great interest in reduction of the number of local governments, mainly through consolidation. What are the pros and cons of consolidation, and how can they be determined? To shed light on this question, ideally we would like to build an analytic framework in which we can identify and quantify the major advantages and disadvantages of local government consolidation; discuss and evaluate those which lend themselves only to qualitative statements at this time; and evaluate and compare the overall costs and benefits of such consolidation. Furthermore, under ideal conditions we would hope to identify some of those groups who are likely to lose or gain from consolidation.[5]

Three major virtues have been claimed for local government consolidation: savings due to economies of scale, improved conditions for coordinated and orderly planning for growth, and equity in financing government services.

Analytical as well as empirical issues of economies of scale have been examined in Chapters 7 and 8 and can be summarized as follows: Although

TABLE 12.4   *Local Government Units, Selected Years 1942–1967*

Year	Counties	Townships and Towns	Municipalities	School Districts	Other Special Districts	Total
1942	3,050	18,919	16,220	108,579	8,299	155,067
1952	3,049	17,202	16,778	67,346	12,319	116,694
1957	3,047	17,198	17,183	50,446	14,405	102,279
1962*	3,043	17,144	17,997	34,678	18,323	91,185
1967*	3,049	17,107	18,051	21,782	21,264	81,253
Net change 1942–1967	(−1)	(−1,812)	(+1,831)	(−86,797)	(+12,965)	(−73,814)
1967 divided by 1942	(1.00)	(.90)	(1.11)	(.20)	(2.56)	(.52)

* 1962 and 1967 data include Alaska and Hawaii.

SOURCE: *U.S. Census of Government*, 1942, 1952, 1957, 1962, and 1967.

consolidation of very small local government units is likely to result in benefits from scale economies, such consolidation into huge local governments is likely to produce major diseconomies. In this respect, local governments appear to be distinctly different from private industry, except for bonding and for water, gas, electric power, and sewage disposal services. Most local government services require relatively close geographic proximity of service units to service recipients; this prevents the establishment of huge primary schools, fire houses, police stations, or libraries. Local government services are also labor intensive, with wages and salaries often accounting for more than two-thirds of the current costs. Further concentration of manpower can increase the bargaining power of labor and this, in turn, increases costs. While some economies result from bulk purchases of supplies and equipment, such savings can be outweighed by inefficiencies resulting from top-heavy administration and the ills of political patronage in very large governments. Therefore, in terms of economies of scale, governments serving from 50,000 to 100,000 urbanites might be most efficient.

The second claim for consolidation relates to coordinated and orderly planning for growth. Through consolidation of government units, spillovers are internalized and can be more explicitly taken into consideration in planning and nursing the orderly growth of the area. This advantage of consolidation is somewhat counteracted by a sacrifice of freedom to act individually and independently. Perhaps the most serious questions in this context have been raised by James R. Schlesinger, who is convinced that "large organizations suffer from a geometric increase in the difficulty of *a*) successfully communicating intentions and procedures, *b*) establishing a harmonious system of incentives, and *c*) achieving adequate cohesion among numerous individuals and sub-units with sharply conflicting wills."[6] He goes on to point out that "large organizations find it hard to anticipate, to recognize, or to adjust to change. . . . Changes in the environment can only be appreciated by small groups initially. To influence a large organization—to get the prevailing doctrine changed—is a time consuming process, and by the time it is accomplished the new views will themselves be on the verge of obsolescence. This may account for the organizational propensity to zig and zag."[7] If large organizations are centralized there can be a declining incentive to consider alternatives and an increasing pressure simply to get decisions made. As a result, as Roland N. McKean points out, large centralized governments may be tempted to neglect the variety of choices open to them. More importantly, they may be inclined to underestimate uncertainties.[8]

A third virtue claimed for consolidation is equity. Since in a metropolitan area many costs and benefits spill over municipal and district boundaries, benefits accruing to certain residents of the area are not matched by their tax contributions. Furthermore, since some tax jurisdictions are havens for industry, others for rich residents, and still others for poor residents, consolidation permits bringing the tax base of the entire area more nearly in line with the principle of ability to pay. However, it must be conceded that equity is a somewhat ambiguous concept. Since reliance is placed on both income- and wealth-related taxes for financing urban government services, equity can at best be attained with regard to one or the other, but not to both, unless income and wealth bases are highly correlated. There is also a philosophical issue: Do we benefit from giving all urbanites the same public service, since not everyone has the same preference functions?

But even if we agree that increased equity is important as an objective, various fiscal arrangements can be relied on to attain this objective without a change in government structure. Federal and state subsidies to local urban governments have worked in this direction and have produced similar results, as shown in studies by Jesse Burkhead and Donald J. Curran. Their case studies of Cuyahoga County, Ohio, and Milwaukee County, Wisconsin, indicate that in the postwar period, per capita expenditures of urban governments have grown increasingly similar.[9]

Under certain circumstances consolidation of local governments is likely to have other distinct shortcomings besides those of diseconomies of scale and overcentralization. Thus, consolidation tends to reduce, if not eliminate, consumer choice with regard to local government services. The presence of numerous governments makes it possible for people to select their places of residence according to their tastes in education, police protection, etc. Wholesale consolidation would eliminate these choices, except to the extent that the services could be procured privately.

A further distinct cost of consolidation is that it removes people from their government. Small local government has sentimentally, and perhaps correctly, been extolled as the last bastion of "town meeting" government. It is the only level at which people in government can effectively meet and engage in democratic dialogue with citizens.

In a large country with rapidly growing urban populations and increasing complexity of life under the best of circumstances, the distance between the governing and the governed tends to be very great. As a result many people feel frustrated and disenfranchised. Some may conclude that they have no way of affecting government decisions although such decisions heavily affect them. Sociologists and psychologists have concluded that in extreme cases of frustration people tend to turn to illegitimate forms of protest—civil disobedience, riots, assassinations, etc.—in order to get their government to listen to them.[10] The movement to break up huge, faceless urban government was spearheaded in the late 1960s by Negroes who wanted more voice and participation in school affairs. While some advantages are clear, some short-comings also are evident, the most important of which are perhaps socio-political, namely the furthering of segregation.

Considering the various pros and cons, the conclusion of the Royal Commission on Local Government in Greater London makes much sense:

> . . . As many local functions as possible should be given to local authorities of the smallest practicable size. Our reason for this is that we believe that local authorities should be small enough to maintain and promote a sense of community in local affairs, and, if possible, to stimulate the practical interest of electors. On the other hand, we believe that they must be large enough and strong enough financially to carry the necessary staffs for the performance of their functions. The ideal size logistically varies beween function and function, and some round average must be produced. We thought that the optimum size would be a minimum of about 100,000 inhabitants, and a maximum of about 250,000, and we thought that these boroughs should be achieved partly by keeping existing boroughs unaltered and partly by amalgamations of the smaller boroughs, urban district councils and rural district councils.[11]

In the postwar period, in spite of early strong advocacy of consolidation, hardly any large-scale mergers and few small mergers have taken place.[12] What are some of the reasons?

The first point one might want to make is that consolidation did not offer as many advantages as the first protagonists claimed. Furthermore, metropolitan areas are heterogeneous in their interests and outlooks. While newspapers, real estate interests, banks, retail trade, railroads, and utilities are often vociferous in favor of consolidation, large manufacturers that sell in the national market and fear higher taxes, and residents who are afraid that further traffic congestion, air pollution, juvenile delinquency, etc., will be stimulated by industrial growth, appear to oppose it.

Also, the race issue might have played some part in that white suburbanites were fearful that consolidation would open the gates to Negroes, spreading low-income groups throughout residential areas and resulting in the deterioration of public services and increases in costs.

Another reason has been advanced by Donald J. Curran, who maintains that "spontaneous integration of the localities swings on the fulcrum of individual self interest."[13] His Milwaukee study does not find any trend toward uniformity in resources of different urban governments. Since local governments would be more unlikely to spontaneously forgo advantages in resources, and therefore tax base, grave impediments to consolidation exist. He concludes that the resources position of the central city, i.e., Milwaukee proper, the position of which has steadily worsened both in property base and in state payments, further darkens the outlook for consolidation.

Finally, consolidation is a revolutionary step—a great departure from the experience of most American urbanites. As such it engenders pervasive uncertainties, and many voters appear reluctant to opt for a future that might profoundly affect the quality of their living.

Even though large-scale consolidation of urban governments is not in the cards, some compromises have appeared. Among them are countywide purchasing efforts, regional planning councils, and the "Lakewood Plan," whereby cities purchase certain services from an urban county.[14]

The Federal government has taken a number of steps that can encourage areawide cooperation. For example, in the National Capitol Transportation Act of 1960, the Congress declared that the continuing policy and responsibility of the Federal government is to encourage and aid in planning and developing a unified and coordinated transit system for the Capitol region.[15] The Act of 1965 authorizes a system of rail rapid transit to be built within the District of Columbia but fully capable of extension beyond the District boundaries and not to exceed $431 million. To this end $150 million were appropriated and a $50 million bond issue was authorized.[16]

In the same manner, Congress has encouraged interstate and regional cooperation in the planning, acquisition, and development of outdoor recreation resources,[17] and the Housing and Urban Development Act of 1965 explicitly requires "significant effective efforts" by all available public and private resources in projects designed to beautify and improve open space and other public lands in the nation's urban areas.[18]

STATE AND LOCAL FISCAL OUTLOOK

Interest in identifying and measuring possible effects of alternative public policy decisions on the fiscal outlook of state and local governments stems from a variety of reasons. First, a powerful analytic framework for assessing the fiscal resources of state and local governments should aid in appraising the fiscal outlook over, let us say, a five- to ten-year period and in evaluating the nature and scope of alternatives open to governments. Second, within such a framework we should be able to consider different judgments regarding possible state and local government expenditure and revenue policies. Finally, with the aid of alternative policy assumptions, we might be able to develop a planning process that is responsive to changing economic and social needs.

Most state and certain local governments are big businesses, and we must be concerned about the efficient management and effective planning of their resources. To this end, we require evaluation and projection of revenues which might be raised and expenditures which might be made in the future. Also, because of the size of some of the government units, the private sector of the economy seeks good information on the future budgets of these governments. State and local governments require not only evaluation of the expenditures and revenues in their main budgets for the next several years, but also consideration of all their expenditures and revenue sources over a longer period of five or ten years. The statement of the fiscal outlook should relate to the activities of both the private sector and other levels of government. A government's fiscal outlook should be formulated to facilitate budgetary decisions and multiyear financial planning; in addition, the outlook of a state should facilitate economic development planning and determination of the speed with which social aspirations can be achieved. In other words, the statement of the fiscal outlook is not a substitute for, but is a basic ingredient of, the overall economic and social planning of government.

The fiscal outlook statement should not represent a mechanical extrapolation of revenue and expenditure trends. Instead, as mentioned in the discussion of multiyear program budgeting, the statement should be developed so as to assist the decision maker in assessing and evaluating the effects of past policy actions and in determining what policy shifts will be needed. During the entire postwar period, state and local governments have had to contend with rising factor prices that have become virtually automatic expenditure escalators. Fortunately, revenues also have escalated, as a result of increases in the value of the tax base over time. But other factors are the principal determinants of expenditure levels—number of service recipients, service quality, service conditions, technology (or productivity), and, in the case of state governments, state aid to local governments. Likewise, revenues can be affected by the tax system, structure, base, and rates, as well as by financial aid which can be expected from higher levels of government.

Thus, state and local government officials are deeply concerned that the existing tax system and its structure, in conjunction with whatever other sources of revenue they may have, will produce revenue that is insufficient to finance the services that are likely to be demanded from them in years to come. Their anguish and cries about future fiscal crises mean that pressures are strong for future service demand and expenditures to exceed future revenues. The first issue, then, is whether the existing tax system and structure—without change in rates, rate structure, or tax base definition—are likely to produce tax yields that will meet service demands and expenditures.[19]

In more precise terms, the question is: In a future period will "prescribed" revenues balance "preempted" expenditures? Prescribed revenues are revenues that allow for changes over time in the valuation of the tax base (assuming no change in tax base definition), but not for changes in tax rates, system, or structure. Financial aid from higher levels of government is also included in prescribed revenues. The revenue determinants, other than intergovernmental aid, are policy variables.

Preempted expenditures are expenditures at the current authorized level adjusted for changes in factor price level, number of service recipients, service conditions, and technology. In the case of state expenditures, state aid to local governments is held at the legally authorized level. Furthermore, and most importantly, the quality of services is not permitted to change. Of the expenditure determinants, the following are policy variables—quality, technology, state aid, and, to some extent, the number of service recipients.

We specified above that preempted expenditures do not allow for quality improvements. Yet, people's aspirations for government services usually stimulate "aspiration" expenditures, which allow for quality improvements and which usually exceed by far both preempted expenditures and prescribed revenues. In such cases, where people aspire to and demand more and better services, the government must make some difficult decisions. Since subnational governments have limited tax bases, priorities must be established among aspired services, and decisions must be made about how rapidly the priorities should be met. Estimates for various public programs must therefore include both the preempted expenditures and the aspired program improvements. Such standards can be estimated with the aid of detailed studies of public attitudes as well as the judgments of experts about the demand for and supply of specific programs.

In addition to prescribed revenues and preempted and aspired expenditures, there are "preferred" revenues and expenditures. They are the result of a compromise and are preferred in terms of balancing people's demand for public services and what people are collectively willing to pay for the services.

In the short run, changes in aspired and preferred government expenditures are perhaps most directly related to income elasticity of government expenditures and size of population to be served. Expenditure elasticity is defined as the ratio of a percentage change in government service expenditures to the corresponding percentage change in constituents' income. Expenditure elasticity indicates by how much expenditures will increase as a result of increases in income over time.[20]

Tax revenue changes from one year to the next can be related to the income elasticity of tax revenue, for short revenue elasticity, and the tax base. As was pointed out in Chapter 4, the coefficient of revenue elasticity is the ratio of a percentage change in tax revenue to the corresponding percentage change in taxpayers' income. Since projections of prescribed revenue assume constant tax rates, we can rely on a coefficient of tax base instead of revenue elasticity. Revenue elasticity is important in projecting preferred revenues.

A FISCAL OUTLOOK MODEL

We seek a model that permits us to compare the results of explicit changes in expenditure and revenue policy variables, with a view to equating expenditures and revenues in a future period. The model developed here excludes capital expenditures and the revenues raised by bond issues to meet new liabilities or repayments on existing liabilities.

We begin by considering total expenditures the simple product of expenditures per service recipient and the number of service recipients:

$$E^0 = e^0 M^0 \tag{12.3}$$

where

$E =$ total current expenditures
$e =$ average expenditure per service recipient
$M =$ number of service recipients

Superscripts refer to the time periods, i.e., 0 is base period and i is the number of years after the base period.

To obtain preempted expenditures we must adjust the terms on the right-hand side of equation 12.3 for the expected annual rates of increase in the four factors mentioned above. Preempted expenditures for any year are then:

$$E_p{}^i = e^0 M^0 [(1 + m)(1 + f)(1 + s)(1 + t)]^{i} \text{ }{}^{21} \tag{12.4}$$

where

$E_p =$ preempted current expenditures
$m =$ annual rate of change in number of service recipients
$f =$ annual rate of change in factor prices
$s =$ annual rate in real terms of change in service conditions per service recipient
$t =$ annual rate in real terms of changes in technical conditions affecting costs per service recipient

On the revenue side, if we disregard that there are various revenue sources, prescribed revenues can be defined as

$$R_p{}^i = r^0 B^0 [(1 + N_B y)(1 + p)]^i + a^0 M^0 [(1 + m)(1 + f)(1 + q)]^i \tag{12.5}$$

where

$R_p =$ prescribed revenues
$r =$ tax rate
$B =$ value of tax base
$N_B =$ tax base elasticity (elasticity of per capita tax base with respect to per capita income—see Chapter 4)
$y =$ annual rate of change in per capita personal income

$p =$ annual rate of population change

$q =$ annual rate of change in expenditures per service recipient (in real terms)

$a =$ aid per service recipient from higher level of government

If preempted expenditures exceed prescribed revenues within this framework, a number of alternatives can be articulated, and estimates can be provided of what changes in policy variables would bring future expenditures into balance with future revenues. For example, such a balance can be brought about by adjusting the level of expenditures—which often means changing the quality of the service offered—or by increasing revenue through changes in the definition of the tax base, increases in the rates applicable to the already defined tax base, or addition of new taxes. These are the major variables subject to the government's control. Federal or state aid may be increased through appeals to the legislature, but this factor is not really a decision variable of the lower level of government.

To this point we permitted expenditures to increase largely because of exogenous factors, such as price level changes and changes in the size of the population served. The demand for services and expenditures by government can also increase because the population served demands a higher level of service. Particularly, as a result of higher incomes and aspirations, the quality and character of service and the mix of services demanded will change. These aspired expenditure levels are likely to be higher than the preempted expenditures, especially when per capita income is rising.

Aspired expenditures can be defined as

$$E_A{}^i = (1 + N_e y^i) E_p{}^i \qquad (12.6)$$

where

$E_A =$ aspired expenditures

$N_e =$ expenditure elasticity (elasticity of per capita expenditures with respect to per capita income)

The symmetry of this model can be seen in that both revenue and expenditure sides are affected by changes in factor prices, population, and incomes and by responses to income changes.

Ideally we would apply this model to make separate projections of preempted and aspired expenditures for each service, or preferably for each program, as well as of preempted revenues from each revenue source. For this purpose, relevant expenditure, tax base, and revenue elasticity coefficients, as well as service recipient and tax base projections for future years, would be essential. After such separate projections are made, we should carefully consider the projections as a group in toto, keeping in mind the complementary and (or) competitive relations that exist between them.

Although the tax sources of a given state or local government are relatively few, its functions or programs are very numerous. For this reason, it may be efficient to consolidate functions into perhaps five groupings. A grouping that has the advantage of common demand characteristics is the following:

Education, cultural activities, and recreation services

Public health, hospital and welfare services

Protection services

Street services

Water and sewage services

Next we will present two partial case studies as illustrations. First we will concern ourselves with an example of the fiscal outlook of a single local program—education—and then with an example of the overall fiscal outlook of a state government.

School District Fiscal Outlook

We have selected a school district as our first example; since it basically furnishes a single service and uses a single local tax base, it is a relatively simple case. Service recipients of equations 12.1 and 12.2 are students. In implementing equation 12.2 we will assume that during the period under consideration changes in service conditions and in technology make moves in opposite directions and of about equal magnitude and thus cancel each other out. Per-student state aid changes reflect either changes in factor prices only or changes in the level of state support as well as in factor prices.[22]

To estimate the fiscal outlook of a school district, we will slightly expand equation 12.5. Specifically, we will separate the residential from the nonresidential tax base. Thus.

$$R_p{}^i = r^0\{B_r{}^0[(1 + y\,N_r)(1 + p)]^i + B_c{}^0(1 + d\,N_c)^i\} \\ + a^0 M^0[(1 + m)(1 + f)(1 + q)]^i \qquad (12.7)$$

where

N_r = residential tax base elasticity (elasticity of residential per capita tax base with respect to per capita income)

N_c = nonresidential tax base elasticity (elasticity of nonresidential per capita tax base with respect to dollar output of firms)

d = annual rate of change in dollar output of firms

We will consider prescribed revenues and preempted and aspired expenditures for the Los Angeles Unified School District over the period 1966–1967 through 1971–1972. Because the financing of schools is a complex mixture of factors, the data in the following tables have been simplified. Although the data therefore do not directly represent the Los Angeles circumstances, every attempt has been made to use numbers that are relevant to this district so that we have a reasonable simulation of reality.

According to our formulation, in fiscal 1966–1967 the district spent about $382 million from its general fund to teach 644,000 students with the aid of more than 25,000 employees. Preempted expenditure projections through 1971–1972 are presented in column 1 of Table 12.5. They assume annual enrollment increases of 1.18 percent for grades below the seventh grade and 3.37 percent for the seventh through the twelfth grades. Current 1966–1967 expenditures per student in average daily attendance ($521 for kindergarten through sixth grade and $681 for seventh through twelfth grades) are increased for each of the succeeding five years by 3.2 percent. This figure represents the rate of increase in factor prices based on the 1958–1966 average annual rate of increase in the implicit price deflator for state and local government purchases.

Prescribed revenue projections in columns 2 and 6 were made on the assumption that assessed valuation of all property, residential and nonresidential, will increase annually at 5.1 percent, the average rate over the preceding nine years; assuming the property tax base elasticity to be 1, revenues also will increase annually at 5.1 percent.[23] In addition, state aid per student of $172 for kindergarten through sixth grade and of $146 for seventh through twelfth grades is increased annually by 9 percent, the average annual increase in per capita state expenditures for California during 1950–1967; the 1966–1967 tax rate per $100 assessed valuation was $3.6072.[24] It was further assumed that in each year the local tax rate is increased or decreased to achieve balance, eliminating any surplus or deficit in that year. Hence, in the first year, 1967–1968, where a $4.5 million surplus would occur without a tax rate change, we assume that the tax rate is decreased by $0.0553 to $3.5519 as shown in columns 4 and 5.

The projected 1971–1972 preempted expenditures and prescribed revenues (columns 1 and 2) yield a surplus of $4.5 million in the first year and $7.5 million by the fifth year. If property tax rates were not reduced, a $4.5 million surplus would result in the first year and one of $32 million would result in the fifth year, permitting a 1.1 percent and a 6.4 percent quality improvement, respectively (columns 6–8).

Next, in Table 12.6, aspired expenditures are projected and related to prescribed revenues, assuming, as in column 6 of Table 12.5, that local tax rate remains constant and assuming a 9 percent annual increase in state aid. The rate at which aspired expenditures increase is a product of the rate of growth in per capita income and the expenditure elasticity discussed above. For this example, we have used the average real rate of increase in Los

TABLE 12.5 *Preempted Expenditures and Prescribed Revenues, 1966–1967 to 1971–1972 (in thousands of dollars)*

	(1)	(2)	(3)	(4)	(5)	(6)	(7)	(8)
Year	Preempted Expenditures*	Prescribed Revenues†	Imbalance	Tax Rate to Balance per $100 Assessed Valuation	Change in Tax Rate per $100 Assessed Valuation	Prescribed Revenues‡	Surplus Available for Aspired Increases	Surplus as % of Preempted Expenditures
0 1966–1967	$382,002	$382,004	+$ 2	$3.6072		$382,004	+$ 2	
1 1967–1968	403,359	407,851	+ 4,492	3.5519	−$.0553	407,851	+ 4,492	1.1
2 1968–1969	425,949	431,015	+ 5,067	3.4926	− .0593	435,737	+ 9,788	2.3
3 1969–1970	449,832	455,597	+ 5,764	3.4284	− .0642	465,881	+ 16,049	3.6
4 1970–1971	475,073	481,652	+ 6,578	3.3587	− .0697	498,516	+ 23,442	4.9
5 1971–1972	501,739	509,143	+ 7,404	3.2841	− .0746	533,776	+ 32,037	6.4

* Assumptions (a) through (e) apply.

† Assumptions (a), (b), and (f) through (j) apply.

‡ Same assumptions as †, plus the assumption that local tax rate is held at $3.607.

Assumptions are as follows:

a assumes 1.18% annual increase in students in grades K–6.

b assumes 3.37% annual increase in students in grades 7–12.

c assumes $521 expenditure per student in grades K–6.

d assumes $681 expenditure per student in grades 7–12.

e assumes 3.2% annual increase in factor prices.

f assumes $172 state aid per student in grades K–6.

g assumes $146 state aid per student in grades 7–12.

h assumes 5.1% annual increase in assessed valuation.

i assumes $3.6072 per $100 assessed valuation for tax rate.

j assumes state aid increases annually by 9 percent, i.e., average annual rate of increase per capita in State of California expenditures during 1950–1967.

TABLE 12.6 Aspired Expenditures and Prescribed Revenues, 1966–1967 to 1971–1972 (in thousands of dollars)

	(1) Aspired Expenditures*	(2) Prescribed Revenues†	(3) Imbalance	(4) Cumulative Tax Rate Increase to Balance per $100 Assessed Valuation‡	(5) Annual Tax Rate Increase to Balance per $100 Assessed Valuation	(6) Aspired Expenditures§	(7) Imbalance	(8) Cumulative Tax Rate Increase to Balance per $100 Assessed Valuation	(9) Annual Tax Rate Increase to Balance per $100 Assessed Valuation
Year									
0 1966–1967	$382,002	$382,004	+$ 2			$382,002	+$ 2		
1 1967–1968	419,090	407,851	− 11,239	$.1383	$.1383	411,426	− 3,575	$.0440	$.0440
2 1968–1969	460,025	435,737	− 24,287	.4227	.2844	442,987	− 7,249	.1289	.0849
3 1969–1970	503,812	564,881	− 37,931	.8454	.4227	476,822	− 10,941	.2581	.1292
4 1970–1971	553,461	498,516	− 54,945	1.4280	.5826	513,079	− 14,563	.4125	.1544
5 1971–1972	607,104	533,776	− 73,328	2.1677	.7397	551,913	− 18,137	.5955	.1830

* Assumes annual increase of 3.9% in expenditures per student. (The annual increase in expenditures per student in Los Angeles schools in real terms in 1956–1967 was 2%. In 5 years the real rate exceeded 2%; the average real rate for those 5 years was 3.9%.)
† See assumptions related to footnote ‡ of Table 12.5.
‡ Increase over $3.6072 per $100 assessed valuation.
§ Assumes annual expenditure increase of 2 percent.

Angeles school expenditures per pupil for the five years with the highest growth rate from the eleven-year period 1965–1967. This rate was 3.9 percent and is equivalent to unity elasticity factor combining with a 3.9 percent rate of increase in per capita income. With aspired expenditures as indicated in column 1 of Table 12.6, the $3.61 tax rate must be increased by 14 cents in the first year and by 74 cents by the fifth year to bring revenues and expenditures into balance. (See columns 4 and 5 of Table 12.6). Thus, if the district waited until the fifth year to raise taxes, the initial rate of $3.61 would have to be increased by $2.17, or 60 percent.

At the same time, a moderate annual benefit increase of 2 percent (equal to the average annual real rate of expenditure increase during 1956–1957) based on a slower rate of growth in per capita income, combined with a unitary expenditure elasticity, requires relatively small rate increases: 4 cents in the first year or 18 cents by the fifth year. By the fifth year the initial tax of $3.61 per $100 assessed valuation would have to be increased by 60 cents, or 17 percent, in order to balance projected prescribed revenues (columns 6–8 of Table 12.6).

State Fiscal Outlook

In applications of the fiscal outlook model to a state government we should use a model which explicitly reflects the interactions between the state government and the local governments in the decision-making process. In the school district study above, state aid policy was a given; it was an exogenous factor as far as the balancing of the budget was concerned. Alternatively, when evaluating state fiscal actions, we can take the behavior of local governments, as well as that of the Federal government, as a given. However, if the model is to simulate the budgeting process and to reveal trade-offs in a realistic fashion, then we must consider the interactions of the different government units. To do this we need to state the response of localities to aid from above and the response of the state to local allocative decisions in a behavioral equation. We saw in Chapter 6 that the response of localities to grants-in-aid has not been definitively determined either in theory or by empirical effort.

An alternative, which avoids explicit financial interactions among governments, is a consolidated overview approach where the components of state expenditures and revenues are not considered, but only the aggregate figures are developed. This approach is useful for limited purposes, chiefly for estimating the magnitude of government's role in the economy without concern for the mix of services or for revenue methods. This somewhat monolithic view of the public sector may be valid in cases where authority and responsibility are arranged in a tight hierarchy. But in states with many strong agencies, local governments, and authorities that have revenue sources independent of the central state government, the predictive value of the consolidated approach is questionable.

An alternative approach, between the extremes of the consolidated overview and specific behavioral interactions among governments, is described below. This approach builds up the fiscal outlook from various components of expenditures and revenues. It first considers expenditure needs and aspirations and revenue possibilities for the state as a whole, and then allocates the fiscal responses to each government level on the basis of analyses of how the various levels shared their response in the past and might share it in the future. In this way the differential effects of income changes or population changes on various activities can be separated and greater verisimilitude can be achieved. This approach is appropriate when we consider that not only the state government but other governments also provide services for meeting the entrepreneurial needs of business and the social needs of households and for improving the economic potential of the state—through programs affecting physical and human resource development, taxes, and regulatory provisions— as well as for facilitating operations of local government.

Just as in the school district case, in the state example preempted expenditures and prescribed revenues are estimated, and then aspired expenditures are estimated. Conjectures about future aspiration levels of state government services are based on examination of past trends and on judgment. Finally, various choices can be explicitly articulated, and how the different revenue sources would have to change in order that aspired expenditures may be met can be shown. Although total expenditures and revenues are discussed, they are derived from different degrees of disaggregation.

In our hypothetical illustration[25] we consider a state government where the most recent budgetary expenditure was at a level of $5 billion. About half of the state's expenditures are assumed to be for state aid to local governments, a proportion which has prevailed since the mid-fifties. Total state expenditures have increased 15 percent per year since 1960, growing much faster than the state personal income or total Federal expenditures during the same period. About 85 percent of state expenditures were for operating purposes and 15 percent for construction, a relation which has not changed appreciably over the past decade.

The state government's total revenues in its latest budget are assumed to be about $4.5 billion, more than twice the level prevailing ten years earlier. Three-fourths of the state government's revenues flow through the general fund: one-third from income taxes, one-fourth from user taxes and fees (including the sales tax), one-tenth from business taxes, and the remainder from miscellaneous sources. The state's tax structure is demonstrated as being responsive to changes in overall economic activities. Thus, when economic activity is rising rapidly, state revenues increase at a still more rapid pace.

One reason for the relatively high income elasticity of revenues is the heavy reliance on the personal income tax, which has been contributing an increasing proportion of state revenues. The state's revenue also has benefited from the rapid growth of Federal grants, mainly for health, education, welfare, and highway purposes.

While ideally we would like to make explicit assumptions about and to project separately major expenditure programs, available information forces us to concentrate on expenditure functions. On the revenue side, explicit assumptions are made about revenue elasticities, and projections are provided for each revenue source. Illustrative assumptions are given in Table 12.7.

TABLE 12.7　*Assumptions for State Expenditures and Revenues Projections*

Preempted Expenditure Assumptions	Expected Annual Rate of Change in Expenditure Determinants
Current Expenditures:	
Functions:	
General government	
Health	
Housing	
Natural resources and recreation	Population $+1.1\%$
Public safety	Government wages and prices $+3.6\%$
Sanitation and utilities	
Unallocated	
Transportation	
Services to agriculture, business, labor	Employment $+1.3\%$ Government wages and prices $+3.6\%$
Education department	Public school enrollment $+1.0\%$ Government wages and prices $+3.6\%$
State university	University enrollment $+9.5\%$ Government wages and prices $+3.6\%$
Public welfare	Families with real income less than $5,000 per year -3.3% Consumer price index $+1.7\%$
Capital Expenditures:	
Functions:	
General government	
Health	
Housing	
Natural resources	Population $+1.1\%$
Public safety	Construction and investment goods price level $+2.4\%$
Sanitation and utilities	
Unallocated	
Total local government capital	
Education department	Employment $+1.3\%$
Services to agriculture, business, labor	Construction and investment goods price level $+2.4\%$
State university	Construction and investment goods price level $+2.4\%$
Transportation	Construction and investment goods price level $+2.4\%$

TABLE 12.7 *Assumptions for State Expenditures and Revenues Projections—*
Continued

Prescribed Revenue Assumptions	Expected Annual Rate of Change in Revenue Determinants	
	Revenue Elasticity (assumed constant)	
State government estate tax		
State government miscellaneous revenues	1.0	
Local government other revenues		
Local government mortgage tax		
State income tax	1.8	
Insurance premium tax	1.3	
Sales tax	1.05	
Motor fuel tax	0.7	
Highway use tax		times Personal
Motor vehicle tax	0.4	Income
Alcoholic beverage tax		increase, 5.7%
Liquor and wine	0.7	
Sparkling wine	2.0	
Pari-mutual tax		
Other taxes	1.2	
Stock transfer tax		
Lottery tax		
Assessments	1.6	
Local property tax	0.475	
Corporate franchise tax		
Corporate and utilities taxes	Revenue	times Business
Unincorporated business tax	Elasticity	Output
Real property transfer tax	of 1.34	increase, 5.5%
Alcoholic beverage tax		
Beer	Population (14 years and older)	
Cigarette tax	Cigarette consumption +2.0%	

SOURCE: National Planning Association, *New York Fiscal Outlook* (Washington, D.C., 1968), pp. 60–62.

The state's preempted expenditures in 1975 are estimated to amount to $7 billion, with about 80 percent of the increase accounted for by price rises and the remainder by an increase in the number of service recipients. State aid to localities in 1975 would be 60 percent above its current level. Prescribed revenues would amount to $8 billion in 1975. About 20 percent of the revenue increase would be accounted for by expected increases in Federal grants. In 1975, yields from income taxes would be twice the 1968 level, business taxes would be 75 percent higher, and user taxes and fees would be 40 percent higher. As a result, 1975 prescribed revenues are expected to exceed preempted expenditures by $1 billion.

Aspiration expenditures are estimated for moderate and substantial bene-fit improvements by assuming that the rate of benefit improvements achieved in the first half of the sixties could be characterized as substantial, whereas the improvements in the second half of the fifties were moderate. Assuming that the benefit improvements would continue to be substantial, then 1975 aspiration expenditures would be estimated at $15 billion. However, if benefit improvements were to be moderate, the aspiration expenditures would be estimated at $10 billion.

Under such assumptions, the state would require $3 billion for moderate expenditure improvements (that is, above the preempted level of expendi-tures) and $8 billion for substantial benefit improvements. This, in turn, would require $2 billion additional revenues (above the prescribed levels) for moderate improvements and $7 billion additional for substantial improve-ments.

How could the additional revenues be raised and what might be a pre-ferred expenditure-revenue level? The prescribed 1975 revenue level implicitly assumed $2 billion Federal aid to the state; this in turn assumed an annual national economic growth of 4.5 percent and a national unemployment rate of 3.8 percent. A more rapid national growth rate accompanied by higher levels of state expenditures could result in more Federal aid to the state, say $2.5 billion. As a result, moderate benefit improvements would require $1.5 billion in additional state-raised revenues, and substantial improvements would require $6.5 billion. With business taxes in the state close to the national average, a moderate rise in their rate would probably not jeopardize the state's attraction for new business, particularly in light of the improved services that would be forthcoming. However, even a 20 percent increase in business tax rates would increase business taxes by only $200 million to $300 million above the prescribed revenues which have been estimated.

For this reason, the personal income tax is likely to be the most promis-ing source of revenue to bridge the gap between aspiration expenditures and prescribed revenues for 1975. Estimating the personal income tax elasticity to be 1.8 and 1975 personal income levels to be 50 percent above current levels, the income tax payment in 1975 would almost double the current level even with no change in rates. A tax rate increase which would be fairly substan-tial, but which would still be within the bounds of increases that have occurred in the past, might result in a 2.5 percent increase in tax payments for every 1 percent increase in personal income. Such a rate increase would add $1 billion to $1.5 billion of income tax revenue to the prescribed reve-nues for 1975. This would be sufficient to meet the moderate aspiration levels, but far short of the substantial aspiration. Unless significant new revenue sources were exploited, it is unlikely that the substantial aspiration standards would be achieved in this hypothetical case.

NOTES

CHAPTER 1

1. For details see Werner Z. Hirsch, *A Statistical Sketch of State and Local Government Activities* (Los Angeles: University of California, Institute of Government and Public Affairs, 1967), MR–105.

2. Richard A. Musgrave, *The Theory of Public Finance* (New York: McGraw-Hill, 1959), pp. 43–44; and Julius Margolis, "The Demand for Public Services," in Harvey S. Perloff and Lowdon Wingo, Jr., (eds.), *Issues in Urban Economics* (Baltimore: Johns Hopkins, 1968), pp. 541–548.

3. H. A. Washington (ed.), *The Writings of Thomas Jefferson* [Washington, D.C.: U.S. Congress (printers), 1853–1854], vol. VII, p. 216.

4. *Ibid.*, vol. I, p. 82.

5. *Ibid.*, vol. VII, p. 256.

6. Richard Ruggles, "The Federal Government and Federalism," in Harvey S. Perloff and Richard P. Nathan (eds.), *Revenue Sharing and the City* (Baltimore: Johns Hopkins, 1968), pp. 40–48.

7. For example, the courts and law enforcement agents to no small extent provide a visible, tangible service: an environment and rules by which a civilized society lives and thrives. The policeman who directs car traffic or helps school children across the street produces a direct final product, in the first case speeding up traffic and in the second preventing accidents. Furthermore, it is not easy to decide whether financial transfers from one household to another involve tangible or intangible services.

8. Musgrave, *op. cit.*, pp. 6–27.

9. Alvin H. Hansen and Harvey S. Perloff, *State and Local Finance in the National Economy* (New York: Norton, 1944), pp. 11–12.

10. Ralph Turvey, "Side Effects of Resource Use," in Henry Jarrett (ed.), *Environmental Quality in a Growing Economy* (Baltimore: Johns Hopkins, 1966), p. 47.

11. By superior government we mean a state or Federal jurisdiction that would internalize the interjurisdictional spillovers.

CHAPTER 2

1. Benefit-cost analysis will be presented in more detail in Chaps. 11 and 12.

2. Marion Clawson, *Methods of Measuring the Demand for and Value of Outdoor Recreation* (Washington, D.C.: Resources for the Future, 1959), Reprint no. 10.

3. In this section we take the government price policy as a given. For a discussion of pricing and the demand information generated by user charges, see Chap. 3.

4. Wayne E. Boyet and George S. Tolley, "Recreation Projections Based on Demand Analysis," *Journal of Farm Economics*, vol. 48 (November, 1966), pp. 984–1001.

5. About the best work is that of Herbert E. Klarman, *The Economics of Health* (New York: Columbia, 1965); and Grover Wirick, Jr., and R. Barlow, *The Economics of Health and Medical Care (1964 Symposium)* (Ann Arbor: University of Michigan Press, 1964).

6. Robert Campbell and Barry N. Siegel, "The Demand for Higher Education in the United States, 1919–1964," *American Economic Review*, vol. 57 (June, 1967), pp. 482–494.

7. Robert L. Wilson, "Livability of the City: Attitudes and Urban Development," in F. Stuart Chapin and Shirley F. Weiss (eds.), *Urban Growth Dynamics* (New York: Wiley, 1962), pp. 359–399.

8. James M. Buchanan, *Public Finance in Democratic Process* (Chapel Hill: University of North Carolina Press, 1967).

9. William C. Birdsall, "A Study of the Demand for Public Goods," Richard A. Musgrave (ed.), *Essays in Fiscal Federalism* (Washington, D.C.: Brookings, 1965), pp. 235–294.

10. *Ibid.*, pp. 238 and 247.

11. *Ibid.*, pp. 262–263.

12. John F. Due, *Government Finance: Economics of the Public Sector*, 4th ed. (Homewood, Ill.: Irwin, 1968).

13. James Q. Wilson and Edwin C. Banfield, "Public Regardingness as a Value Premise in Voting Behavior," *American Political Science Review*, vol. 58 (December, 1964), pp. 856–887.

14. Robert R. Alford and Eugene C. Lee, "Voting Turnout in American Cities," *American Political Science Review*, vol. 62 (September, 1968), p. 803.

15. Charles M. Tiebout, "A Pure Theory of Local Expenditures," *Journal of Political Economy*, vol. 64 (October, 1956), pp. 416–424.

16. Julius Margolis, "The Demand for Urban Public Services," in Harvey S. Perloff and Lowdon Wingo, Jr. (eds.), *Issues in Urban Economics* (Baltimore: Johns Hopkins, 1968), pp. 548–552.

17. Roland N. McKean, "Unseen Hand in Government," *American Economic Review*, vol. 55 (June, 1965), pp. 498–500.

18. Anthony Downs, *Inside Bureaucracy* (Boston: Little, Brown, 1967).

19. Due, *op. cit.*

20. Albert Breton, "A Theory of the Demand for Public Goods," *Canadian Journal of Economics*, vol. 32 (November, 1966).

21. Otto A. Davis and George H. Haines, "A Political Approach to a Theory of Public Expenditure: The Case of Municipalities," *National Tax Journal*, vol. 19 (September, 1966), pp. 259–275.

22. James M. Buchanan and Gordon Tullock, *The Calculus of Consent* (Ann Arbor: University of Michigan Press, 1962).

23. Anthony Downs, *An Economic Theory of Democracy* (New York: Harper, 1957).

24. Kenneth J. Arrow, *Social Choice and Individual Values*, 2d ed. (New York: Wiley, 1963).

25. An all-or-nothing demand schedule.

26. Due, *op. cit.*, pp. 31–32.

27. David Easton, *Varieties of Political Theory* (Englewood Cliffs, N.J.: Prentice-Hall, 1966).

CHAPTER 3

1. Ronald Teeples, *Some Problems Concerning the Magnitude of State and Local Government Revenues from User Charges* (Los Angeles: University of California, Institute of Government and Public Affairs, 1968), MR–108, p. 3.

2. The distinction is made clear in the following section. *Ibid.*, pp. 3–13.

3. *Ibid.*, pp. 3–8.

4. The plurality of norms can readily be demonstrated by the traditional influence of normative notions on water supply: Private gain should not be made from its sale; every person should have all he wants; water sources should be collectively owned; the effects on scenery and beauty should be more highly valued; a uniform quality must be maintained; etc.

5. Roland N. McKean and J. R. Minasian, "On Achieving Pareto Optimality—Regardless of Cost?" *Western Economic Journal*, vol. 5 (December, 1966), pp. 14–23.

6. *Ibid.*

7. Historically, many government "tax" systems and "tax forming" schemes were such enterprises.

8. In most cases average variable costs are charged, since capital outlays are not financed out of sales receipts.

9. In the case of a long-run average cost schedule that declines throughout the entire relevant range of demand, fair pricing would result in underproduction. See the following marginal cost pricing section.

10. R. H. Coase, "Regulated Industries: Discussion," *American Economic Review*, vol. 54 (May, 1964), pp. 194–197; G. J. Stigler and C. Friedland, "What Can Regulators Regulate?" *Journal of Law and Economics*, vol. 5 (October, 1962).

11. P. O. Steiner, "Peak Loads and Efficient Pricing," *Quarterly Journal of Economics*, vol. 71 (November, 1957), pp. 585–610; Ralph Turvey, "Marginal Cost Pricing in Practice," *Economica*, vol. 31 (November, 1964), pp. 423–432;

Jack Hirshleifer, "Peak Loads and Efficiency Pricing: Comment," *Quarterly Journal of Economics,* vol. 72 (August, 1958), pp. 451–462; James M. Buchanan, "Peak Loads and Efficiency Pricing: Comment," *Quarterly Journal of Economics,* vol. 80 (August, 1966), p. 463; and William Vickrey, "Some Objections to Marginal Pricing," *Journal of Political Economy,* vol. 56 (June, 1948), pp. 218–238.

12. Admittedly this rule will not allow consumers who want a lower quality to bribe the manager (through higher profits) and other consumers (through a lower price) to give up the *imposed* quality. The quality of passages was specified by defining "capacity" for the manager. Both safety and degree of congestion are still variables of the output that are subject to rational choice *given* that the bridge exists. Therefore, the manager might also be instructed to alter capacity and then follow the above rule, eventually selecting that "capacity" which yields the greatest return to the bridge operation *(assuming that full knowledge of quality on the part of consumers has been assured).*

13. This should not be interpreted to mean that consumers of the government output would be subjected to constantly fluctuating price schedules. Price changes and complications in price schedules involve costs which both consumers and the producer will attempt to avoid—at least up to some point. See Ralph Turvey, "Peak Load Pricing," *Journal of Political Economy,* vol. 76 (January-February, 1968), pp. 101–113.

14. This situation is usually assumed to result from continually decreasing long-run marginal cost, but it may also occur for constant or even eventually rising long-run marginal cost.

15. Steiner, *op. cit.,* pp. 585–586.

16. Again, since price changes and information are costly, some shortages and surpluses of output will be efficient; to avoid all such wastes would be too costly. But for our purposes this complication can be ignored.

17. "Peak use" and "off-peak use" of a given facility might be considered distinct outputs where the good is defined as a dated unit of service.

18. Hirshleifer, *op. cit.,* pp. 423–432.

19. Unless the good whose consumption is being subsidized is sufficiently inferior with respect to real increases in the household's income.

20. James M. Buchanan, *The Public Finances* (Homewood, Ill.: Irwin, 1960), pp. 503–516.

21. Free services to farmers include programs of detecting, diagnosing, controlling, and eradicating agricultural pests and diseases; soil tests; research on insect and pest control and on seed and stock improvement; and free inspection and dealer licensing. In addition, counties as well as states have sponsored and subsidized fairs for many years.

22. William S. Vickrey, "Pricing in Urban and Suburban Transport," *American Economic Review,* vol. 53 (May, 1963), pp. 452–465.

23. *Ibid.*

24. Roland N. McKean, "The Unseen Hand of Government," *American Economic Review*, vol. 55 (June, 1965), pp. 496–506.

25. These schools include such services as instruction for hairdressers, bartenders, barbers, mechanics, artists, models, musicians, and computer programmers.

26. M. Friedman, *Capitalism and Freedom* (Chicago: University of Chicago Press, 1962), chap. VI; E. G. West, "Tom Paine's Voucher Scheme for Public Education," *Southern Economic Journal*, vol. 33 (January, 1967), pp. 378–382.

27. By facilities we mean playgrounds, meeting rooms, auditoriums, gymnasiums, athletic fields and equipment, etc.

28. Enforcement of antipollution laws with respect to water and air (although permits may be sold to operate certain pollutant-emitting devices), monitoring of air and water for radiological counts, insect and vermin control on public property (especially the sewer system), inspection of private hospitals, mosquito control, etc.

29. Kjeld Philip, *Intergovernmental Fiscal Relations* (Copenhagen: Institute of Economics and History, 1954), p. 60.

CHAPTER 4

1. For a detailed discussion, see the sections "The Thrust of This Volume" in Chap. 1 and "Interjurisdictional Spillovers and Nonoptimal Spending" in Chap. 6.

2. See especially the section "Characteristics and Rationale of User Charges" in Chap. 3.

3. Richard A. Musgrave and Alan T. Peacock (eds.), *Classics in the Theory of Public Finance* (London: Macmillan, for International Economic Association, 1958); Richard A. Musgrave, *The Theory of Public Finance* (New York: McGraw-Hill, 1959), pp. 61–115.

4. Musgrave, *ibid.*, pp. 211–217.

5. Interesting theoretical and empirical incidence studies include: Richard A. Musgrave and Darwin W. Daicoff, "Who Pays the Michigan Taxes?" *Michigan Tax Study: Staff Papers* (Ann Arbor: University of Michigan, 1958), pp. 131–183; Harold M. Groves and W. Donald Knight, *Wisconsin's State and Local Burden* (Madison: University of Wisconsin Tax Study Committee, 1959); Oswald H. Brownlee, "Estimated Distribution of Minnesota Taxes and Public Expenditure Benefits," *University of Minnesota Studies in Economics and Business* (Minneapolis: University of Minnesota Press, 1960), no. 21; and Werner Z. Hirsch, Elbert W. Segelhorst, and Morton J. Marcus, *Spillover of Public Education Costs and Benefits* (Los Angeles: University of California, Institute of Government and Public Affairs, 1964).

6. The prices of identical factors of production and of identical products do not vary among locations within the region.

7. Assume that liabilities and benefits have been established for a long period, so that neither firms nor households have an incentive to alter their locations.

8. Examples of the former are selling and finance, which greatly benefit from face-to-face communication. Examples of the latter are wholesale functions that find that a particular location provides the least costly distribution to retail outlets throughout the metropolitan area.

9. James M. Buchanan, *The Public Finances* (Homewood, Ill.: Irwin, 1960), pp. 251–260.

10. For details see Richard Goode, "The Income Tax and the Supply of Labor," *Journal of Political Economy*, vol. 57 (1949), pp. 428–437; George F. Break, "Income Tax Rates and Incentives to Work and Invest," in Joseph Scherer and James A. Papke (eds.), *Public Finance and Fiscal Policy* (Boston: Houghton Mifflin, 1966), pp. 537–547; G. Cooper, "Taxation and Incentives in Mobilization," *Quarterly Journal of Economics*, vol. 66 (1952), pp. 43–66; and A. Marvin Kosters, *Effects of an Income Tax on Labor Supply* (Santa Monica, Calif.: RAND, January, 1968), P–3757.

11. For an evaluation of these arguments see Richard Goode, *The Individual Income Tax* (Washington, D.C.: Brookings, 1964), pp. 25–28; and Irving Fisher, "Income in Theory and Income Taxation in Practice," *Economica*, vol. 5 (January, 1937), pp. 1–55.

12. See Musgrave, *op. cit.*, chaps. 12 and 14; also John F. Due, *Government Finance: Economics of the Public Sector*, 4th ed. (Homewood, Ill.: Irwin, 1968), chap. 7.

13. Arnold C. Harberger, "The Incidence of the Corporate Income Tax," *Journal of Political Economy*, vol. 70 (June, 1962), pp. 215–240; Marian Krzyzaniak and Richard A. Musgrave, *The Shifting of the Corporation Income Tax* (Baltimore: Johns Hopkins, 1963); Marian Krzyzaniak, *Effects of Corporation Income Tax* (Detroit: Wayne State University Press, 1966); Carl Shoup, "Incidence of the Corporation Income Tax: Capital Structure and Turnover Rates," *National Tax Journal*, vol. 1 (March, 1948), pp. 12–17; and John G. Cragg, Arnold C. Harberger, and Peter Mieszkowski, "Empirical Evidence on the Incidence of the Corporation Income Tax," *Journal of Political Economy*, vol. 75 (December, 1967), pp. 811–821.

14. Most frequently the required percentage is a weighted average of three ratios: the value of property owned by the corporation in the state to the value of all property owned by the corporation; wages paid in the state to all wages paid; and corporate sales in the state to all corporate sales.

15. John F. Due, *The Theory of Incidence of Sales Taxation* (New York: King's Crown, 1942); Earl Rolph, "A Proposed Revision of Excise Tax Theory," *Journal of Political Economy*, vol. 65 (April, 1957), pp. 102–112; James M. Buchanan, *Fiscal Theory and Political Economy* (Chapel Hill: University of North Carolina Press, 1960); and Robert L. Bishop, "The Effects of Specific and Ad Valorem Taxes," *Quarterly Journal of Economics*, vol. 82 (May, 1968), pp. 198–218.

16. Henry M. Levin, "An Analysis of the Economic Effects of the New York City Sales Tax" (Washington, D.C.: Brookings, February, 1967), Reprint 127; and William Hamovitch, "Sales Taxation: An Analysis of the Effects of Rate Increases in Two Contrasting Cases," *National Tax Journal*, vol. 19 (December, 1966), pp. 411–420.

17. The tax is proposed on ethical grounds—that land value is created by "circumstances" of the world rather than by purposeful behavior of landowners, and thus increments in land value are "unearned." Furthermore, many increments in land value are created by government expenditures, making such a tax a benefit levy, at least in part.

18. Among those economists who agree that land taxation will alter the allocation of land among uses there is disagreement on the normative policy effects of land taxation. For example, the "single land tax" advocates in the tradition of Henry George believe that "too much" land is held idle and "too great" dispersion of urban structures results in the absence of land value taxation.

19. Dick Netzer, *Economics of the Property Tax* (Washington, D.C.: Brookings, 1966), pp. 32–66.

20. Earl R. Rolph and George F. Break, *Public Finance* (New York: Ronald, 1961), p. 343.

21. If the amount of investable funds shifted out of construction is so great that the rate of return on investment throughout the region's economy is reduced, the size of the existing stock of structures need not be reduced as much, since new construction is made more profitable by reductions in the cost of investable funds.

22. Raymond L. Richman, "The Incidence of Urban Real Estate Taxes under Conditions of Static and Dynamic Equilibrium," *Land Economics*, vol. 43 (May, 1967), pp. 172–180.

23. James Heilbrun, *Real Estate Taxes and Urban Housing* (New York: Columbia, 1966), p. 92.

24. Harold M. Somers, "Sales Taxation and the Economist," in *Tax Changes for Shortrun Stabilization, Hearings before the Subcommittee on Fiscal Policy of the Joint Economic Committee* (89th Cong., 2d Sess., Mar. 16, 17, 18, 22, and 30, 1966).

25. In designing tax policies that leave at least one party better off, one always assumes the relevant group to be residents of the tax jurisdiction.

26. For example, municipal taxes on gross earnings are much more readily collected from wage earners than from self-employed persons.

27. These references appear as footnotes in the earlier portions of this chapter.

28. It should be kept in mind that textbook discussions of "distortions" usually presuppose a state of ideal efficiency. Therefore real-world tax policy concerns will usually be attempts to redress "under or over" production and (or) consumption by administering countervailing distortion'

29. Musgrave, *op. cit.*, part 4, pp. 405–615; M. J. Bailey, *National Income and the Price Level* (New York: McGraw-Hill, 1962), chaps. I–III, VI, and IX; and Armen A. Alchian and William R. Allen, *Exchange and Production: Theory in Use* (Belmont, Calif.: Wadsworth, 1969), chap. 20.

30. On the expenditure side, we have the following counterparts to the revenue determinants: Income elasticity of government service expenditures (expenditure elasticity) is defined as the ratio of a percentage change in the cost of government services demanded over the corresponding percentage change in constituents' income. Policy determinants of expenditures include service quality and quantity, service conditions, technology, and financial aid to lower levels of government. Nonpolicy expenditure determinants include factor prices, constituents' income, and population size.

31. We have ruled out negatively sloped revenue supply functions by assuming that increases in constituents' income never lead to an absolute decrease in revenue yield.

32. The regional taxation income concept requires further clarification, both as to whose income and what components it should include. As to the first issue, we are basically interested in the income of the jurisdiction's taxpayers, i.e., all those who pay taxes to the jurisdiction regardless of place of residence.

As to the nature of income, we would like to include in regional income not only household personal income but also changes in net worth. Changes in net worth can be either realized or unrealized; the latter are usually neglected by revenue collectors. Household personal income plus realized changes in net worth are approximated by the Internal Revenue Service's concept of total income, i.e., line 9 of its Form 1040.

33. By adding a fourth category, "all other revenue sources," we make it possible to generalize the model from one of taxes to one of all revenue sources; the latter would include user charges, intergovernmental transfers, and gifts.

34. In this formulation, any taxable income not directly related to households supplying factor inputs is apportioned to households.

35. Using the earlier notations, and since $R = rb$, we can expand the revenue elasticity formula 4.1:

$$N_Y = \frac{\dfrac{\Delta R}{R}}{\dfrac{\Delta Y}{Y}} = \frac{\Delta R}{\Delta Y} \cdot \frac{Y}{R}$$

into

$$\frac{\Delta rB}{\Delta Y} \cdot \frac{Y}{rB} = \frac{\Delta b}{\Delta Y} \cdot \frac{Y}{B} = \frac{\dfrac{\Delta B}{B}}{\dfrac{\Delta Y}{Y}} \tag{4.8}$$

i.e., income elasticity of tax base.

36. Progressive taxation can be defined as taxation that takes a higher proportion of income (or wealth) from those with large incomes (or wealth) than from those with small incomes (or wealth). O. H. Brownlee and Edward D. Allen, *Economics of Public Finance* (Englewood Cliffs, N.J.: Prentice-Hall, 1954), p. 19.

37. The empirical estimation of equation 4.12 poses numerous difficulties. Personal income tax payments by income groups can be derived from state income tax rate schedules. However, the state income tax rates levied on taxable income must be translated into average effective tax rates by relating taxable income to a household income concept, which includes changes in realized net worth and retained corporate earnings.

Much basic material regarding expenditure taxes by income groups can be found in Federal income tax returns. Federal income tax law permits taxpayers to deduct state and local sales taxes on the basis of a stipulated formula, but taxpayers can claim larger sales tax deductions if they stipulate their purchases. An alternative method would rely on expenditure surveys.

Serious difficulties arise in connection with wealth taxation. For certain groups in the population, especially the aged, there is little relation between income and property. Furthermore, the relationship between estate taxes and income is not too clear.

The fourth revenue group has two major components, one of which, user charges by income groups, should be determined by expenditure surveys. Intergovernmental transfers, the second major component, are often inversely related to income; estimates can be based on the specific program under which transfers are made available to state and local governments.

38. However, it must be recognized that because reassessment of properties (stock) is infrequent, the value of the service of the asset (flow) is inadequately reflected.

39. For a detailed discussion of these and other models, see Werner Z. Hirsch and Sidney Sonenblum, *Selecting Regional Information for Government Planning and Decision-making* (New York: Praeger, 1970).

CHAPTER 5

1. In Chap. 3, we offered a careful definition of user charges and attempted to estimate their magnitude for 1965–1966. In this chapter, where we attempt to shed light on the productivity of taxes, and therefore need historical data, we are forced to rely on official statistics and their definitions.

2. Alan Williams, *Public Finance and Budgetary Policy* (London: G. Allen, 1963), pp. 16 and 19. Mr. Williams's framework focuses on who pays and who should pay, i.e., equity questions, which do not dominate local and state government concerns. Operationally, the Williams approach requires that the property taxes on residential and business property be separated, which is empirically impossible.

3. John Shannon, *Recent Developments on the State Personal Income Tax Fund* (Washington, D.C.: Advisory Commission on Intergovernmental Relations, 1965), p. 10.

4. Joseph A. Pechman, *Federal Tax Policy* (Washington, D.C.: Brookings, 1966), pp. 205–206; and Advisory Commission on Intergovernmental Relations, *State and Local Taxes: Significant Features, 1968* (Washington, D.C.).

5. Kenneth Allen and Richard F. Fryman, "Comparison of Revenues and Expenditures in Income and Non-income Tax States in 1962," *National Tax Journal*, vol. 17 (December, 1964), pp. 357–364.

6. Advisory Commission on Intergovernmental Relations, *State and Local Taxes: Significant Features: 1966 to 1969* (Washington, D.C., 1968), p. 23.

7. While such nonpecuniary income differentials as living in a pleasant community should perhaps be added to the income tax base, the benefits are highly subjective and no ready way can be found to tax such consumption. However, when the differential is generally recognized, it will tend to be capitalized in land values and in this manner be indirectly reflected in rent incomes and the property tax base.

8. Advisory Commission on Intergovernmental Relations, *State and Local Taxes: Significant Features, 1968*, pp. 3, 45–46.

9. James A. Maxwell, *Financing State and Local Government* (Washington, D.C.: Brookings, 1965), p. 86.

10. As shown in Chap. 4, price decreases are expected under these circumstances for the most geographically specialized resource services.

11. Harold M. Groves and C. Harry Kahn, "Stability of State and Local Tax Yields," *American Economic Review*, vol. 42 (March, 1952), p. 87.

12. Lee Soltow, "The Historic Rise in the Number of Taxpayers in a State with Constant Tax Law," *National Tax Journal*, vol. 8 (December, 1955), p. 379.

13. Dick Netzer, "Financial Needs and Resources over the Next Decade: State and Local Governments," *Public Finances: Needs, Sources, and Utilization* (Princeton: National Bureau of Economic Research, 1961), pp. 36–38.

14. Robert Harris, *Income and Sales Taxes: The 1970 Outlook for State and Localities* (Chicago: Council of State Governments, 1966).

15. Neil M. Singer, "The Use of Dummy Variables in Estimating the Income-elasticity of State Income Tax Revenues," *National Tax Journal*, vol. 21 (June, 1968), pp. 200–204.

16. Selma J. Mushkin and Gabrielle C. Lupo, "Project 70: Projecting the State-Local Sector," *Review of Economics and Statistics*, vol. 49 (May, 1967), p. 243.

17. The economic rationale for corporate income taxes is questionable. Ultimately, the burden of every tax must be realized by some individual, and therefore we can find little economic justification for government instituting a tax on a particular form of business organization through the fiction that it is a legal person. A

superior method would be to tax individuals or households directly through the income tax on personal income receipts. Taxing for the privilege of doing business in the corporate form derives mainly from ease of tax administration and a somewhat fallacious notion of ability to pay. James M. Buchanan argues that since corporations carry on most of the business in the United States, corporate investment constitutes a nationwide, established practice rather than a special privilege. Since government should not allow a real differential advantage to any special person, no special tax treatment should be accorded owners of other business forms and no special disadvantage should be placed on corporate owners. James M. Buchanan, *The Public Finances* (Homewood, Ill.: Irwin, 1960), p. 297.

18. See footnote 17.

19. Alan K. Campbell, "Taxes and Industrial Locations in the New York Metropolitan Region," *National Tax Journal*, vol. 11 (September, 1958), p. 209.

20. In addition to general sales and specific excise taxes, there are rare multiple-stage taxes which include turnover taxes and value-added taxes. Turnover taxes are penalties on money transactions at all stages of the production process and thus have the distinct disadvantage of promoting vertical integration in the production-distribution process. This tax was almost exclusively used outside the United States and has steadily been abandoned for the value-added tax. The base of the value-added tax is defined as sales revenues minus selected costs at each production level. Michigan used a variant of the value-added tax (called the business activities tax) in lieu of a corporate income tax from 1953 to 1967; this business activities tax became Michigan's second-largest source of general funds revenue.

21. Advisory Commission on Intergovernmental Relations, *State and Local Taxes: Significant Features, 1968*, pp. 1–9. In a study made in Wisconsin in 1959 it was estimated that a typical 2 percent sales tax that did not except food and medicine would yield more than the Wisconsin state income tax, which ranged from 1 percent to 7 percent and provided tax credits in lieu of personal exemptions of $7 for single persons and $14 for married couples. Quoted in Pechman, *op. cit.*, p. 209.

22. *Ibid.*, pp. 47–48.

23. *Ibid.*, p. 2.

24. William Hamovitch, "Sales Taxation: An Analysis of the Effects of Rate Increases in Two Contrasting Cases," *National Tax Journal*, vol. 19 (December, 1966), pp. 411–420.

25. The major difference in sales tax coverage between the two areas was that Alabama taxed and New York City exempted household expenditures on food and housing.

26. Harry E. McAllister, "The Border Tax Problem in Washington," *National Tax Journal*, vol. 14 (December, 1961), p. 374.

27. Mushkin and Lupo, *op. cit.*, p. 243.

28. Maxwell, *op. cit.*, pp. 116–118.

29. Advisory Commission on Intergovernmental Relations, *State and Local Taxes: Significant Features, 1968,* pp. 4, 59, 60.

30. These money claims are for fixed amounts of money in the case of bonds, but for variable amounts in the case of equity shares which are claims to income flows.

31. Personal property taxes are levied primarily on the capital value of automobiles, furniture, appliances, jewelry, raw materials inventories, and finished goods inventories. These tax liabilities will be handled separately below.

32. David Ricardo, *The Principles of Political Economy and Taxation* (Homewood, Ill.: Irwin, 1963).

33. Maxwell, *op. cit.*, p. 127.

34. U.S. Bureau of the Census, *Census of Government: Property Tax Rates in Selected Major Cities and Counties* (May, 1968), CG–P–5, pp. 1–3.

35. *Ibid.*, p. 1.

36. The partial exemptions mentioned earlier relate to this issue.

37. Debt liabilities are not ignored in the accrual concept of income measurement.

38. Buchanan, *op. cit.*, pp. 461–462.

39. Joint Economic Committee, *Impact of the Property Tax: Its Economic Implications for Urban Problems,* prepared by Dick Netzer, 90th Cong., 2d Sess. (Washington, D.C.: GPO, 1968).

40. See the section, "Who Pays: Tax Shifting and Incidence," in Chap. 4.

41. Dick Netzer, *Economics of the Property Tax* (Washington, D.C.: Brookings, 1966), p. 185.

42. Jesse Burkhead, *State and Local Taxes for Public Education* (Syracuse N.Y.: Syracuse University Press, 1963), pp. 53–70.

43. Robert J. Lampman, "How Much Government Spending in the 1960's?" *Quarterly Review of Economics and Business,* vol. 1 (February, 1961), pp. 7–17.

44. Eugene P. McLoone, "The Facts of Tax Elasticity and the Financial Support of Education" (Ph.D. dissertation, University of Illinois, 1961).

45. Mushkin and Lupo, *op. cit.*, p. 243; see illustrations I and II.

46. Selma J. Mushkin, *Property Taxes: The 1970 Outlook* (Chicago: Council of State Governments, 1965), p. 23.

47. Mushkin and Lupo, *op. cit.*, p. 243.

48. Raymond W. Goldsmith, *The National Wealth of the United States in the Post-war Period* (Princeton: Princeton University Press, for National Bureau of Economic Research, 1962), table A–5.

49. Netzer, *op. cit.*, p. 140.

50. *Ibid.*, pp. 141–142.

51. *Ibid.*, p. 146.

52. *Ibid.*, p. 152.

53. Advisory Commission on Intergovernmental Relations, *State and Local Taxation of Privately Owned Property Located on Federal Areas* (Washington, D.C.: GPO, 1965), pp. 14–15.

54. Advisory Commission on Intergovernmental Relations, *State and Local Taxes: Significant Features, 1968*, pp. 17 and 52–57.

55. *Ibid.*, p. 58.

56. Ursula K. Hicks, "Autonomous Revenue for Local Government," *Western Economic Journal*, vol. 6 (June, 1968), p. 179.

57. Arnold C. Harberger, "A Federal Tax on Value-added," *The Taxpayer's Stake in Tax Reform* (Washington, D.C.: Chamber of Commerce of the United States, 1968), p. 26.

58. George F. Break, "Financing of Local Government" (Sacramento, Calif.: Advisory Commission on Tax Reform: Researcher's Tentative Report, October, 1968).

59. Robert D. Ebel, "The Michigan Business Activities (Value-added) Tax: A Retrospective Analysis and Evaluation," *Proceedings of the 1968 Conference of the National Tax Association*. The use of the value-added tax in the United States has been quite limited. After employing it for about fifteen years, during which time it had become the second-largest source of general funds revenue, the State of Michigan abolished its quasi-value-added tax. In 1967, West Virginia seriously considered a value-added tax to replace its gross receipts tax, but the proposal lost by a two-vote margin in the State Senate. See Robert D. Ebel and James A. Papke, "A Closer Look at the Value-added Tax: Propositions and Implications," *Proceedings of the 1967 Conference of the National Tax Association*, pp. 155–171.

60. Henry Aaron, "The Differential Price Effects of a Value-added Tax," *National Tax Journal*, vol. 21 (June, 1968), pp. 162–175.

61. U.S. Bureau of the Census, *Census of Government: Taxable Property Values, 1966* (1967), pp. 42 and 74.

62. Ronald B. Welch, *A Look Ahead*, a paper delivered at the Sixth Annual Conference of the Committee on Taxation, Resources and Economic Development (Milwaukee, Wis., July 8, 1967).

63. Arnold C. Harberger, "Issues of Tax Reform for Latin America," *Fiscal Policy for Economic Growth in Latin America* (Baltimore: Johns Hopkins, 1965), pp. 119–120.

64. *Ibid.*, p. 422.

CHAPTER 6

1. Roscoe C. Martin, *The Cities and the Federal System* (New York: Atherton, 1965), p. 111.

2. Advisory Commission on Intergovernmental Relations, *State and Local Finances, 1966 to 1969* (Washington, D.C.: GPO, 1968), M–43, p. 20.

3. But as Norman Beckman points out"...the approaches vary. The state is used as a channel in '701' planning assistance to smaller communities, a priority-setting body in sewage treatment and hospital construction grants, a planning body in the Federal-aid highway program, a partner in the River Basin Commission title of the Water Resources Planning Act, and an approving body in the Land and Water Conservation Fund. For most programs of the Department of Housing and Urban Development, most states have done little more than pass enabling legislation. The Water Works and Sewage Disposal Plants grant and loan program of the Farmers Home Administration requires no state action of any kind." Norman Beckman, "For a New Perspective in Federal-State Relations," *State Government*, vol. 39 (Autumn, 1966), p. 260.

4. U.S. Bureau of the Census, *Census of Government, 1967: State Payments to Local Governments* (1968), vol. 6, no. 4, pp. 1–4.

5. Admittedly, states differ as to the revenues they permit local governments to collect.

6. U.S. Bureau of the Census, *Census of Government, 1967: State Payments to Local Governments, op. cit.*, p. 2.

7. *Ibid.*, pp. 3–4.

8. William J. Baumol, "Urban Services: Interactions of Public and Private Decisions," in Howard G. Schaller (ed.), *Public Expenditure Decisions in the Urban Community* (Baltimore: Johns Hopkins, 1963), p. 4.

9. For a detailed discussion see Alan Williams, "The Optimal Provision of Public Goods in a System of Local Government," *Journal of Political Economy*, vol. 74 (February, 1966), pp. 18–33; and William C. Brainard and F. Trenery Dolbear, Jr., "The Possibility of Oversupply of Local 'Public' Goods: A Critical Note," *Journal of Political Economy*, vol. 75 (February, 1967), pp. 86–90.

10. This view has been taken by Werner Z. Hirsch, Elbert W. Segelhorst, and Morton J. Marcus, *Spillover of Public Education Costs and Benefits* (Los Angeles: University of California, Institute of Government and Public Affairs, 1964).

11. George F. Break, *Intergovernmental Fiscal Relations in the United States* (Washington, D.C.: Brookings, 1967), p. 76.

12. Werner Z. Hirsch, "Local versus Areawide Urban Government Services," *National Tax Journal*, vol. 17 (December, 1964), pp. 331–339; and Break, *op. cit.*, p. 69.

13. Of course it can be argued that as educated individuals become a larger

proportion of society they vote for more public schooling than others want, thereby imposing costs on importing communities.

14. Walter W. Heller, *New Dimensions of Political Economy* (New York: Norton, 1966), pp. 64–65.

15. For a more elaborate classification scheme, see Kjeld Philip, *Intergovernmental Fiscal Relations* (Copenhagen: Institute of Economics and History, 1954), pp. 92–103.

16. I. M. Labovitz, *Number of Authorizations for Federal Assistance to State and Local Governments under Laws in Force at Selected Dates during 1964–66* (Washington, D.C.: Library of Congress, 1967).

17. Heller, *op. cit.*, pp. 145–147.

18. Douglas H. Eldridge, "Equity, Administration and Compliance and Intergovernmental Fiscal Aspects," in *The Role of Direct and Indirect Taxes in the Federal Revenue System* (Princeton: Princeton University Press, 1964), p. 191.

19. Break, *op. cit.*, p. 35.

20. *Ibid.*, p. 41.

21. Advisory Commission on Intergovernmental Relations, *Federal-State Coordination of Personal Income Taxes* (Washington, D.C.: GPO, 1966).

22. Break, *op. cit.*, p. 28.

23. Federation of Tax Administrators, *Federal-State Exchange of Tax Information* (1962), pp. 15 and 19.

24. See Ronald K. Teeples, "A Model of a Matching Grant-in-aid Program with External Tax Effects" (Los Angeles: University of California, Institute of Government and Public Affairs, 1968), OR–145; and James A. Wilde, "The Expenditure Effects of Grant-in-aid Programs," *National Tax Journal*, vol. 21 (September, 1968), pp. 340–348, for the assumptions relating to this preference function. Wilde also has an extensive bibliography of recent work in this area.

25. David L. Smith, "The Response of State and Local Governments to Federal Grants," *National Tax Journal*, vol. 21 (September, 1968), pp. 349–357.

26. Solomon Fabricant, *Trends of Government Activity in the United States since 1900* (New York: National Bureau of Economic Research, 1952), pp. 122–131.

27. Glenn W. Fisher, "Interstate Variation in State and Local Government Expenditure: A Preliminary Analysis," *National Tax Journal*, vol. 14 (December, 1961), p. 349.

28. Seymour Sacks and Robert Harris, "The Determinants of State and Local Government Expenditures and Intergovernmental Flows of Funds," *National Tax Journal*, vol. 17 (March, 1964), pp. 75–85.

29. *Ibid.*, pp. 84–85.

30. Jack W. Osman, "The Dual Impact of Federal Aid on State and Local Government Expenditures," *National Tax Journal*, vol. 19 (December, 1966), p. 366ff.

31. *Ibid.*, p. 371.

32. *Ibid.*

33. George A. Bishop, "Stimulative versus Substitutive Effects of State School Aid in New England," *National Tax Journal*, vol. 17 (June, 1964), p. 134.

34. *Ibid.*, p. 142.

35. Smith, *op. cit.*, p. 356.

36. Robert F. Adams, "The Fiscal Response to Intergovernmental Transfers in less Developed Areas of the United States," *Review of Economics and Statistics*, vol. 48 (August, 1966), p. 311.

37. *Ibid.*

38. Tax collection cost, as distinct from tax effort, will be discussed below.

39. For a discussion and quantification of the tax effort concept, see Advisory Commission on Intergovernmental Relations, *Measures of State and Local Fiscal Capacity and Tax Effort* (Washington, D.C.: GPO, 1962).

40. Teeples, *op. cit.*, part II.

41. James M. Buchanan, "Federalism and Fiscal Equity," *American Economic Review*, vol. 40 (September, 1950), pp. 583–599; A. D. Scott, "A Note on Grants in Federal Countries," *Economica*, vol. 17 (November, 1950), pp. 416–422; and James M. Buchanan, "Federal Grants and Resource Allocation," *Journal of Political Economy*, vol. 60 (June, 1952), pp. 208–217, followed by further comments by Scott and Buchanan in the same journal (December, 1952), pp. 534–538.

42. U.S. Department of Commerce, Area Redevelopment Administration, *Migration into and out of Depressed Areas* (September, 1964), p. 21.

43. Break, *op. cit.*, p. 147.

44. See "Wealth Base" in Chap. 4.

45. An interesting history of federalism can be found in Harry N. Scheiber, *The Conditions of American Federalism: An Historian's View* (Washington, D.C.: Subcommittee on Intergovernmental Relations, Oct. 15, 1966).

46. Herbert Kaufman, "Administrative Decentralization and Political Power," *Political Administration Review*, vol. 29 (January-February, 1969), p. 3.

47. *Ibid.*, pp. 11–12.

48. Thus it is becoming possible for state governments to establish minimum standards of student achievement in basic subjects and to estimate costs in each district of programs that should allow students to meet or surpass the standards. This activity could be financed jointly by Federal and state governments. Leaving local school districts free to reach or surpass minimum standards, the state government could institute a biennial or triennial performance audit. Those districts that fail the test might be warned and placed on probation for a year; if the districts fail to meet the test, monies could be withdrawn from them, or, on a temporary basis, changes could be made by the state government.

CHAPTER 7

1. Clarence E. Ridley and Herbert A. Simon, *Measuring Municipal Activities* (Chicago: International City Managers Association, 1938).

2. *Ibid.*, p. 2.

3. Henry D. Lytton, "Recent Productivity Trends in the Federal Government: An Exploratory Study," *Review of Economics and Statistics*, vol. 41 (November, 1959), pp. 341–359.

4. Bureau of the Budget, *Measuring Productivity of Federal Government Organizations* (Washington, D.C.: GPO, 1964).

5. My ideas of defining quality were greatly influenced by Irving Hoch of Resources for the Future.

6. I owe this distinction to Morton J. Marcus of the Institute of Government and Public Affairs, University of California, Los Angeles.

7. For examples see F. Welch, *Measurement of the Quality of Schooling* (Chicago: University of Chicago, Investment in Human Capital Series), Paper no. 65:12; Albert H. Bowker, "Quality and Quantity in Higher Education," *Journal of the American Statistical Association*, vol. 60 (March, 1965), pp. 1–15; and Allan M. Cartter, "Qualitative Aspects of Southern University Education," *Southern Economic Journal*, vol. 32, part 2 (July, 1965), pp. 39–69.

8. Warren Y. Kimball, "Population Density and Fire Company Distribution," *Fire Journal* (March, 1965), pp. 39–41.

9. Lanneth I. Goldin, "Three Aspects of Highway Efficiency," *Journal of Transportation Economics and Policy*, vol. 2 (September, 1968), p. 8.

10. Werner Z. Hirsch and Elbert W. Segelhorst, "Incremental Income Benefits of Public Education," *Review of Economics and Statistics*, vol. 47 (November, 1965), pp. 392–399.

11. James C. T. Mao, "Efficiency in Public Urban Renewal Expenditures through Benefit-Cost Analysis," *Journal of American Institute of Planners*, vol. 32 (March, 1966), pp. 95–108.

12. Welch, *op. cit.*; Bowker, *op. cit.*; Cartter, *op. cit.*

13. Mao, *op. cit.*

14. Henry J. Schmandt and G. Ross Stephens, "Measuring Municipal Output," *National Tax Journal*, vol. 13 (December, 1960), pp. 369–375.

15. Martin S. Feldstein, "Hospital Bed Scarcity: An Analysis of the Effects of Interregional Differences," *Economica*, vol. 32 (November, 1965), pp. 393–409; and Harold A. Cohen, "Variations in Cost among Hospitals of Different Sizes," *Southern Economic Journal*, vol. 33 (January, 1967), pp. 355–366.

16. Welch, *op. cit.*

17. This formulation appears especially fruitful for an analysis of state and local

government production, where technological changes are relatively infrequent. For private firms distinguished by exceptionally rapid technological progress, I have proposed separating entrepreneurship into risk taking and technical decision making. Werner Z. Hirsch, "Technological Progress and Microeconomic Theory," *American Economic Review*, vol. 59 (May, 1969), pp. 36–43.

18. George J. Stigler, *The Theory of Price* (New York: Macmillan, 1946), pp. 41–51.

19. We could also use a mean value, i.e., average achievement test score, as an output measure.

20. A. A. Walters, "Production and Cost Functions: An Econometric Survey," *Econometrica*, vol. 31 (January-April, 1963), p. 11.

21. *Ibid.*, pp. 11–13.

22. *Ibid.*, p. 8.

23. Harry Markowitz, "Industry-wide, Multi-industry, and Economy-wide Process Analysis," in T. Barna (ed.), *The Structural Interdependence of the Economy*, proceedings of an International Conference on Input-Output Analysis, July, 1954, University of Pisa, Italy (New York: Wiley, 1956), pp. 119–150.

24. Benjamin Stevens and Walter Isard, "An Interregional Linear Programming Model," *Journal of Regional Science*, vol. 1 (Summer, 1958), pp. 60–98; Benjamin Stevens and Robert Coughlin, "A Note on Inter-areal Linear Programming for a Metropolitan Region," *Journal of Regional Science*, vol. 1 (Spring, 1959), pp. 75–83; Britton Harris, "Linear Programming and Projection of Land Use," Penn-Jersey Transportation Study (1963), Philadelphia, P J Paper no. 20, pp. 1–30 and charts; and William Garrison and D. F. Marble, "Analysis of Highway Networks: A Linear Programming Formulation," *Highway Research Board Proceedings* (1958), no. 37, pp. 1–17.

25. Walter Isard and Robert E. Coughlin, *Municipal Costs and Revenues* (Wellesley, Mass.: Chandler-Davis, 1957).

26. Sanitary Engineering Research Project, *Analysis of Refuse Collection and Sanitary Land Fill Disposal* (Berkeley: University of California, December, 1952), Technical Bulletin no. 8, ser. 37.

27. Walters, *op. cit.*, pp. 17–19.

28. Lawrence R. Klein, *A Textbook of Econometrics* (Evanston, Ill.: Row, Peterson, 1953).

29. Robert M. Solow, "Investment and Technical Progress," in Kenneth Arrow *et al.* (eds.), *Stanford Symposium on Mathematical Methods in the Social Sciences, 1959* (Stanford, Calif.: Stanford, 1960), pp. 89–104.

30. Herbert J. Kiesling, "Measuring a Local Government Service: A Study of School Districts in New York State," *Review of Economics and Statistics*, vol. 49 (August, 1967), pp. 356–367.

31. The socioeconomic groups were children of professional persons, proprietors,

managers and officials; clerks and kindred workers; skilled workers; semiskilled workers; and unskilled workers and servants.

32. *Ibid.*

33. By far the best statistical fit was obtained in relation to all students of grades 10 and 11, where the adjusted coefficient of multiple determination was .810. *Ibid.*

34. Martin T. Katzman, *Distribution and Production in a Big City Elementary School System* (Ph.D. dissertation, Yale University, 1967).

35. *Ibid.*, pp. 52–53.

36. It should of course be kept in mind that school decision makers are not interested in maximizing the output desired by Katzman and Kiesling. Thus the techniques and input combinations will reflect the maximization of other school outputs.

37. Phoebus J. Dhrymes and Mordecai Kurz, "Technology and Scale in Electricity Generation," *Econometrica*, vol. 32 (July, 1964), pp. 287–315.

CHAPTER 8

1. Charlotte DeMonte Phelps, "The Impact of Tightening Credit on Municipal Capital Expenditures in the United States," *Yale Economic Essays*, vol. 1 (Fall, 1961), pp. 274–321.

2. Werner Z. Hirsch, "Cost Functions of an Urban Government Service: Refuse Collection," *Review of Economics and Statistics*, vol. 47 (February, 1965), pp. 87–92.

3. X_2 is a quantity proxy, X_3 and X_4 are quality variables, and the other three variables reflect service conditions affecting input requirements. Since we are dealing with a short-run cost function of a reasonably homogeneous metropolitan area in one year, there is no need to introduce either the state of technology or input factor prices as independent variables.

4. Kong Kyun Ro, "Determinants of Hospital Costs," *Yale Economic Essays*, vol. 8 (Fall, 1968).

5. Ann R. Horowitz, "A Simultaneous-equation Approach to the Problem of Explaining Interstate Differences in State and Local Government Expenditures," *Southern Economic Journal*, vol. 34 (April, 1968), pp. 459–476; and James M. Henderson, "Local Government Expenditures: A Social Welfare Analysis," *Review of Economics and Statistics*, vol. 50 (May, 1968), pp. 156–163.

6. Gerhard Colm *et al.*, "Public Expenditures and Economic Structure," *Social Research*, vol. 3 (February, 1936), pp. 57–77.

7. Solomon Fabricant, *The Trend of Government Activity in the United States since 1900* (New York: National Bureau of Economic Research, 1952), pp. 112–139.

8. Glenn W. Fisher, "Determinants of State and Local Government Expenditures: A Preliminary Analysis," *National Tax Journal,* vol. 14 (December, 1961), pp. 349–355.

9. Seymour Sacks and Robert Harris, "Determinants of State-Local Government Expenditures and Intergovernmental Flows of Funds," *National Tax Journal,* vol. 17 (March, 1964), pp. 75–85.

10. Glenn W. Fisher, "Interstate Variation in State and Local Government Expenditure," *National Tax Journal,* vol. 17 (March, 1964), pp. 57–74.

11. Ernest Kurnow, "Determinants of State and Local Expenditures Reexamined," *National Tax Journal,* vol. 16 (September, 1963), pp. 252–255.

12. For example, see Edward F. Renshaw, "A Note on the Expenditure Effect of State Aid to Education," *Journal of Political Economy,* vol. 68 (April, 1960), pp. 170–174; Werner Z. Hirsch, "Determinants of Public Education Expenditures," *National Tax Journal,* vol. 13 (March, 1960), pp. 29–40; Sherman Shapiro, "Some Socioeconomic Determinants of Expenditures for Education: Southern and Other States Compared," *Comparative Education Review,* vol. 6 (October, 1962), pp. 160–166; and Jerry Miner, *Social and Economic Factors in Spending for Public Education* (Syracuse, N.Y.: Syracuse University Press, 1963).

13. Harvey E. Brazer, *City Expenditures in the United States* (New York: National Bureau of Economic Research, 1959), Occasional Paper 66.

14. Stanley Scott and Edward Feder, *Factors Associated with Variations in Municipal Expenditure Levels* (Berkeley: University of California, Bureau of Public Administration, 1957).

15. George B. Pidot, Jr., *The Public Finances of Metropolitan Government in the Metropolitan United States* (Ph.D. dissertation, Harvard University, 1966).

16. *Ibid.,* p. 230.

17. Robert C. Wood, *Fourteen Hundred Governments* (Cambridge, Mass.: Harvard, 1961); Seymour Sacks *et al., Financing Government in a Metropolitan Area: The Cleveland Experience* (Glencoe, Ill.: Free Press, 1961); Werner Z. Hirsch, *Measuring Factors Affecting Expenditure Levels for Local Government Services* (St. Louis: Metropolitan St. Louis Survey, 1957).

18. W. E. Whitelaw, *An Econometric Analysis of a Municipal Budgetary Process Based on Time Series Data* (Cambridge, Mass.: Harvard Program on Regional and Urban Economics, September, 1968).

19. Horowitz, *op. cit.,* pp. 474–476.

20. James M. Henderson, "Local Government Expenditures: A Social Welfare Analysis," *Review of Economics and Statistics,* vol. 50 (May, 1968), pp. 156–163.

21. Robert L. Harlow, "Factors Affecting American State Expenditures," *Yale Economic Essays,* vol. 7 (Fall, 1967), pp. 263–308.

22. Clearly, there can be different combinations of these three basic types.

23. The following consolidation plans have received most attention: annexation by the core city, city-county consolidation, federation or borough plans, urban or metropolitan county plans, single- or multipurpose metropolitan district plans. Decentralization includes complete legal separation, borough plans, etc.

24. The characteristics of a fire house are slightly different in that some portion of the fixed plant, i.e., the fire fighting equipment, is divisible and adaptability is limited. A fire house extends its scale of operation by adding a fire engine and the number of firemen who operate it.

25. Don Patinkin, "Multiple-plant Firms, Cartels and Imperfect Competition," *Quarterly Journal of Economics*, vol. 61 (February, 1947), pp. 173–205.

26. Werner Z. Hirsch, "Expenditure Implications of Metropolitan Growth and Consolidation," *Review of Economics and Statistics*, vol. 41 (August, 1959), pp. 232–241.

27. Joe S. Bain, *Barriers to New Competition* (Cambridge, Mass.: Harvard, 1956).

28. T. R. Saving, "Estimation of Optimum Size of Plant by Survivor Techniques," *Quarterly Journal of Economics*, vol. 75 (November, 1961), pp. 569–607.

29. John Riew, "Economies of Scale in High School Operation," *Review of Economics and Statistics*, vol. 48 (August, 1966), pp. 280–287.

30. Jesse Burkhead, *Input and Output in Large City High Schools* (Syracuse, N.Y.: Syracuse University Press, 1967), pp. 48–56.

31. Ro, *op. cit.*, p. 245.

32. Harold A. Cohen, "Variations in the Cost among Hospitals of Different Sizes," *Southern Economic Journal*, vol. 33 (January, 1967), pp. 355–366.

33. For such an analysis, ideally we would like to have time series data of government growth without consolidation or of government consolidation without external growth. Unfortunately, such data are not available and researchers attempting to estimate quasi-long-run average unit cost functions have been forced to use cross-section data.

34. Hirsch, "Cost Functions of an Urban Government Service: Refuse Collection," *op. cit.*, pp. 87–92.

35. The partial correlation coefficient relating per capita expenditure and population size was .22, which is statistically insignificant for a sample size of nineteen. Henry J. Schmandt and G. Ross Stephens, "Measuring Municipal Output," *National Tax Journal*, vol. 8 (December, 1960), p. 374.

36. Kiesling, *op. cit.*

37. Robert E. Will, "Scalar Economies and Urban Service Requirements," *Yale Economic Essays*, vol. 5 (Spring, 1965), pp. 1–62.

38. *Ibid.*, p. 33.

39. *Ibid.*, p. 43.

40. *Ibid.*, p. 60.

41. *Ibid.*, p. 59.

42. Hirsch, "Expenditure Implications of Metropolitan Growth and Consolidation," *op. cit.*, pp. 239–240.

43. Walter Isard and Robert E. Coughlin, *Municipal Costs and Revenues* (Wellesley, Mass.: Chandler-Davis, 1957), p. 76.

44. Marc Nerlove, *Returns to Scale in Electricity Supply* (Stanford, Calif.: Stanford University, Institute for Mathematical Studies in the Social Sciences, 1961), p. 11.

45. K. S. Lomax, "Cost Curves for Gas Supply," *Bulletin of the Oxford Institute of Statistics*, vol. 13 (1951), pp. 243–246.

46. J. Johnston, *Statistical Cost Analysis* (New York: McGraw-Hill, 1960).

47. Among those who claim to have been unable to detect significant scale economies is Harvey E. Brazer, who stated: "... There is little, if any, demonstrable positive relationship between the population size of cities and their levels of expenditures per capita when other independent variables are taken into account and the sample studied is a large one." Brazer, *op. cit.*, p. 66.

48. Nels W. Hanson, "Economy of Scale as a Cost Factor in Financing Public Schools," *National Tax Journal*, vol. 17 (March, 1966), pp. 92–95.

49. Harvey Shapiro, "Economies of Scale and Local Government Finance," *Land Economics*, vol. 34 (May, 1963), pp. 175–186.

CHAPTER 9

1. For example, Martin Katzman finds that one of the major goals of the Boston public schools is to provide Irishmen with employment in the schools. Although this is a goal that one normally would not specify, it is only one of a large number of important goals that schools are likely to have. Martin T. Katzman, *Distribution and Production in a Big City Elementary School System* (Ph.D. dissertation, Yale University, 1967), p. 102.

2. The view expressed here does not consider urban public service supply functions as either superfluous or nonexistent. This extreme view is implied (erroneously, I think) in a statement by Otto A. Davis when he says, "... Economists attempting to understand this [allocation] process would do well to discard at least a part of their notions of demand and supply and, hence, the implicit implication that a pricing mechanism is the allocative device in the public sector." Otto A. Davis, "Empirical Evidence of Political Influences upon the Expenditure Policies of Public Schools," in Julius Margolis (ed.), *The Public Economy of Urban Communities* (Baltimore: Johns Hopkins, 1965), p. 111. There is a difference between saying that there is no direct relationship between the marginal cost and the supply function, on the one hand, and that economists should discard parts of their supply notions.

3. Eugene J. Devine, "Manpower Shortages in Local Government Employment," *American Economic Review*, vol. 59 (May, 1969), pp. 538–545.

4. Joseph A. Kershaw and Roland N. McKean, *Teacher Shortages and Salary Schedules* (New York: McGraw-Hill, 1962).

5. A. A. Alchian, K. J. Arrow, and W. M. Capron, *An Economic Analysis of the Market for Scientists and Engineers* (Santa Monica, Calif.: RAND, June, 1958), RM–2190–RC.

6. See G. C. Archibald, "The Factor Gap and the Level of Wages," *Economic Record*, vol. 30 (November, 1954), pp. 187–199; Eugene J. Devine and Morton J. Marcus, *Monopsony, Recruitment Costs and Job Vacancies* (Los Angeles: University of California, Institute of Government and Public Affairs, 1966), MR–74; and Devine, *op. cit.*, pp. 538–545.

7. Walter Isard and Robert E. Coughlin, *Municipal Costs and Revenues* (Wellesley, Mass.: Chandler-Davis, 1957); Werner Z. Hirsch, and Marc Nerlove, *Returns to Scale in Electricity Supply* (Stanford, Calif.: Stanford University, Institute for Mathematical Studies in the Social Sciences, 1961).

8. Advisory Commission on Intergovernmental Relations, *Performance of Urban Functions: Local and Areawide* (Washington, D.C., September, 1963), p. 6.

9. Werner Z. Hirsch, "Local versus Areawide Urban Government Services," *National Tax Journal*, vol. 17 (December, 1964), pp. 331–339.

10. This analysis is based on Carl S. Shoup, "Standards for Distributing a Free Governmental Service: Crime Prevention," *Public Finance*, vol. 19 (1964), pp. 383–392.

11. Stephen L. Mehay and Donald C. Shoup, "Missions and Outputs of Police Agencies" (Los Angeles: University of California, Institute of Government and Public Affairs, 1969), OR–143.

12. For instance, it was found that income, unemployment rate, and family structure are significant variables in explaining variations in juvenile delinquency rates among neighborhoods within a large city and among communities; B. M. Fleisher, "The Effect of Income on Delinquency," *American Economic Review*, vol. 56 (March, 1966), pp. 118–137.

13. Mehay and Shoup, *op. cit.*, pp. 32–34.

14. Shoup, *op. cit.*, pp. 386–390.

15. Anthony Downs, *An Economic Theory of Democracy* (New York: Harper, 1957), chaps. 11–14, pp. 207–278.

16. Kenneth A. Martyn, *Report on Education to the Governor's Commission on Los Angeles Riots*, Los Angeles (November, 1965).

17. Katzman, *op. cit.*, p. 78.

18. Patricia C. Sexton, *Education and Income* (New York: Viking, 1961).

19. Katzman, *op. cit.*, pp. 80–81.

20. Of course, a reporting phenomenon is encountered. Only insofar as the same percentage of total crimes is reported to the police in each division can reported crime rates be used for comparison, and even then crimes are unweighted.

21. Mehay and Shoup, *op. cit.*, p. 33.

CHAPTER 10

1. Irving Hoch, *The Economics of Vertical Transportation, Air Rights and Land Use* (Washington, D.C.: Resources for the Future, 1968), p. 2.

2. Edward M. Bassett, *Zoning* (New York: Russell Sage, 1940), pp. 52–53.

3. Jacob B. Ukeles, *The Consequences of Municipal Zoning* (Washington, D.C.: Urban Land Institute, 1964), pp. 28–29.

4. Most municipalities can accomplish a zone change by ordinance on recommendation of their planning commission. The zone variance is designed to relieve a hardship imposed by zoning. The conditional use permit makes provision for certain community services uses at special types of locations and not anticipated in zoning plans.

5. U.S. Department of Commerce, *A Standard City Planning Enabling Act*, Secs. 6, 7 (1928).

6. See the section, "The Thrust of This Volume," in Chap. 1.

7. Roland N. McKean, *Public Spending* (New York: McGraw-Hill, 1968), pp. 25–29.

8. Edwin S. Mills, "An Aggregative Model of Resource Allocation in a Metropolitan Area," *American Economic Review*, vol. 57 (May, 1967), pp. 197–210; and Donald L. Martin, "An Economic Theory of Urban Decentralization," paper given at a seminar at the University of California, Los Angeles, May, 1966.

9. Irving Hoch, "The Three Dimensional City," a paper presented at a Resources for the Future Forum in Washington, D.C., November, 1967.

10. Local transportation is defined to include automobile purchase and operation, public transit, and car pools. Utilities include gas and electricity, water, sewage, garbage removal, and telephone service.

11. U.S. Bureau of Labor Statistics, *Survey of Consumer Expenditures: 1960–61*, "Consumer Expenditures and Income: Urban States, 1960–61," Supplement 3, part A to BLS Report, 237–38, July, 1964, table 29a.

12. Otto A. Davis, "Economic Elements in Municipal Zoning Decisions," *Land Economics*, vol. 39 (November, 1963), p. 376.

13. Ukeles, *op. cit.*, p. 32.

14. Not infrequently in American politics, a mayor apparently appoints persons to the board of zoning adjustment after they have made contributions to the mayor's campaign fund.

15. Davis, *op. cit.*, p. 381.

16. *Ibid.*, p. 379.

17. James M. Buchanan, "A Behavioral Theory of Pollution," *Western Economic Journal* (December, 1968), pp. 347–358.

CHAPTER 11

1. Charles E. Lindblom, *The Intelligence of Democracy: Decision Making through Adjustment* (New York: Free Press, 1965).

2. Aaron Wildavsky, *The Politics of the Budgetary Process* (Boston: Little, Brown, 1964), p. 131.

3. Some of the effort in California is summarized in State of California Department of Finance, *Programming and Budgeting System* (Sacramento, 1968). John W. Reynolds and Walter G. Hollander, "Program Budgeting in Wisconsin" in the *Planning-Programming-Budgeting System: Progress and Potentials* hearings before the subcommittee on economy in government of the Joint Economic Committee, Congress of the United States (Washington, D.C.: GPO, 1967), pp. 243–248, well describes the effort in Wisconsin. A more sophisticated municipal effort is taking place in New York City, as can be seen from The City of New York, Bureau of the Budget, *FY 1969–1970 Program, Budget Instruction* (1968).

4. Harry P. Hatry and John F. Cotton, *Program Planning for State, County, and City* (Washington, D.C.: State-Local Finances Project of the George Washington University, 1967).

5. Stephen L. Mehay and Donald C. Shoup, "Missions and Outputs of Police Agencies" (Los Angeles: University of California, Institute of Government and Public Affairs, 1969), OR–143, p. 3.

6. Only when deficits were realized were the expenditures of municipal enterprises and special districts included on a net basis. Thus, for local transit and for some water districts and municipally operated airports (where receipts exceed expenditures, including depreciation), no entry was made in the program budget account. It is easy to make a case for including gross figures. The approach used here merely reveals those activities which may be assumed to rely wholly or in part (through subsidies) on local governments to maintain operations. In a sense, by treating them this way we have decided not to subject them to analysis. As a result we are in no position to know whether these businesslike activities funded through user charges are efficient or not.

7. For example, Roland N. McKean, "Cost-Benefit Analysis and British Defense Expenditure," *Scottish Journal of Political Economy*, vol. 10 (February, 1963), pp. 17–35; Charles J. Hitch and Roland N. McKean, *The Economics of Defense in the Nuclear Age* (Cambridge, Mass.: Harvard, 1960), pp. 109–118; Arthur Smithies, *Government Decision-making and the Theory of Choice* (Santa Monica, Calif.: RAND, 1964), P–2960; Roland McKean, *Efficiency in Government through*

Systems Analysis (New York: Wiley, 1958) ; and Jack Hirshleifer, J. C. DeHaven, and J. W. Milliman, *Water Supply* (Chicago: University of Chicago Press, 1960).

8. Julius Margolis, "The Demand for Urban Public Services," in Harvey Perloff and Lowdon Wingo, Jr. (eds.), *Issues in Urban Economics* (Baltimore: Johns Hopkins, 1968), p. 556.

9. See the section, "Interjurisdictional Spillovers and Nonoptimal Spending" in Chap. 6.

10. This section draws heavily on Hitch and McKean, *op. cit.*, pp. 109–118.

11. McKean, *Efficiency in Government through Systems Analysis, op cit.*; Hirshleifer, DeHaven, and Milliman, *op. cit.*; Joe S. Bain, R. Caves, and J. Margolis, *The Northern California Water Industry* (Baltimore: Johns Hopkins, 1966) ; John V. Krutilla and Otto Eckstein, *Multiple Purpose River Development* (Baltimore: Johns Hopkins, 1958) ; and Otto Eckstein, *Water Resources Development: The Economics of Project Evaluation* (Cambridge, Mass.: Harvard, 1958).

12. Alan P. Carlin and William E. Hoehn, *The Grand Canyon Controversy—1967: Further Economic Comparisons of Nuclear Alternatives* (Santa Monica, Calif.: RAND, March, 1967), P–3546.

13. Throughout the discussion, benefit-cost ratios will be given as ratios to 1.

14. Carlin and Hoehn, *op. cit.*, p. 17.

15. Robert K. Davis, *The Range of Choice in Water Management: A Study of Dissolved Oxygen in the Potomac Estuary* (Baltimore: Johns Hopkins, 1968).

16. Federal Water Pollution Control Administration, *Delaware Estuary Comprehensive Study* (Philadelphia, 1966).

17. For a discussion of cost allocation, the work of Otto Eckstein, *op. cit.*, is informative.

18. For a thoughtful review on many of these problems, see Jack L. Knetsch and Robert K. Davis, "Comparisons of Methods for Recreation Evaluation," in Allen V. Kneese and Stephen C. Smith (eds.), *Water Research* (Baltimore: Johns Hopkins, 1966), pp. 125–142.

19. J. Michael Kavanagh, "Programmatic Benefit-Cost Analysis of Local Youth Recreation Programs" (Los Angeles: University of California, Institute of Government and Public Affairs, 1968), OR–142.

20. C. D. Foster and M. E. Beesley, "Estimating the Social Benefit of Constructing an Underground Railway in London," *Journal of the Royal Statistical Society*, vol. 126 (1963), pp. 46–58.

21. T. M. Coburn *et al.*, "The London-Birmingham Motorway," *Technical Paper*, 46 (London: Road Research Laboratory, 1960).

22. See Herbert Mohring, "Urban Highway Investments," in Robert Dorfman (ed.), *Measuring Benefits of Government Investments* (Washington, D.C.: Brookings, 1965), pp. 231–291; James R. Nelson, "The Value of Travel Time," in

Samuel B. Chase (ed.), *Problems in Public Expenditure Analysis* (Washington, D.C.: Brookings, 1968), pp. 78–118; Nathaniel Lichfield and Honor Chapman, "Road Proposals for a Shopping Center," *Journal of Transport Economics and Policy*, vol. 2 (September, 1968), pp. 2–42; and Anthony Downs, *Uncompensated Non-construction Costs Which Urban Highways and Urban Renewal Impose upon Residential Households* (Chicago: Real Estate Research Corporation, 1968).

23. Nathaniel Lichfield and Julius Margolis, "Benefit-Cost Analysis as a Tool in Urban Government Decision Making," in Howard G. Schaller (ed.), *Public Expenditure Decisions in the Urban Community* (Baltimore: Johns Hopkins, 1963), pp. 140–143.

24. E. O. Olsen, *Estimating the Value of Any Government Housing Program to the Tenant* (Santa Monica, Calif.: RAND, 1968), D–18101.

25. James C. T. Mao, "Efficiency in Public Urban Renewal Expenditures through Benefit-Cost Analysis," *American Institute of Planners Journal*, vol. 32 (March, 1966), pp. 95–106; Nathaniel Lichfield, *Cost-Benefit Analysis in Urban Redevelopment* (Berkeley, Calif.: Real Estate Research Program, 1962), Research Report 20; Nathaniel Lichfield, *Cost-Benefit Analysis in Town Planning: A Case Study of Cambridge* (Cambridge, Cambridgeshire, and Isle of Ely County Council, 1966); and Nathaniel Lichfield, "Cost-Benefit Analysis in Town Planning," *Urban Studies*, vol. 3 (November, 1966), pp. 215–249.

26. Jerome Rothenberg, *Economic Evaluation of Urban Renewal* (Washington, D.C.: Brookings, 1967), pp. 176–197.

27. For a comprehensive review see Theodore W. Schultz, *The Economic Value of Education* (New York: Columbia, 1963).

28. For details see Werner Z. Hirsch and Morton J. Marcus, "Some Benefit-Cost Considerations of Universal Junior College Education," *National Tax Journal* (June, 1966), pp. 48–57. The 1.66 and 0.64 ratios for one year of junior college education are somewhat smaller than those for two years given in the reference.

29. Burton A. Weisbrod, "Preventing High School Dropouts," in Robert Dorfman (ed.), *Measuring Benefits of Government Investments* (Washington, D.C.: Brookings, 1964), pp. 117–161.

30. *Ibid.*, p. 147.

31. Herman P. Miller, "Income and Education: Does Education Pay Off?" in Selma J. Mushkin (ed.), *Economics of Higher Education* (Washington, D.C.: GPO, 1962), pp. 129–146; Shane J. Hunt, "Income Determinants for College Graduates and the Return to Educational Investment," *Yale Economic Essays*, vol. 3 (1963), pp. 305–357; Orley Ashenfelter and Joseph D. Mooney, "Graduate Education, Ability and Earnings," *Review of Economics and Statistics*, vol. 49 (February, 1968), pp. 78–86; and Burton Weisbrod and Peter Karpoff, "Monetary Returns to College Education, Student Ability, and College Quality," *Review of Economics and Statistics*, vol. 50 (November, 1968), pp. 491–497.

32. Herbert E. Klarman, *The Economics of Health* (New York: Columbia, 1965), p. 167.

33. U.S. Department of Health, Education and Welfare, *Application of Benefit-Cost Analysis to Motor Vehicle Accidents* (August, 1966).

34. Ronald Ridker, "Strategies for Measuring the Cost of Air Pollution," in Harold Wolozin (ed.), *The Economics of Air Pollution* (New York: Norton, 1966), pp. 87–101; and Hugh O. Nourse, "The Effect of Air Pollution on House Values," *Land Economics*, vol. 42 (May, 1967), pp. 181–189.

35. Bryan C. Conley, "Application of Program Budgeting to the Welfare Function of Local Governmental Units in Metropolitan Los Angeles" (Los Angeles: University of California, Institute of Government and Public Affairs, 1968), OR–139 B.

36. *Ibid.*, pp. 76–85.

37. See David Novick (ed.), *Implementation and Operation in Program Budgeting* (Cambridge, Mass.: Harvard, 1965), Part III, pp. 285–370.

38. Bertram M. Gross, "The New Systems Budgeting," paper delivered at the 1968 annual meeting of the American Political Science Association; Allen Schick, "Systems Politics and Systems Budgeting," paper delivered at the 1968 annual meeting of the National Political Science Association; and H. Rosenzweig, "Defense Planning, Programming and Budgeting: A New Look" (unpublished paper).

39. David Novick, *Program Budgeting* (Cambridge, Mass.: Harvard, 1965), p. 380.

40. Charles L. Schultze, *The Politics and Economics of Public Spending* (Washington, D.C.: Brookings, 1968), pp. 97–101.

41. *Ibid.*, p. 99.

42. Donald C. Shoup and Ruth P. Mack, *Advance Land Acquisition by Local Governments* (Washington, D.C.: GPO, 1968), p. 82.

43. Werner Z. Hirsch, "The Budget as an Instrument for Medium and Long-range Planning and Programming of Education," *Budgeting, Programme Analysis and Cost-effectiveness in Educational Planning* (Paris: Organization for Economic Co-operation and Development, 1968), pp. 92–110.

44. One interesting effort can be found in Richard J. O'Brien, *School Submodel for Large Urban Schools* (Washington, D.C.: U.S. Office of Education, National Center for Educational Statistics, 1967), Technical Note 38.

CHAPTER 12

1. The material in this section was taken from "Local Impact of Industrialization on Local Schools," *Review of Economics and Statistics*, vol. 46 (May, 1964), pp. 191–199. For further explanations of regional input-output analysis see Werner Z. Hirsch, "Interindustry Relations of a Metropolitan Area," *Review of Economics and Statistics*, vol. 41 (November, 1959), pp. 360–369.

2. These income figures are likely to differ substantially from the typical per

family income earned by workers in these industries, since the income figures presented in this study incorporate the incomes of those who are indirectly employed to support production of a particular industry.

3. For greater detail see Werner Z. Hirsch, Elbert W. Segelhorst, and Morton J. Marcus, *Spillover of Public Education Costs and Benefits* (Los Angeles: University of California, Institute of Government and Public Affairs, 1964), from which much of the material in this and the next section was taken.

4. Clayton is a major shopping, financial, and government center for St. Louis County and the western section of the City of St. Louis. Its retail shops cater to the wealthiest clientele in the metropolitan area and it has state and regional offices of national firms as well as numerous medical facilities. These characteristics contribute to Clayton's property wealth and make possible its high level of public school expenditures: $833 per pupil in average daily attendance in 1959–1960, compared with the national average of $369. Median family income in Clayton was $10,925 in 1959, 74 percent higher than the St. Louis County median of $6,275. The large number of regional offices of national organizations, which periodically transferred personnel, tended to contribute to what was probably an unusually high rate of population migration.

5. Material on pp. 32–40 in part is taken from Werner Z. Hirsch, "Expenditure Implications of Metropolitan Growth and Consolidation," *Review of Economics and Statistics*, vol. 4 (August, 1959), pp. 232–241, and "The Supply of Urban Public Services," in Harvey S. Perloff and Lowdon Wingo, Jr. (eds.), *Issues in Urban Economics* (Baltimore: Johns Hopkins, 1968).

6. James R. Schlesinger, *Organizational Structures and Planning* (Santa Monica, Calif.: RAND, Feb. 25, 1966), P–3316, p. 1.

7. *Ibid.*, p. 19.

8. Roland N. McKean and Melvin Anshen, "Limitations, Risks, and Problems," in David Novick (ed.), *Program Budgeting* (Cambridge, Mass.: Harvard, 1965), pp. 285–307.

9. Jesse Burkhead, "Uniformity in Governmental Expenditures and Resources in a Metropolitan Area: Cuyahoga County," *National Tax Journal*, vol. 16 (December, 1961), pp. 337–348; and Donald J. Curran, S.J., "The Metropolitan Problem: Solution from Within?" *National Tax Journal*, vol. 16 (September, 1963), pp. 213–223.

10. David O. Arnold, *The American Way of Death: The Roots of Violence in American Society* (Los Angeles: University of California, Institute of Government and Public Affairs, 1968), MR–113.

11. Sir Edwin Herbert, "The Reorganization of London's Government," *The Metropolitan Future: California and the Challenge of Growth*, Conference no. 5 held at Berkeley, September, 1963 (Berkeley: University of California, 1964), pp. 9–10.

12. Dade County, Fla., and Toronto, Canada, are the two most prominent consolidations on the American continent in the postwar period. Numerous difficulties were experienced in the Dade County consolidation.

13. Curran, *op. cit.*, p. 221.

14. Vincent Ostrom *et al.*, "The Organization of Government in Metropolitan Areas," *American Political Science Review*, vol. 55 (December, 1961), pp. 831–842; and Robert Warren, "A Municipal Services Market Model of Metropolitan Organization," *Journal of the American Institute of Planners*, vol. 30 (August, 1964), pp. 193–204.

15. *Public Law 86–669.*

16. *Public Law 89–173.*

17. *Public Law 88–29.*

18. *Public Law 89–117.*

19. In a closed economy with only a single government, service recipients are identical with taxpayers. Although in an open economy some of those who demand services from a given government jurisdiction live outside it, their number and expenditure characteristics are germane to the projection of future expenditures of that jurisdiction. Likewise, some of the taxpayers of a given jurisdiction live outside it, and they must be considered in determining the tax base of that jurisdiction's tax revenue.

20. Expenditure elasticities are not completely satisfactory factors to project aspired expenditures if the elasticity measure is derived from past behavior of governments. Ideally, we would want a measure of the change in the demand for a government service in response to income changes. The expenditure elasticity as defined above is based on observed expenditures, a result of compromises between aspired expenditures and prescribed revenues.

21. In many respects this function resembles cost functions discussed in Chap. 8, where also such terms as service conditions are defined.

22. Changes in state support can be interpreted as a state policy to increase quality or an attempt to reduce the state's share of the burden of support for the public schools. Since state aid appears in some states to have been a reasonably stable percentage of state expenditures over time, for simplicity's sake we will treat aid as a fixed percentage.

23. Dick Netzer, *Economics of the Property Tax* (Washington, D.C.: Brookings, 1966), pp. 184–190.

24. In the years 1966–1967 the Los Angeles Unified School District had a tax rate of $3.9147 per $100 assessed valuation. At the same time the general fund tax rate, that is, excluding the taxes raised for bond redemption, was $3.2123. The tax rate of $3.6072 actually used in this analysis was derived by taking preempted expenditures derived for year zero less state aid derived for year zero to indicate the amount of funds necessary to balance the budget or come close to balancing it in year zero. This balancing amount was assumed to be the local contribution and was then divided by the tax base to derive the $3.6072 rate actually used.

25. Although the figures used are illustrative, the procedure described has actually been applied in at least one instance.

INDEX